Suicide as a Dramatic Performance

Suicide as a Dramatic Performance

David Lester
Steven Stack
editors

Routledge
Taylor & Francis Group
LONDON AND NEW YORK

First published 2015 by Transaction Publishers

Published 2017 by Routledge
2 Park Square, Milton Park, Abingdon, Oxon OX14 4RN
711 Third Avenue, New York, NY 10017, USA

Routledge is an imprint of the Taylor & Francis Group, an informa business

Copyright © 2015 by Taylor & Francis.

All rights reserved. No part of this book may be reprinted or reproduced or utilised in any form or by any electronic, mechanical, or other means, now known or hereafter invented, including photocopying and recording, or in any information storage or retrieval system, without permission in writing from the publishers.

Notice:
Product or corporate names may be trademarks or registered trademarks, and are used only for identification and explanation without intent to infringe.

Library of Congress Catalog Number: 2015004387

Library of Congress Cataloging-in-Publication Data

Suicide as a dramatic performance / edited by David Lester & Steven Stack.
    pages cm
    Includes bibliographical references.
    ISBN 978-1-4128-5694-2 -- ISBN 978-1-4128-5661-4 1. Suicide--Case studies. I. Lester, David, 1942- editor. II. Stack, Steven, editor.
    HV6545.S828 2015
    362.28--dc23

                                                                2015004387

ISBN 13: 978-1-4128-5694-2 (hbk)

Contents

1	Introduction *David Lester & Steven Stack*	1
2	Ritual, Dramatic Performance, and Suicide: An Anthropological Perspective *Joseph Rubenstein*	5
Part 1.	The Suicide Note	
3	The Presentation of the Self in Suicide Notes *David Lester & Bijou Yang*	13
4	Dramatic Suicide Notes *David Lester*	21
5	The Body as a Suicide Note *David Lester*	41
6	Suicide and the Communicative Condition: Audience and the Idea of Suicide *Jermaine Martinez*	51
Part 2.	The Location of the Suicidal Act	
7	The Location of the Suicidal Act *Steven Stack*	73
8	Suicide Away from Home *Steven Stack*	77
9	Hotel Suicide and the Drug Subculture *Steven Stack*	95

10	Back to Nature: Suicide in Natural Areas *Steven Stack*	109
11	Suicide in the Grand Canyon National Park *Steven Stack & Barbara Bowman*	129
12	Suicide in Public *David Lester*	151
13	Suicide on Television and Online *David Lester*	159

Part 3. The Methods Chosen for Suicide

14	The Methods Chosen for Suicide *David Lester*	167
15	The Rehearsal: Nonfatal Suicidal Behavior as a Precipitant of Suicide *John F. Gunn III*	183
16	Suicide by Fire: Ethnicity as a Predictor of Self-Immolation in the United States *Steven Stack & Seth B. Abrutyn*	193
17	Have Gun, Will Travel *Steven Stack*	211
18	Unusual Suicides *Steven Stack*	223
19	Methods of Suicide Around the World *Steven Stack*	243

Part 4. Cultural Scripts for Suicide

20	Russian Roulette and Duels *David Lester*	259
21	Death by Seppuku *David Lester*	267

22	Self-Immolation as a Protest *David Lester*	273
23	Victim-Precipitated Homicide *David Lester*	285
24	Sati *David Lester*	305
25	Suicide as the Liberation of the Soul *David Lester*	319
26	Conclusion *David Lester & Steven Stack*	323
About the Authors		333
Senior Author Index		335
Subject Index		341

All the world's a stage,
And all the men and women merely players;
They have their exits and their entrances,
And one man in his time plays many parts . . .
—William Shakespeare, *As You Like It*

1

Introduction

David Lester & Steven Stack

Gertrude Stein once said, "A rose is a rose is a rose." For many of those who study suicide, it might similarly be said, "A suicide is a suicide is a suicide." We talk of the risk of suicide and the rate of suicide, implying that all suicides are the same. Of course, suicide is engaged in by different people—men and women, the young and the old, and psychiatrically disturbed and nondisturbed people. But the nature of their act is rarely examined.

Consider two suicidal acts. On November 25, 1970, in Tokyo, Japan, Yukio Mishima, aged forty-five and a successful Japanese novelist, decided to take his paramilitary force, invade an army base, and persuade the soldiers there to overthrow the Japanese government and restore the Emperor to absolute power. The soldiers refused to follow his commands. Mishima then committed seppuku. He took a knife and ripped his abdomen open, and then his loyal assistant decapitated him.

What a death! Mishima orchestrated his suicide, and the report of his suicide by the media captured worldwide attention. The setting of his suicide, the manner of his suicide, and the timing of it all added to the dramatic aspects of the act.

Consider the suicidal attack on the twin towers of the World Trade Center on September 11, 2001, by two planes led by Mohamed Atta. This act of martyrdom for an Islamic cause created images that haunt us still today. The planes hitting and damaging the towers, the response of those rushing to the towers, the collapse of the towers, and the scenes of people fleeing the scene—all of these images added to the impact that Atta and his team had hoped to create. However you might label or judge those involved in this attack, you cannot deny the drama created by their actions.

This book is intended to view suicide from this dramatic perspective. We will examine to what extent suicidal acts (or at least some suicidal acts) can be viewed from a theatrical perspective. We will explore how suicides can choose the timing, setting, method, and other circumstances of their suicide to heighten the impact on others and to frame their suicide in a way that they choose.

What happens in the hours, minutes, and second before a suicide? If others are present, what are the interactions? On January 29, 1977, Freddie Prinze, the television actor, shot himself in a room with his business manager present. On December 1, 2012, Jovan Belcher, a linebacker for the Kansas City Chiefs NFL team, shot himself in the parking lot of a football stadium after talking to his coach, Romeo Crennel. What is the nature of the interactions between the suicidal individual and the bystanders? And what role does this interaction have on the outcome?

Let us give an example from the study of murder. Only one study has looked at the interpersonal interactions between murderer and victim. Luckenbill (1977) analyzed the act of murder as a dynamic interchange between the murderer and the victim. In Stage 1, the victim does something that the offender defines as an offense to "face," an insult, a refusal to comply, or a nonverbal gesture. In Stage 2, the offender interprets the victim's action as personally offensive, often with the victim and bystanders providing information for this interpretation (in 60% of the incidents). In Stage 3, the offender makes a retaliatory move to restore face, such as a verbal or physical challenge (in 86% of the incidents) or an actual murderous act (in 14% of the incidents). In Stage 4, the victim responds either with noncompliance (41%) or an attack (30%). The bystanders (present in 70% of the incidents) may at this point encourage the attack (57%) or remain neutral (43%). In Stage 5, the victim is killed. In Stage 6, the offender may flee (58%), stay voluntarily (32%) or, in rare cases, be held at the scene by the bystanders (10%). This type of study has never been conducted on suicide carried out in the presence of others.

Those who die by suicide alone leave a suicide note. Does this suicide note provide insights into the mind of the suicides? Or it designed merely to present themselves to others in a particular way? There are other ways that the suicidal person can communicate to others, such as using Twitter and YouTube, or even live on television. Does the timing of the suicidal act have significance? Does the suicide choose daytime or nighttime? It has been claimed that there is a birthday effect in suicide, that many suicides kill themselves close to the time of their birthday. What does this signify?

What about the way suicides dress themselves? Are there common choices of clothing and does the choice of clothes have any psychological meaning? The thirty-nine members of the Heaven's Gate cult, who died by suicide together on March 26, 1997, all clothed themselves identically and positioned themselves in their beds in the same way.

Suicides choose a location for their suicide. This is typically at home, but many die by suicide away from home. Very little is known about the characteristics of those who choose to die away from home. What factors, psychological, social, and cultural, influence this choice? Wasserman and Stack (2008) have written on the notion of *lethal locations* and noted that the choice of certain locations influences the chances of another person interrupting the suicidal act. People who rent a motel room for their suicidal act, for example, are less likely to have their suicide interrupted by someone who will try to prevent the suicide. All else being equal, people choosing to die by suicide alone in the wilderness (e.g., deep in the trail system of a national park) will be less likely to be interrupted than are persons choosing to de by suicide at home where significant others may try to stop them. Some locations almost insure death, while other locations may make a successful suicide less likely. In short, suicidal intent, a major concern to clinicians, varies with the chosen location for suicide. Locations vary in their lethality and implied suicidal intent just as the methods chosen for suicide (e.g., guns versus poison) vary in their lethality.

The issues we discuss may seem offensive to some of those concerned with preventing suicide. Focusing on the dramatic aspects of suicidal acts may seem tangential to the physical and mental pain of those dying by suicide. But, as we will see, these aspects of the act often give us clues into their mental state, clues that might be helpful in understanding and preventing other suicides. In the theater, the issues involved in staging a play are handled by the scenographer. Thus, this book might have been called *The Scenography of Suicide*, where the scenographers are none other than the suicides themselves.

The goal of this book is to explore the scenographic aspects of the suicidal act. It is hoped that the ideas and issues discussed here will provoke readers to think about suicidal acts in a new way and stimulate new and innovative research into suicide.

References

Luckenbill, D. (1977). Criminal homicide as a situated transaction. *Social Problems*, 25, 176–86.

Wasserman, I., & Stack, S. (2008). Lethal locations. *Death Studies*, 32, 757–67.

2

Ritual, Dramatic Performance, and Suicide: An Anthropological Perspective

Joseph Rubenstein

Most discussions of suicide correctly begin with Emile Durkheim's *Le Suicide* (1897). His four-fold sociological typology—egoistic/altruistic/anomic/fatalistic—has precipitated a rich conversation for more than a century, albeit with considerable criticism and emendation.

Anthropologists question the conservative "Western" bias informing Durkheim's types. Altruistic suicide, for example, certainly a "self-killing," might be viewed more morally neutral and even positively outside the Durkheimian structure. It seems problematical to stigmatize the suicide bomber for identifying too much with his social world, and to call the Western soldier sacrificing his life to save others a "hero." "Assisted suicide" is for some humane and not counter to Judeo-Christian ideology. Recontextualizing suicide is an on-going project. This chapter argues that many types of suicides might be better understood in the framework of ritual drama. This performative approach implies "agency" and a spectrum of control, interpreting suicide as a distinctly human act in a social and cultural context.

Suicide as dramatic performance addresses the more reductive causal explanations of suicide by sociology and biology. The anthropologist Turner (1969) asks us to look at the "process" and "premise" of ritual action and not the product which, in this case, is self-death.

The shift is subtle. Turner would not deny that an individual's inability to "master social surroundings" leads to tension and "social disunity." Equally important, however, is the individual's *recognition* of this conflict and the construction of a ritual performance, a "social drama" (Turner, 1974), in order to resolve it—either on his own terms, or with the help of a practitioner.

A performative approach suggests an understanding of suicide less guided by the more rigid sociological types mentioned above that miss, as Geertz (1957) writes, "the framework of beliefs, expressive symbols, and values in terms of which individuals define their world, express their feelings, and make their judgments." (p. x)

Is it possible that "performing suicide" can lead to an authentic and dramatic "transcendence of life"? Or are the feelings so distorted, the judgment so impaired that the performance appears more "ritualistic" than ritual. The trappings of theatricality may be apparent, but the last act does not lead to a transformation. Rather, it leads to an incomplete ending. Rarely is anything resolved; rarely is anything left whole.

The Structures of Suicidal Drama

Suicidal Scripts

Suicidal dramas, ancient or modern, sacred or secular, require "scripts." Again, as Durkheim (1912/1961) argued, rituals perpetuate the social structures of society, and their rules show us how to comport ourselves. Thus, the suicidal script *mechanically* adheres to the conventions of society. But that takes us only so far and views scripts/rituals as endlessly circular celebrations of the fixed order. Durkheim's text may be a blueprint, but the real work of building a performance remains.

It is in the *rehearsal* (long or short) that the suicidal actor comes to understand the goal of his performance—which is immortality—through the sacrifice of oneself and often of others. Many texts are, by now, well known and culture bound—the Japanese *kamikaze* pilot, the Buddhist self-immolator, the Muslim suicide bomber, the United States mass shooter, and the more frequent, less spectacular, quiet and isolated self-deaths.

The rehearsal or actor training is the "process" that precedes the acting out of the suicide. Playwright and director Grotowski's (1968) "poor theater," which derived from his study of traditional ritual dramas, understood that the actor gained self-awareness, clarity of character perhaps for the first time, in this liminal period (Ven Gennep, 1909/1960). This "betwixt and between," well understood in anthropology, is as "real" and perhaps more real than the final action. Grotowski wrote that the actor rehearsed to finally eliminate conflict, to feel whole. He felt that, if the actor were transparent enough, it would be akin to "self-sacrifice." Suicide, then, is never *for* the other, but always *in relation to* the other.

Suicidal Messages

Others are always involved in suicides. Messages are sent. Moore and Myerhoff (1977, p. x) write, "Clearly, in a complex specialized and differentiated society, rites often . . . are used to show a limited commonality, or even to create it."

In choreographer Anna Halprin's performances throughout the 1980s, beginning with *Search for Living Myths and Rituals Through Dance and Environment*[1] and concluding with *The Planetary Dance*,[2] there is a focused communicative message she hopes will spread beyond the event. She writes about the *Vortex Dance,* part of her *Circle the Earth* cycle (May 29–June 1, 1985 through 1994), "We join as a whole in the center of the space, to build a symbol of our collective strength." (Halprin, 1995, p. 243).

Halprin's performances moved from a mountain to the entire planet in an embodied message to join the world in peace. Whether it was successful or not is beside the point. Behind the ritual was a momentary belief ("a common pulse with a common purpose") that by participating in the performance we could be transformed, renewed in our fundamental humanity. The medium was the message.

The suicidal drama, whether collectively enacted or individually performed, always has, as Moore and Myerhoff enumerate in the formal properties of ritual, a "social message." Any aspect of behavior, they write, can be ritualized. Suicide requires ritual form to accomplish its meanings. It is the vessel from which we all drink to make sense of the act.

Suicide understood in this way draws us in so that we are forced to share the drama. Even the novel suicidal script eventually is repeated and becomes part of our collective memory, "tradition" if you will. "It was like a bad movie," the audience says as SWAT teams arrive, TV cameras are deployed, and a kind of stage is cordoned off.

We cannot avert our eyes and, to use playwright and actor Artaud's (1958) notion, truly this is a "theater of cruelty." How close is it to Artaud when we watch the suicidal standoff? He writes of "cruel theater" that "wakes us up. Nerves and heart." We experience "immediate violent action." The message? Surrender to this act. Feel it.

Suicidal Properties

Suicide as ritual drama is constructed of several formal properties. Definitions of ritual are legion, but, to stay with Moore and Myerhoff, the elements below allow us to see suicide's performative structure:

1. Repetition
   The "tradition"
2. Acting
   "Self-conscious" behavior, not spontaneous
3. "Special" behavior or stylization
   Symbols or actions used in novel or extraordinary ways
4. Order
   Acts in the drama, from beginning to end, including rehearsal
5. Evocative presentational style; staging
   We are made "attentive" either during or after

Goffman's *The Presentation of Self in Everyday Life* (1959) is noted for its dramaturgical model of social life. The role playing of the suicide actor, again, reminds us that the individual committed to taking his own life does so in "relation" to an audience:

1. Performance
   In "performance" a social message is conveyed, to oneself and others, about the situation. Whether the actor is aware of it or not, "impression management" is occurring and the audience is attributing meaning.
2. Setting
   Scenery, props, and location are central to the performance.
3. Manner
   "Playing" the role. How consistent is the performance given with what we know about the actor? Inconsistent performances require a more complex reading of the script.
4. Front
   The "script" which is often predetermined for the actor.
5. Front Stage, Back Stage
   Front Stage: Role playing for an audience.
   Back Stage: "Who he truly is."

Suicide: Remedy or Poison?

How, finally, to understand a suicide? Is it a remedy or a poison? Goffman reminds us that performance requires a kind of consensual agreement between the actor and the audience. We "suspend our disbelief" and allow the play to proceed. Suicide, however, in most cases, is defined as a "poison," and we are ready to intervene, to jump on stage to stop the performance—*to disbelieve*. It is almost never a "remedy," but rather a tabooed action, explicit or implicit.

To say it is against the law to commit suicide implies there is a punishment to be meted out for breaking the taboo. Apart from those who assist suicide, or the stigmatized friends and relatives unable to stop it, it is hard to imagine what further harm might be done to one who has successfully committed suicide.

Perhaps it would be better to conclude by asking about the role of the suicidal actor. What is the meaning of his performance, and what dangers are unleashed when the drama proceeds? We would rather it not proceed, for committing suicide "breaks the rules," a remedy consigning us to "anomie," *a nomos*, without order. For Durkheim, a poison.

But it is in the void that we find another possibility in the suicide performance. A performative model of suicide discovers an ambivalent structure in the void. Yes, the rules are broken in that short or long period when the pills take hold, the moment before the trigger is pulled, or in the protracted siege. Death resolves the indeterminacy. It is the remedy *and* the poison that, for the moment before the end, injects order into a slowly dissolving life.

Notes

1. Jan. 31-May 2, 1981 Choreographed and Performed by: Anna Halprin and San Francisco Dance Workshop with people of the Bay Area
2. 1987 Choreography: Anna Halprin. Performers: People of the Bay Area and communities worldwide

References

Artaud, A. (1958). *The theater and its double*. New York: Grove.

Durkheim, E. (1897). *Le suicide*. Paris, France: Felix Alcan.

Durkheim, E. (1912/1961). *The elementary forms of the religious life*. New York: Collier.

Geertz, C. (1957). Ritual and social change: a Javanese example. *American Anthropologist, 59*, 32–54.

Goffman, E. (1959). *The presentation of self in everyday ife*. Garden City, NY: Doubelday.

Grotowski, J. (1968). *Towards a poor theater*. New York: Simon & Schuster.

Halprin, A. (1995). *Moving toward life*. Hanover, NH: Wesleyan University Press.

Moore, S. F., & Myerhoff, B. G. (Eds.) (1977). *Secular ritual*. Assen, the Netherlands: Van Gorcum.

Turner, V. W. (1969). *The ritual process: Structure and anti-structure*. Ithaca, NY: Cornell University Press.

Turner, V. W. (1974). *Dramas, fields, and metaphors: Symbolic action in human society.* Ithaca, NY: Cornell University Press.
Ven Gennep, A. (1909/1960). *The rites of passage.* Chicago, IL: University of Chicago Press.

Part 1

The Suicide Note

3

The Presentation of the Self in Suicide Notes[1]

David Lester & Bijou Yang

In taking any psychological test, there is always the possibility that, instead of responding truthfully, individuals wish to present a particular view of themselves. To detect this, the Minnesota Multiphasic Personality Inventory (MMPI), for example, has subscales to detect presenting a healthy self (faking good) and presenting a pathological self (faking bad). Research has supported the ability of people to fake the image that they present to others. For example, Braginsky, Braginsky, and Ring (1969) demonstrated that schizophrenic inpatients could choose whether or not to report major symptoms (such as hallucinations) depending on the expected outcome (being placed on a locked ward versus being released). In a second study, Braginsky and Braginsky (1971) found that adolescents in a mental hospital could vary their mental age on intelligence tests by three years, again depending on the outcome (being placed in a pleasant versus unpleasant program at the institution).

Individuals present various images on a daily basis as a result of their different roles and corresponding functions they perform. We are used to switching from one image to another and choosing the image to fit the occasion, and there is no reason to doubt that this is true when we die. In modern times, the popularity of online social media sites such as Twitter and Facebook have allowed people to craft the narrative of their lives and present themselves to friends and family, and to the world, in a particular light. This fits a popular television message: "Image is everything." In contrast, some psychological tests ignore this behavior and assume that the individual's self-presentation is not faked. For example, the Thematic Apperception Test (TAT), a projective test, asks respondents to tell stories to pictures shown to them. The interpretation of their stories assumes that the stories will reveal accurate information about the respondents' psychodynamics. The scoring does not take into account the possibility that the respondents' stories are affected by the desire of the respondents to present a particular image of themselves. A recent volume, in which suicidologists were asked to write 1,500 words about themselves (Pompili, 2010), resulted in a very diverse set of protocols. Some were very personal, revealing details of the writer's life, and others listed professional accomplishments. Some avoided personal information but were brief scholarly articles on a particular topic. Occasional chapters revealed strong emotions such as anger. These chapters illustrate the different ways writers present the self.

Suicide notes have been examined in the past in a way similar to TAT stories in that researchers assume that suicide notes reveal accurate information about the psychological states of those dying by suicide and the reasons for their suicide. As a result, researchers have not viewed suicide notes as a possible means by which the suicides consciously present a particular self-image. A broader way of stating this hypothesis is to propose that those writing suicide notes have a hidden agenda. The present chapter argues that suicide notes may often be a result of a decision (conscious or unconscious) to present the self in a particular way and may not, therefore, provide clues to the psychodynamics of the suicidal act.

In the following sections, five topics are covered: (1) examples of the hypothesis of the chapter using suicide bombers and kamikaze pilots; (2) an exploration of whether the suicidal act and the suicide note can be construed as a presentation of the self to other; (3) pseudocides (i.e., those who fake their own suicide); (4) an analysis of one suicide note in detail: and (5) an examination of the classification of suicide notes by Jacobs for its relevance for the present hypothesis. The final section draws some conclusions.

Crafted Self-Images by Suicide Bombers and Kamikaze Pilots

A good example of the presentation of the self in suicide communications comes from videos recorded by suicide bombers prior to their departure to be released to the media after the suicide attack. Best (2010) analyzed the content of some of these videos and noted that they focus on the political nature of the act and that they cast the act as altruistically motivated. However, Best also noted that the videos show evidence of editing, and this editing is done by persons unknown (for example, by those who sent the suicide bomber on his or her mission or by the media outlets that broadcast the video). Although the videos seem to be produced for the public, unedited versions may have contained messages for the suicide bomber's family and indications of the individual's state of mind. Most commentators on suicide bombers focus on the official motivation for the suicide bombing provided by the suicide bomber or the organization that planned the attack. There is reluctance by scholars to analyze the psychodynamic processes that led the individual to become a suicide bomber, as Lester, Yang and Lindsay (2004) have noted, and a reliance on what the individual says in the video as the truth rather than as an attempt by the suicide bomber to present himself in a particular manner.

A similar problem arises with analyses of the letters sent home by Japanese kamikaze pilots from the Second World War. Orbell and Morikawa (2011) analyzed the themes in these letters, a meaningful project, and classified the themes into mentions of an honorable or beautiful death, expressions of familial love, and so on. But to consider these letters as insights into the psychodynamics of pilots is perhaps misguided. These letters were written in the presence of other members of the unit and superiors, with the awareness that they might be read by superiors. As a result, the letters are most likely to be presentations of the self rather than windows into the minds of the pilots. For example, in one of the most conforming populations in the world, where what others think of you is of paramount importance, no Japanese pilot wrote that he was doing this because he was too scared not to volunteer, according to Orbell and Morikawa. No pilot wrote home that he was experiencing panic or somatic symptoms of terror. No pilot said that he had had a lifetime history of depression and that going on a kamikaze mission was a way of committing suicide in a covert manner.

Suicide Notes as Public Statements

As Etkind (1997) argued, suicide notes are meant to be public. They are written for others to read and sometimes to be published. Etkind noted that writing suicide notes became more common after newspapers in Europe started publishing them in the eighteenth century. MacDonald and Murphy (1990) observed that suicides, expecting their suicide notes to appear in the newspapers, saw that they had access to a mass audience, and suicides could craft their suicide note so as to achieve sympathy or revenge, or perhaps to project an image that others would remember. Etkind presented suicide notes from those accused of misdeeds and noted that they often did not admit guilt, but rather presented themselves as victims of persecution. For example, Major Henry Hubert manufactured evidence to convict a Jewish officer, Captain Alfred Dreyfus, of treason, yet Hubert's suicide note in 1898 made no admission of guilt. Some suicide notes are written to advance a cause, perhaps arguing for assisted-suicide or for political reasons. Percy Bridgman, a Nobel Prize winner in physics, committed suicide in 1961 while suffering from cancer and wrote, "It isn't decent for society to make a man do this thing himself. Probably this is the last day I will be able to do it myself." Bridgman's note is often used by those advocating physician assisted-suicide. Jo Roman (1980) wrote a book, as well her suicide note, arguing for the establishment of places where people could go in order to commit suicide peacefully in pleasant surroundings. Craig Badialis and Joan Fox committed suicide after a Vietnam Peace Moratorium rally at Glassboro State College in New Jersey on October 16, 1969 (Asinof, 1971), and left notes that advocated peace (but which were suppressed by the local authorities). Etkind (1997, p. i) argued that, instead of being intensely personal documents, many suicide notes should be read as social acts.

Suicides can indeed be choreographed. Etkind described the 1944 suicide of Lupe Velez, a Hollywood actress known as the Mexican Spitfire. She was divorced from Tarzan's Johnny Weismuller and pregnant by a man who was unwilling to marry her. She ordered a Mexican feast; decorated her bedroom with satin sheets, flowers, candles, and a crucifix; and ingested seventy-five Seconals. Her note was addressed to the lover, blaming him for her death and that of their unborn child.

Some suicides occur in public, along with public statements intended to shape the image presented to others. Yukio Mishima committed seppuku in 1970 in front of a regiment of soldiers after urging them to rise up and restore the Emperor to his rightful, powerful place in Japan. Bud Dwyer, the state treasurer in Pennsylvania, was convicted in 1986 of taking a three hundred thousand-dollar kickback after awarding a state contract and faced a fine and a fifty-five-year prison sentence. On January 22, 1987, one day before sentencing, he shot himself in his office in front of newspapers and television reporters, proclaiming his innocence.

Pseudocides

Some people fake their suicide, leaving a suicide note and then disappearing, moving elsewhere to start a new life. These instances include occasional notes left on the Golden Gate Bridge in San Francisco for which no one saw anyone jump off the bridge. Seiden and Tauber (1970) studied these notes and found that they differed from notes left by suicides. They tended to be longer, gave more realistic reasons for suicide (such as financial and legal problems), had less positive emotion, and made less mention of death and suicide than the genuine notes. Here is one short suicide note from a man who was a member of the board of San Francisco supervisors who turned up a year later selling bibles in Houston: "Loved ones: My nerves are shot. Please forgive me. Chris." (Etkind, 1997, p. 61)

An Illustration of the Thesis

To illustrate the thesis of this chapter, here is a genuine suicide note from a man in his nineties who committed suicide.

> A terrible fright! I woke up this morning at 9 o'clock and looked over to my spouse's bed, and she doesn't move. On closer inspection, she is dead. She had been ailing in the afternoon and stayed in bed, but had in the evening freshened herself up and enjoyed her supper. She was, on the contrary, for the most part buoyant following her stay in the hospital. I gave her the medication. She did cough a lot, but she finally calmed down. I lay down and then fell asleep. After I awoke, see above. What the cause of her decease is I cannot determine. I shall leave everything in the room the way it is. I myself am, at my age of 93, utterly unhappy and have no desire to continue living, above all as I have often been ill for years now. Why should I go on now? I wish to add that my spouse was just in the clinic and had just been released by [Dr. Y]. following a thorough examination. Our marriage has lasted since 1926 and might doubtless be termed good. My married son lives in [address]. He is a teacher, but very often ill, is not allowed to visit us. His grief! Instead, his wife helped out in our household while my spouse was undergoing surgical treatment (eye operation) and returned home when my spouse was released. As I said, I have no desire to continue living and am going to take my life with some medical drugs I collected years ago. I have not informed anyone of my spouse's death as my own will follow immediately. In deepest mourning, Karl.

At first reading, this note suggests an elderly, possibly frail man with not many years left to live, acting impulsively on discovering that his wife has died. His son is not well, and he may feel that he would be a burden to his son and daughter-in-law if they had to take care of him. The death of his wife means that he has lost a very important social tie. This elderly man, therefore, seems to fit neatly into Joiner's (2005) theory of suicide which proposes that perceived burdensomeness and thwarted belonging are the two most important causal factors for suicide.

But let us look at this note from a "presentation of the self" perspective. First, the note carefully lays out the facts and the man's decision-making processes. He is presenting himself as calm and rational. He is not a crazy, elderly man with dementia. Second, he knows (or strongly suspects) that his son and daughter-in-law will read this note. How will they feel? His son may feel guilty, and perhaps his father wants him to! Although the son is ill, he has not visited his parents, nor have his parents visited him. He left taking care of his parents in an emergency to his wife. Has he telephoned or written regularly to them? How long ago is it since his parents were invited to visit and stay with him? Did he make his parents feel welcome if they did visit, or did he make them feel that they were an inconvenience?

The man's suicide seems to be a sudden decision, but he and his wife may have talked about what they would do if one of them died. In one's nineties, illnesses are common, and the day-to-day tasks of living quite difficult. Suicide may have been a well-thought-out plan.

Alternatively, could this be a murder-suicide or double suicide, with the suicide note intended to mislead the police? After all, the wife is in her nineties, and a natural death is very likely. Is the medical examiner going to conduct as thorough an investigation as he or she would if the couple were in their thirties or forties? Moreover, a double suicide is not a crime and, even if it is murder-suicide, the murderer is dead, and why upset the children any more than would a natural death followed by suicide?

Studies have found that the authorities sometimes show concern for the survivors. For example, Carpenter, et al. (2011) found that coroners in Queensland (Australia) were less likely to carry out a complete autopsy on a suicide if the family had concerns about the procedure or if the religion of the deceased had proscription against autopsies.

Jacobs's Classification of Suicide Notes

Since the circumstances leading to suicide are subject to a wide variation, it is plausible to assume that suicide notes may be determined by the desire to present the self in a particular way. According to Jacobs (1967) suicide notes can be classified into four types: (1) the person has a terminal illness, (2) the person accuses another of causing his or her death, (3) last will and testaments, and (4) first form notes. It is this last category that is relevant to the present hypothesis. By and large, in this type of note, suicides try to reconcile the image of themselves as to-be-trusted people (who have been given the sacred trust of life) with the fact that they are about to break this trust through the act of suicide.

Jacobs summarized several components that might be found in first-form suicide notes:

- The person is faced with extremely distressing problems.
- He views this state of affairs as part of a long history of such distressing crises.
- He believes that death is the only solution to his problems.
- He has become increasingly socially isolated so that he cannot share his distress with others.
- He has overcome his internalized moral constraint that categorizes suicide as irrational or immoral.
- He has succeeded in this since his social isolation makes him feel less constrained by societal rules.
- He has constructed some verbal rationalization that enables him to view himself as a to-be-trusted person, in spite of his trust violation, by defining the problems as not of his own making or as open to no other solution.
- He has made some provision that his problems will not occur after death.

It is typically found that these notes beg forgiveness or request indulgence. They show that the problems that have led to this decision are not of his own making. These notes communicate the history of these problems, how they have grown beyond endurance, and the necessity of death. Finally, the writer includes that he is fully aware of what he is doing but knows that the reader will not understand his reasons. While Jacobs felt that this expressed the genuine thoughts, desires, and emotions of the suicide, the present hypothesis would view the suicide note as deliberately presenting the image of a rational and reasonable person making a sensible decision.

Conclusions

Suicide notes may not simply reflect the motivations and psychological state of the person committing suicide, but rather they may be constructed so as to present an image to the person's significant others. In this case, the suicide is committing a psychosomatic fallacy, a term coined by Shneidman and Farberow (1957) to describe the situation where a person confuses the self as experienced by the self with the self as experienced by others. The suicide in this case is concerned with the reactions of others even though he or she will not be around to witness these reactions. It is not possible to prove that a particular suicide note is the result of a desire to present the self in a particular manner. Likewise it is hard to prove that the note is *not* the result of a desire to present the self in a particular manner. We should use caution, therefore, when using suicide notes as a means of understanding the psychodynamics of the suicidal mind.

Note

1.   This chapter is based on Yang and Lester (2011).

References

Asinof, E. (1971). *Craig and Joan*. New York: Viking.

Best, S. (2010). Liquid terrorism: altruistic fundamentalism in the context of liquid modernity. *Sociology*, 44, 678–94.

Braginsky, B., Braginsky, D., & Ring, L. (1969). *Methods of adness*. New York: Holt, Rinehart & Winston.

Braginsky, D., & Braginsky, B. (1971). *Hansels and Gretels*. New York: Holt, Rinehart & Winston.

Carpenter, B., Tait, G., Adkins, G., Barnes, M., Naylor, C., & Begun, N. (2011). Communicating with the coroner. *Death Studies*, 35, 316–37.

Etkind, M. (1997). . . . *Or not to be*. New York: Riverhead Books.

Jacobs, J. (1967). A phenomenological study of suicide notes. *Social Problems*, 15, 60–72.

Joiner, T. E. (2005). *Why people die by suicide*. Cambridge, MA: Harvard University Press.

Lester, D., Yang, B., & Lindsay, M. (2004). Suicide bombers. *Studies in Conflict & Terrorism*, 27, 283–95

MacDonald, M., & Murphy, T. R. (1990). *Sleepless souls*. New York: Oxford University Press.

Orbell, J., & Morikawa, T. (2011). An evolutionary account of suicide attacks. *Political Psychology*, 32, 297–322.

Pompili, M. (2010). *Suicide in the words of suicidologists*. Hauppauge, NY: Nova Science.

Roman, J. (1980). *Exit house*. New York: Seaview Books.

Seiden, R., & Tauber, R. (1970). Pseudocides versus suicides. *Proceedings of the 5th international conference for suicide prevention*, pp. 219–22. Vienna, Austria: International Association for Suicide Prevention.

Shneidman, E. S., & Farberow, N. L. (1957). The logic of suicide. In E. S. Shneidman & N. L. Farberow (Eds.) *Clues to suicide*, pp. 31–40 New York: McGraw-Hill.

Yang, B., & Lester, D. (2011). The presentation of the self: an hypothesis about suicide notes. *Suicidology Online*, 2, 75–79.

4

Dramatic Suicide Notes

David Lester

We have seen in the previous chapter how people may construct their suicide notes in a way to present a particular image or even to transform their image. They often want to shape how others remember them. There are many other ways in which people leave memorials to themselves.

A Suicide Note on YouTube

Amanda was a fifteen-year-old teenager who posted a video on YouTube in which she presented a sequence of flash cards to tell of her experience of being blackmailed and bullied. She had sent a picture of her breasts to a man she met online who then circulated it around the Internet. She uploaded the video to YouTube on September 2, 2012, and committed suicide on October 10, 2012. By October 13, her video had received 1.6 million views. It is difficult to remove a video from the Internet because others make copies and circulate them. Interestingly, when I asked my college's IT unit to download the video onto a flash drive, it took them over an hour to find out how to do it. Students at the college knew how to do it immediately, with the appropriate software already downloaded on their computers and smart phones.

When in eighth grade, Amanda sent the picture of her breasts to a man she met on video chat. He then blackmailed her by threatening to circulate it. He did so, and the police informed Amanda and her family about this. Amanda experienced anxiety and depression and had panic attacks. The family moved to a new home, and Amanda attended a new school, but Amanda began to use alcohol and drugs. A year later, the man created a Facebook page with Amanda's photo as the profile image and circulated it to her classmates. Amanda attempted suicide with bleach and was treated at an emergency department, after which abusive messages were posted by her classmates on her own Facebook page. The family moved again, but Amanda began to engage in self-mutilation and again attempted suicide. Eventually she killed herself.

Amanda's suicide received worldwide attention in the media. On October 19, a vigil was held across Canada. A Facebook memorial page was created which has received millions of "likes," but abusive postings still occurred. Amanda's mother established a trust fund in Amanda's name to fight cyber-bullying. Guidelines from the Centers of Disease Control and from suicide prevention organizations state that sensationalizing and glorifying suicide makes it more likely that a suicide will generate more suicides in the community. However, sensationalizing and glorifying suicide is often the norm today.

What is also noteworthy is that Amanda uploaded the YouTube video five weeks prior to her suicide. The messages on the flash cards outlined her plight and stated that she had already made two prior suicide attempts. She provided, therefore, thirty-nine days in which people could have intervened. The American Association of Suicidology has recommended the use of ten warning signs for impending suicidal behavior, using the mnemonic IS PATH WARM: suicidal ideation, substance abuse, purposelessness, anxiety, trapped, hopelessness, worthlessness, anger, recklessness, and mood changes. Previous research by Gunn, Lester, and McSwain (2011) have shown that these signs are valid for predicting suicidal ideation and behavior. For the present chapter, I had two judges read Amanda's flash cards from her YouTube video, and they found eight or nine of these signs as present. Anger was missing, and the two judges did not agree on purposelessness.[1] It is clear, therefore, that Amanda would be judged to be at high risk for suicide by a suicide expert viewing her video. However, there is no indication that any of those who viewed the video attempted to intervene and prevent Amanda's suicide.[2] Here is what she wrote on the flashcards.

Hello
I've decided to tell you about my never ending story
In 7th grade I would go with friends on webcam
meet and talk to new people
then got called stunning, beautiful, perfect, etc . . .
then wanted me to flash . . .
so I did . . . 1 year later . . .
I got a msg on facebook
From him . . . don't know how he knew me . . .
It said . . . if you don't put on a show for me I will send ur boobs

he knew my adress, school, relatives, friends, family names
Christmas break . . .
Knock at my door at 4 AM
It was the police . . . my photo was sent to everyone
I then got really sick and got . . .
Anxiety, major depression, and panic disorder
I then moved and got into Drugs & Alcohol . . .
My anxiety got worse . . . couldn't go out
A year past and the guy came back with my new
list of friends and school. But made a facebook page
My boobs were his profile pic . . .
Cried every night, lost all my friends and respect
people had for me . . . again . . .
Then nobody liked me
name calling, judged . . .
I can never get that photo back
It's out there forever . . .
I started cutting . . .
I promised myself never again . . .
Didn't have any friends and I sat at lunch alone
So I moved schools again . . .
Everything was better even though i still sat alone
at lunch in the library everday.
After a month later I started talking to an old guy friend.
We back and fourth texted and he started to say he . . .
Liked me . . . led me on . . . he had a girlfriend . . .
then he said come over my gf's on vacation
so I did . . . huge mistake . . .
He hooked up with me . . .
I thought he liked me . . .
1 week later I get a text get out of your school
His girlfriend and 15 others came including hiself . . .
The girl and 2 others just said look around nobody likes you
In front of my new school (50) people
A guy then yelled just punch her already
So she did . . . she threw me to the ground a punched me several times
Kids filmed it. I was all alone and left on the ground.
I felt like a joke in this world . . . I thought nobody deserves this
I was alone. I lied and said it was my fault and my idea
I didn't want him getting hurt, I thought he really liked me.

but he just wanted the sex . . . someone yelled punch her already
Teachers ran over but I just went and layed in a ditch and my dad
found me.
I wanted to die so bad . . . when he brought me home I drank bleach . . .
It killed me inside and I thought I was gonna actully die.
Ambulence came and brought me to the hospital and flushed me
After I got home all I saw was on facebook—She deserved it, did you
wash the mud out of your hair?–I hope shes dead
nobody cared . . . I moved away to another city to my moms.
Another school . . . I didn't wanna press charges because I wanted
to move on.
6 months has gone by . . . people are posting pics of bleach, clorex
and ditches.
tagging me . . . I was doing a lot better too . . .They said . . .
She should try a different bleach, I hope she dies this time and isn't
so stupid.
They said I hope she sees this and kills herself . . .
Why do i get this? I messed up but why follow me . . .
I left your guys city . . . Im constantly crying now . . .
Everyday I think why am i still here?
My anxiety is horrible now . . . never went out this summer
All from my past . . . lifes never getting better . . . cant go to school
meet or be with people . . . constantly cutting. Im really depressed
Im on anti deppresants now and councelling and a month ago this
summer
I overdosed . . . in hospital for 2 days . . .
Im stuck . . . whats left of me now . . . nothing stops
I have nobody . . . I need someone :(
my name is Amanda Todd
[picture of wrist with cuts]
[stay strong]

A Suicide Note on Twitter

Ashley, an eighteen-year-old, died by suicide[3] after sending 145
tweets in the twenty-four hours prior to her suicide. In these tweets,
she alleged that she had been sexually abused from ages fourteen to
seventeen by her father. After trying to bring the abuser to justice, she
had received news that her alleged abuser would not be prosecuted.
After Ashley's death, her mother said that Ashley felt that the investigation into her abuse had made her feel like a suspect rather than

the victim that she was. The investigating authorities were accused of being insensitive and for sending her back to the home where the alleged abuse took place because they claimed that they could not remove her. Child and Protective Services conducted a five-month investigation but were unable to confirm that the abuse had taken place (*CBS News*, November 15, 2011). The authorities, of course, denied any wrongdoing. However, after Ashley's suicide, they claimed that they would look further into her allegations. As of March 2012, no action had been taken.

On the day of her death, Ashley told her friend who drove her to school that she was feeling ill. From 6:44 AM to 2:08 PM she sent 144 tweets. She had over five hundred followers, but it is not known whether any were monitoring her that day. During the sequence of tweets, there was a break of 139 minutes after 10:42 AM and another twenty-one-minute break after 1:47 PM. No one seems to have intervened in those periods and, again, it is not known whether anyone knew of what was transpiring. At 2:08 PM in her last tweet, Ashley said, "Take two. I hope I get this right."

Ashley came from a dysfunctional family. Ashley's mother had accused her own father of molesting her, and Ashley's grandmother had accused her father of molesting her. Ashley's mother married two men in 1998, one of whom sexually assaulted Ashley and was sent to prison for eleven years. Ashley's mother then met a married man who was separated, and she broke into his house with intent to murder his wife. She was sent to prison, and Ashley moved in with her father.

Other noteworthy events in Ashley's life were that she nearly drowned in a bucket of water at eleven months of age. Ashley had also been the victim of bullying in sixth grade because of her weight. She began to cut her wrists, and she developed an eating disorder. She turned to pills and marijuana to cope. After her mother's release from prison, Ashley was taken on outings with family members, including an uncle who was a registered sex offender and who was later arrested for abusing an eleven-year-old relative. According to Ashley's grandmother, Ashley had a nervous breakdown in 2009, after which her father obtained psychiatric treatment for her and transferred her to a charter school. There she made friends but continued to cut, and her eating disorder switched from anorexia to bulimia. She had a series of mini-romances and confessed to her friends that she had lost her virginity around age fourteen. She had a serious romance with a young boy who apparently found out that Ashley's father was sexually abusing her. Malisow, a newspaper reporter, could not get this boy to talk to him, and so Malisow noted that this information has not been confirmed.[4] The boy ended the relationship. Ashley apparently told her friends that her father had caught her with drugs and blackmailed her into performing oral sex, but her friends were never sure how much of what Ashley told them was true.

At her new school, she made one good friend and apparently told this friend that her father would rent her out to his friends. Toward the end of her life, Ashley had reconnected with her boyfriend, but the relationship broke up again. She then received the news that no charges would be brought against her father. Ashley tried to obtain some counseling, but there was no insurance to pay for it. She had been looking forward to a part in the school production of *Hairspray*, but her poor grades meant that she probably would not be allowed to participate.

Gunn and Lester (2012) ran Ashley's Twitter postings through a computer program that analyzed words used in hourly intervals. There was a trend toward a decrease in the use of the pronoun "I" and a significant decrease in all references to the self over time. There was also a trend toward an increase in terms reflecting positive emotions. Although this may seem surprising, a similar trend was observed in two tape recordings made by a young man in the hours before he died by suicide (Lester, 2010).

On reading the posts, it becomes clear that Ashley attempted to write the posts using rhymes. For example: 10:21 AM "I went to the bathroom and locked the door;" 10:22 AM "I took apart a razor I had gotten from the store."

Here are her tweets.

Nov 6
10:50 PM: "I fuckked up my own suicide" yeah tell me about it . . .
Nov 7
6:44 AM: Staying home today. Can I reach 1000 tweets??? I'm thinking yes!
9:45 AM: just woke up
9:45 AM: Don't feel too well
9:45 AM: There is somebody in my dreams
9:46 AM: I want them gone
9:46 AM: How can we control our dreams?
9:46 AM: Hummm wish somebody would text me
9:47 AM: Kinda lonely right now

Dramatic Suicide Notes

9:47 AM: There was so much more I wanted to do
9:48 AM: Ahhh well time to move on
9:48 AM: My thought process is too crazy
9:48 AM: I totally think I'm bipolar
9:49 AM: Or just crazy
9:49 AM: Idk.
9:49 AM: Humm I remember why we broke up
9:50 AM: I shall do it again
9:50 AM: Because this time I don't have a bf
9:50 AM: And I really don't care anymore
9:51 AM: I should get ready then
9:51 AM: Should have gotten everything last night
9:52 AM: Still just trying to raise my numbers
9:52 AM: So I met this boy
9:52 AM: He was very cute you see
9:52 AM: Quite popular too
9:53 AM: Me and this boy started talking
9:53 AM: Then we talked a lil more
9:53 AM: Then he let me in his front door
9:54 AM: We walked up the stairs where everything was quite
9:54 AM: And he whispered 'you look beautiful' into my ear
9:55 AM: Shivers moved down my spine
9:55 AM: And then he began to kiss my neck
9:56 AM: I know you're thinking 'why did she go'
9:57 AM: And all I can say is my father told me so
9:57 AM: So he kissed me sweet and laid me down on his bed
9:58 AM: I started to shake he said 'give me head'
9:58 AM: I laughed at him and said 'I'm a vegetarian'
9:59 AM: Then I wondered why I had really come to him.
9:59 AM: See I've been in this situation before
10:00 AM: When a boy I loved said he would leave if I didn't give it up
10:00 AM: And I told my friends I had done it even though it wasn't true
10:01 AM: Because he was telling everybody the same things too
10:01 AM: But here is the honest truth
10:01 AM: I never did it till I was sixteen
10:02 AM: I did not know the boy
10:02 AM: And I never got to know him
10:02 AM: He was older stronger and high at the time
10:03 AM: He probably will never admit I was a crime

Suicide as a Dramatic Performance

10:03 AM: His breath smelt sour like smoke and his kisses became rough

10:04 AM: Then I tried to sit up and say 'I've had enough'

10:04 AM: My attempt of getting free were feeble

10:05 AM: I decided to scream 'please stop'

10:05 AM: but he just took a pillow to my face and put me in the dark

10:06 AM: First to go were my shoes. I feel my feet go cold

10:06 AM: Next my pants, he was so bold.

10:07 AM: It hurt so much as he entered me

10:07 AM: Guys I'm telling you my first time was taken from me

10:08 AM: He noticed and said 'are you a virgin?'

10:08 AM: I nodded through tears as he kept barging in

10:09 AM: He finished and was done with me

10:09 AM: I lay on his bed lifeless

10:10 AM: He let me stay there and sleep

10:10 AM: Then he offered me some weed

10:10 AM: I said 'no thank you I don't do that either'

10:11 AM: He said 'girl you're no fun. See you later'

10:12 AM: I started to get dressed and he came back in

10:12 AM: He came close; i tried to get away from him

10:12 AM: He told me 'dont be scared'

10:13 AM: and like an idiot I believed him

10:13 AM: He asked if I liked it

10:14 AM: I shrugged my shoulders

10:14 AM: He leaned in for a kiss, and I let him

10:15 AM: He laid me down and rubbed my back

10:15 AM: I cried in his pillow. He cried back

10:15 AM: He said he was sorry

10:16 AM: I said 'it's okay'

10:16 AM: we laid there together just bathing in our fears

10:17 AM: I don't know why. But I saw the human in him.

10:17 AM: He was probably just as broken as me

10:18 AM: He drove me to my park

10:18 AM: I got on the swirly slide. I just laid there and cried

10:19 AM: I finally walked home

10:19 AM: My father opened the door

10:19 AM: Asked me 'how was it'

10:20 AM: I said 'i'll never forget it . . .'

10:20 AM: as he pressed for questions. I grew impatient

10:20 AM: Said 'dad in so tired can I just go to bed'

Dramatic Suicide Notes

10:21 AM: he dismissed me and I trudged up the stairs.
10:21 AM: My legs hurt. And my heart was filled with despair
10:21 AM: I went to the bathroom and locked the door
10:22 AM: I took apart a razor I had just gotten from the store
10:22 AM: I did what I had to do to forget.
10:23 AM: It seems it's been my only way since sixth grade
10:24 AM: When the kids called me fat even though I was a double zero
10:24 AM: And I began to watch my weight like it was a MTV show.
10:25 AM: I cried as I remembered how I'd starve for days
10:25 AM: And my parents never noticed
10:26 AM: So I laid there and watched the blood gather on the floor
10:26 AM: Then my weak hands reached for the door
10:27 AM: I ran into my little sister she saw and shook her head.
10:27 AM: Then she looked at me and said. 'Just don't let them see sissy.'
10:27 AM: she kissed my head and walked away
10:28 AM: I swear after that night I was never the same
10:28 AM: My dad became to want 'favors' from me too
10:29 AM: He would use it to bribe me if I wanted to hang out after school
10:30 AM: I didn't know that I should have told somebody what he was doing to me
10:30 AM: Sex just became second nature to me
10:31 AM: My father let me as long as he got details sometimes I'd even have to let him see
10:32 AM: I was just a young girl. Who quickly became afraid of men.
10:32 AM: Then years past and it never stopped.
10:32 AM: Finally on day I began to pop
10:33 AM: I sent a boy away
10:33 AM: And told my father enough was enough
10:33 AM: He cried and said 'I'm just so weak'
10:34 AM: I looked at him and saw the brokenness too
10:34 AM: I took pity on him and became the fool
10:35 AM: Things never changed they just got worse
10:35 AM: Till one day I met a boy who in the end hurt my heart worst
10:36 AM: We met in my typical situation
10:36 AM: We were both undressed within a matter of seconds.
10:37 AM: But I could tell he was different.
10:37 AM: I pledged myself by not hooking up with complete strangers.
10:38 AM: But for him I was eager

10:38 AM:	But there was something different about this guy
10:39 AM:	He returned the favor and actually said goodbye
10:40 AM:	On the bus ride home we sat next to each other. Talked for hours on end
10:40 PM:	We held each other's hands and told each other our favorite bands
10:41 PM:	He looked me dead in the eyes and asked if I would please consider seeing him again
10:42 PM:	I went home filled with smiles and cheer
1:01 PM:	Annyways. The guy eventually asked me to be his girl
1:02 PM:	And things were great for a while
1:04 PM:	But my dad got in the way. And ruined everything. One day I just couldn't do it. So I told my boyfriend my secret
1:06 PM:	What happened next was a blur. I told him not to tell. We tried to act normal. We had been dating for over a month when I took his virginity
1:07 PM:	I fell in love for the first time. But my secret was too much for him. He needed time to think. I thought I was going to lose him.
1:09 PM:	A lot happened. But all that matters is that my secret was about to become puplic. Him & my friends made me tell
1:10 PM:	All my efforts to keep a normal life were crumbling right before my eyes.
1:11 PM:	I remember telling my closest teacher and CPS and the police and dectectives. I remember having to tell them everything about my dad
1:35 PM:	It was my boyfriend who told my mom. And she came to get me.
1:37 PM:	Weeks passed then I got the call. They said. 'Sorry but there isn't enough evidence' I hung up.
1:38 PM:	That's when I changed. I didn't care anymore. And the people I was meeting gave me no reason to.
1:39 PM:	The guys I've been with, ha none of them care. They just look at me like I'm just some other hoe.
1:40 PM:	To that I say. I guess I am. I don't know how else to be. It's not my fault. Somebody else chose that for me.
1:47 PM:	Well that's. The story of how I came to be who I am. Well the condensed version. I'd love to hear what you have to say. But I won't be around
2:08 PM:	Take two. Hope I get this right

Mitchell Heisman's 1,905-Page Suicide Note

Mitchell Heisman, aged thirty-five, shot himself in the head on the steps of Memorial Church on the campus of Harvard University at 11 AM on September 18, 2010, in front of some twenty tourists. The day was Yom Kippur, and a service was being held in the church. The gun was described as a silver 38-caliber revolver, and Mitchell fired once into his right temple. Before dying by suicide, Mitchell left a suicide note online that was a formatted book of 1,905 pages, entitled *Suicide Note*, and he e-mailed copies before he died to perhaps up to four hundred people.

Mitchell was born in 1975 in New York City, attended elementary school in Monroe Township in New Jersey, and graduated with a BA in psychology from the University of Albany (according to an article in *The Harvard Crimson* (Newcomer & Srivatsa, 2010)). At the time of his death he was living in an apartment in Somerville, a town neighboring Cambridge, where Harvard University is located.

His mother, seventy-six years old, knew he was writing a book, and he seemed happy about finishing it, she told reporters. However, she did not know anything of its contents. She was expecting Mitchell to help her move in October. She gave *The Harvard Crimson* permission to reveal his name because she knew that Mitchell would want that.

According to Abel (2010), Mitchell was erudite, wry, and handsome. He had a sister, and his mother said that he was a gregarious child but became introverted at twelve after the death of his father from a heart attack. At college, he was described as bookish. After graduating, Mitchell worked at bookstores in Manhattan, acquiring a personal library of thousands of books. Five years before his death, he moved to Somerville to focus on writing and to be near a good library.

Mitchell worked in several bookstores in the area and lived on an inheritance from his father. He led a Spartan existence, eating chicken wings, microwaved meals, and energy bars. He did date, but avoided long-term relationships. He went to a gym daily and took Ritalin, which his mother thought may have led to depression. A roommate described Mitchell as quiet and considerate, never angry.

Mitchell had spent five years working on his book, sometimes for twelve hours a day. It has 1,433 footnotes and a twenty-page bibliography. He had 1,700 references to God and 200 to Friedrich

Nietzsche. Abel felt that this paragraph in the book summed up Mitchell's thesis.

> Every word, every thought, and every emotion come back to one core problem: life is meaningless. The experiment in nihilism is to seek out and expose every illusion and every myth, wherever it may lead, no matter what, even if it kills us.

The Internet has several threads discussing Mitchell, but the majority focus on the contents of the book and whether it is a meaningful discussion of philosophical and other issues, including human nature, society, religion, technology and science. One commentator on www.styleforum.net thought that *Suicide Note* was a masterpiece of modern philosophy and brilliantly written, ending with a thesis of nihilism and rejection of hope. On the other hand, others judged Mitchell's book to show a complete misunderstanding of the topics it covers (encyclopediadramatica.es). Mitchell writes that it is highly unlikely that he will be able to defend his work, suggesting that he planned to die by suicide once he had finished writing the book.

An Analysis of the Suicide Note

Mitchell's book is called *Suicide Note*. Therefore, it is critical is to view it in this light rather than as a work of philosophy. What clues can we glean about Mitchell's beliefs and goals from this book?

First of all, Mitchell believes that his work will be repressed by the society (p. 15), perhaps by silent, inconspicuous, and innocuous methods of repression (p. 17). This statement and those made later in the book suggests mild paranoia. Hardly anything gets repressed in our society. It leads me to wonder whether he tried to get scholarly papers published but journals rejected them. Perhaps he tried to get this book, or an earlier version, published and had it rejected. Rejection is common in the scholarly world, and it is very likely that Mitchell's rambling essays (and book) would not have been found acceptable in the scholarly world. But that does not mean that society wants to suppress his ideas. He says that he will likely be unable to defend the book's content (p. 18), which hints of his eventual suicide.

Mitchell casts his work as a theoretical application of sociobiology to politics, especially liberal democracy. He quickly asserts that he is a nihilist (p. 20) and that he disputes the idea that choosing life is inherently superior to choosing death (p. 22). Others think that choosing death is irrational, but Mitchel disputes this. He views eliminating this bias as analogous to eliminating sexism and racism (p. 24). Mitchell wants to overcome the will to live and liberate death from its subordination to the tyranny of life (p. 25). It seems, therefore, that Mitchell is going to focus this book on persuading himself intellectually that it is rational and desirable to choose to die, even by suicide. Mitchell soon makes his philosophy clear—life is meaningless (p. 28)—and so he wants his nihilism to convince us (and himself) to will death through truth and truth through death (p. 30).

> Life is exploitation. In order to end exploitation, we must end life. In order to end exploitation, we must will death. (p. 182)

> Equality equals death. (p. 185)

The first part of the book is on God who, Mitchell believes, does not exist, at least as conceived by conventional religious systems of thought (p. 33). He views the Christian Bible as science fiction (p. 40). He goes into great detail disputing the existence of God, and, in doing so, he spends many pages on Jews and the Jewish religion. Is Mitchell anti-Semitic? Not in the ordinary sense. But he sees a "correlation" between Jews and the most vociferous and persistent critics of sociobiology in which he believes (p. 103). Since he must intellectually attack the critics of sociobiology, in his view, he also must attack Jewish thought.

Because Mitchell sees all of the modern revolutions (meaning in the last few thousand years) as having a sociobiological basis in ethnic or racial discord (p. 173), he attempts to examine these revolutions in great detail. The book itself begins with a long essay on the nonexistence of God, followed by a long mediation on Hitler and the Nazis. As he discusses the topics he planned to cover, he seems to move toward a position of nihilism. He quotes from Nietzsche:

> For why has the advent of nihilism become necessary? . . . because nihilism represents the ultimate logical conclusion of our great values and ideals. (p. 575)

In the next section, Mitchell draws parallels between the Norman conquest of the Anglo-Saxons in 1066, the English civil war in the 1600s (a temporary conquest by the "Anglo-Saxons" over the "Normans"), and the American civil war in the 1800s (a more permanent conquest by the "Anglo-Saxons" over the "Normans").[5] He views the conquered Anglo-Saxon Puritans as having a slave morality (and mentality), and he postulates an Anglo-Jewish convergence resulting from sociobiological evolution. Mitchell's sympathy lies with the Anglo-Saxons, and he agrees with the view that the Norman conquest in 1066 was an act of aggression and a calamity.

Mitchell believes in the potential for a major war with deaths in the billions (a "gigadeath"). He believes in the prospect of capitalism making intelligent machines that will make work obsolete and that the liberal democratic era will end because the *Homo sapiens* era will come to an end when humans are genetically engineered into a new species, rendering human equality obsolete. Martin Manley (discussed below) saw future catastrophes in very personal terms, whereas Mitchell sees them more abstractly. Martin is concerned with his own decline into possible dementia, whereas Mitchell is concerned with gigadeaths. Mitchell entitled his chapter, "How the Anglo-Saxon defeat of 1066 has universalized into the prospective defeat of the entire biological human race." (p. 1536) His chapter on page 1659 is entitled "Marx was wrong (and the human-capitalist system will self-destruct)." (p.1659)

Finally, Mitchell has a chapter titled "The Punchline." (p. 1739) He first focuses on sociobiology. He notes that sociobiologists, such as Edward Wilson, have been accused of racism, sexism, Nazi ideology, and conservative positions in politics. But for Mitchell, value judgments must be eliminated. He notes that the Nazi extermination camps were genetically adaptive for the Germans. He asserts that he does not claim that the destruction of European Jews was good or bad because that would be a value judgment, but he does claim that Jews do object to sociobiology. Mitchell values facts and science. He writes:

> By addressing issues wherein the value of self-preservation conflicts with value of scientific investigation, I will test this hypothesis by actively seeking out what are, for me, the most self-destructive scientific truths. (p. 1757)

However, just when I thought that Mitchell was going to discuss the views of DeCatanzaro (1981) and others who have applied sociobiology to the topic of suicide, Mitchell goes back to the Norman conquest of England in 1066! Indeed, Mitchell seems to have not come across sociobiological writing on suicide.

The rambling nature of Mitchell's *Suicide Note* raises the question of what psychiatric disorder he has, if any. Is this book a product of obsessiveness, of mania, or what? Why can't Mitchell focus on what is presumably the issue at hand—his death by suicide? He repeats his defense of sociobiology which he sees not as nonsense, but rather as making too much sense. He labels sociobiology as an "outlaw science," meaning that its proponents are persecuted. This is, of course, an exaggeration. It is criticized, but criticism does not equate with persecution. Eventually, Mitchell comes back to self-destruction.

> Life is a prejudice that happens to be talented as perpetuating itself. To attempt to eliminate this source of bias is to *open your mind to death*. (p. 1828)

> I cannot fully reconcile my understanding of the world with my existence in it. There is a conflict between the value of objectivity and the facts of my life. This experiment is designed to demonstrate a point of incompatibility between "truth" and "life" . . . such that it leads to a voluntary and rational completion of this work in an act of self-destruction. (pp. 1830–31)

The question that arises at this point is whether Mitchell will justify his suicide using sociobiological ideas, that is, will his death increase the chances of the survival of his genes in future generations by unburdening his kin so they can propagate their genes, which overlap with his own genes. Apparently not. Mitchell comes to view suicide as leading to equality.

> Rational self-destruction is identical with the logic of the progress of equality. (p. 1850)

> Suicide, then, is the fulfillment of the American experiment as the fulfillment of the idea of equality. . . . Rational self-destruction is posited here as the actualization of an experiment to test a tentative nihilism. (p. 1852)

Mitchell then begins a personal analysis. (p. 1858) He notes that even before the age of twelve, his age when his father died, he was inclined to view everything materially. Emotions were material processes; his father was a "purely material phenomenon" (p. 1858).[6] Mitchell says he has Asperger's Syndrome. However, he notes that he is more complex than that since he has the capacity for social intelligence, by which presumably he means that he can interact with others in a meaningful way. After his father's death, Mitchell says that he had a "kind of moral collapse" in which his materialistic, physical view of himself and the world became combined with a "nihilistic inability to believe in the worth of any goal" (p. 1861). His most basic assumption was "that life is meaningless and that I am an animal-machine."

> If life itself is without ultimate meaning, and is not fundamentally rationally superior to death, then perhaps the test of the worth of life is found in willing death and self-destruction. (p. 1864)

Mitchell cannot believe that psychotherapy can "cure" nihilism. He also saw that his emotions could get in the way of his plans, and so he did not accord them any meaning or significance. Eventually, life lost its cogency for Mitchell.

> If life is truly meaningless and there is no rational basis for choosing among fundamental alternatives, then all choices are equal and there is no fundamental ground for choosing life over death. (p. 1873)

> Now, before I blow my brains out, I should like to point out that the most basic issue at the very center of this work is. . . . nihilism. (pp. 1874–1985)

Discussion

Whereas Martin Manley, discussed below, forced himself into dying by suicide by setting up his website, sending out suicide notes, and shooting himself while on the telephone with the police department, Mitchell forced himself into suicide by intellectual argument. Martin argued for his own suicide in his website, but that was only a part of it. Martin also talked of possibly being a burden in the future, of having to endure personal and societal catastrophes, and of being able to leave those to whom he felt close some material benefits. Mitchell relied solely on intellectual arguments.

Yet Mitchell did have a purpose in his life—at least for those years when he worked on his 1,900-page book. The problem was that, once the book was finished, he had no goal in life. He was like those who retire and die quickly thereafter from natural causes, in part because there is no longer any meaning in their lives.

The Suicidal Act

Mitchell's roommates and family thought he was writing a book on the Norman conquest of England in 1066. No one had any inkling that Mitchell was planning to kill himself. A month before his death, he got his roommate to witness his will. Two days before his death, Mitchell was elated and told his roommates that he had finished his book.

The day before his death, he bought stamps and prepared packages to send the CD with his book to friends and family, as well as e-mails after his death.

For his death, Mitchell dressed in a white tuxedo, white shoes, a white tie, and white socks, covered by an ill-fitting trench coat. He told his roommates that the white clothes were a Jewish tradition. He apologized if he had ever done anything to offend his roommate and hoped that his roommate would forgive him. He then went to Harvard Yard, a green area in the midst of the Harvard University campus, on the Jewish festival of Yom Kippur, and shot himself in the head on the steps on Memorial Church on the campus of Harvard University, at 11 AM in front of some twenty tourists, with a silver revolver.

The choice of a white tuxedo, a public venue that is well-known (both a church and a university campus), and to shoot himself in the head (a messy death) in front of others, clearly shows Mitchell's desire to bring attention to his death by suicide.

Martin Manley's Website

Martin Manley died by suicide on August 15, 2013, on his sixtieth birthday. For the previous eighteen months, Manley had created a website on Yahoo discussing his decision to die by suicide, and he posted many autobiographical details of his life. Although Yahoo took down Manley's website after his death, mirror sites were created, and the postings survived. Prior to creating his website, Martin had worked at the *Kansas City Star* as a sports reporter.

I analyzed Manley's website (Lester, 2014) and argued that his decision to die by suicide was rational. Manley did not appear to be suffering from any psychiatric disorder. The major reason he gave for his choice was that he was beginning to have memory lapses, and he feared developing dementia and being alone in a nursing home for such patients. I argued that a reading of his website shows a wonderfully intelligent and humorous individual, with no signs of dementia.

In the same way as Mitchell Heisman, discussed above, Martin left a memorial to himself—a website rather than a scholarly work. In the final entries on the website, he wrote as if he was already deceased. Before he killed himself, Martin sent personalized suicide notes to his friends that arrived on the day that he died. Martin wanted to spare his landlord and his sister from having to discover his body, and so he carefully arranged his death. He went to the parking lot of his local police station, at 5 AM, and he called the police station to report a suicide at the south end of their parking lot. Then he shot himself in the head. The police ran out of the building and found his body.

In many ways, Martin, although he was firm in his decision to end his life, also forced himself into going through with his decision. He sent out personalized letters to friends, and he called the police station. To back out at that point would make him look ridiculous. Instead, he hoped to shape his image after death with his website, a website which presents an image of Martin as a witty, intelligent, and creative individual.

Discussion

Each of the individuals discussed in this chapter left a "suicide note," a memorial to themselves. Amanda and Ashley left postings on social media (Twitter and YouTube) which not only serve as memorials to them and as suicide notes, but which can also be seen as cries for help. Despite their postings, no one intervened to prevent Ashley's death, and not enough was done to prevent Amanda's. On the other hand, Mitchell's online book and Martin's website were not known to others until after their deaths. They were, therefore, suicide notes and memorials rather than cries for help.

I will discuss the role of social media in staging one's suicide in chapter 13, but the people discussed here left dramatic "suicide notes." In addition, both Mitchell and Martin staged the last moments of their life carefully, with meticulous planning. They also gave consideration to the feelings of their friends and relatives. Many of those who experience the suicide of a loved one are left with one question: "Why?" Martin and Mitchell, answered that question, and they died in such a way as to spare their loved ones from the trauma of their death.

Notes

1. Previous research on these signs (Lester, McSwain, & Gunn 2011) has shown that judges have a difficult time distinguishing between hopelessness and purposelessness.
2. The Canadian law enforcement authorities do apparently monitor the Internet to some extent, since they notified Amanda's family that pictures of her were circulating on the Internet.
3. She died by asphyxiation using helium and a plastic bag, a method she had researched on YouTube and Wikipedia.
4. http://www.houstonpress.com/2012-03-08/news/ashley-billasano-twitter-teen-suicide/

5. Mitchell equates Normans with masculinity and Anglo-Saxons with femininity.
6. His father and grandfather were engineers.

References

Abel, D. (2010). What he left behind: A 1,905-page suicide note. September 27. (www.boston.com)

DeCatanzaro, D. (1981). *Suicide and self-damaging behavior.* New York: Academic.

Gunn, J. F., & Lester, D. (2012). Twitter postings and suicide. *Suicidologi,* 17(3), 28–30.

Gunn, J. F., Lester, D., & McSwain, S. (2011). Testing the warning signs of suicidal behavior among suicide ideators using the 2009 National Survey on Drug Abuse and Health. *International Journal of Emergency Mental Health,* 13, 147–54.

Lester, D. (2010). The final hours. *Psychological Reports,* 106, 791–97.

Lester, D. (2014). *Rational suicide: Is it possible?* Hauppauge, NY: Nova Science.

Lester, D., McSwain, S., & Gunn, J. F. (2011). A test of the validity of the *IS PATH WARM* warning signs for suicide. *Psychological Reports,* 108, 402–4.

Newcomer, E. P., & Srivatsa, N. N. (2010). Suicide note found online. *The Harvard Crimson,* September 22. (www.thecrimson.com)

5

The Body as a Suicide Note[1]

David Lester

Those about to die by suicide often leave a suicide note, that is, words written on paper, although these days the note may be written on a computer or tablet or posted on Facebook or Twitter. However, the suicide also leaves a body, and this communicates information to the individual's loved ones and bystanders. This chapter explores the choices made by the suicidal individual in how they present their body.

Suicide Notes Written on Skin

On rare occasions, suicides write a suicide note on their skin. Demirci, et al. (2009) reported on two cases of suicides by hanging in Turkey who had written on their bodies. The words in their first case, a thirty-two-year-old married man, were "donkey," "do not," "wash" and "*Hodja*." A Hodja is a holy man who washes a corpse and wraps it in a shroud before burial. The second case was a thirty-two-year-old married woman who ingested insecticide. She was a victim of physical abuse from her husband, and she wrote a note on her left leg saying that she could not stand the abuse any more.

Austin and Byard (2013) found notes written on the skin of two suicides out of the 498 that they studied in Australia. One was an eighteen-year-old man who died by hanging with "I failed" and "It was my fault, I destroyed myself" written on his right forearm (he was left-handed). The second was a thirty-year-old man who died by hanging with a plastic bag over his head, who wrote "Ug-Lee, Lone-Lee, Dead-Lee, Sorry" on the back of his left hand. Austin and Byard also found three other cases in the medical examiner's files: a fifty-two-year-old man (hanging) who wrote "cremation OK" on his left hand; a fifty-five-year-old man who died from carbon monoxide poisoning who wrote "I love [x] and look after our [x]" on his left arm; and a thirty-eight-year-old man who died by jumping from a building, who wrote "RIP" on his chest.

There are no clues as to how soon before the suicidal act these "notes" were written. If they were written long before the suicidal act, they may have been a cry for help to any who might have seen the writing. Since these notes are not addressed to anyone in particular, skin messages may indicate loneliness and a lack of (or isolation from) friends and family. The messages may have served as reminders to the individual—this is what I am going to do. They may also indicate a lack of forethought and preparation, if written immediately prior to the act, with pen and paper not readily available.[2]

Related to this are two cases reported by Byard and Charlwood (2014). In the first case, a young man, nineteen years old, hanged himself. On his shoulder, he had a heart shaped tattoo with a name and "RIP." The name was that of his brother who had died by suicide, also using the same method (low suspension hanging) and in the same shed nine years and two days earlier. In the second case, a forty-seven-year-old woman committed suicide by hanging. She had a tattoo on her hip with a name and birth and death dates. The name was that of her daughter who had killed herself by hanging in the same shed one year and five days earlier. Both of these cases suggest an anniversary reaction to the suicides of their family members, and both used the same method and location for their own suicide as their significant other.

What We Wear

Do people dress in a particular way when they decide to die by suicide? Gaylord and Lester (1994) reported on the fifty-six suicides and seventy-six attempts that occurred on the Mass Transit Railway (MTR) subway in Hong Kong from 1979 to 1991. For general security reasons, the MTR installed surveillance cameras in the subway stations, and several clues were identified indicating that an individual might be planning to jump in front of the train, such as standing by the wall where the train enters the station, putting items such as bags down as the train approaches (whereas ordinary passengers pick up their bags) and hiding their faces with hats, scarves, or some other disguise. However, one clue is how the individual is dressed. A prostitute will usually be dressed in ornate red silk, adhering to the belief that her ghost, when it returns to harm her enemies, will be made stronger. Elderly Chinese planning to jump to their deaths will wear traditional ethnic garments or their best clothes. Others wear unusual make-up or disguise, or hide their face with a broad hat or scarf. Some remove their shoes and jewelry, carry family picture or items of sentimental value such as stuffed toys or old dolls. Couples in a suicide pact may be linked together by handcuffs or ropes. When the subway staff members notice these cues, they approach the individual and attempt to engage them in conversation, eventually turning to crisis intervention. Interestingly, Gaylord and Lester noted that those who jump from high buildings to their death do not usually dress in this way.[3]

In the 1970s, a cult developed in California known as "Heaven's Gate," led by Marshall Applewhite and his nurse, Bonnie Nettles, who came to believe that they were the two witnesses mentioned in the Book of Revelation in the Bible (11:3). They attracted others who believed their story, and the cult developed the belief that Earth was going to be recycled (cleaned, renewed, and refurbished). They decided that they had to leave immediately by dying, and they hoped thereby that their souls would reach an alien spacecraft associated with the Hale-Bopp comet. Thirty-nine members of the cult committed mass suicide by poison in Rancho Santa Fe, California, and were found by police on March 26, 1997. On March 22, the first group of fifteen members committed suicide by drinking vodka and applesauce laced with phenobarbital and pulling plastic bags over their heads. The remaining members removed the plastic bags and draped purple shrouds over the bodies. The following day, the process was repeated with fifteen more members. On the third day, the process was repeated with seven members, after which the two remaining members died by suicide. They were found with the plastic bags still over their heads. All of their heads were shaved clean of any hair. Each body had a five-dollar bill and three quarters in the shirt pocket. Since their goal was move to the next level, they did not consider their acts to be suicide. They expected to be united with God, and so it would have been suicidal, in their view, not to take their own lives (VanSteenhuyse, 2013).

The group began in the spring of 1975 in Los Angeles where Applewhite (who had been a choirmaster in Texas) and Nettles (together known as Bo and Peep or Do and Ti) exhorted people to give up sex, alcohol, and tobacco and leave their families.[4] The group moved to the Rogue River in Oregon, then to Wyoming and Colorado. They camped and sometimes worked as store clerks and waitresses, and later as designers of web pages for the Internet. They saved enough to buy several campers, and their group numbered in the hundreds. Applewhite was dictatorial. The group members had to ask permission get their car keys and drive, and he sometimes condemned them to silence for days. They were assigned partners on a rotating basis, but not allowed to get romantically involved. However, those who dropped out were treated with respect rather than scorn.

The bodies had begun to decompose by the time they were discovered. Each was lying in their own bunk bed, faces and torsos covered by a square piece of purple cloth. All wore identical black shirts and sweat pants, black-and-white Nike Decades athletic shoes, and armbands with the words "Heaven's Gate Away Team." They dressed alike with identical loose fitting shirts and pants while they were alive, perhaps as a symbol of their equality. Their identical apparel a symbol of their common bond. Lester (2002) noted that, unlike those whom Jack Kevorkian assisted in suicide, the Heaven's Gate members who died were 50% women (compared to 71% of Kevorkian's suicides) and younger (means ages forty-six versus fifty-eight). However, the Heaven's Gate suicides had a greater proportion of women than suicides in general in the United States.

These issues have been addressed in some types of murder. Van Brunt and Lewis (2014) have explored why rampage murderers in the United States dress the wear they do. They noted that rampage murderers are often characterized by misogyny and objectification of the targets that they seek to kill. They typically wear black, olive and camouflage clothes that are easily available in stores and online. As Van Brunt and Lewis noted, pink and yellow outfits are not stocked by stores! Psychologically, the clothing they choose indicates their desire to be pseudo-commandos and to facilitate them achieving a warrior mentality. They emulate heroes, or rather antiheroes, as they are portrayed in movies, such as Darth Vader in the *Star Wars* movies and Batman, leaving an image for their victims and onlookers, an image that is often left on their online websites and Facebook pages. As Lester (2010b) has noted, many rampage murders die by suicide, a proportion as high as 35%.

Naked Suicide

Some suicides are naked when they die. Simon (2008) presented three cases of patients (two women and one man) who hung themselves while in a psychiatric hospital (two cases) or at home (one case) and who were naked when they died in this way, but he was unable to provide any reasons for their nakedness (and he did not report what percentage of suicides by hanging were naked). Simon found similar cases in the media, including a construction worker who fell down an elevator shaft from the fourth floor downwho was naked (Klein, 2007). Simon speculated that the nakedness suggests that the death was a suicide rather than an accidental death.

Why might suicides be naked or partially unclothed? Simon noted that some methods for suicide require partial undressing, such as exposing the site where the wound is to be inflicted, as in a stabbing. If ropes are unavailable a suicide may use the clothing to provide a noose, such as a prisoner in a jail cell. Since people undress to take a bath or shower, suicides in the bathtub or shower may be naked. Simon suggested that nakedness is more common in those who use hanging, overdoses and drowning in the bathtub for suicide but not in those who drown in the ocean. Nakedness is less common in those who jump, use gas, or use firearms. Simon thought that jumpers who are naked are more likely to be psychotic or substance abusers or under the influence of command hallucinations that suggest being naked when jumping.

Simon listed possible implications of a suicidal individual choosing to be naked

- Rebirth and cleansing[5]
- Self-abasement and masochistic surrender
- Atonement and guilt
- Exhibitionism
- Eroticization of death
- Anger to shock survivors
- Impulsivity (while incidentally undressed)
- Tidiness to minimize any mess
- Disorganization from intoxication and other states
- Psychosis, including command hallucinations

As well as nakedness suggesting impulsivity in the suicidal act, Simon noted that clothes strewn about also suggest impulsivity, whereas neatly arranged clothes suggest planning. Impulsiveness is common in suicidal acts. Simon, et al. (2001) found that 24% of attempted suicides made their suicide attempt within five minutes of having suicidal ideation, and Deisenhammer, et al. (2009) found that 48% made the attempt ten minutes or less after thinking about suicide. Cheah, Schmitt, and Pridmore (2008) reported the case of a young man who had embezzled some money and lost it gambling. He was crossing a bridge and, one-third of the way across, began to worry about his crime. At the top of the bridge (forty-nine meters high) he decided to commit suicide and jumped. The planning process, therefore, took only a few seconds. As soon as he jumped, he regretted his decision, got into the pin-drop position (legs straight and toes pointed) and survived the jump. (Only three jumpers out of thirty-two had survived this jump in the past.)

It is traumatic for the significant others of a suicide to find the body. Some methods for suicide (such as firearms) disfigure the body, increasing the trauma for those finding the body. Simon suggested that nakedness can add to this trauma and suggests that naked suicides want to cause distress to the survivors. Simon thought that depressed individuals might also choose to die naked as an expression of utter despair, desolation, and worthlessness. He noted the case of a patient with psychotic depression who believed that he was the cause of the world's calamities and planned to die by suicide while naked to atone for his sins like a sacrificial lamb. There can also be erotic overtones to dying naked. Simon noted that many artistic depictions of classic suicides, such as that of Cleopatra, show them naked.[6] Marilyn Monroe, who committed suicide on August 5, 1962, by overdose, was naked, but it has been noted that she typically slept naked.[7]

Simon presented the case of a naked woman who attempted drowning in a bathtub who, in psychotherapy, came to realize that her attempt was a rebirth and reunion fantasy with her mother who had died by suicide using drowning when the patient was nine years old.

Finally, the tidiness of dying naked is illustrated by Willard Hershberger, who was the backup catcher for the Cincinnati Reds. Hershberger killed himself at the Copley Plaza Hotel in Boston on August 3, 1940, after feeling that he had lost important games for his team (Barbour, 1987). When he failed to show for a game, a friend of Hershberger went to the hotel and found him in the bathroom. He had covered the floor with towels and slashed his throat with his roommate's safety razor while leaning over the bathtub. Hershberger's father had killed himself November 21, 1929. He had been depressed for several weeks, with financial worries and a demotion at work. He shot himself in the chest in the bathroom of his house at 2:30 AM with a shotgun, leaving a bloody mess for his family to find. His son had tried to be tidier in his death. Barbour did not report whether Hershberger was clothed or naked.

Simon made the clinical observation that any individual who attempts suicide naked should be considered a greater risk for later completed suicide than attempters who remain clothed for their attempt.

Concern for One's Physical Appearance

Lester (1969) explored several explanations for why women who die by suicide more often choose less disfiguring methods (such as overdoses which, incidentally, are also less lethal). One possibility is that women want their physical appearance to be attractive after death. The less disfiguring methods for suicide are also, on the whole, less lethal, and so there is a greater chance of surviving those methods. Diggory and Rothman (1961) explored the values destroyed by death by presenting seven consequences to a variety of people, such as "I could no longer have any experiences" and "I could no longer care for my dependents." One consequence was "I am afraid of what might happen to my body after death." This was typically the least feared consequence, but women feared this significantly more than men.

Lester (1988a) repeated the study of Diggory and Rothman with 429 undergraduate students and, in addition, asked them what method they might choose for suicide and whether they chose that method because it was quick, painless, does not disfigure, or is easily available. Women were more likely to choose overdose more than did men, firearms less often, and carbon monoxide/car exhaust equally often. The women rated painlessness, less disfigurement and availability as more important reason for their choice of method, and availability as less important. Students who chose firearms were less concerned about disfigurement, and men had less concern over disfigurement than the women. In another study, Lester (1988b) had students rate different methods for suicide, and they rated suicide by firearms (versus an overdose) as messy (versus tidy), as well as quick (versus slow), painful (versus painless), difficult (versus easy), irreversible (versus reversible), dramatic (versus banal), and masculine (versus feminine). This difference is consistent with a report by a former warden of the prison at Sing Sing Correctional Facility in Ossining (New York) that women about to be executed often asked, as a last wish, to have their hair done.

Firth (1961) described a common method for suicide in the Pacific Ocean island of Tikopia. The individual takes a fish line or some other kind of thin cord, ties it to a point in the house, and then runs away from the fastening point, thereby strangling himself. It is said, Firth noted, that people who hang themselves are said to defecate, leaving the interior of the house messy. Part of the motivation for suicide is to preserve the social personality intact (that is, how one is perceived by others) and to avoid despair and shame. Suicidal individuals, therefore, want to maintain their dignity. In Tikopia, suicides typically refrain from eating for a day or so prior to dying so that they do not defecate.

It is very difficult to find reliable information on this possibility. There are accounts of people who are about to be executed for having committed serious crimes wear diapers. For example, in an account of the execution of Sandra Smith in South Africa who was executed for robbery and murder (www.rowdiva.com/sandra.html), the article notes that, like all female prisoners in South Africa who are executed, she was forced to wear a diaper. Reports indicate that North Carolina required all prisoners about to be executed to wear a diaper (www.crimejusticeandamerica. com/death-row-trivia). The same seems to be true for South Carolina (storiesofsummerville.blogspot.com/2009/05/execution-of-christine-hill.html?zx-3ed). Denno (1994), in a law review article, has noted that defecation and micturition occur during electrocution.

Other bodily excretions occur with hanging. In the past, when individuals were executed by hanging in public, the crowds would look for the erections and ejaculations that often accompanied the hanging. Some men hang themselves for sexual purposes since the hanging heightens their sexual arousal. Sometimes, the individual cannot free himself from the rope and dies. The clothing of these individuals often provides clues to the police as to whether the man's death was accidental, suicide, or murder. Those doing this for sexual reasons are more often naked or wearing female clothing, and there are sexual aids and pornography nearby. Simon (2008) noted that women are also typically naked when inducing asphyxia for sexual purposes.[8]

Discussion

The choice of clothing (or lack of clothing) may be an important decision made by those who are planning to die by suicide. It may also provide clues as to the motivations and psychological state of the suicidal individual. Yet this aspect of the circumstances of the suicidal act is rarely noted so that research into the meaning of the choice is rare. Future research should remedy this omission.

Notes

1.   This title was suggested to me by Christine Quigley, who maintained a wonderful website on death entitled *Quigley's Cabinet* (quigleyscabinet. blogspot.com/search/label/suicide), and she graciously gave me permission to use it in this book.

2. Bijou Yang suggested these possibilities.
3. Recently, in order to cut the cost or air conditioning, the MTR has installed platform doors, thereby reducing the incidence of suicide at their subway stations (Lester 2010a).
4. Nettles died of cancer in 1985.
5. Simon noted that, when Jesus was resurrected, his clothes were left behind.
6. Simon noted that Cleopatra is usually shown being bitten by a snake, with obvious Freudian symbolism.
7. Some believe that Marilyn was murdered, but her death was classified officially a suicide after an investigation by the Los Angeles suicide prevention center staff and the medical examiner.
8. Simon (2008) also noted a phenomenon in which individuals who die from hypothermia sometimes feel overheated immediately prior to losing consciousness and dying, and so discard their clothing (Wedin, et al. 1979).

References

Austin, A. E., & Byard, R. W. (2013). Skin messages in suicide. *Journal of Forensic & Legal Medicine, 20*, 618–20.

Barbour, J. (1987). The death of Willard Hershberger. *The National Pastime, 6*(1), 62–65.

Byard, R. W., & Charlwood, C. (2014). Commemorative tattoos as markers for anniversary reactions and suicide. *Journal of Forensic & Legal Medicine, 24*, 15–17.

Cheah, D., Schmitt, G., & Pridmore, S. (2008). Suicide, misappropriation and impulsivity. *Australian & New Zealand Journal of Psychiatry, 42*, 544–46.

Deisenhammer, E. A., Ing, C. M., Strauss, R., Kemmler, G., Hinterhuber, H., & Weiss, E. M. (2009). The duration of the suicidal process. *Journal of Clinical Psychiatry, 70*, 19–24.

Demirci, S., Dogan, K. H., Erkol, Z., & Gunaydin, G. (2009). Unusual suicide note written on the body. *American Journal of Forensic Medicine & Pathology, 30*, 276–79.

Denno, D. W. (1994). Is electrocution an unconstitutional method of execution? *William & Mary Law Review, 35*, 551–692.

Diggory, J. C., & Rothman, D. Z. (1961). Values destroyed by death. *Journal of Abnormal & Social Psychology, 63*, 205–10.

Firth, R. (1961). Suicide and risk-taking in Tikopia society. *Psychiatry, 24*, 1–17.

Gaylord, M. S., & Lester, D. (1994). Suicide in the Hong Kong subway. *Social Science & Medicine, 38*, 427–30.

Klein, A. (2007). Unclothed worker dies after four-story plunge. *Washington Post, January 11*, B5.

Lester, D. (1969). Suicidal behavior in men and women. *Mental Hygiene, 53*, 340–45.

Lester, D. (1988a). Why do people choose particular methods for suicide? *Activitas Nervosa 30*, 312–14.

Lester, D. (1998b). The perception of different methods of suicide. *Journal of General Psychology, 115*, 215–17.

Lester, D. (2002). Cult suicide and physician-assisted suicide. *Psychological Reports*, 91, 1194.

Lester, D. (2010a). *Preventing suicide: Closing the Exits revisited.* Hauppauge, NY: Nova Science.

Lester, D. (2010b). Suicide in mass murderers and serial killers. *Suicidology Online*, 1, 19–27.

Simon, O. R., Swann, A. C., Powell, K. E., Potter, L. B., Kresnow, M. J., & O'Carroll, P. W. (2001). Characteristics of impulsive suicide attempts and attempters. *Suicide & Life-Threatening Behavior*, 31 (Supplement 1), 49–59.

Simon, R. I. (2008). Naked suicide. *Journal of the American Academy of Psychiatry & the Law*, 36, 240–45.

Van Brunt, B., & Lewis, W. S. (2014). Costuming, misogyny, and objectification as risk factors in targeted violence. *Violence & Gender*, 1, 1–11.

VanSteenhuyse, E. (2013). Heaven's Gate: An exploration of the Christian, apocalyptic nature of the space destined suicidal cult. https://www.academia.edu/6781181/Heavens_Gate_An_Exploration_into_the_Christian_Apocalyptic_Nature_of_the_Space_Destined_Suicidal_Cult

Wedin, B., Vanggard, L., & Hirvonen, J. (1979). Paradoxical undressing in fatal hypothermia. *Journal of Forensic Sciences*, 24, 1129–33.

6

Suicide and the Communicative Condition: Audience and the Idea of Suicide

Jermaine Martinez

Lester (2001) observed that the "communicative aspects of suicide have certainly been implied in suicide research" (p. 49). Furthering what he identifies as a deficit in understanding suicide in relation to formal theories of communication, Lester turned to a well-established textbook on communication theory by Littlejohn (1983) to shed light on how nonfatal suicidal behavior can be conceptualized through theories of nonverbal communication. I want to build on this fruitful approach and make communication central in understanding suicide. In particular I offer a dialogical communicative perspective on the motives implied by committing suicide. Agreeing with Hayakawa (1957) who referred to suicide as "... a last desperate act of communication" (p. 50), I have in mind only completed suicides accompanied with suicide notes. Such suicide phenomena suggest that written and physical suicidal communiqués have, as a rule, some kind of implicit or explicit audience-directed thinking that precedes the act. Given this communicative condition, suicide is a type of symbolic action similar to other human actions, but suicide is distinguished by the way in which a suicidal person imagines the audience for whom suicide will take on some intended expressive significance. A deeper understanding of suicide becomes possible when viewed as a symbolic action directed toward an audience (real or imagined).

This chapter begins by offering a brief sketch of the questions raised by a cultural anthropological approach to understanding the motives of suicide set forth by Kral (1994, 1995) and Kral and Dyck (1995).

I will dive deeper into this perspective by introducing a dialogical and dramatic communicative perspective on both the motive of suicide and the ideation of suicide. Then I will offer a brief, but suggestive, exploratory reading of suicide notes to help concretize the communicative perspective I am offering.

The Question about Suicidal Motives and Lethality

There is much psychologically grounded research on suicide, but anthropological, cultural, and sociological approaches to the study of suicide have also gained currency (cf. Cole 1996; Durkheim, 1951; Good, 1992; Kleinman, 1988; Strauss, 1992). In this chapter, I will review the anthropological approaches of Kral (1994, 1995) and Kral and Dyck (1998) who review and build off these seminal papers in exploring the causes of suicide. Exploring the conditions for the possibility of suicide, namely motivation and ideation, Kral moves away from purely psychological perspectives.

In his article, "Suicide as Social Logic," Kral (1994) extends Shneidman's (1985) theoretical approach to suicidal motivation. Shneidman argued that the common stimulus for suicide is unendurable psychological pain, pain a person is "seeking to escape" (p. 124). In this view, suicide is an attempt at cessation when an individual's own level of pain exceeds a threshold "that is unique to that individual" (p. 125). Kral agreed that psychological pain is a motivator of suicide, but he reminded us that, despite the wealth of knowledge that exceeding pain thresholds accompanies suicide, "the vast majority of people do not choose to die once they exceed their stress thresholds" (1994, p. 246). In short, exceeding a psychological pain threshold does not necessarily lead to suicide.

There is another aspect to consider. Whereas this perturbation can be seen as the necessary condition for suicide, it is not yet a sufficient condition without what Shneidman (1985) referred to as lethality. For Shneidman, lethality referred to a scalable degree of "risk to rescue ratio" inherent in any chosen method of suicide. Lethality refers to the deadliness of the methods chosen for suicide. For example, holding a gun to a head has a high level of lethality whereas overdosing with barbiturates has a low level of lethality. Kral (1994), however, deepened the notion of lethality by offering a more pragmatic view. Kral emphasized the volunteerism of lethality, observing, "*Lethality is the killer* . . . it is the intentionality and singularity of suicide as an option to end perturbation" (p. 246). Elsewhere, Kral and Dyck (1995) wrote that lethality "refers to the conscious decision to end one's life. . . . it is simply the choice of suicidal death as a plan of action" (p. 201). For Kral, much research in suicidology has focused on the understanding and treatment of perturbation, but little research has been given to understanding lethality, that is, to how people come to *choose* suicide as an option from among a repertoire of ways to cope with perturbation (see also Baechler, 1979).

As a way of answering how the idea of suicide becomes a real, sensible response to perturbation, Kral (1994) demonstrated how suicide conforms to a "social logic." By "social logic" Kral meant the person/culture dialectic of social learning and imitation whereby normative cultural beliefs serve as foundations for individual choice and action. Kral's theoretical perspective stems from the sociological work of Tarde (1898) who viewed societal norms as the context in which individual human behavior and identities are formed. Put simply, society provides socially acceptable scripts of knowing, believing, doing, expressing, and experiencing, without which individual performances (including improvising on those norms) would be impossible in any meaningful sense. The self, and likewise suicide, is understood in this sense as a social construction. Although Kral observed that viewing suicide as a socially constructed idea is nothing new, his point was that suicide is a learned choice of action and does not originate simply in the head any more than do societal fashions, fads, or trends. If we are to understand how people come to view the idea of suicide as a viable option, Kral argued we need to account for the social conditions in which the idea of suicide becomes available, relevant, and appropriate for the suffering person to accomplishing the specific, goal-directed purpose of suicide.

The fundamental question Kral (1994) presented us for consideration is: "Why suicide? . . . How does one actually choose that option, that idea?" (p. 249) Kral and Dyck (1995) answered this question in an indirect manner by reviewing evidence and research that demonstrated the social aspects of suicide such as the Werther effect, the well-documented rise in suicides resulting from unrequited love following the publication of Goethe's novel in 1774 (Phillips, 1974). These instances of "suicide clusters" or "copy cat" suicides occur following the suicide of a famous or well-beloved figure (Takahashi, 1993) or following news stories about suicide (Phillips, Carstensen, & Paight, 1989). Kral and Dyck also pointed out the role of social influence in personally chosen methods of suicide, such as the increase in suicides by gunshot, burning, or poisoning (Gould, Wallenstien, & Davidson,

1989), as well as research that shows people in different cultures seem to have different "popular" methods of suicide, such as death by firearm in Canadian and American men while in Switzerland and the Southwest Pacific islands of Tikopia hanging is the preferred method (DeCantazaro, 1981; Lester, 2008). Ultimately, Kral's work offers a solid argument for how culture influences both the choice to perform suicide and the method of doing so.

Although imitation can account for how social logics are maintained, in what specific forms do those "references to similarity" play out in the minds of persons? If some people are drawn to suicide while others are not, what is the life-blood that nourishes suicide as an idea for some? I want to hazard an answer, demonstrating that the life-blood of the social logic of suicide is a desire to be *in communication with an audience*. Suicide as a social idea is inseparable from communicative actions dramatically rehearsed and performed, introspectively or behaviorally, and always implies an audience for whom such communicative actions are offered for social sanction. We can move deeper into the question "why suicide?" by asking, "For whom is suicide?" Who is the audience for whom suicide is an appropriate and acceptable choice of action as a response to perturbation? In short, by understanding the dialogical dimension of communication, we are able explore the concept of "audience" as a way of illuminating the performative aspects of suicide motivation and ideation.

The Communicative Condition: Dialogue and Audience

Lester (2001) urged that we attend to the communicative functions of nonfatal suicide behaviors. Lester's first step into such communicative territory suggested that "functionalist" conceptions of communication seem to resonate more with nonfatal suicidal behavior especially because research has shown that nonfatal suicide behaviors often involve communicative intent. Given this emphasis on intentionality, a functionalist approach does seem to make intuitive sense. But I want to direct attention to something more than a functional perspective on communication and instead paint an image of "communication as a condition." The distinction made here between "communication as function" and "communication as condition" are reflective of an enduring disciplinary debate about the nature of communicative intention and its role in determining when communication occurs.

In the early 1990s, methodological shots were fired across the bow of a well-established principle of communication, namely, the classic axiom of communication that "one cannot *not* communicate" (Watzlawick, Beavin, & Jackson, 1967. Hereafter WBJ). WBJ argued that communication requires no intention for communication to occur. This view equated human behavior with communication. Any verbal and nonverbal action involves nonconsciously directed communicative aspects of which receivers, in principle, are often all too privy. Thus, one cannot *not* communicate. We are at all times subject to the evaluative appraisals of others, especially in our most unwitting moves (Goffman, 1969). Indeed, even when no other is physically present, this does not absolve our actions from both tacit and conscious consideration of the evaluative "judgments" and "looks" of others (Steiner, 1986; Sartre, 1984). These views of communicating give expression to communication as a "condition." We are communicative through and through, insofar as others can always interpret the full range of our expressive actions beyond our conscious intention. Given this, this communicative condition gives shape and form to our own expressive actions. In sum, communication occurs all the time as a natural part of human association and does not require conscious intention for one to be communicating.

This view stimulated the study of the nonverbal aspects of communication. The discipline accepted the axiom, and research continued apiece. But Motely (1990) challenged this long-standing axiom of communication, arguing that other traditional postulates about communication seem to contradict the axiom and that the discipline had too much unwarranted faith in WBJ's axiom. He proposed instead that *other-directed intention* is required for communication to occur. He noted that "traditionally" communication has been characterized in the following way. (1) People have a "repertoire of symbols" with which they attempt to represent internal "symptoms." (2) Communication is characterized by the encoding of messages, that is, persons select, formulate, and execute a speech plan always activated by considerations of "other-directedness." (3) Communication is an interactive process, that is, it requires a response from another person. Thus "passive, noninteractive, receiver-independent behaviors" indicate contexts in which one can *not* communicate. Finally, (4) communication has a fidelity characteristic, or an assessment of agreement or disagreement, confirmation or disconfirmation, that is not only required but expected from a receiver whenever communication occurs. For Motley, other-directed intention is the distinguishing mark of traditional postulates of communication, its very activating condition. If there is no one physically present for a sender, then we cannot speak of communication occurring. A sender can *not* communicate by simply removing the physical presence of others or by not considering other peoples' responses because, for Motely, communication requires "intent."

The conscious decision to end one's life appears to resonate best with Motley's sender-oriented view of communication, particularly because of its focus on the "other-directedness" of the act. Suicide can be viewed as a goal-directed activity involving "escape," "revenge," or "punishment of the self" and can involve the communication of intent (Baumeister, 1990; Menninger, 1938; Shneidman, 1985). But we can benefit from making use of both functional and condition-oriented perspectives on communication in order to understand the phenomenon of suicide. Suicide can be understood as a conscious intention to communicate as well as a "production" of the communicative condition.

Let us view suicide as a communicative, dramatic act. Viewing suicide as a dramatic act means that, at its core, suicide is expressive communication. Let us understand the act of suicide as a way of speaking by examining the phenomenon of the act of speaking itself. The Russian philosopher Bakhtin (1986) reasoned more thoroughly about the phenomenon of speech communication than many thinkers of the twentieth century. In his seminal essay, "On the Problem of Speech Genres, " Bakhtin broke with the tradition of viewing speech as simply a functional activity of using words to craft expressions. He distinguished between "utterances" and "sentences." He argued that traditional linguistics, particularly the work of de Saussure, assumed speech to be the production of sentences transmitted linearly to a listener. For Bakhtin, this was a simplification and misunderstanding of the phenomenon of speaking, as if knowing sentences was to know the phenomenon of speech communication. For Bakhtin, the most basic unit of speech communication is not the sentence but the "utterance" (p. 67). The utterance is always a situationally concrete event of speaking, of literally making vocalized noises for a purpose that presupposes at all times the presence of some audience. Dialogue, literally the give and take of communication between persons, is the primordial condition that makes utterances possible *as utterances*. Sentences, on the other hand, are an abstract moment of ongoing, real-time, purpose-directed utterances of daily living. Sentences are repeatable in a way that utterances can never be. The utterance is itself not a sentence, nor words, nor grammar, nor even syntax, but is rather a whole-bodied expression at once tied to an unrepeatable context of purpose and audience-directed use. The distinguishing mark of the "utterance" cannot be found in the utterance at all, but in its eventfulness as an expressive and whole-bodied action "shaped" by an audience toward whom it is directed.

This way of thinking about speech is also quite rhetorical, which is to say that we speak because there is a desire to accomplish something by expression. As Burke (1950) observed about the basic rhetorical situation:

> In its essence communication involves the use of verbal symbols for purposes of appeal . . . speaker, speech, and spoken-to, with the speaker so shaping his speech as to 'commune with' the spoken to [as] the precondition of all appeal. (p. 271)

The purposes for which utterances are created (to admonish, to shame, to blame, to exhort, to praise, to request, etc.) are constantly shifting in everyday speech and cannot be reduced to any kind of linguistic category. But utterances are parasitic upon reifications of utterances. Bakhtin referred to these as "speech genres," or generic forms of utterances that ossify into available resources for individual acts of speaking (pp. 61–67). One way to understand what a speech genre "is" in the context of suicide is to think of them as the methods of suicide. Kral noted, for instance, that "a gun to the head" has become a genre of suicide that a person privately chooses from a public reper-toire. It is important to note that the purposes of an utterance are not reducible to these repeatable genres, that is, the genres do not cause a person's purpose. Rather, within these genres, "'everything repeatable and reproducible proves to be material, a means to an end,'" which is "the purpose for which it [the utterance] was created" (Bakhtin cited in Morson and Emerson (1990, p. 127)). A purpose is dialogical, referring to the unfolding, nonrepeatable, real, social, concrete context of actual-ity. There is a rich dramatic element here, as genres can be understood as social dramatic scripts. Burke (1967) offered an extremely elegant view of this communicative condition. He wrote:

> Where does the drama get its materials? From the unending conversa-tion that is going on at the point in history when we are born. Imagine that you enter a parlor. You come late. When you arrive, others have long preceded you, and they are engaged in a heated discussion, a discussion too heated for them to pause and tell you exactly what it is about. In fact, the discussion had already begun long before any of them got there, so that no one present is qualified to retrace for you all the steps that had gone before. You listen for a while, until you

> decide that you have caught the tenor of the argument; then you put in your oar. Someone answers; you answer him; another comes to your defense; another aligns himself against you, to either the embarrass-ment or gratification of your opponent, depending upon the quality of your ally's assistance. However, the discussion is interminable. The hour grows late, you must depart. And you do depart, with the discussion still vigorously in progress. It is from this "unending conversation" that the materials of your drama arise. (pp. 110–11)

Thus, sentences exist, common colloquial forms of speaking exist, cultural expressions of various kinds exist (including the act of suicide). These genres of speech, or expressive actions, exist dormant in the background, awaiting their use in the event of utterance making, existing only as a real person's purposive, whole-bodied utterance appealing to an audience whose fundamental character is to be a responsive dialogical partner.

Interestingly, Bakhtin's (1986) distinction between utterance and sentence also coincides with a distinction between the dictionary meanings of words, or words known in their repeatable, reduced, and abstract meanings (i.e., sentences), and the *real* "contextual" meanings of words that are tied irreducibly to the nonrepeatable context of use shaped by desires for communicating with an audience (i.e., utterances) (pp. 160–161). "Contextual meaning" is meaning derived from the actu-ality of a felt "sense of a situation" (Morson & Emerson, 1990, p. 127). Given that some views of communication tend to reduce speech to the speaking of words as lexical units (i.e., sentences), the contextual mean-ings of words are often subordinate to dictionary meanings. Although many people today are convinced, for instance, that "the *real* meaning of a word is found in the dictionary," they do not seem to be aware of the fact that *they, everyday, must participate* in making meanings with others as a condition of expression and comprehension (Thayer, 1997).

For Bakhtin, however, those dictionary "meanings" are abstract meanings. They are empty *potentials* waiting to be "exploited" by a real human, on a real occasion of utterance making for a particular purpose, where utterances are shaped by the anticipated responses of an audience. In those moments of actual speaking, the abstract meaning becomes contextualized in the concrete utterance, an utterance that is always in an unrepeatable dialogue with a real audience in a real, living actuality. Of views that understand the unrepeatable and inexhaustive meanings of actual audience shaped utterances, Bakhtin wrote: "this meaning . . . cannot be peaceful and cozy (one cannot curl up comfort-ably and die within it)" (Bakhtin, 1986, p. 160). What a provocative statement about abstract meaning and death! Following Bakhtin along this path, then, it stands to reason that those views convince us that the meaning of any utterance can be found in the abstract and repeatable meanings of sentences. Those—*those*—are the types of meanings within which *one can curl up comfortably and die*.

Meaning exists inseparably from its production within ongoing unending conversations, unrepeatable actual dialogue with others. This dialogical perspective of Bakhtin reflects an important correction to views of communication that are convinced that a pure form of identification with one's audience, or pure understanding, is achievable through communication, as if one "could just find the right words." Words, as always utterances, have no abstract or universal meaning (save as sentences). Thus a search for "the right words" (i.e., the word that will have pure meaning and will mean what "I want it to mean") is often futile because such a search is more about finding words *per se* (sentence/dictionary meanings) and less about the *actual* spoils of communication—desiring and sensing a particular response from a real, actual audience through utterances. This difference between a desire to "find the right words" (i.e., lexical units, sentences) and a desire to feel connected to others often goes unattended to by those feeling unheard, Indeed, they often tragically continue to search for the "right words," as if an abstract, sentence could produce an understanding that only real, concrete utterances are capable of producing.

Bakhtin (1986) noted that, given our communicative condition, "For the word (and consequently for the human being) there is nothing more terrible than a lack of response" (p. 127). Research has revealed that a good number of suicides are often rooted in feeling unable to cope with deep feelings of isolation, feelings of being alone, or feelings of being misunderstood (Stravynski & Boyer, 2001). In normal health, to avoid such dialogical shocks of being unheard, of being unable to "find the right words," Bakhtin postulates that we often posit a "third party" whom the speaker "with greater or lesser awareness" presupposes an "absolutely just responsive understanding ... either in some metaphysical distance or in distant historical time" (p. 126). This is what he calls the "superaddressee." This is very much like imagining an audience who understands your utterances completely. Yet the "superaddressee" is often not imagined in a very explicit or intentional act on our part, but rather it is an audience deeply taken for granted as perpetually always on our side. For Bakhtin, every dialogue we have "takes place as if against the background of the responsive understanding of an invisibly present third party who stands above all the participants in the dialogue (partners)" (p. 126). The superaddressee actively and sympathetically responds to our speech in just the right way (Morson & Emerson, 1990, p. 135). This presumptive "third party" serves a vital communicative function. It assures that one's speech always has a "loophole" of sorts, recourse to an idealized response—to being heard. With a superaddressee always on our side, we can push against any finalization of utterances by always being able to imagine some audience for whom even the most idiosyncratic utterances can "make sense." Might suicide be viewed as a solution to a "crisis in communication," that is, might feelings of being unheard, isolated, worthless, or alone, become so insurmountable only because one's superaddressee has been imagined in such a way as to not offer a satisfying response—perhaps even that one's superaddressee has been imagined as an audience for whom suicide is seen as the only appropriate response?

Finally, one last aspect of the communicative condition is that it is compatible with classic sociology, particularly the researches of Durkheim, Dewey, and Mead. Our sense of the wholeness of our selfhood, according to these views, is constituted by our relationships with significant others. One cannot become "whole" alone (consider also the arguments of Buber, in his seminal *I and Thou* (1970)). The person is a kind of "production" of communicative interactions with an audience. As such, and as already mentioned, it is not possible to purely identify with an audience, to literally be merged in understanding. This is not only due to physically impossible, but because we are always already in human association, a search for such "understanding" is more like a forgetting of our communicative condition rather than an attempt to regain some communicative paradise lost. Furthermore, the communicative condition requires that communication occur between two simultaneous agents at a minimum (Frank, 2000 p. 153). We need dialogical partners who are *not us* for dialogue to occur at all. Such communicative conditions are, in part, what produce life's dramatic hue. It is precisely because one cannot *not* communicate that we can get caught up in others' interpretive assessments, making it possible thereby to experience dimensions of our own selfhood in those non-repeatable performed utterances aiming for authentication. Thus, we read in Goffman (1959):

> ... [The] self is a *product* of a scene that comes off, and is not a *cause* of it. The self, then, is a performed character, is not an organic thing

that has a specific location, whose fundamental fate is to be born, to mature, and to die; it is a dramatic effect arising diffusely from a scene that is presented, and the characteristic issue, the crucial concern, is whether it will be credited or discredited (pp. 252–253).

Accreditation, or disaccreditation, of any expressive line taken derives its authentication by others, by an audience that matters, because they are *not* me. Bakhtin has written the importance of this *outsideness* of others for helping render our selfhood whole. He wrote:

> What do I gain by having the other fuse with me? He will know and see but what I know and see, he will but repeat within himself the tragic dimensions of my life. Let him rather stay outside because from there he can know and see what I cannot see or know from my vantage point, and he can thus enrich essentially the event of my life. (cited in Todorov, 1988, p. 108).

As a result of being always and already in communication with others, a desire to connect with others is more like a kind of "self-interference" (Burke, 1950, pp. 267–294) where we first postulate a division between others and ourselves so that we might encounter the other as "other" and seek a rejoining that allows for certain dimensions of selfhood to be experienced (feelings of connectedness, for instance). Therefore, because existential wholeness can never be accomplished for oneself alone but always for *oneself with another*, the desperate act of suicide is parasitic upon these communicative conditions, begging the following questions: Who is the other for whom the act of suicide is imagined to be a response? And how is the audience for an act of suicide imagined such that the act of suicide is felt to be a response to a crisis of a communicative wholeness lost?

"Just the Right Way": Communicative Conditions in Suicide Notes

Next, I will demonstrate communicative themes at work in suicide notes as a way of concretizing my claims and addressing the questions I raised above. For those people who die by suicide and leave suicide notes, their last words betray evaluative and rhetorical choices in the sense that they chose to say this, *not* that. They can be viewed as forms of appeal and, as such, are seeking to regain a felt loss of communicative wholeness with others.

Keeping the preceding conceptual discussion in mind, let us examine how the communicative condition features in suicide notes. What follows is in no way an exhaustive study of notes. Rather, it is an exploratory and tentative approach to suggesting a more rigorous examination of how the communicative condition can give insight into suicide and suicide notes. The hope is to provoke discussion on how the suicidal person imagines the form and degree of responsiveness of an audience for whom their communicative act (utterance) seeks accreditation. The following examples are taken from Etkind (1997), Shneidman (1985), Jacobs (1967), and Messner and Buckrop (2000). Other excerpts are taken from a collection of suicide notes analyzed in Michael Kral's *Culture & Mental Illness* seminar at the University of Illinois Urbana-Champaign in 2011. Those notes were copies of original notes from a study of conducted by Leenaars, Wilde, Wenckstern, and Kral (2001) and are indicated below with asterisks.

In an anonymous entry at the start of chapter 3 of Etkind's book, one person's final words were simply, "No comment." What an incisive identification of the central communicative crisis of suicide, namely that, under the perturbation of loneliness, one senses no possibility of having a fulfilling responsive understanding from an audience. Yet it is clear that this expression, having been written by the person prior to suicide, still communicates a "commentary" and so assumes an audience of some kind. Given no particular person being addressed, the audience is an anonymous one, but tragically not of the "superaddressee" kind that might hint at some understanding of the act in ways that are understood "in just the right way." Rather, this person's last words are representative of a "self-interference" of an impossible attempt to find the "right words." Betrayed here also is a lack of differentiating between sentences/dictionary meanings and contextual meanings/utterances. Thus, the simple two-word note displays a sense of ambivalence. In the utterance "No comment," we can read generic figures of shameful self-evaluation, such as "I am not worthy of comment" or "I am not worth listening to." Yet this person is also imagining an audience who will find their dead, lifeless body, thereby betraying that, even in suicide, one knows that one's body gives off expressions. In this sense it is not hard to imagine this person having a reflective flash of dramatic consideration of how their body will "be found." This transforms the contextual meaning of "No comment" into a kind of instruction for how those encountering the body should make sense of it—specifically, "I am not worthy of comment." This kind of abstract participation with absentee dialogical partners is a crucial condition for solving the "crisis of communication," for in dying, in literally removing themselves from dialogue with actual responses of a real audience, this last utterance will forever be an abstract, empty possibility. This person can literally "curl up comfortably and die." Even in this simple two-word communiqué, we can see the audience as a shaping force of the expressive act.

We can further see how the audience and cultural resources shape suicide as a communicative act in the following note by Fanny Godwin. The suicide note read:

> I have long determined that the best thing I could do was to put an end to the existence of a being whose birth was unfortunate and whose life has only been a series of pains to those persons who have hurt their health in endeavoring to promote her welfare. Perhaps to hear of my death may give you pain, but you will soon have the blessing of forgetting that such a creature ever existed. (Shneidman, 1985, p. 105)

The evaluation of herself in the most biological of terms as an "existence," a "creature," and as a "being" betrays a crisis in communicative wholeness. If existential wholeness is not achieved alone, but for oneself with another, then a tragic kind of self-forgetting, or more to the point, a deeply felt sense of being divided from significant others, provokes a crisis. This is a "communicative" perspective on Shneidman's (1985) concept of "cognitive constriction" (p. 35), for Goodwin has here postulated a division between herself and others, but what is lacking is the "productive" kind of redemptive rejoining that makes more positive experiences of selfhood possible, a *difference* necessary for one to feel the self-worth of being a responsive dialogical participant in an enduring unending conversation.

Once again there is ambivalence at work. She addresses her act to a particular other for whom her whole existence is said to not matter, but indeed her life clearly *does* matter. Her life "matters" so much that she feels it would be "a blessing" to forget it. The rhetorical allusions of sanctification in her note betray her selfhood in terms that she herself cannot appreciate, namely as something sacred and important for others (see Goffman (1967)). How does she not notice this importance? How has she come to feel so disconnected from others?

In her case, the audience imagined here is one for whom a "just right" response has presumably not been forthcoming up to this point. As she says, her birth has brought nothing but "pain for others." As such, this communiqué betrays a search for the "right words," a desire to communicate with an audience. The disconnection she positions between herself and others is felt so deeply that the act of suicide is a last desperate utterance, expressing the depths of her remorse, of her loneliness. Again, one can imagine a flash of dramatic consideration about how her actions would communicate to her audience. Paradoxically, this not only demonstrates a tacit knowledge of the communicative condition, but also a fundamental forgetting of those communicative conditions. It is for this reason, moreover, that Goodwin's feelings of burden found rhetorical expression in the reductionist style of biological frameworks. Things in biological process have no agency. Framing her life through the abstract meanings of biological processes that require no real participation for them to exist (unlike human utterances and contextual meaning), Goodwin can curl up comfortably and die.

Many suicide notes express their inability to communicate with others, to be heard in the just the right way. They express their feelings of isolation and aloneness. This is somewhat paradoxical given that the communicative condition implies that one's selfhood is always a production achieved with others and the fact that they intend to communicate to someone, whose response presumably matters, via their death. This loneliness is often framed as an inability to find the "right words," rather than feeling unheard. The self-interference necessary for the possibility of a search for "right words" is a determination, or a deeply felt sense, that one's audience is deeply unresponsive. For instance one suicide note reads:

> It is hard to say why you don't want to live. I have only one reason. The three people I have in the world which I love don't want me. Tom, I love you so dearly but you have told me you don't want me and don't love me. (Jacobs, 1967, p. 67)

Other letters begin in this way:

> I do not really know how to word this.*

> I have no words for you because I love you so much.*

> I love you so much. I don't know how to say it to you . . . *

> I was crying for help and nobody answered of course you all thought I was joking, I wasn't. Don't forget to tell everyone the punch line. (Messner & Buckrop, 2000, p. 10)

> I have been waiting and hoping maybe you go out of your way to show me that you are sorry for what you did but you don't even think about

> it I take it if s not important enough to do so. If you really did [care] you would make the time. So I feel like you're forcing me to make a move. (Messner & Buckrop, 2000, p. 9)

These people give voice to an inability to find the "right words" that will lead to feeling heard. Ironically, however, the notes presumably express something, and their act of suicide itself will also continue to communicate. They can feel as though they are still participants in the conversation, even beyond their death. Here is a clue into the nature of the audience for these particular persons. They are addressing an idealized audience whom they imagine will never understand their feelings. But yet, in crafting these words, these people are well aware that there is a responsive audience being addressed, although seemingly constricting their view of the audience as primarily a nonresponsive one.

Obviously the dead will no longer be capable of receiving a response, of participating in the unending conversation. The death by suicide materializes those feelings of isolation and disconnection in a final tragic utterance that removes all possibility of participation in a dialogue with others, of feeling heard. The note left, like the lifeless body, is, therefore, not like active utterances, but more like monologues, empty possibilities awaiting actual audience-centered and purpose-driven human utterances. Thus, from the perspective of the suicidal person, insofar as death renders impossible the experience of an actual response, we can expect to find traces in these notes of a sense of one's superaddressee, that invisible third party who exists in metaphysical spaces and understands us in "just the right way." Insofar as suicide and a suicide note addresses an idealized audience, it is to *this* audience that the performance of suicide is accredited as an appropriate response to their suffering.

Suicide as a communicative act has the dramatic form of a sentence, insofar as it is addressed to an idealized audience who will never actually be experienced. We might, therefore, consider the communicative act of suicide and the suicide note as cultural idioms parasitic upon notions of communication convinced that "transmission" of the "right words" is the pathway for solving a crisis in communicative wholeness. The audience is imagined to be one who will simply passively receive an idealized message in just the right way. This is why, in some suicide notes, we read instructions, or "metamessages" (Bateson, 1972) about how one should interpret their death and what should be done with their body. For instance, some might express, "I hope you do not cry*,"

"Bury me without delay," and "Please don't think I'm a coward for doing what I am about to do." Or, as one person wrote:

> I love you very much but I can't live anymore making you life a mess. You need to call Sam about our back taxes that you don't know about. I cannot manage money. There seems like there is never enough. No matter what I do I mess things up. Without me you won't need to worry about house or anything anymore. (Messner & Buckrop, 2000, p. 12)

Here the audience is given instructions on how this death is to be interpreted as a benefit. Its rhetorical dimension is to persuade the audience that they are better off with the writer dead. The metamessage here is, "Death is a good thing for the intimates in my life."

Another person wrote:

> My life would have been a failure anyway. I guess I could have changed, but I just didn't have the will power. I'm sick of suffering and sick of seeing you suffer . . . Pall bearer . . . you will find me in the garage.*

This person gives an account of how their failures have been burdens to others, and so their death will bring ease to the suffering of these others. The metamessage is "Take my death as a blessing." These attempts to persuade their audience to react in one way, and not another, reveals their tacit awareness of the communicative condition, that is, they are addressing an audience whom they know will continue to be responsive persons participating in living, unique, contextual meanings well beyond their death. But these contextual considerations are contradicted by what they actually write in their notes, for beyond consideration is the strong likelihood that their death will in fact bring *more* suffering. If the superaddressee is the imagined third party who will respond to our speech in just the right way, then it is clear that these people are writing to an idealized third party audience.

Suicide and suicide notes can be read as final communiqués and felt as "final" by those uttering them, in the sense that, once deceased, the suicidal person will be unable to hear actual living responses to their final utterance. Yet their crafted notes and their decision to commit suicide presuppose awareness of some responsive audience and the conversation within which their act will "live on" through the living responses of others. It will be as if their utterance is imbued with abstract, universal meaning. Perhaps with a sense of relief (or "curling up in comfort"), they can die feeling that their words will be heard "in just the right way."

Conclusion: Are the Concepts of Communicative Conditions and Audience Useful?

I began this essay by noting with Lester (2001) that communicative aspects of suicide are implied in suicide research. I then reviewed the anthro-psychological perspective of Kral (1994) and Kral and Dyck (1995). Suicide ideation as the interiorizing of cultural scripts begged the question regarding what form or shape such ideation takes in the minds of persons who chose suicide as a "sensible" response to perturbation. I asked in what specific forms do those ideations play out in the minds of people and what is the life-blood that nourishes suicide as an idea for some? I then reviewed a long-standing debate regarding communication intention and drew a distinction between communication as a function and the communicative condition. I concluded by suggesting that both an intent to communicate and that one cannot *not* communicate are useful perspectives for understanding the performative aspects of suicide. I turned to the work of Bakhtin to elucidate what I meant by the communicative condition and found that "audience" figures as the primary motivator of human communication. As such, the act of suicide and suicide notes have, *as a rule,* an implicit or explicit audience-directed thinking that precedes the act. Given this communicative condition, suicide is a type of symbolic action as are other human actions, but it is distinguished by the way in which a suicidal person imagines the audience for whom their actions will take on their intended expressive significance.

By exploring such an audience-centric perspective, I hope to provoke discussion of the dramatic dimensions of the "why" and "how" of suicide, or the perturbation theory of suicidal motivation and the lethality theory of suicidal ideation. Can suicide usefully be viewed as solution to a "crisis in expression" that, seen from the perspective of the suicide, takes the form of an extreme rhetorical appeal intended for some audience? My brief notations of suicide note excerpts suggest that tacit and explicit considerations of an audience influence both the act of suicide and the crafting of suicide notes, and that the choice of suicide as an expressive action is parasitic upon deeply held cultural beliefs that communication with others should aspire to being a pure and transcendent connection.

The suicidal act and the posthumously read note are both expressive acts intended for an audience or, in short, suicide is an act "drawn out" from persons by their notions of the audience and their desire for communication. I am suggesting, therefore, based on this brief analysis of notes, that suicide paradoxically involves a communicative motive to achieve "pure understanding" with others, but preceded by a primordial forgetfulness that we are always already embedded within audiences with whom we are in communication.

Lurking in the background of feelings of interpersonal isolation or a deep disconnection with others, that so often accompany the "psych-ache" of suicide, is assent to an ideal of communication that creates a desire to feel completely understood in "just the right way." Given a more conditional view of communication, I have suggested that suicide is a suffering person's idea of achieving a communiqué. However, not in the sense of a "last word" that expresses some inner pain in a perfect form, that is, that the message that will be understood in "just the right way" by some audience. Rather, suicide and suicide notes can be viewed as communiqués that paradoxically take the form of a monologue, a constricted view of their suicidal utterances as idealized, abstracted, and sentential. Insofar as death renders the sufferer physically absent to experiencing concrete audience responses or human association, such abstract meanings, these "empty possibilities," are actualized (i.e., taken up as a living utterance one last time) and taken to their formal and material conclusion in the sheer act of successful suicide. Thus, nestled within the idea of "suicide as social logic" are communicative motives at work that dramatically, paradoxically, and tragically render a "perfect" idealized (i.e., imagined) audience for whom suicide is socially sanctioned as a self-warranted choice among a repertoire of choices.

References

Baechler, J. (1979). *Suicides*. New York: Basic Books.

Bakhtin, M. M. (1986). *Speech genres and other late essays*. Austin, TX: University of Texas Press.

Bateson, G. (1972). *Steps to an ecology of mind*. Chicago, IL: University of Chicago Press.

Baumeister, R. F. (1990). Suicide as escape from self. *Psychological Review, 97*, 90–113.

Buber, M. (1970). *I and thou*. New York: Scribner.

Burke, K. (1950). *A rhetoric of motives*. New York: Prentice-Hall.

Burke, K. (1967). *The philosophy of literary form: studies in symbolic action*. Baton Rouge, LA: Louisiana State University Press.

Cole, M. (1996). *Cultural psychology: A once and future discipline.* Cambridge, MA: Belknap Press of Harvard University Press.

DeCatanzaro, D. (1981). *Suicide and self-damaging behavior.* New York: Academic Press.

Durkheim, E. (1951). *Suicide: A study in sociology.* Glencoe, IL: Free Press.

Etkind, M. (1997). *. . . Or not to be: A collection of suicide notes.* New York: Riverhead Books.

Frank, A. W. (2000). Illness and autobiographical work: Dialogue as narrative destabilization. *Qualitative Sociology,* 23, 135–56.

Goffman, E. (1959). *The presentation of self in everyday life.* Garden City, NY: Doubleday.

Goffman, E. (1967). *Interaction ritual: Essays on face-to-face behavior.* Garden City, NY: Doubleday.

Goffman, E. (1969). *Strategic interaction.* Philadelphia, PA: University of Pennsylvania Press.

Good, B. (1992). Culture and psychopathology: Directions for psychiatric anthropology. In T. Schwartz, G. White & C. A. Lutz, (Eds.), *New directions in psychological anthropology,* pp. 181–205. Cambridge, MA: Cambridge University Press.

Gould, M. S., Wallenstein, S., & Davison, L. (1989). Suicide clusters: a critical review. *Suicide & Life-Threatening Behavior,* 19, 17–29.

Hayakawa, S. (1957). Suicide as a communicative act. *ETC,* 15, 46–50.

Jacobs, J. (1967). A phenomenological study of suicide notes. *Social Problems,* 15, 60–72.

Kleinman, A. (1988). *Rethinking psychiatry: From cultural category to personal experience.* New York: Free Press.

Kral, M. (1994). Suicide as social logic. *Suicide & Life-Threatening Behavior,* 24, 245–55.

Kral, M. (1995). Suicide and the internalization of culture: Three questions. *Transcultural Psychiatry,* 35, 221–33.

Kral, M., & Dyck, R. (1995). Public option, private choice: Impact of culture on suicide. In B. Mishara (Ed.), *The impact of suicide,* pp. 200–14. New York: Springer.

Leenaars, A., De Wilde, E., Wenckstern, S. & Kral, M. (2001). Suicide notes of adolescents: A life span comparison. *Canadian Journal of Behavioural Science,* 33, 47–57.

Lester, D. (2001). Nonfatal suicidal behavior as a communication. *Crisis,* 22, 49–51.

Lester, D. (2008). Suicide and culture. *World Cultural Psychiatry Research Review,* 3(2), 51–68.

Littlejohn, S. W. (1983). *Theories of human communication.* Belmont, CA: Wadsworth.

Menninger, K. (1938). *Man against himself.* New York: Hartcourt Brace.

Messner, B. A., & Buckrop, J. J. (2000). Restoring order: interpreting suicide through a Burkeian lens. *Communication Quarterly,* 48, 1–18.

Morson, G. S., & Emerson, C. (1990). *Mikhail Bakhtin: Creation of a prosaics.* Stanford, CA: Stanford University Press.

Motely, M. T. (1990). On whether one can(not) communicate: An examination via traditional communication postulates. *Western Journal of Speech Communication,* 54, 1–20.

Phillips, D. P. (1974). The influence of suggestion on suicide: substantive and theoretical implications of the Werther effect. *American Sociological Review,* 39, 340–54.

Phillips, D. P., Carstensen, L. L., & Paight, D. J. (1989). Effects of mass media news stories on suicide, with new evidence on the role of story content. In C. R. Pfeffer (ed.), *Suicide among youth: Perspectives on risk and prevention,* pp.101–16. Washington, DC: American Psychiatric Press.

Sartre, J. (1984). *Being and nothingness.* New York: Washington Square Press.

Shneidman, E. S. (1985). *Definition of suicide.* Northvale, NJ: Jason Aronson.

Steiner, G. (1989). *Real presences.* Chicago, IL: University of Chicago Press.

Strauss, C. (1992). Motives and models. In R. D'Andre & C. Strauss (Eds.), *Human motives and cultural models,* pp. 1–20. New York: Cambridge University Press.

Stravynski, A., & Boyer, R. (2001). Loneliness in relation to suicide ideation and parasuicide. *Suicide & Life-Threatening Behavior,* 31, 32–40.

Takahashi, Y. (1993). Suicide prevention in Japan. In A. A. Leenaars (Ed.), *Suicidology: Essays in Honor of Edwin S. Shneidman.* Northvale, NJ: Jason Aronson.

Tarde, G. (1898). *La logique sociale.* Paris, France: Felix Alcan.

Thayer, L. O. (1997). *Pieces: Towards a revisioning of communication/life.* Greenwich, CT: Ablex.

Todorov, T. (1988). *Mikhail Bakhtin: The dialogic principle.* Minneapolis, MN: University of Minnesota Press.

Watzlawick, P., Beavin, J. M., & Jackson, D. D. (1967). *Pragmatics of human communication.* New York: Norton.

Part 2

The Location of the Suicidal Act

7

The Location of the Suicidal Act

Steven Stack

The staging of suicide involves a location. Where do people decide to end their lives? There are many options, including at home versus away from home. If at home, there is a question of which room? Some choose exterior areas such as a detached garage or yard. If not at home, options include a friend's home, a park or open area, one's motor vehicle, or checking into a hotel to end one's life in a private room.

The choice of a place for suicide could be random, following no socio-demographic patterns. Perhaps, for example men and women would be equally likely to die by suicide at home, equally likely to end their lives in a park, or in a hotel room.

Table 7-1 presents data on the locations of suicides in 2010 from the recently released National Violent Death Reporting System (NVDRS) for 2010 (Parks, et al., 2014). It is based on suicides from sixteen states. The CDC coded information received from county coroners and medical examiners on a variety of circumstances surrounding suicides including the location.

Most persons (75.4% in 2010) decided to end their lives at home. The CDC coders who construct the NVDRS do not code the place of suicide within the home. In the Detroit suicide project, the most common room for suicides was the bedroom, with the body typically found in the bed (Wasserman & Stack, 2008).

Nevertheless, a quarter of those who die by suicide choose to end their lives away from the familiar surroundings of their homes. This part of the book uses the NVDRS data to assess what patterns, if any, underlie this basic choice for staging one's suicide. For example, are

Table 7-1. Location of suicides, 2010; NVDRS; sixteen States; adapted from Parks, et al. (2014).

Location (Stage for the suicide)	Number of suicides	Percentage of suicides
House or apartment	7,662	75.4%
Natural area	415	4.1%
Street/highway	322	3.2%
Motor vehicle	233	2.3%
Hotel/motel	196	1.9%
Park/playground/sports/athletic area	156	1.5%
Jail/prison	134	1.3%
Parking lot/public garage/public transport	122	1.2%
Commercial/retail area	70	0.7%
Railroad tracks	56	0.6%
Hospital or medical facility	52	0.5%
Industrial or construction area	40	0.4%
Supervised residential facility	37	0.4%
Farm	30	0.3%
Office building	27	0.3%
Abandoned house/building or warehouse	10	0.1%
Preschool, school, college, school bus	6	.05%

men, whose traditional sex role is centered more around work and less around home, more likely than women to select a stage for their suicide outside of the home? Some men, for example those who use firearms, choose to travel away from home to end their lives.

A major stage for suicide outside of the home is nature, including national parks, state parks, metropolitan parks, beaches, and waterfalls. One out of every six suicides outside of home (4.1% in 2010) occurred in natural areas. Chapter 10 focuses on those who die by suicide in natural areas. Natural areas often provide a "lethal location" for suicides because they are remote places with few or no people who might act as potential rescuers—persons who might intervene and stop a suicide in progress. Chapter 11 describes the suicides that occur in national parks.

Chapter 9 summarizes research on suicide in hotels and presents the first national epidemiological study of suicide in the nation's hotels using four years of NVDRS data. Given that previous studies on hotel suicide was carried out at the local level, patterns found in small local samples may not always replicate broader, more representative national data.

References

Parks, S. E., Johnson, L. L., McDaniel, D. D., & Gladden, M. (2014). Surveillance of violent deaths: National violent death reporting system, 16 states, 2010. *Morbidity & Mortality Weekly Report, 63*(SS01), 1–33.

Wasserman, I., & Stack, S. (2008). Lethal locations: An application of opportunity theory to motel suicide. *Death Studies, 32,* 757–67.

8

Suicide Away from Home

Steven Stack

A major issue in suicidology is assessing the degree of intent to die in suicide attempts (Lester, 2000; Miller, Azrael, & Barber, 2012). The method used for suicide has been proposed as one clue for the degree of intent to end one's life. People who choose to shoot themselves in the head are choosing for a highly lethal technique that is almost certain to succeed. In contrast, those who take a handful of Tylenol pills may succeed or may not since the effect is not immediate. Death will not come for hours or even weeks and only after liver failure. In a recent analysis based on national data on suicide and suicide attempts for one year, 85% of attempts by firearms were successful, 69% of hanging/suffocation attempts, and 31% of suicide attempts by jumping/falls. In contrast, only 2% of suicide acts by poison resulted in death, and just 1% of acts by cutting resulted in death (Miller, Azrael, & Barber, 2012).

While the method for suicide can be a measure of intent, the location selected for suicide, whether it be a living room, workplace, hotel, or a remote area in a national park, can also indicate the intent to die. Some locations are considered more lethal than others, and one factor in determining this is the probability of bystander intervention in a suicide attempt.

Along these lines, Wasserman and Stack (2008) applied a general theory of criminology and deviant behavior, opportunity theory (Cohen & Felson, 1979), to the issue of the lethality of locations for suicide. In criminology, opportunities for getting away with a crime are enhanced by the absence of guardians. Robbers, for example, prefer to select victims who are alone, unprotected, and generally more vulnerable than persons traveling with others. A key concern in suicidal actions is the presence of rescuers or guardians and, in addition, whether these persons are motivated enough to try to stop or rescue the person on the brink of suicide (Wasserman & Stack, 2008; Weisman & Worden, 1972).

When suicidal persons contemplate suicide, a basic consideration is where the act should take place. What stage will be selected? A key division, empirically, is whether one should engage in the suicidal act in the familiar surroundings of one's home or travel to some other stage such as a park, railroad tracks or a hotel. All else being equal, the choice of one's home as a stage for suicide is considered less lethal since this is where significant others, including family and neighbors, might notice the act and be motivated enough to intervene to stop it. However, little is known about those who choose to stay home versus those who travel to a distant stage for suicide.

Previous research on the location for suicide is sparse. A ten-year review of research on suicide found only a single investigation exploring factors related to location (Lester, 2000). Due to data limitations, the few studies that do exist have generally operationalized location in a manner different from a simple dichotomy—at one's residence versus somewhere other than one's residence. Given constraints of official data available to previous investigators, studies usually define "away from home" in terms of dying in a different county or even a different state from that of the suicide's residence (e.g., Gross et al., 2007; Lester & Frank, 1990; Windfuhr, et al., 2010). They tend to stress long distances away from home, and these long-distance travelers have been termed "suicide tourists" (Gross, et al., 2007).

Because of data limitations, those who travel a short distance away from home (within the same city or county) to a nearby stage for suicide, such as a parking garage, hotel, or lake, unfortunately, are not classified suicides "away from home" in previous research, even though these local suicides do involve travel to some other (nearby) location where motivated rescuers are less likely to be present. The present chapter argues that these suicides need to be counted as "away from home." They are likely to be in "lethal locations" where rescuers are less likely to be present. Suicides happening away from home include those within the area of residence (e.g., city or county) as well as ones outside the area of residence. The NVDRS provides an opportunity for fine-tuning this aspect of the opportunity theory of suicide with respect to location.

Given that there is very little theoretical work on location and suicide, the present chapter is largely exploratory. Preliminary interpretations of the findings will be suggested that may serve as guides for future research and suggest hypotheses for new work.

Methodology

All data are from the National Violent Death Reporting System (NVDRS). Files for each of four years, 2003, 2004, 2005, and 2006, were obtained from the Centers for Disease Control. The number of states covered in the NVDRS catchments area increased from seven in 2003 to seventeen by 2006. CDC staff coded data received from the states. The data sources included files from county medical examiners, county coroners, local police reports, death certificates, hospital records, child fatality reviews, and abstractor completed reports (CDC, 2008). The data set includes measures of demographic variables such as age, gender, ethnicity, and marital status. In addition, there are data on social and related problems including economic strains, legal strains, health problems, and deaths of loved ones. Measures of psychiatric morbidity use data from toxicology reports on the presence of alcohol and drugs, as well as mental health issues such as depression and previous suicide attempts.

Demographic Variables

First, predictors of differences between suicides away from home and suicides at home were sought in regard to demographic variables (gender, ethnicity, marital status, age, and urban location). Previous investigations have found that gender predicts suicide far away from home. Given previous work on gender (Gross, et al., 2007; Lester & Frank, 1990), the present study predicted that the percentage of suicides away from home involving women will be less than the percentage of suicides away from home involving men.

NVDRS codes for ethnicity (Caucasian/white, Hispanic American, African American, Native American, and Asian American) were used to assess the extent to which ethnicity can differentiate away from home suicides from at-home suicides. Marital status was measured in terms of a series of dichotomous variables (married, single, widowed, and divorced). Urban location was measured as residence in a county of 500,000 persons or more, coded as 1, while counties of less than 500,000 were coded as 0 (Wasserman & Stack, 2011).

Social Strains

Social strain measures encompassed a variety of constructs, including deaths, economic strains, legal strains, and strains in social relationships. Each NVDRS strain category is defined in table 8-1. Table 8-1 also provides an example of each of these problem areas.

Table 8-1. Definitions and examples of the NVDRS categories of social problems or strains (CDC, 2008).

Problem or strain category	Definition	Example
Death of a loved one	The suicide was reportedly distressed over the death of a friend or family member during the last five years through a means other than suicide.	The suicide has been depressed since the death of his wife two years ago.
Financial problem	Financial problems that appeared to play a precipitating role in the suicide.	The suicide was experiencing bankruptcy, overwhelming debts, or a home foreclosure.
Job problem	At the time of the suicide the person was having a problem at work (such as tensions with a coworker, poor performance reviews, increased pressure, feared layoff) or was having a problem with joblessness (e.g., was recently laid off).	The suicide was in the midst of a sexual harassment action at work. The suicide was recently laid off from work.
Intimate partner problems	Problems in marriages, relationships with an ex-spouse, cohabitants, or other intimate relationships such as courtships.	The suicide was engaged in a bitter custody dispute with her ex-husband
Strains with friends, other family	Assorted problems and strains between the suicide and his/her friends or family members. These do not include suicides involving intimate partners.	A twenty year old was recently kicked out of his house by his parents because of arguments and drug use.
Criminal/legal problems	These include recent and/or pending issues with the criminal justice system. They include recent or impending arrest, police pursuit, and forthcoming court dates involving criminal offenses.	The suicide was awaiting a criminal court date for a drunken driving charge.
Victim of violence	This includes being the victim of violence that occurred during the month before their suicide.	The suicide had been physically assaulted by their spouse the week of the suicide.
Health problem	The suicide had experienced physical health problems that were linked to the suicide.	The suicide was diagnosed with pancreatic cancer and was told she had two months to live.

Psychiatric morbidity

Psychiatric morbidity was measured by a series of eleven variables available in the NVDRS. Five variables were from the toxicology reports and measured the presence (1) or absence (0) of alcohol, amphetamines, cocaine, marijuana, and opiates. Problem drinking was coded as a dichotomous variable (0, 1) and was present if the victim was perceived by self or others to have a problem with, or was addicted to, alcohol. The person was coded as having a drug abuse problem if the person was perceived by self or others to have a problem with, or was addicted to, drugs other than alcohol (0, 1). Depression was assumed to be present (0, 1) by CDC coders if the person was perceived by self or others as depressed at the time of the suicide. A report of a previous suicide attempt was also coded as a dichotomous variable (0, 1). The presence or absence of a mental disorder (other than alcohol or drug abuse) was coded as a dichotomous variable (0, 1). Finally, a dichotomous variable was created which measured if the suicide was currently undergoing treatment for a mental disorder (0, 1).

Results and Preliminary Interpretations

Demographic Predictors of Suicide away from Home

Eight of the twelve demographic variables significantly differentiated at-home from away-from-home locations for suicide (see table 8-2).

Gender

Gender was a significant predictor of suicide at home; 79.7% of females and 71.6% of males ended their lives at home.

Ethnicity

Three of the five categories of ethnicity predicted suicide location. Caucasians were more likely than other ethnic groups to die by suicide at home (74.2% vs. 68.9%). Two groups were less likely to die by suicide at home, African Americans (66.5% vs. 73.9% other races), and Asian Americans (66.9% vs. 73.5%) other races. The percentage of Hispanic Americans and Native Americans dying by suicide at home was essentially the same as that of other ethnic groups.

The tendency for some ethnic groups to die by suicide away from home may be related to the nature of the residence and family size. To the extent that an ethnic group is marked by a large household size, households located in multi-family residences with an abundance of neighbors, or residences nested in crowded areas, the likelihood of the

Suicide as a Dramatic Performance

Table 8-2. Demographics of suicide: Comparison of the percentage of persons dying by suicide at home in a given demographic group versus comparison group.

Demographic group	Percent who die by suicide at home	Percent who die by suicide at home	Chi-square test of significance
Gender			
	Males 71.6%	Females 79.7%	170.4*
Ethnicity			
	Caucasians 74.2%	Other ethnicities 68.9%	60.6*
	Hispanic Americans 71.8%	Other ethnicities 73.5%	2.07
	African Americans 66.5%	Other ethnicities 73.9%	59.7*
	Native Americans 75.3%	Other ethnicities 73.3%	1.04
	Asian Americans 66.9%	Other ethnicities 73.5%	14.4*
Marital status			
	Married 73.7%	Other 73.2%	0.9
	Single 69.9%	Other 75.0%	90.9*
	Widowed 85.1%%	Other 72.5%	152.4*
	Divorced 75.5%	Other 72.8%	19.3*
Urban	Urban county 72.8%	Other counties 73.6%	1.8
Age (mean)	Mean at home: 42.4 years	Mean away from home: 46.4 years	

* $p < .05$

presence of motivated rescuers increases. Further work is needed to test these notions.

Marital Status

The choice of a stage for suicide was predicted by three marital statuses: single, widowed, and divorced. Only 69.9% of single persons died by suicide at home compared to 75.0% of all others. While older single persons may live alone, many young single persons still live with their parents. Perhaps single individuals who live with parents are especially motivated to travel away from home for their suicides since parents are generally considered to be motivated guardians who would try to prevent the suicide.

More widowed persons died by suicide at home than nonwidowed persons (85.1% vs. 72.5%). To the extent that widows and widowers are relatively old and live alone, their children being adults with residences of their own, motivated rescuers are less likely to be present in the home. As such, there is less reason for the widowed to travel to some other site for suicide in order to avoid being stopped by rescuers. In addition, travel may be difficult for some of the widowed population. Persons who are frail, who can no longer drive, who are blind, and so on, would find it more difficult to travel to a site for staging their suicides.

As in the case of the widowed, divorced persons lack a spouse. As such, if all else is equal, they have less reason to die by suicide away from home to avoid being stopped by a motivated guardian. The data in Table 8-2 are consistent with this thesis. Divorced persons were significantly more likely than nondivorced persons to die by suicide at home (75.5 vs. 72.8%).

There was no significant difference between the percentage of married persons dying by suicide at home and the corresponding percentage for persons of other marital statuses (73.7% vs. 73.2%). This result is counterintuitive since married persons, all else being equal, have a motivated guardian (their spouse) living at home. It would be anticipated that married persons might be more likely to choose a stage away from home—a natural area, a hotel, an abandoned building, a bridge, or a parking garage, where a motivated rescuer would be less likely to be present. It is plausible, however, that married persons may plan their suicide at times when their spouse is absent from the home place. Possibly, some who are especially angry at their spouse, who may be seen as the cause of their suicide, may want to expose the spouse to the act of suicide. In rare cases, the suicide has killed their spouse at home in a homicide-suicide event. Further work is needed to test these possible explanations.

Urbanism was unrelated to the percentage of persons who die by suicide at home, but persons dying by suicide at home were older (46.4 years) than persons traveling away from home for suicide (42.4 years).

Social Stress as a Predictor of Location

Table 8-3 provides the results for the associations between social strains and location of suicide. Death of a loved one predicted location: 80.2% of those suffering this loss die by suicide at home compared to only 72.9% of those do not experience death of a loved one. Given that death of a loved one can involve a spouse or some other potential rescuer who

Table 8-3. Social strains and suicide location. Comparison of the percentage of persons dying by suicide at home by problem area.

Social strain	Percent suicides at home, strain is not present	Percent suicides performed at home, strain is present	Chi-square test of significance
Death of a loved one	72.9%	80.2%	45.3*
Financial strain	73.0%	76.6%	17.7*
Job problem	73.0%	77.1%	24.6*
Intimate partner problem	72.3%	76.4%	52.1*
Other relationship problem	73.1%	75.9%	10.0*
School problem	73.3%	76.3%	1.3
Legal problem, (criminal justice)	74.9%	58.1%	375.0
Legal problem, other, (civil offense)	73.4%	72.9%	0.14
Violence victim	73.3%	81.0%	5.4*
Poor health	70.5%	84.6%	498.6*

* $p < .05$

lives in the home, such a loss reduces the number of potential rescuers from the home, thereby increasing the lethality of the home and decreasing the need to travel to be isolated from persons who might stop the suicide. There may be, however, covariation between death of a loved one and widowhood. Future work needs to sort out exactly who the loved one is—a spouse, a lover, a child, a close friend, and so forth.

Both measures of economic strain predicted location of suicide. While the differences were not large, both persons with financial problems (76.6%) or job problems (77.1%) were more likely to die by suicide at home than their counterparts.

Both measures of strains in social relationships predicted location of suicide. Persons with intimate partner problems (76.4%) and persons with other relationship problems (75.9%) were more likely to choose home for the stage of their suicides than their counterparts. School problems were unrelated to suicide location.

Persons involved in legal strains in the criminal justice system were especially less likely than others to die by suicide at home (58.1% vs. 74.9%).

This is one of the strongest predictors of suicide location. There may be, however, covariation between such criminal justice strains and age, since many persons charged with crimes are young and still living with parents. In addition, some of these persons are undergoing processing and in jail. Jail is a frequent site of suicides away from home. Future work is needed to sort out these alternative explanations. In contrast to criminal cases, involvement in other or civil legal cases did not predict suicide location.

Victims of violence were more likely to die by suicide at home—81.0% compared to 73.3% of those who are not victims of violence.

Poor physical health was a significant predictor of location. Only 70.5% of suicides who lack a physical health problem died by suicide at home. In sharp contrast, among those afflicted with physical health issues fully 84.6% chose to die by suicide at home. Intuitively, some persons with severe health problems may be too frail to travel. These might include the blind, the crippled, and persons with suspended driver's licenses due to health problems. Physical health problems can thwart the ability to travel in general, particularly to a site for suicide.

Psychiatric Predictors of Location

Table 8-4 provides the bivariate results on the relationship between measures of psychiatric disorders and location of suicide. Nine of the eleven measures of psychiatric morbidity predicted suicide at home. Five of the seven measures of substance abuse predicted location of suicide. With the exception of the presence of marijuana, these substance abuse measures were associated with a greater incidence of suicide at home. For example, 76.4% of those suicides whose blood contained alcohol from a toxicology report staged their suicides at home compared to 72.5% who did not have alcohol reported in their toxicology report but died by suicide at home; 80.9% of those with an opioid present in the blood died by suicide at home whereas only 72.7% of those without an opioid in their blood died by suicide at home. The presence of amphetamines or cocaine did not differentiate between the at-home and away-from-home suicides.

All four measures of mental problems (depression, suicide attempt, mental health problems, and current treatment) predicted suicide at home. For example, 79.0% of depressed persons chose home as a location for their suicides compared to 69.5% of nondepressed persons, and 75.4% of those with a previous suicide attempt chose home for the location of their suicide compared to 72.9% of those lacking a previous

Suicide as a Dramatic Performance

Table 8-4. Psychiatric strains and suicide location. Comparison of the percentage of the persons dying by suicide at home in the absence of the psychiatric strain.

Psychiatric strain	Percent of persons without the strain who die by suicide at home	Percent of persons with the strain who die by suicide at home	Chi-square test of significance
Substance abuse indicators			
Alcohol present	72.5%	76.4%	44.3*
Amphetamines present	73.4%	73.1%	0.21
Cocaine present	73.4%	73.2%	0.19
Marijuana present	73.5%	68.3%	10.3*
Opiate present	72.7%	80.9%	83.2*
Perceived alcohol problem	72.2%	79.7%	114.1*
Perceived drug problem	73.0%	75.6%	11.7*
Perceived depression problem	69.5%	79.0%	341.5*
Previous suicide attempt	72.9%	75.4%	13.3*
Reported mental health problem	71.2%	77.0%	125.4*
Undergoing current treatment for mental health problem	71.6%	77.8%	120.9*

*p < .05

suicide attempt. Persons with a reported mental disorder as well as persons in current treatment for a psychiatric disorder were also more likely to die by suicide at home than their counterparts.

In summary, persons dying by suicide at home were more likely to have psychiatric or substance abuse issues than persons without psychiatric or substance abuse problems. Most of the differences were not large. Nevertheless, the data suggest that persons who chose to die by suicide away from their home place (in natural areas, hotels, parking garages, or other locations) were in somewhat better mental condition than those dying by suicide at home. Possibly one needs a

Suicide Away from Home

Table 8-5. Multiple logistic regression analysis.

Variable	Logistic regression coefficient	Standard error	Odds ratio
Demographic			
Gender: Female	-0.35*	0.03	0.7
Ethnicity			
Asian American	0.32*	0.09	1.38
African American	0.15*	0.06	1.16
Caucasian	0.08	0.05	1.09
Other Ethnic = reference			
Marital status			
Single	-0.13*	0.03	0.86
Widowed	-0.54*	0.07	0.57
Divorced	-0.54*	0.07	0.57
Married = reference			
Age	-0.008*	0.001	0.99
Problems of living			
Death of a loved one	-0.1	0.06	0.9
Financial problem	-0	0.04	0.99
Job problem	-0.13*	0.04	0.87
Intimate partner problem	-0.36*	0.03	0.69
Other relationship problem	-0.17*	0.04	0.83
Legal problem with criminal justice	0.68*	0.04	1.97
Victim of violence	-0.31	0.19	0.72
Health problem	-0.63*	0.04	0.52
Psychiatric morbidity:			
Toxicology: alcohol present	-0.2*	0.03	0.81
Toxicology: marijuana present	0.13	0.08	1.14
Toxicology: opiate present	-0.27*	0.05	0.76
Reported alcohol problem	-0.34*	0.04	0.71
Reported substance abuse problem	-0.07	0.04	0.92
Depression	-0.3*	0.03	0.73
Previous suicide attempt	0.07	0.04	1.07

(*Continued*)

Table 8-5. (Continued)

Variable	Logistic regression coefficient	Standard error	Odds ratio
Any mental health problem	-0.09	0.05	0.91
In current treatment	0.08	0.05	0.92
Constant	-0.11	0.07	–

$*p < .05$
Nagelkerke r-squared = .081
-2 Log likelihood = 33675.1*
Cases correctly predicted: 73.77%

boost of energy in order to travel to an alternative location on the day of one's suicide. Those lacking in energy, being of depressed mood, may not have the strength to make the effort to travel for their suicide. An understanding of the roots of these linkages between mental health and location for suicide needs further research.

Of the thirty-two variables explored, twenty-four were able to differentiate at-home from away-from-home suicides. All three variable groups provided many significant factors linked to location. At least two thirds of the variables in each set predicted location: eight of the twelve demographic variables, seven of the ten social strain variables, and nine of the eleven psychiatric variables.

Multivariate Analysis of Predicting Location at Home

In order to sort out the independent predictors of suicide at home, a multivariate logistic regression analysis was undertaken. Only those variables that had a significant association at the bivariate level were entered into the multivariate analysis. The results of the multivariate analysis are provided in Table 8-5. Here the dependent variable is suicide away from home, equal to 1, versus at home, equal to 0.

Eight demographic variables were entered. Controlling for the other predictor variables, seven of these eight demographic factors remained significant predictors of the location of suicide. From the odds ratio, females were 30% less likely than males to die away from home. Two ethnic groups were more likely to die by suicide away from home. African Americans were 16% and Asian Americans 38% more likely to die by suicide away from home than the other reference groups. The three measures of marital status that were significant predictors of location in the bivariate tables remained significant in the multivariate analysis. Controlling for the other variables, singles were 14% less likely, the widowed 43% less likely, and the divorced 43% less likely to die by suicide away from home than were married persons. Finally, the odds of traveling away from home decreased 1% for each year of age.

Five of the eight social problems or strains remained significant predictors of location. From the odds ratios, four of these strains reduced the likelihood of traveling away from home to stage their suicide: job problems (13% less likely), intimate partner problems (31% less likely), other relationship problems (17% less likely), and health problems (48% less likely). In contrast, one social problem increased the odds of travel away from home for suicide. Persons having a problem with the criminal justice system were 97% more likely to die by suicide away from home.

Only four of the nine measures of psychiatric morbidity remained significant after controlling for the other predictor variables. All four reduced the odds of suicide away from home. Depressed persons (27% less likely to travel), persons with a reported alcohol problem (29% less likely to travel), and persons who test positive for alcohol in their toxicology test (19% less likely to travel) were all less likely to travel than persons lacking these mental health markers. Persons under the influence of opiates were 24% less likely to die by suicide away from home for suicide than persons not under the influence of opiates at the time of their death.

Overall, of the twenty-five significant predictors of location at the bivariate level, sixteen remained significant at the multivariate level. Of the three sets of predictors, the demographic variables held up best, with seven of the eight still predictive of suicide location, and the model provided a good fit to the data. The model correctly predicted 73.8% of the cases as being at home or away from home.

Conclusions

The present investigation called attention to a neglected area of lethality, namely the location of the suicide. As with methods of suicide, where some methods are more lethal than others, some locations are believed to be more likely to result in death than others. A key aspect of the stage or location selected for a suicide may be the probability of there being a motivated rescuer or guardian present.

Persons who go through the trouble of traveling a distance away from their homes are judged, as a group, to be more intent on dying. In general, they are minimizing their chances of being stopped in their efforts to die by suicide by picking locations free of motivated guardians, mainly their significant others and neighbors. As such, their efforts are considered more lethal than those who choose to die by suicide at home where the chances of the presence of a motivated guardian are greater.

The analysis proceeded through three sets of variables (twelve demographic variables, ten social strains, and eleven psychiatric variables) as possible predictors of location of suicide. Twenty-four of these thirty-three predictors differentiated at-home from away-from-home suicides. The results concerning the social and the psychiatric predictors are new since none of the few available previous studies systematically considered these as possible predictors of location of suicide.

Women, in particular, are more likely than men to die by suicide at home. This finding is consistent with traditional gender role stereotypes that women are homemakers, building their identities, more so than men, around the home. Since the home is a less lethal location, that women differentially select the home as a location for their suicide is consistent with the evidence that they are less intent on dying than are men (Stack & Wasserman, 2009). Two American-based previous studies also found women less likely than men to die by suicide away from home (Gross, et al., 2007; Lester & Frank, 1990). However, a previous investigation of suicides in England, using a somewhat different measure for away from home based on health areas, found no gender difference (Windfuhr, et al., 2010). A future analysis of the NVDRS could be undertaken to employ a similar definition of resident versus nonresident suicide locations as in Windfuhr, et al., (2010) to see if the results on gender reported here remain significant.

The present investigation found that two ethnic minorities, African Americans and Asian Americans, were more likely than other ethnic groups to die by suicide away from home. However, Lester and Frank (1990) found no significant difference between blacks and whites in the percentage that traveled out of state for the stage of their suicides. Future research is needed to see if this discrepancy between studies is an artifact of how "away from home" is measured—anywhere outside of one's residence (present study) versus out of state (Lester & Frank, 1990). A previous national study of England also found that ethnic minorities were more likely to travel, in this case travel outside of the health registration area, to die by suicide (Windfuhr, et al., 2010). Ethnic minorities made up 11% of nonresident (traveling) suicides compared to only 5% of resident suicides. Ethnic minority status may be related to household size, a measure of the probability of the presence of motivated rescuers, as well as residence type (single family versus multi-family housing units). Persons living in apartment complexes may be more motivated to travel to avoid detection (or embarrassment and shame) by their neighbors. Further research is needed to explore these possible explanations for the link between ethnic minority status and the odds of traveling to a stage for suicide.

Another demographic factor predicting suicide location was marital status. Widows and divorced persons, as well as single persons, were less apt to die by suicide on a stage away from home. Widows, divorced persons, and single persons (especially if they are middle-aged adults) have a higher probability of living alone than married persons. To the extent that traveling to a stage away from home is motivated by avoiding motivated rescuers, there is less motivation for such travel if one lives alone. The finding is largely consistent with research from England where 39% of nonresident suicides lived alone compared to 44% of resident suicides (persons who died by suicide in their health area of residence) (Windfuhr, et al., 2010). However, Lester and Frank (1990) found that 4.7% of out of state suicides involved single persons compared to only 2.5% of married persons. Again, future work is needed to see if this discrepancy is due to measurement differences in "away from home."

Little systematic research is available on the extent to which problems of living are related to suicide away from home. One of the strong predictors of dying by suicide at home in the present investigation was a health problem. This particular finding was also found in the national study of location of suicide in England. Windfuhr, et al. (2010) found that 14% of the suicides of nonresidents of the health area versus 18% of suicides of residents in the health area were characterized by a long-term illness. Persons incapacitated or semi-incapacitated from a health problem are less able to arrange the logistics for traveling to a suicide stage outside of the home. Future work that looks at the details regarding the type of illness and the presence of incapacitation is needed to rigorously assess his hypothesis.

The present study provides the first systematic, national epidemiological findings on possible links between psychiatric factors and suicide location. Previous studies were unable to address this aspect of the epidemiology of suicide location since the data in their respective databases lacked psychiatric measures. Since the NVDRS contains such information, the present study was able to provide the first results for this possible set of predictors of suicide location. Persons meeting the generalized definitions of psychiatric morbidity were more likely to choose their homes as their stage for suicide than persons not marked by the same feature of psychiatric morbidity. This consistent trend, that the more disturbed persons are the ones who stay put and die by suicide at home, is in need of future study. It is possible that it may take extra psychic energy to travel to a suicide site away from home. Possibly less disturbed and/or more energetic people are the ones more likely to travel to suicide sites.

Caution needs to be exercised in interpreting the results in terms of the opportunity theory of deviance (Wasserman & Stack, 2008). While traveling away from home can be driven by efforts to avoid potential motivated rescuers or guardians at home, there are other possible motives. These can include a desire for a significant other not to see the suicide or the dead body. This was mentioned in a suicide note in a previous study on hotel suicide (Hanzlick, Masterson, & Walker, 1990). According to the man's suicide note, he chose to die by suicide in a hotel so that his daughter would not find the body.

There are also additional reasons for travel in the case of traveling to well-known suicide hotspots. Motivations to travel to hotspots may include destigmatization of the act of suicide. Knowing that others have died by suicide at a hotspot may convey a sense of comradeship in death and combat feelings of loneliness. In some cases, persons might travel long distances to a suicide hotspot such as a bridge or cliff where others have ended their lives. The natural beauty of some hotspots, such as the Golden Gate Bridge, Skyway Bridge in Florida, and many less well-known local bridges in natural areas, can also destigmatize suicide (Stack, 2014). Hotels can also serve as hotspots. While there are many hotels available in Atlanta, about half of the hotel suicides by jumping were in just one, suggesting a possible magnet-like attraction to the one hotel (Hanzlick et al., 1990). Qualitative work with suicide attempters is needed to ascertain exactly what kinds of motivations underlie their selection of a stage for their suicide. This is true not only for hotspots but for location of suicide in general.

Future research is needed to explore the different types of suicide away from home. In particular, suicides in natural areas deserve some attention. Natural areas are a frequent location of suicides away from home. This topic is taken up in chapter 10. Furthermore, suicides in hotels constitute another frequent location of suicides away from home. The hotel room is similar to a bedroom in a home. It typically has a bed, bureau, nightstand, and an adjacent bathroom. From the present results, women prefer to stage their suicides at home. Given that the bedroom is the most commonly selected room for suicides at home, it may be that suicidal women may be more attracted to hotel locations. Even though women prefer to stage their suicides at home more than men, certain locations away from home could be differentially selected by women. Chapter 9 explores this and other aspects of hotel suicide.

References

Centers for Disease Control. (2008). *National Violent Death Reporting System coding manual.* Washington, DC: Department of Health and Human Services.

Cohen, L., & Felson, M. (1979). Social change and crime rate trends: a routine activities approach. *American Sociological Review,* 44, 588–607.

Gross, C., Piper, T. M., Bucciarelli, A., Tardiff, K., Vlahov, D., & Galea, S. (2007). Suicide tourism in Manhattan, New York City, 1990–2004. *Journal of Urban Health,* 84, 755–65.

Hanzlick, R., Masterton, K., & Walker, B. (1990). Suicide by jumping from high rise hotels: Fulton County Georgia, 1967–1986. *American Journal of Forensic Medicine & Pathology,* 11, 294–97.

Lester, D. (2000). *Why people iill themselves.* Springfield, IL: Charles C. Thomas.

Lester, D. & Frank, M. L. (1990). Suicide and homicide far away from home. *American Journal of Forensic Medicine & Pathology,* 11, 298–99.

Miller, M., Azrael, D., & Barber, C. (2012). Suicide mortality in the United States: The importance of attending to method in understanding population level disparities in the burden of suicide. *Annual Review of Public Health,* 33, 393–408.

Stack, S. (2014). The impact of suicide crisis phones on bridge suicide: Prevention vs. contagion on Skyway Bridge, Tampa Florida. Paper read at the annual meetings of the *Midwest Injury Prevention Association.* Ann Arbor, MI, September 30.

Stack, S., & Wasserman, I. (2009). Gender and suicide risk: The role of wound site. *Suicide & Life-Threatening Behavior,* 39, 13–20.

Wasserman, I., & Stack, S. (2008). Lethal locations: An application of opportunity theory to motel suicide. *Death Studies,* 32, 757–67.

Wasserman, I., & Stack, S. (2011). Race, urban context, and Russian roulette: Rindings from the national violent death reporting system. *Suicide & Life Threatening Behavior,* 41, 33–40.

Weisman, A. D., & Worden, J. W. (1972). Risk-rescue rating in suicide assessment. *Archives of General Psychiatry,* 26, 553–60.

Windfuhr, K., Bickley, H., While, D., Williams, A., Hunt, I. M., Appleby, L., Kapur, N. et al. (2010). Nonresident suicides in England: A national study. *Suicide & Life Threatening Behavior,* 40, 151–58.

9

Hotel Suicide and the Drug Subculture

Steven Stack

Henry Morselli (1882), one of the founders of suicidology, considered exploring regularities in the methods of suicide and the places where suicide occur to be a fundamental task in the epidemiology of suicide. Using data from twenty-two European nations and regions, he was able to demonstrate patterns in these features of suicide. In particular, the evidence on the locations of suicide did not change over the time frames analyzed and, for example, the places for suicide selected by men and women followed regularities. For example, in Prussia, 9.2% of men selected the woods as a place for their suicides in 1872, 8.6% in 1873, 9.3% in 1874, and 9.6% in 1875. The percentage of female suicides located in the woods was always much lower and ranged between 1.1% to 1.7% over the same period. Hotels were used by 1.4% of male suicides compared to 0.9% of female suicides in 1872. The percentage of hotel suicides for males never exceeded 2% and the corresponding percentage for female was always less than 1%. Morselli did not provide any systematic explanation for the patterns in places chosen for suicide.

Unlike Morselli, subsequent sociological work on suicide was less concerned with the location or place of suicide. Durkheim's (1897/1965) dismissal of a range of social factors, including location, media impacts, and alcohol as risk factors for suicide, has been cited as a cause of the neglect of these risk factors for decades after Durkheim (Pope, 1976; Stack, 1982), and perhaps the location of suicides has been neglected for the same reason (Lester, 2000; Stack 2000a, 2000b).

The present chapter focuses on what influences the selection of hotels as a stage for suicide. The most recent available data coming from the NVDRS for the year 2010 show that hotels constituted the fourth most common location for suicide (Parks, et al., 2014).

Hotels were the location for 1.9% of all suicides, trailers, homes, and apartments 75.4%, streets and highways 3.2%, and inside a vehicle 2.3%. In 2010, 196 persons ended their lives through suicide in motels and hotels (Parks, et al., 2014).

The general opportunity theory of deviance and criminology has provided a framework for analyzing hotel suicide (Wasserman & Stack, 2008). In the criminological literature, the probability that criminal behavior will take place is enhanced by the lack of a guardian. For example, daytime household burglary soared after World War II as millions of housewives entered the labor force. This left a higher percentage of homes unguarded during the day, creating opportunities for successful burglaries (Cohen & Felson, 1979).

The probability that an attempt at suicide will be successful (resulting the end of life) increases if there are no significant others or persons around to intervene. For example, a parent or sibling might call 911 if they find that a teenager has taken an overdose of Tylenol at home. Help will arrive and, hopefully, death from an overdose will be prevented. Even for suicide with firearms, persons in the home might be able to talk a would-be shooter out of suicide or perhaps disarm the potential shooter. However, if the potential suicide decides to travel away from home where there is essentially no chance of intervention by a significant other, the odds of a successful, completed suicide are enhanced. If an overdose is taken away from home, for example, in a locked hotel room or in a remote area deep in a national park, the odds of death are increased. There are no bystanders to call for help.

Hotels provide a lethal location since a hotel room is a secure, private location where the door can be locked to all outsiders, and behavior in the locked hotel room is not readily observable by others. In contrast, suicides at home or on the street are more likely to be witnessed by bystanders or guardians who might intervene. For example, even suicides in parked vehicles can be prevented if seen by passers-by. Bystander interventions to stop suicides, while neglected in academic research, have been illustrated in many feature films. For example, in the film *Forest Gump*, the main character is about to attempt suicide by firearm in a car parked in a no-parking zone. An officer, in the process of issuing a parking ticket, intervenes and stops the suicide.

The construct of a guardian in the opportunity theory of general deviance is similar to the concept of motivated rescuer found in several papers on suicide way from home. Weisman and Worden (1972) speak in terms of a risk-rescue ratio in assessing the intent to kill oneself. The rescue component refers to the presence of guardians or bystanders who might attempt to stop the suicide. Weisman and Worden saw the hotel room as an example of a place with a relatively low chance for rescue.

Relatively little is known about those who die by suicide in hotels. A search using Medline with the subject "suicide" and a keyword of "hotel" (accessed June 1, 2014) received only twenty-two hits. Some of these described individual case studies of suicides in hotels, such as a complex suicide carried out through a combination of electrocution and drug poisoning in Japan (Yamazaki, et al., 1997) and a case study of a man dressed in a Judo outfit who, after stabbing himself multiple times, set himself on fire and jumped out of his hotel room window with the judo belt wrapped tightly around his neck (Schlenger, et al., 2008). Some studies grouped together suicides with all other deaths occurring in or around hotels, and this makes it difficult to describe deaths from suicide that actually happened in a hotel as opposed to a parking lot or a casino attached to a hotel (e.g., Jason, Taff, & Boglioti, 1990). Only three studies focusing on deaths from suicide inside a hotel and reporting more than one case were found.[1] The essentials of the previous three, comparable studies are provided in table 9-1.

The samples of hotel-based suicides in previous work are small, ranging from twenty-three to sixty-one cases. The rate of suicide in hotels, taking into account the number of guests per year, is very high (Gemar, et al., 2008; Zarkowski & Avery, 2006). The suicide rate for residents of Clark County (which contains Las Vegas) who had registered as hotel guests was 271 per 100,000 per year (Gemar et al., 2008). This is over twenty times the national suicide rate, which hovers between ten and twelve. The suicide rate for Las Vegas County in general was sixteen. In like manner the suicide rate for local residents who registered in the hotels of Seattle (King County) was very high, 223 compared to only 11.7 for King county residents as a whole (Zarkowski & Avery, 2006). In this sense, hotels might be considered "hotspots" for suicide. Gemar, et al. (2008) speculated that the popular movie, *Leaving Las Vegas*, in which the star, Nicholas Cage, died by suicide in a hotel room in Las Vegas, might have influenced the incidence of hotel suicide.

Demographic patterns behind hotel suicide are marked by mixed findings, perhaps because of the small samples. For example, gender is not significantly associated with hotel suicide in Detroit, but it is apparently in Las Vegas (Wasserman & Stack, 2008; Gemar, et al., 2008).

Table 9-1. Previous major studies of hotel suicides in the United States.

Author (Year)	Location	Number of hotel suicides (years of study data)	Control or comparison group	Key findings
Gemer, et al. (2008)	Las Vegas/Clark County, NV	61 (2003–2005)	872 non-hotel suicides	Suicide rate of local residents registered in hotels: 271 per 100,000 guests per year. Suicide rate of Las Vegas general population: 16.6. Females: account for 21% of nonhotel suicides vs. 16% hotel suicides. Widows account for 8% of nonhotel suicides, but only 3% of hotel suicides.
Wasserman & Stack (2008)	Detroit, Wayne County, MI	27 (1997–2005)	1,430 non-hotel suicides	Race differentiated hotel from nonhotel suicides with 4% of hotel suicides involving blacks vs. 28% of nonhotel suicides involving blacks. Marital status predicted hotel suicide: 22% of hotel suicides were single vs. 45% of nonhotel suicides. Neither age nor gender predicted hotel suicide. Of 8 problem areas, only substance abuse differentiated hotel suicides (30% substance abusers) vs. nonhotel suicides (2% substance abusers).
Zarkowski & Avery (2006)	Seattle, WA	23 (2002–2004)	619 non-hotel suicides	Suicide rate of local residents registered in hotels: 223 per 100,000 guests; Suicide rate for the general local population: 11.7.

Most investigations do not provide tests of statistical significance, and so it is not possible to judge whether or not reported differences in the epidemiology of hotel versus nonhotel suicide are due to chance.

A key limitation of previous research is that it did not go beyond demographic variables (age, gender, residence, and marital status) in an effort to differentiate hotel from nonhotel suicides. Social and economic stress factors, such as intimate partner problems and financial problems, as well as measures of psychiatric morbidity (e.g., substance abuse and depression), were not considered in most studies. Wasserman and Stack (2008) did consider measures of social problems and psychiatric factors, but their sample of cases was small (n = 27). Larger samples are needed.

Multivariate analyses seeking to isolate the independent predictors of hotel suicide are largely unavailable in previous work. However, Wasserman and Stack (2008) determined that substance abuse was a leading predictor of hotel suicide. Controlling for demographic and other possible predictors of hotel suicide, substance abusers were 2.6 times more likely than non–substance abusers to die by suicide in hotel rooms.

The present analysis extends the previous work in several respects. It is based on a much larger sample of cases of hotel suicides (more than six hundred) so that findings are more reliable. It follows the lead of Wasserman and Stack (2008) in assessing three sets of variables (demographic variables, social problems, and psychiatric morbidity) in a search of significant predictors of hotel suicide. Special attention is drawn to drug-related variables since these were important predictors of hotel suicide in Detroit. In addition, through the use of the NVDRS, it is able to include less urban areas, whereas previous studies have been based on large urban areas (Detroit, Las Vegas, and Seattle). It is plausible that new patterns might emerge as less urbanized areas are included in the analysis.

Methodology

The methodology for the study is the same as that described in chapter 8, using the NVDRS data set. The dependent variable in the present study is the location of the suicide. Suicides staged in hotels or motels are coded as "1" and suicides happening in all other locations are coded as "0." There were 648 suicides in hotels and 29,922 suicides in other locations. Special attention is drawn to factors related to a drug subculture. These include the presence of opiates in the body of the suicide measured by the toxicology reports. In addition, attention is drawn to the perception that the suicide had a drug abuse problem.

Results and Preliminary Interpretations

Table 9-2 provides the results for the demographic variables. Gender predicted choosing a hotel as a stage for suicide: 2.8% of females versus 1.9% of males ended their lives in a hotel. A hotel room is similar to a bedroom in a house. There is a bed, nightstand, bureau, and an adjacent bathroom. To the extent that women are home-oriented, according to traditional sex-role stereotypes, when a woman desires to die by suicide away from home, she might be attracted to the home-like atmosphere of the hotel room. From the previous analysis on suicide away from home, it was determined that women are less likely than men to stage their suicides away from home. The hotel room is apparently the exception to this general rule.

Three measures of ethnicity predicted hotel suicide. Caucasian Americans were more likely (2.2% vs. 1.7%), while both Hispanic Americans (1.4% vs. 2.2%) and African Americans (1.6% vs. 2.2%) were

Table 9-2. The percentage of persons dying by suicide at a hotel, NVDRS, 2003–2006. n = 30,570 suicides.

Demographic Group	Percent who died by suicide at a hotel	Percent who died by suicide at a hotel	Chi-square test of significance
Gender			
	Males 1.9%	Females 2.8%	17.9*
Ethnicity			
	Caucasian Americans 2.2%	Other ethnicities 1.7%	4.7*
	Hispanic Americans 1.4%	Other ethnicities 2.2%	3.96*
	African Americans 1.6%	Other ethnicities 2.2%	2.93*
Marital status			
	Widowed 0.7%	Other 2.2%	20.08*
	Divorced 2.4%	Other 2.0%	4.21*
Urban	Urban county 2.8%%	Other counties 1.8%	29.62*
Age (Mean)	(mean at hotel: 42.97 years)	(mean at other locations: 45.42 years)	

* $p < .05$

less likely than other ethnicities to pick a hotel for a site for suicide. Native American and Asian American ethnicities were not significant predictors of hotel suicide, and so they are omitted from the table. Hotels charge room fees so it might be anticipated that ethnic groups with relatively low incomes (e.g., Hispanics Americans and African Americans) would be less likely to choose hotels for staging their suicides.

Two measures of marital status predicted hotel suicides: 2.4% of divorced persons chose to die by suicide in a hotel compared to 2.0% of all others. In contrast, widowed persons were less likely to die by suicide in a hotel (0.7% of widows vs. 2.2% all others). Two other marital statuses (married and single) did not differentiate hotel from nonhotel suicides and so are omitted from the table. Widows, having lost their significant other or housemate, have less motivation than others to seek a location that is free from any potential rescuers. Given the absence of a spouse who has passed away, their home environments are more likely than those of other persons to be guardian-free.

Urban location was a significant predictor of staging a suicide in a hotel: 2.8% of the persons choosing a hotel for a suicide were located in highly urban counties whereas only 1.8% of persons residing in less urban counties picked a hotel for the site of their suicides. This particular finding might be anticipated from another aspect of opportunity theory. Urban counties are likely to have more hotels than the less urban counties. For example, larger cities generally need more hotels available for conferences and business and tourist travelers. Given the greater availability of hotels, it is likely that relatively more people might choose a hotel as a stage for their suicides.

Two social and health strains differentiated the hotel suicides from suicides at other locations. As shown in table 9-3, the death of a loved one lowered the odds of traveling to a hotel to end one's life. Of those experiencing the death of a loved one, 1.2% staged their suicide in a hotel compared to 2.2% of those who had not lost a loved one. This finding is consistent with an opportunity theory. To the extent that the loved one was living in the same household as the suicide, there is less need to travel to a hotel to avoid detection by a significant other. Hotels were selected by only 1.3% of those suffering from a health problem. For those without a health problem, 2.2% selected a hotel for the site of their suicides. Since health issues might hamper travel, we would expect those without physical health issues to choose hotels more often as the location for their suicides.

Other social stresses were not significant predictors of location of suicide at a hotel, including financial problems, job problems, intimate partner problems, other relationship problems, legal problems with the criminal justice system, other legal problems, and being the victim of a violent crime.

A major theme in the relationship between psychiatric variables and choosing a hotel as a suicide stage involved hard drugs (see table 9-4). Of those who tested positive for cocaine, 3.8% of the persons testing positive for cocaine ended their lives in hotels compared to only 2.0% of other persons. If any opiate was present in the suicide, 4.2% chose a hotel for the location to end life compared to only 1.9% of persons who were opiate-free and chose a hotel for the location to end their lives.

Table 9-3. Social strains and suicide location.

Problem area	Percent suicides at a hotel, strain is not present	Percent suicides at a hotel, strain is present	Chi-square test of significance
Social strains			
Death of a loved one	2.2%	1.2%	7.20*
Poor health	2.3%	1.3%	24.63*

*p < .05

Table 9-4. Psychiatric strains and suicide location.

Psychiatric strain	Percent of suicides without the strain at hotels	Percent of suicides with the strain at hotels	Chi-square test of significance
Toxicology reports, substance abuse indicators			
Alcohol present	2.0%	2.5%	5.26*
Cocaine present	2.0%	3.8%	19.84*
Opiate present	1.9%	4.2%	59.48*
Perceived reported drug problem	2.0%	3.0%	19.2*
Perceived reported depression problem	2.4%	1.7%	17.7*
Presence of a suicide note	1.6%	3.3%	83.7*

*p < .05

Hotel Suicide and the Drug Subculture

Table 9-5. Multiple Logistic Regression Analysis.

Variable	Logistic regression coefficient	Standard error	Odds ratio
Demographics			
Gender: female = 1	0.25*	0.09	1.29
Ethnicity			
Caucasian American	0.01	0.19	1.01
African American	-0.32	0.25	0.72
Hispanic American	-0.53	0.29	0.58
Other ethnicity = reference			
Marital status			
Widowed	-0.91*	0.27	0.4
Divorced	0.07	0.09	1.07
Married and other = reference			
Age	-0.001	0.002	0.99
Urban county	0.41*	0.08	1.51
Social & Related Problems of Living			
Death of a loved one	-0.33	0.22	0.71
Health problem	-0.59*	0.12	0.55
Psychiatric Morbidity			
Toxicology: alcohol present	0.09	0.09	1.09
Toxicology: cocaine present	0.32*	0.15	1.38
Toxicology: opiate present	0.67*	0.11	1.95
Reported substance abuse problem	0.22*	0.11	1.25
Depression	-0.35*	0.08	0.69
Left a suicide note	0.72*	0.08	2.07
Constant	-4.11*	0.22	–

*$p < .05$
Nagelkerke r-squared = .046
-2 Log Likelihood = 6016.6*
Cases correctly predicted: 97.88%

In a similar fashion, persons reported to have a drug problem were more likely than those who had no drug problem to choose hotel rooms. However, these and other significant relationships may not hold up under controls. To answer that issue we turn to a multivariate analysis.

Table 9-5 presents the results of the multivariate logistic regression analysis. Controlling for the other variables, three of the demographic factors remained significant predictors of suicide at a hotel. Females were 29% more likely than men to stage their suicide at a hotel. Widows, as anticipated, were 60% less likely than other persons to die by suicide at a hotel. Persons residing in urban counties were 51% more likely to die by suicide in a hotel than persons not living in urban counties. Only one of the two significant predictors of life stressors remained significant in the multivariate analysis. Persons with health issues were 45% less likely than persons without health issues to choose a hotel for their suicides.

Most of the psychiatric predictors from the bivariate analysis remained significant in the multivariate analysis. In particular, persons testing positive for any opiate-based drug were 95% more likely to choose a hotel for their suicides than persons not testing positive for opiates. Based on the investigative reports, persons thought to have a drug addiction problem were 25% more likely than others to end their lives in a hotel. Persons leaving suicide notes were 1.9 times more likely than persons not leaving notes to pick a hotel for the location of their suicide.

Given the strong findings linking drug use to hotel suicide, it is important to determine if hotel suicides are disproportionately performed through drug overdoses as a method. To assess this issue, the analysis from table 9-5 was rerun with an additional binary variable where 1 represents the suicides that used poison and 0 for those that used any other method. Controlling for the other predictors of hotel suicide, persons using poison[2] were 2.6 times more likely than others to end their lives in a hotel room.

Table 9-6 summarizes the link between the use of poison as a method of suicide and the selection of a hotel as a location for suicide: 4.6 of those who use poison as a method for suicide choose a hotel for their act, whereas only 1.6% of those who use other methods select hotels for their suicides. There were exactly 260 persons (of the 648 ending their lives in hotels) who used poison as a method and the hotel as a

Table 9-6. The association between the use of poison as a suicide method and the selection of a hotel as a location for suicide.

	All other suicide methods	Poison as a suicide method
Other location	98.4%	95.4%
Hotel location	1.6%	4.6%
	100.0%	100.0%
	Chi-square: 201.23, p <.000	

Hotel Suicide and the Drug Subculture

location for suicide. In a further analysis, 82.7% of those testing positive for opiate use, in particular, used poisons to end their lives in hotels. In hotel suicide, suicide by poison is more frequent than suicide by guns. In fact, only 1.1% of persons using guns for suicide (the most common method in the United States), chose to die by suicide in hotels, whereas 3.2% of persons using by other methods (e.g., poisons or hanging) ended their lives in hotels. These analyses suggest that suicide in hotels is tied to a drug subculture, that is, persons who die by suicide in hotel rooms are more likely to have a substance abuse problem. Further, they are more likely than others to end their lives through ingesting poisons (possibly including the drugs that they are using to get high).

The association between selecting a hotel as a location for one's suicide and the use of poison as a suicide method is consistent with an opportunity theory of suicide. To the extent that it takes a significant amount of time to die from an overdose, it is important to make as certain as possible that there will be no rescuers present to thwart one's suicide. Ingesting a lethal dose of poison inside a locked hotel room lowers the probability of detection. This stage for suicide is relatively high in lethality in terms of the location as well as the method.

Conclusions

The present study found that females were more likely than males to stage their suicide in hotels. This finding is consistent with that of Kposowa and McElvain (2006) who mentioned, in passing, that 9.3% of women compared to 2.2% of men died by suicide in hotels. The location was a California county (Riverside), which is not as urban as the locations upon which most of the previous work is based. Hotels provide an environment similar to a bedroom in a home where many suicides take place. According to gender role stereotypes, women are more home-centered than men, which may explain the female attraction to hotels as a stage for suicide. Nevertheless, qualitative work is needed to specify what it is about hotels that attract suicidal women.

Stressful life events and conditions were largely unable to differentiate hotel from nonhotel suicides. However, the presence of physical health problems did exert a significant impact on suicide location. Physically ill persons were less likely to pick a hotel for their suicides.

A key finding of the present investigation was that substance abuse, principally of hard drugs, predicted hotel suicide. This finding is consistent with the multivariate analysis of hotel suicide in Detroit where hotel suicides were over twice as likely to have drug problems than suicides in other locations (Wasserman & Stack, 2008). Possibly, drug users are attracted to hotels to stage their suicide in order to avoid interference by rescuers. This is especially an important concern for those who use drugs or poisons to end their lives. The time to death is longer, generally, for those who ingest poisons than those who use quick methods such as firearms or hanging. Hence, it is even more important for person's using drugs to find a quiet location free of bystanders who might interfere with the suicide.

Further analysis determined that persons using drugs as a method of suicide were two times more likely than persons using other methods to pick a hotel as a location for the event. This same pattern was mentioned in a study of suicide in Riverside County, California. Suicides in hotels were 4.9 times more likely than their counterparts in other locations to use drugs as a method of suicide (Kposowa & McElvain, 2006).

Some caution should be exercised in interpreting the finding wherein persons leaving suicide notes are twice as likely as others to stage their suicide in a hotel. There is the possibility that part of this difference may be due to a lower probability that suicide notes will be destroyed or removed from the scene in hotels. At the typical location, the home, family members and significant others of a suicide may seize and conceal a suicide note before the police or authorities arrive on the scene. In some cases, persons close to the deceased may have a motive for hiding or destroying the note. For example, if the note blames a significant other for the suicide, the significant other may wish to hide the note to avoid reprisals from friends of the deceased. This is less likely to be the case in a hotel where persons unknown to the deceased, such as maids, discover the body and the note. Such anonymous persons have no stake in wanting to conceal the suicide note. While there is apparently little academic work on this issue, motives for concealing suicide notes are often provided in cinematic representations of suicide (Stack & Bowman, 2012).

The present study was guided by the opportunity theory of suicide, with an emphasis on the absence of motivated rescuers in hotel rooms. There are other reasons why persons might seek a hotel room for suicide. Hanzlick and Ross (1987) assessed reasons for selecting a hotel from narratives in the suicide notes left by hotel suicides in Atlanta. One note specifically mentioned a desire to conceal his suicide from his daughter, while another sought to avoid media exposure. For some altruistic persons, there may be a desire to die by suicide in a hotel room to spare significant others the chore of cleaning up any unpleasant aftereffects of the suicide.

Notes

1. A fourth investigation was excluded since it dealt only with eleven hotel suicides by nonresident persons who drove long distances to the city of Atlanta (Hanzlick & Ross 1987). This subsample of hotel suicides makes it less comparable to the other three studies, which included both resident and nonresident suicides. A fifth study was excluded since it was limited to persons who jumped to their deaths from hotels (Hanzlick, Masteron, & Walker 1990).
2. Poison refers to ingested solid and liquid substances as a cause of death.

References

Cohen, L., & Felson, M. (1979). Social change and crime rate trends: A routine activities approach. *American Sociological Review*, 44, 588–607.

Durkheim, E. (1897/1965). *Suicide*. New York: Free Press.

Gemar, K., Zarkowski, P., & Avery, D. (2008). Hotel room suicide: Las Vegas and Clark County. *Social Psychiatry & Psychiatric Epidemiology*, 43, 25–27.

Hanzlick, R., Masteron, K., & Walker, B. (1990). Suicides by jumping from high rise hotels: Fulton County Georgia, 1967–1986. *American Journal of Forensic Medicine & Pathology*, 11, 294–97.

Hanzlick, R., & Ross, W. K. (1987). Suicide far from home: the concept of transjurisdictional suicide. *Journal of Forensic Science*, 32, 189–91.

Jason, D. R., Taff, M. L., & Boglioli, L. R. (1990). Casino-related deaths in Atlantic City, New Jersey, 1982–1986. *American Journal of Forensic Medicine & Pathology*, 11, 112–23.

Kposowa, A., & McElvain, J.P. (2006). Gender, place, and method of suicide. *Social Psychiatry & Psychiatric Epidemiology*, 41, 435–43.

Lester, D. (2000). *Why people kill themselves*. Springfield, IL: Charles C. Thomas.

Morselli, H. (1882). *Suicide: An essay on comparative moral statistics*. New York: D. Appleton.

Parks, S. E., Johnson, L. L., McDaniel, D. D., & Gladden, M. (2014). Surveillance of violent deaths: National Violent Death Reporting System, 16 states, 2010. Morbidity & Mortality Weekly Report, 63, 33.

Pope, W. (1976). *Durkheim's suicide: A classic reanalyzed*. Chicago. IL: University of Chicago Press.

Schlenger, R., Kaatsch, H. J., & Grellner, W. (2008). Unusual circumstances in a fourfold complex suicide. *Kriminologie*, 221, 149–58.

Stack, S. (2000a). Suicide: a 15-year review of the sociological literature. Part I. Cultural and economic factors. *Suicide & Life Threatening Behavior*, 30, 145–62.

Stack, S. (2000b). Suicide: a 15-year review of the sociological literature. Part II. Modernization and social integration perspectives. *Suicide & Life Threatening Behavior*, 30, 163–76.

Stack, S., & Bowman, B. (2012). *Suicide movies: Social patterns, 1900–2009*. Cambridge, MA: Hogrefe.

Wasserman, I., & Stack, S. (2008). Lethal locations: an application of opportunity theory to motel suicide. *Death Studies*, 32, 757–67.

Weisman, A. D., & Worden, J. W. (1972). Risk-rescue rating in suicide assessment. *Archives of General Psychiatry,* 26, 553–60.
Yamazaki, M., Terada, M., Ogura, Y., Wakusugi, C., & Mitsukuni, Y. (1997). A suicidal case of electrocution with hypnotic drug poisoning: An autopsy report." *Japanese Journal of Legal Medicine,* 51, 95–101.
Zarkowki, P., & Avery, D. (2006). Hotel room suicide. *Suicide & Life Threatening Behavior,* 36, 578–81.

10

Back to Nature: Suicide in Natural Areas

Steven Stack

During the Great Depression in the 1930s, many Japanese individuals took a three-and-a-half hour ferry boat ride to the island of Oshima, fifty miles southwest across the bay from Tokyo. While most were tourists, there were many who were seeking to end their lives. The island featured the majestic Mount Mihara, a volcano rising 2,461 feet above sea level. Suicidal persons were apparently attracted to Mount Mihara for at least two reasons: its natural beauty (the first religion in Japan was Naturism (Iga, et al., 1978)), and probable copycat effects.

On February 11, 1933, Miss Kiyoko Matsumoto, a student at Jissen Girl's College, had traveled with her companion, Miss Tomito, to Oshima. Miss Matsumoto had written, "I am bewildered to distraction of the complexities of maturing womanhood." Her suicide, by jumping into the fires of Mount Mihara, was assisted by her companion, Miss Tomito. Newspaper coverage of the event was extensive. In the ten months that followed in 1933, at least 143 additional persons plunged to their deaths on Mount Mihara.

The curiosity of the Japanese people was aroused. So many people wanted to visit the site of the suicides that rides aboard the ferryboat had to be booked weeks in advance. Many tourists were apparently hoping to see another suicide during their tour of the island. In 1934 alone, at least another 167 persons plunged to their deaths, although one report cited eight hundred. More than a thousand suicide attempts were thwarted, however, by motivated rescuers, including the police (*Chicago Daily Tribune*, 1936; *Fortune*, 1935; *Time*, 1935).

In efforts to stop the suicides, watchmen with telescopes were stationed at intervals around the wide top of the volcano's crater. Many attempts at suicide were interrupted, but the death toll nevertheless increased. The circumference of the top of the volcano measures seven miles. Once a watchman spied a likely suicidal individual, help could not always get there in time to prevent another suicide.

Many persons planning to end their lives did not purchase round-trip tickets, so the government passed a ban on the sale of one-way tickets. However, this only enhanced the profits of the ferryboat owners, the Tokyo Bay Steamship Company. Ultimately it was estimated that more than one thousand people ended their lives at Mount Mihara, a natural area serving as a suicide hotspot for several years. While this is a sensational, yet neglected, example of a large number of suicides in a natural area, it suggests that a certain sector of a population may be drawn to nature for staging their suicides.

In Japan, there are other hotspots for suicide in natural areas, including the Black Forest at the base of Mount Fuji. About thirty or more persons choose the Black Forest each year as a location for their suicide, more than the number who die by suicide at the Golden Gate Bridge in San Francisco (Takahashi, 1988). During the Japanese recession in 1998, a record number of seventy-three bodies were retrieved from the Black Forest, up from fifty-five a year earlier (Strom, 1999).

Little is known, however, about the kinds of persons drawn to Mount Mihara and other natural areas selected for suicide. Most reports on suicide in nature cover only basic demographic variables (age and gender) and the frequency of suicides in a hotspot or national park (Heggie, et al., 2008; Heggie & Amundson, 2009; King & Frost, 2005; Morselli, 1882; Newman, et al., 2010; Ross & Lester, 1991; Takahashi, 1988). As we shall see, hotspots and national parks contribute only a very small proportion of suicides that occur in natural areas. It is not known if the patterns behind suicides in hotspots and national parks will be similar to a more general sample of suicides in all natural areas, including nonhotspots and areas not part of the national park system.

Most persons would have to travel a long distance to such areas. As it turns out, most of the suicides in nature occur at locations other than hotspots and national parks. Nevertheless, research and public fascination has been disproportionately focused on hotspots in nature such as the Golden Gate Bridge National Recreation Area and the Black Forest (Lester, 1971; Takahashi, 1988; Yeh & Lester, 2010). Indeed, there has even been a feature film on suicide in the Black Forest (*The Forest*, 2011) as well as on suicide at the Golden Gate Bridge (*The Bridge*, 2009).

The present study makes several contributions to the literature on suicide in nature. First, it expands the analysis to a representative sample of all suicides in any natural area in the United States. This includes suicides in national parks, but also suicides in all other natural areas. Second, it is able to provide a more thorough description of suicides in natural areas than the past research. Through the use of the NVDRS, it provides information on a greater number of demographic characteristics of the suicide (age and sex, but also ethnicity, marital status and urban place of death). In addition, the present study is also able to provide epidemiological data on additional categories of risk and protective factors for suicide including social strains (e.g., death of a loved one and financial problems) and psychiatric morbidity (e.g., depression). Most previous work was not able to include these variable sets. Third, the present study applies a general theory of deviant behavior, opportunity theory, to the problem of suicide in natural areas. In addition, it applies theoretical propositions on gender (fear of crime and sex role socialization to outdoor activities) to interpret the specific findings on gender and location of suicide (e.g., Burger, 1998; Snedker, 2012; Warr, 1985).

Back to Nature

A theoretical frame that guides much of the analysis is the opportunity-routine activities theory of deviance (e.g., Cohen & Felson, 1979; Wasserman & Stack, 2008). Suicide in nature is a suicide away from home, and so there is less of a chance that persons will be present to stop the suicide in a natural area. As such, suicides in nature can be partially interpreted from an opportunity theory of deviant behavior and criminality reviewed in chapters 8 and 9. In this view, three phenomena need to come together in order for a crime to be committed: (1) the presence of a motivated offender, (2) a suitable target, and (3) the absence of motivated guardians (Cohen & Felson, 1979). If one goes to a national forest and hikes down a trail to the remote areas of the forest, there will probably be no one around to interfere with a suicidal action. In particular, motivated guardians, such as family and friends, are certainly unlikely to be present. Hence, like hotel rooms far away from home, national forests and many sites in nature constitute a "lethal location"—a remote area where the probability of the presence of "motivated rescuers" who might stop the suicide is relatively low. Motivated rescuers are more likely to be present in other locations, such as the residence of the suicidal individual.

In the case of nature, a suitable place for suicide can entail a structure for the suicidal act. For example, if one seeks to jump or fall as a method of suicide, natural areas, such as national parks in the Rocky Mountains or canyon country in the American West, have cliffs and high points that are suitable for the suicidal act. In addition, natural areas such as the Great Lakes, the Atlantic Ocean, and thousands of inland lakes and rivers offer opportunities for drowning. Indeed, if one seeks to end their life by drowning, natural areas are among the most suitable places to go. A previous study showed that the presence of oceans on the border of a state predicted the rate of suicide by drowning (Lester, 1989).[1]

Suicide in nature can also be interpreted using the concept of the destigmatization of suicide. Regarding suicide from the Golden Gate Bridge, the natural beauty surrounding the bridge (blue skies, blue waters below, and great views for miles of the passageway to the ocean) may give suicide from the bridge a positive meaning. Suicide set in a beautiful natural area, including those high up with great views, may make the traumatic ending of life through suicide seem less repulsive and scary and, in general, less negative.

The destigmatization of suicide can be maximized through picking not only a beautiful natural area for one's location for suicide, but a specific location where others have ended their lives. A review of cases of suicidal individuals planning to die by suicide at the Golden Gate Bridge, or having had their attempt to jump at the bridge thwarted, noted that they mentioned the beauty of the bridge and its surroundings as a reason for planning their suicide at that location (Bateson, 2012). Another common reason given by suicidal persons for planning a jump at the bridge was put by one individual as, "You're with all those other people." Suicidal people tend to be less connected to others. They often choose to jump off the Golden Gate Bridge in order to join for all eternity a large number of people, hundreds, with whom they have a common bond—a shared suicidal death at that location (Bateson, 2012).

An earlier study based on extended interviews with eight persons who survived the jump from the bridge, also found that they were attracted to the location by its beauty. It was also true that they viewed the bridge as presenting a promise of a certain death (Rosen, 1975).

Previous Work on Suicide in Natural Areas

Previous work on suicide in natural settings such as cliffs, woodland, rivers and oceans is summarized in table 10-1. A historical study of Prussia determined that males were more likely than females to stage their suicides in the woods (Morselli, 1882). In Prussia 9.2% of male

Table 10-1. Previous research studies on suicide in natural areas.

Senior author (year)	Location (years)	Number of suicides (per year)	Percent male	Mean age	Marital status	Other findings
Blaustein (2009)	Golden Gate Bridge (1995–2005)	225 (20.4/yr)	74	40	22 married, 55% never married, 23% divorced	82% white; 40% psychiatric; 25% suicide notes; 22% prior suicide attempts
Heggie (2008)	US Nat'l Parks, (2003–2004)	60 (30/yr)	n.a.	n.a	n.a	42% by guns, 23% hanging, 13% poison; 10% cutting, 12% other methods
Heggie (2009)	US Nat'l Parks, (2005)	18 (18/yr)	n.a.	n.a.	n.a.	n.a.
King (1995)	New Forest, England (1993–1997)	102 (20.4/yr)	na	na	na	63% of suicides die from car exhaust gas
Lester (1971)	Niagara Falls (1958–1967)	71 (7.1/yr) (American side only)	47%	52	n.a.	Peaks in August & September
Morselli (1882)	Woods, Prussia (1872)	217 of 2363 male suicides, 10 of 587 female suicides in woods	9.2% male suicides vs. 1.7% female suicides	n.a.	n.a.	6.4% male suicides vs. 14.1% female suicide occur in rivers. 2.2% male suicides vs. 8.1% female suicides occur in seas and lakes.
Newman (2010)	84 US Nat'l Parks (2003–2009)	194 (27.7/yr) Completed (+92 attempts)	83%	43 (incl attempts)	n.a.	Suicide peaks in June
Ross (1991)	Niagara Falls (1978–1988)	141 (12.8/yr)	59.0%	39.5 men 38 women	n.a.	Mean distance from home: 10 miles
Skegg (2009)	Lawyer's Head Cliff (1996–2006)	13 (1.3/yr)	n.a.	n.a.	n.a.	No suicides during restricted access in 2006–2008
Surtees (1982)	Beachy Head (1965–1979)	115 (7.7/yr)	53%	n.a.	37% married; 51% never married; 8% divorced/separated; 4% widowed	80% history mental illness; Peak July and August
Takahashi (1988)	Black Forest, Japan (1975–1984)	302 (30.2/yr)	72%	Apx. 35	n.a.	35% by hanging, 28% poisons, 17% CO, 12% exposure, 8% other
Yeh (2010)	Golden Gate Bridge, (1999–2009)	224 (20.4/yr)	73%	41.9 yrs	n.a.	Bridge suicides younger (41.9 yrs) than other suicides (53 yrs); no difference in sex or race

Key: n.a. = data not available

suicides were staged in the woods compared to only 1.7% of female suicides. However, when it came to drowning, females were more likely to choose rivers than males (13.3% vs. 6.4%). In addition, women were more likely than men to choose seas and lakes for their suicides (8.1% vs. 2.4%). Subsequent classic works on suicide generally omitted discussions on the location of suicides (e.g., Cavan, 1928; Durkheim 1897/1951).

There are many journalistic reports about two natural areas in the United Kingdom (Beachy Head and the New Forest) that are suicide hotspots. King and Frost (2005) documented a relatively high rate of suicide at these two natural areas. During the years 1993–1997, 102 suicides (20.4 per year) occurred in the New Forest Registration Area, a large park of 145 square miles located on the southern coast of England. The typical method was to park a motor vehicle in a quiet parking area of the New Forest and die inside the motor vehicle by carbon monoxide poisoning. During the same period, there were forty-eight suicides at Beachy Head, a famous site involving jumping from the cliffs into the English Channel. However, the authors did not fully describe the demographic characteristics and motives of the suicides.

An older study by Surtees (1982) described 115 suicides (7.7 per year) at Beachy Head. There was almost no sex difference, with males accounting for 53% of the jumps. In terms of marital status, only 37% were married. Social strains associated with suicide were not covered, but it was noted that 80% of the jumpers had a psychiatric history. These figures would have more meaning if the author could have compared them to a control group, but there was no comparison group.

Skegg and Herbison (2009) presented prevalence data for Lawyers Head, a cliff in New Zealand. They estimated an annual incidence of 1.3 suicides per year, but no data were presented on the demographic or other characteristics of the suicides from the cliff.

In Japan, Takahashi (1988) presented basic demographic data on 302 suicides in the Black Forest, which encompasses ten square miles at the foot of Mount Fuji. The rate, 30.2 per 100,000 per year, is higher than that reported for the Golden Gate Bridge of 20.4 per year (Yeh & Lester, 2010). However, Takahashi was able to provide data only on age and sex: 72% of the suicides were men.

Anecdotal reports describe suicide in other natural areas of Japan. Many reports are from the mass media, but there is often extensive media coverage of the suicide. It is difficult to ascertain if the natural areas themselves attracted suicidal persons, if it was the media publicity, or perhaps some combination of factors that resulted in individuals staging their suicide in nature. For example, Misao Fujimura, a college student from a wealthy family, traveled to Kegon Falls in Nikko, a famed scenic area ninety miles north of Tokyo, to end his life in 1903. His suicide note was actually in the form of a poem carved directly into the trunk of a tree. There was substantial media coverage of Fujimura's suicide, glorifying the act. In the following eight years, over two hundred people ended their lives at the same exact tree (Iga, et al., 1978). At the peak of its popularity as a suicide site, the suicides attracted a large audience of tourists, and an enterprising entrepreneur drove a shaft into the rock to support two Otis elevators and ran a transportation service to the foot of the falls (*Fortune*, 1935).

It is not clear how representative these samples and case studies are of the general population of persons seeking to die in a natural area. Many suicide hotspots like Kegan Falls and Mount Mihara have been covered only in the writings of journalists, and so rigorous, science-based generalizations about suicide are not possible. It is also unknown whether they reflect or differ from suicides in other locations in etiological factors such as social strains and psychiatric morbidity. It is not clear if the extent to which Japanese persons select natural areas is greater than that of persons in other cultures. Nevertheless, it has been speculated that Japanese culture draws on its roots from Naturism, which was the original religion of the Japanese people (Iga, et al., 1978).

It is plausible that Americans might be less likely than the Japanese to select natural settings for suicide. In the United States, there is relatively little research on suicide in natural areas, including the national parks in the United States. Aside from largely descriptive work on suicide from the Golden Gate Bridge, a National Recreation Area (e.g., Bateson, 2012; Blaustein & Fleming, 2009; Yeh & Lester, 2010), little is known about the epidemiology or etiology of suicide in natural areas.[2] Approximately 1,575 suicides have been documented at the Golden Gate Bridge since its opening in 1937 through 2011, an average of twenty-one per year. The annual counts range from two (in 1942) to forty-five (in 1995) (Bateson, 2012). Yeh and Lester (2010) and Blaustein and Fleming (2009) report a prevalence of twenty suicides per year from the bridge, with 74% of the jumpers being male. Bridge suicides are younger than their community counterparts and less likely to be married.

Several investigations provide some limited data on suicides at Niagara Falls and groups of national parks. Two investigations provide basic demographic and prevalence estimates for suicide at Niagara

Falls (Lester, 1971; Ross & Lester, 1991). From the more recent study, which counts suicides on both the American and Canadian sides of the falls, approximately thirteen persons go over the falls each year. Their average age is slightly less than forty, and 59% are males.

Three studies provide some rather limited information on suicide in American national parks. (Heggie, et al., 2008; Heggie & Amundson, 2009; Newman, et al., 2010). The national parks are the setting for about twenty-eight to thirty suicides a year. Of those suicides, 83% are males. In this case, there is some information on suicide methods. There are no data available on most demographic variables and none on social and psychiatric strains among those who die by suicide in our National Parks.

It is important to compare the annual counts of suicide in national parks and suicide hotspots to the larger picture of suicide in all natural areas. To the extent that most natural areas are not hotspots or national parks, we need additional data to fully assess the prevalence, epidemiology, and etiology of suicides in natural areas.

As we shall see, in the present study based on seventeen states, there were 1,321 suicides over a four-year period in natural areas. This is 330 per year in up to seventeen of the fifty states. Given that less than a third of the nation's population lives in the seventeen states covered by the NVDRS, the real number of suicides in natural areas is closer to one thousand per year. The roughly thirty suicides that occur in the national park system each year probably account for about 3% of all suicides in natural areas. Clearly additional work is needed to draw a complete picture of suicide in natural areas, especially if suicides in the national parks are different from suicide in other natural areas.

Methodology

As in earlier chapters, all data are from the NVDRS (CDC, 2008) for 2003–2006. Data on the location of the suicides are from Section 4 of the CDC Codebook involving information from the death certificate of the deceased (CDC, 2008). Specifically the data refer to section 4-28 which corresponds to the variable "Type of Location Where Injured." There are thirty locations listed in the codebook. These include house, bar/nightclub, school bus, and many others. The present study is focused on code number 29: "Natural Area." CDC defines natural areas as including woods, rivers, fields, and beaches. Natural areas are distinguished from city parks and playground,s which are under code 27. Natural areas are also distinguished from sports or athletic areas such as baseball fields, stadiums, and recreation centers, which are under code 14. The principle dependent variable is a dichotomy where suicide located in a natural area equals 1 and all other areas equal 0. The independent variables examined are those used in the earlier chapters and include demographic variables, social strains, psychiatric morbidity, and method for suicide.

Results and Preliminary Interpretations

Table 10-2 presents the results of the bivariate analysis of demographic variables. Results are shown only for those variables which were able to differentiate the suicides in natural areas from those in all other locations. Four of the five demographic variables predicted location, the exception being ethnicity. Gender differentiated the nature-based suicides from those in other locations. Of those who chose natural areas for staging their suicides, 4.6% were males compared to only 3.3% of females. This finding is consistent with the notion that men are more involved in outdoor activities than are women. Men are more likely, for example, to hunt and fish than are females. The greater familiarity of men than women with the outdoors is assumed to influence men's selection of natural areas for their suicides (Floyd, et al., 2006).

In order to compare the findings on gender to previous research it is necessary to present the numbers differently. Looking at gender in terms of the percent of natural area suicides, figures not shown in the

Table 10-2. Demographics of suicide in natural areas. National Violent Death Reporting System, 2003–2006, n = 30,570 suicides.

Demographic Group	Percent who died by suicide at a natural area	Percent who died by suicide at a natural area	Chi-square test of significance
Gender			
	Males 4.6%	Females 3.3%	21.9*
Marital Status			
	Single 5.2%	All others 3.9%	28.5*
	Widowed 1.5%	All others 4.5%	42.7*
	Divorced 3.6%.	All Others 4.5%	9.4*
Urbanism	Urban county 3.2%	Other counties 4.8%	38.4*
Age (mean)	(mean at Natural Area 41.98)*	(mean at other locations: 45.52 years)	

* p < .05

table, males accounted for 83.6% of suicides in natural areas, which suggests that previous research underestimated the effect of gender on suicide in natural areas. In previous studies on hotspots such as Beachy Head, the Black Forest, Niagara Falls, and the Golden Gate Bridge, males accounted for between 47% to 74% of the suicides (Lester, 1971; Ross & Lester, 1991; Surtees, 1982; Takahashi, 1988; Yeh & Lester, 2010). However, the current figure of 84% is almost identical to that found in American national parks (Newman, et al., 2010).

The tendency towards a gendered relationship in selecting a natural area is consistent with work from criminology on gender and fear of crime (Snedker, 2012; Warr, 1985; Yavuz & Welch, 2010). Women have consistently been found to be more fearful of crime victimization than men. This greater fear is associated with lifestyle differences between men and women. For example, while only 8% of men report that they have avoided going out alone, 42% of women report this precaution. To the extent that suicidal persons traveling away from home go out alone to seek a site for suicide, we would anticipate that women would be less likely, in general, to seek a site away from home. In addition, men would, in particular, be more likely than women to seek a site in a remote natural area. An exception to this rule might be natural areas, perhaps especially ones of a romantic nature, that are easily accessible a short distance from the safety of a parked car. The latter would include Niagara Falls, a site sometimes not marked by a gendered relationship to suicide (Lester, 1971). Future work is needed to test this hypothesis.

It is also plausible that gender role socialization to the outdoors may account for part of this gendered relationship. To the extent that men participate in activities, such as hunting and fishing, that bring them to forests and rivers in natural settings more than women, men may be more comfortable than women with the idea of ending their lives in natural settings (Burger, et al., 1998).

Ethnicity (Caucasian American, African American, Asian American, Native American, and Hispanic American) did not differentiate suicides in natural areas from suicides in other locations. In the one study that reported on ethnicity and had a control group, Yeh and Lester (2010) reported that race did not differentiate jumpers from the Golden Gate Bridge from the other suicides in Marin County (whose medical examiner handles the majority of suicides from the bridge).

Persons dying by suicide in natural areas were more likely to be single than those who die by suicide elsewhere. Overall, 4.3% of the suicides (1,321 out of 30,570) occurred in natural areas, whereas 5.2% of single people selected natural areas to stage their suicide. Perhaps, in some cases, this reflects feeling isolated from other people. If so, a bond with nature for life's end may compensate for their loneliness. In contrast, only 3.9% of nonsingle suicides chose natural places. However, this pattern does not hold for persons who are apparently also likely to be alone, the divorced and the widowed. For these two latter groups, suicide in nature was less common than average. Only 1.5% of widows and 3.6% of divorced people chose natural settings. Further work is needed on these apparently conflicting findings.

As expected, where there tends to be more opportunities for suicide in nature (less urban counties), more people chose natural settings for staging their suicide. In urban counties, only 3.2% of the population ended their lives in natural areas, compared to 4.8% of persons dying in nonurban counties.

Finally, persons ending their days at a natural area tended to be younger, as in most past research that reports data on age (e.g., Blaustein & Fleming, 2009; Ross & Lester, 1991; Takahashi, 1988). In the current study, the mean age for persons staging their suicide in nature was 42 years compared to 45.5 years for those who die by suicide at other locations.

Table 10-3 presents the results on social strain variables that were significantly related to suicides located in a natural area. These are the first findings in the literature on this matter. Four of the ten social strains were able to differentiate the suicides in natural areas. Three

Table 10-3. Social strains and suicide location.

Problem Area	The percentage of suicides who *do not* have the strain performed in a natural area	The percentage of suicides who have the strain performed in a natural area	Chi-square test of significance
Social Strains			
Death of a loved one	4.4%	2.3%	17.8*
Poor health	4.7%	2.7%	48.5*
Intimate partner problems	4.5%	3.9%	4.1*
Legal problems, criminal justice system	4.2%	5.1%	5.12*

*p < .05

Suicide as a Dramatic Performance

Table 10-4. Psychiatric strains and suicide location.

	The percentage of suicides who *do not* have the strain performed in a natural area	The percentage of suicides who have the strain performed in a natural area	Chi-square test of significance
Psychiatric Strain			
Toxicology reports:			
Marijuana	4.3%	6.0%	4.98*
Opiates	4.5%	2.8%	15.51*
Reported alcohol problem	4.5%	3.4%	11.2*
Reported drug problem	4.4%	3.6%	5.8*
Depression	4.6%	3.9%	7.4*
Suicide note	4.1%	4.8%	6.7*

*p < .05

social strains lowered the odds of choosing a natural area for one's suicide. Whereas 4.3% of the total sample of the 30,570 suicides chose a site in a natural area, only 2.3% of those who had lost a loved one and 2.7% who were in poor health chose to die in a natural area. From the standpoint of opportunity theory, given that loss of significant others lowers the odds of having a motivated rescuer in one's own home, there is less need for such persons to travel away from home, including travel to a natural area, for their suicides.

Persons having an intimate partner problem were less likely than others to stage their suicides in a natural area (3.9% vs. 4.5%). Finally, one strain actually increased the odds of suicide in a natural area: 5.1% of persons involved in trouble with the criminal justice system located their suicides in natural areas compared with only 4.2% of persons not involved in such trouble.

Table 10-4 presents the findings on psychiatric strain variables that were significantly related to suicides located in a natural area. Six variables of the thirteen in this group were able to significantly differentiate suicides in natural areas from suicides at other locations. From the toxicology reports, 6.0% of persons who tested positive for marijuana died by suicide in natural areas while only 4.3% who did not test positive choose the same location. In contrast, only 2.8% of persons testing positive for opiates staged their suicide in natural areas compared to 4.5%

Table 10-5. Suicide method.

Suicide Method	Percent of suicides in natural areas using a particular suicide method	Percentage of suicides in other locations using that method	Chi-square Test of significance
Cutting	1.9%	2.0%	0.12
Drowning	16.5%	0.5%	2849.3*
Falls/jumps	5.9%	1.9%	103.0*
Fire	0.5%	0.5%	0.03
Firearms	42.7%	51.2%	36.7*
Hanging	22.1%	22.6%	0.20
Motor vehicle	0.4%	1.3%	8.8*
Poison	8.4%	19.1%	95.5*

*$p < .05$

who did not test positive. Thus, persons staging their suicides in national areas appear to have a preference for soft drugs (marijuana) and are less apt to be involved in hard drugs. Persons with either a reported alcohol or drug problem were less likely than their counterparts to stage their suicides in natural areas (3.4% vs. 4.5%, and 3.9% vs. 4.6%, respectively).

Table 10-5 lists the results on the relationship between method used to perform suicide and the location of suicide (natural area versus all other areas). Five of the eight methods of suicide significantly differentiated suicides in natural areas from suicides in other locations. Two methods of suicide were more common in natural areas: drowning and falls. Bodies of water such as lakes, oceans, and rivers are more common in natural areas than other locations, and the presence of waterways in natural areas represents opportunities for suicide by drowning. Fully 16.5% of suicides in natural areas employed drowning as a method of suicide compared to only 0.5% at other locations such as backyard pools and canals that run through downtown areas of large cities. In addition, the availability of structures such as cliffs and mountains in natural areas provides opportunities for suicide by fall. Of all suicides in natural areas 5.9% of all suicides in natural areas involved falls compared to only 1.9% in other locations.

Three methods of suicide are less common in natural areas than other locations: firearms, motor vehicles, and poisons. Firearms were the most common method of suicide, accounting for 42.7% of all suicide in natural areas, but this percentage was lower than the 51.2% of suicides that were carried out by firearms at other locations. Suicides using a motor vehicle as a means of suicide, for example crashing the vehicle into a wall or driving it over a cliff, are rare events. Nevertheless, these were less common in natural areas than at other locations (0.4% vs. 1.3%). Finally, suicide by poison was less common in natural areas than other locations (8.4% vs. 19.1%).

There were no significant differences between natural areas and other locations in the use of other methods. For example, a large percentage of persons staging their suicides in natural areas hung themselves (22.1%). Trees are abundant in many natural areas. However, a nearly identical percentage of suicides by hanging occurred in other locations (22.6%). Structures that can support ropes for suicide by hanging, such as shower heads, overhead rafters in basements, ceiling fans, and trees in the backyard, are abundant at other locations.

Finally, staging one's suicide in natural areas was associated with a greater likelihood of leaving a suicide note (4.8% vs. 4.1%).

A Multivariate Analysis

Table 10-6 presents the results of the multivariate logistic regression analysis. Only those variables (nineteen of the thirty-six variables) significant in the bivariate analyses were entered into the equation. Controlling for the other variables, four demographic variables were still able to differentiate the suicides in nature from suicides in other locations. From the odds ratio, men were 1.52 times more likely than women to select a natural area for suicide. Widows were 60% less likely than married persons to select a natural area for the stage of their suicides. Persons staging their suicides in nature tended to be younger. For each additional year of age, the odds of locating one's suicide in nature are reduced by 1%. As anticipated, persons dying in urban counties were 45% less likely to stage their suicides in natural areas.

Three social strain factors remained significant predictors of suicide location, all associated with lower odds of seeking out a natural area for suicide. Persons who have recently lost a loved one were 38% less likely to die by suicide in natural areas, those with a physical health problem 30% less likely, and those with an intimate partner problem 18% less likely.

Only two psychiatric predictors of location remained significant correlates of location. Persons marked by an alcohol abuse problem were 18% less likely to choose a natural area for the site of their suicide,

Table 10-6. Multiple logistic regression analysis to predict suicide in a natural area.

Variable	Logistic regression coefficient	Standard error	Odds ratio
Demographics			
Gender: male = 1	0.42*	0.08	1.52
Marital status			
Single	-0.06	0.07	0.93
Widowed	-0.89*	0.20	0.4
Divorced	-0.15	0.08	0.86
Married & other = reference			
Age	-0.008*	0.002	0.99
Urban county	-0.59*	0.07	0.55
Social & Related Problems of Living			
Death of a loved one	-0.46*	0.17	0.62
Health problem	-0.34*	0.09	0.7
Intimate partner problem	-0.2*	0.07	0.82
Criminal legal problem	0.09	0.09	1.1
Psychiatric Morbidity			
Toxicology: marijuana present	0.3	0.16	1.35
Toxicology: opiate present	-0.02	0.13	0.97
Reported alcohol abuse problem	-0.18*	0.09	0.82
Reported drug abuse problem	-0.1	0.09	0.9
Depression	-0.04	0.06	0.96
Left a suicide note	0.3*	0.06	1.35
Suicide Method			
Drowning	3.77*	0.12	43.4
Fall/jump	1.34*	0.13	3.8
Firearms	-0.16*	0.07	0.84
Motor vehicle	-1.23*	0.45	0.29
Poison	-0.64*	0.11	0.52
Constant	-2.8*	0.15	–

*$p < .05$
Nagelkerke r-squared = .145
-2 Log Likelihood = 9529.7*
Cases correctly predicted: 95.94%

and those ending their lives in a natural area were more likely (by 35%) to leave a suicide note.

All five measures of method of suicide differentiated between natural areas and other areas for suicide. Persons drowning themselves were forty-three times more likely than those using other methods to die by suicide in a natural area, and persons jumping off cliffs and other high points were 3.8 times more likely than others to end their lives in a natural area. The remaining three methods of suicide all were associated with a lower odds of suicide in a natural area: firearms (16% less likely), motor vehicle (71% less likely) and poison (48% less likely).

Conclusions

The present study offers the first set of national epidemiological data on suicide in natural areas as well as some differences between suicides in natural locations and other locations. Men are significantly more likely than women to die by suicide in natural areas. This finding is consistent with almost all previous investigations. The only exception is a study of suicides from the American side of Niagara Falls in the 1950s and 1960s (Lester, 1971). In that study men were in a slight minority, accounting for 47% of the suicides from the falls. A more recent study of suicides at Niagara Falls, but encompassing both the American and Canadian sides, determined that 59% of the suicides from the falls were accomplished by men (Ross & Lester, 1991).

As previously shown, when women die by suicide away from home, the location is likely to be a hotel room. One is unlikely to be the victim of a violent crime in a locked hotel room. Female perceptions of the chances of being the victim of a violent crime may be linked to a reluctance of women to choose a natural setting for their suicide. Women are reportedly more afraid than men of crime, and they adjust their life styles accordingly. Women are reportedly five times more afraid of going out alone than are men (Snedker, 2012). However, it is possible that certain natural settings where there are other people present (e.g., Niagara Falls) may be more likely to draw suicidal females than remote natural areas where fear of victimization may run high. At Niagara Falls, there is only a short walk from the safety of one's car to the site of the falls for suicide. Future work is needed to test these speculations.

The finding that men are more likely than women to die by suicide in nature is also consistent with traditional sex role stereotype that men are more involved in outdoor activities in rural areas. For example, in a study of South Carolina, only 3.5% of women were hunters compared to 19.7% of men. Men were more likely than women to be involved in fishing, camping, hiking, and canoeing (Burger, et al., 1998; Floyd, et al., 2006). It is likely that gender differences in participation in such outdoor activities in nature might be even greater if data were available on the percentage of men and women who engage in such activities alone. For example, among long-distance hikers, it is rare to find a woman trekking alone (Strayed, 2012). This is an important consideration since suicide is typically carried out alone. If people are accustomed to going into remote natural areas alone, then the odds that they will select such an area may increase.

Controlling for gender, age, and other independent variables, widows were found to be less likely to select a natural setting for their suicides than married persons. Widows are more likely than the general population to live alone without a significant other that might thwart a suicide attempt. As such, the finding on widows is consistent with the opportunity theory regarding the absence of a motivated rescuer as facilitating a suicide. There is less need to travel to a natural area for widows since they are less likely than married persons to have a motivated rescuer at home.

Given less availability of natural areas in urban counties, urban counties tend to host fewer suicides in natural settings than other counties. As in much past research, persons choosing natural areas tend to be younger than persons who die by suicide elsewhere. Older persons are more likely than younger persons to have logistical problems with travel away from home.

As far as the author has been able to determine, the present analysis is the first investigation of its kind to explore social strains as a possible predictor of suicides in natural areas. Consistent with opportunity theory, the death of a loved one lowered the odds of choosing a natural area for suicide. Such persons have less of a need to travel to a natural area for the purposes of avoiding significant others who might try to stop their suicide.

Only one traditional psychiatric factor exerted an effect on selecting a natural area for one's suicide independent of the other variables. Persons who abuse alcohol were less likely to die by suicide in a natural area. There were no significant differences between the suicides located in natural areas and nonnatural areas in current treatment for mental disorders, depression, a previous suicide attempt, or presence of a mental disorder. The studies finding a high degree of mental disorders were of suicide at hotspots (the Golden Gate Bridge and Beachy Head). Possibly apart from hotspots, the importance of mental disorder does not predict suicide location.

The largest odds ratios in the present study involved method of suicide. Persons using by drowning were fully forty-three times more likely to choose a natural area than those using other methods. In part, this may appear to be a tautology since waterways are often thought of as natural areas. Indeed, in results not reported here, 61.8% of the 353 suicides by drowning occurred in natural areas, while 38.2% of the suicides by drowning occurred in other locations such as pools and canals in the central city.

Further work is needed to unravel a motivational profile for suicides in natural areas. For example, persons whose attempts are thwarted could be interviewed to find out why they chose the natural setting. Such work has been done for a specialized subset of person attempting or planning to kill themselves at the Golden Gate Bridge National Recreation Area (Bateson, 2012; Rosen, 1975). This would provide much needed insights on the attractions of natural settings for some suicidal persons. Furthermore, artistic representations may provide insights into the etiology of self-destruction (Stack & Bowman, 2012). Given that there is so little academic research to date on location of suicide, cinematic representations, the most widely consumed art form, may be able to provide insights into the way in which persons select a stage for their suicide.

Notes

1. Many suicides drown in pools and waters in cities not technically defined as natural areas. However, as we shall see, a large proportion of suicides by drowning occur in natural areas.
2. For anecdotal evidence see Whittlesey (1995).

References

Bateson, J. (2012). *The final leap: Suicide on the Golden Gate Bridge.* Berkeley, CA: University of California Press.

Blaustein, M., & Fleming, A. (2009). Suicide from the Golden Gate Bridge. *American Journal of Psychiatry,* 166, 1111–16.

Burger, J., Sanchez, J., Whitfield-Gibbons, J., & Gochfeld, M. (1998). Gender differences in recreational use, environmental attitudes, and perceptions of future land use at the Savannah River site. *Environment & Behavior,* 30, 472–86.

Cavan, R. (1928/1965). *Suicide.* New York: Russell & Russell.

CDC (Centers for Disease Control). (2008). *National Violent Death Reporting System Coding Manual.* Washington, DC: Department of Health and Human Services.

Chicago Daily Tribune. (1936). Japan's firery pit of death. *Chicago Daily Tribune,* May 10, p. D1.

Cohen, L., & Felson, M. (1979). Social change and crime rate trends: A routine activities approach. *American Sociological Review,* 44, 588–607.

Durkheim, E. (1897/1951). *Suicide.* New York: Free Press.

Floyd, M. F., Nicholas, L., Lee, I., Lee, J. H., & Scott, D. (2006). Social stratification in recreational fishing participation. *Leisure Studies,* 28, 351–68.

Fortune. (1935). Profits in suicide. *Fortune.* May, 112–23.

Heggie, T. W., & Amundson, M. E. (2009). Dead men walking: Search and rescue in U.S. national parks. *Wilderness & Environmental Medicine,* 20, 244–49.

Heggie, T. W., Heggie, T. M., & Kliewer, C. (2008). Recreational travel fatalities in US national parks. *Journal of Travel Medicine,* 15, 404–11.

Iga, M., Jamamoto, J., Noguchi, T., & Koshinaga, J. (1978). Suicide in Japan. *Social Science & Medicine,* 12, 507–16.

King, E., & Frost, N. (2005). The New Forest suicide prevention initiative (NFSPI). *Crisis,* 26, 25–33.

Lester, D. (1971). Niagara Falls suicides. *Journal of the American Medical Association,* 215, 797–98.

Lester, D. (1989). The suicide rate by drowning and the presence of oceans. *Perceptual & Motor Skills,* 69, 338.

Morselli, H. (1882). *Suicide: An essay on comparative moral statistics.* New York: D. Appleton.

Newman, S., Akre, D. C. E., Bossarte, R., Mack, K., & Crosby, A. (2010). Suicide in national parks: United States, 2003–2009. *Morbidity & Mortality Weekly Report,* 59, 1546–49.

Rosen, D. (1975). Suicide survivors: A follow-up study of persons who survived jumping from the Golden Gate and San Francisco-Oakland Bay Bridges. *Western Journal of Medicine,* 122, 289–94.

Ross, T. E., & Lester, D. (1991).Suicides at Niagara Falls. *American Journal of Public Health,* 81, 1677–78.

Skegg, K., & Herbison, P. (2009). Effect of restricting access to a suicide jumping spot. *Australian & New Zealand Journal of Psychiatry,* 43, 498–502.

Snedker, K. (2012). Explaining the gender gap in fear of crime. *Feminist Criminology,* 7, 75–111.

Stack, S., & Bowman, B. (2012). *Suicide movies: Social patterns, 1900–2009.* Cambridge MA: Hogrefe.

Strayed, C. (2012). *Wild: From lost to found on the Pacific Crest Trail.* New York: Alfred A. Knopf.

Strom, S. (1999). In Japan, mired from recession, suicide soars. *New York Times,* July 15, 1.

Surtees, S. J. (1982). Suicide and accidental death at Beachy Head. *British Medical Journal,* 284, 321–24.

Takahashi, Y. (1988). Aokigahara-jukai: Suicide and amnesia in Mt. Fuji's black forest. *Suicide & Life Threatening Behavior*, 18, 175.

Time. (1935). Suicide point. *Time*, January 28, pp 30–31.

Warr, M. (1985). Fear of rape among urban women. *Social Problems*, 32, 238–50.

Wasserman, I., & Stack, S. (2008). Lethal locations: An application of opportunity theory to motel suicide. *Death Studies*, 32, 757–67.

Weisman, A. D., & Worden, J. W. (1972). Risk-rescue rating in suicide assessment. *Archives of General Psychiatry*, 26, 553–60.

Whittlesey, L. H. (1995). *Death in Yellowstone*. Lanham, MD: Roberts Rhinehart.

Yavuz, N., & Welch, E. W. (2010). Addressing fear of crime in public space: Gender differences in reaction to safety measures in train transit. *Urban Studies*, 47, 2491–2515.

Yeh, C., & Lester, D. (2010). Suicides from the Golden Gate Bridge: Have they changed over time? *Psychological Reports*, 107, 491–92.

Zarkowki, P., & Avery, D. (2006). Hotel room suicide. *Suicide & Life Threatening Behavior*, 36, 578–81.

11

Suicide in the Grand Canyon National Park

Steven Stack & Barbara Bowman

The Grand Canyon National Park (GCNP), founded in 1919, is located in Northwestern Arizona. Its key feature is a gorge formed by the Colorado River. The gorge is up to eighteen miles wide and six thousand feet deep (Kiver & Harris, 1999). The GCNP hosts 277 miles of the gorge, and thirty miles of the south rim are accessible by road. Along with Mount Everest, it is considered to be one of the seven natural wonders of the world. The present paper provides the first epidemiology of suicide in GCNP and provides comparisons to suicide in other natural areas.

The GCNP is the site of many of the suicides that occur in American national parks. Table 11-1 presents data from Newman, et al. (2010) on the distribution of suicides in our national parks from 2003 to 2009. Only those parks with nine or more suicides are listed for the purpose of brevity. The GCNP ranks third (tied with two other parks) with eleven suicides. No data have ever appeared on the suicide rate in national parks because of difficulties in calculating the full-year equivalent population of a national park.

The present paper draws on the opportunity theory of deviant behavior for its theoretical frame (Cohen & Felson, 1979). Wasserman and Stack (2008) applied opportunity theory to the issue of location of suicide. Hotels were taken as providing opportunity for suicide since generally they are free of motivated guardians or rescuers who would be likely to stop a suicide in progress (see chapters 8, 9, and 10). Remote areas of national parks might also promote suicide for those seeking a location where motivated rescuers are absent.

However, not all suicidal persons go to remote areas in national parks. In the GCNP, many suicides take place at points along the main

Table 11-1. US national parks with nine or more suicides, 2003–2009 (Newman, et al. 2010).

National Park	Location	Number of suicides, 2003–2009
Blue Ridge Parkway	North Carolina & Virginia	15
Colorado National Monument	Colorado	12
Golden Gate National Recreation Area*	California (includes Golden Gate Bridge)	11
Grand Canyon	Arizona	11
Natchez Trace Parkway	Alabama, Mississippi, Tennessee	11
New River Gorge National River	West Virginia	9
Suicides in other national parks contributing (all < 4 suicides)	Various	125
Total suicides		194
Suicides/year		27.7

*Suicides in the Golden Gate Bridge National Recreation Area do not include suicides from the bridge that fall into the water, only those falling into the park.

park road (Estep, 2010; Ghiglieri & Myers 2005), but the physical features and beauty of the park may still play a role in selecting it for a suicide site. Jumping off the canyon's rim, even if just off the main road, increases the opportunities for suicide for two reasons: (1) bystanders, if present, are less likely to be highly motivated rescuers since they are strangers, and (2) one can accomplish the act of suicide by a quick jump taking only seconds. Bystanders find it difficult to stop a suicide that happens very quickly. A jump can be about as fast as raising a pistol to one's head for the purpose of suicide.

From this elementary proposition, it would be expected that the physical presence of ongoing miles of cliffs would be associated with a relatively high rate of suicide by jumping. In like manner, given the desert-like environment of the GCNP, there are few trees, and opportunities for hanging are, therefore, reduced. Thus, the suicide rate by hanging would be expected to be relatively low. Finally, the accessibility of a means for suicide can be applied to the location of suicides in the park. While many suicides might occur in the backcountry of GCNP, it would be anticipated that they might cluster around the thirty miles of easily accessible cliffs on the main road through the park. More generally, opportunities for suicide in nature are also affected by the physical features of a national park, such as beaches on the ocean that promote drowning (e.g., Lester, 1989) and cliffs that can provide opportunities for jumping (e.g., Surtees, 1982).

The present study follows a mixed-methods approach and integrates qualitative data with some basic quantitative information on suicide in the national parks, focusing on suicides in the GCNP. It performs the first comparison between suicides in a national park with suicides from a national sample of suicides in natural areas. Key questions include, Why do some people choose national parks for staging their suicide? What differentiates suicides in the GCNP from suicides in natural areas? And are the suicides in the GCNP guided by the principles of opportunity and accessibility? The present paper also provides the first estimate of the suicide rate in the GCNP.

Previous Research on Suicide in American National Parks

A search through Medline using the keywords "suicide" (in the subject field) and "national park" (in keyword field) turned up only six hits, including one from Uganda. Further searches including a broad category of "mortality" and "injuries" yielded only a few more investigations. Most of the investigations embedded suicide in a study on general mortality and injuries in the parks (Heggie & Amundson, 2009; Heggie, Heggie, & Kliewer, 2008). Research on search-and-rescue missions in the park was a recurrent theme. Most of these studies paid almost no attention to suicide *per se* since there are few cases in comparison to injuries including nonfatal falls, heart attacks, hypothermia, and accidental drowning (Farabee, 2005; Heggie, Heggie, & Kliewer, 2008).

The only national study of suicide in the national parks was one commissioned by the Centers for Disease Control in a joint effort with the National Parks Service (Newman, et al., 2010). During the seven-year span from 2003 to 2009, eighty-four national parks reported 194 suicides. Nationally that is 27.7 per year. However, only 2.3 suicides occurred per park. Some caution needs to be exercised in interpreting these data since there are 393 national parks altogether, and eighty-four parks represent less than one quarter of all parks.

Newman, et al. (2010) determined that 83% of national park suicides involved men, somewhat higher than the nation as a whole where men accounted for 79% of the suicides. The mean age of the park suicides was forty-three years. The peak month for suicides was June, with twenty-one suicides. No other demographic patterns were reported.

The data on suicide method combined the 194 completed suicides with data on ninety-two suicide attempts. For men the most common methods were firearms (36%), falls (19%), not specified (12%), suffocation (includes hanging, 10%), cutting (7%), multiple methods (7%), motor vehicles (6%), and poisoning (5%). For women the most common methods were firearms (21%), falls (19%), poisoning (16%), not specified (14%), multiple methods (13%), motor vehicles (8%), cutting (5%), and suffocation (5%). Hence, firearms and falls were the most common suicide methods for both men and women.

There were no data on social strains or psychiatric factors, including depression and previous suicide attempts. No suicide rate data were provided, even those based on the year-equivalent population of visitors to the national parks. It is difficult to ascertain which national parks are at most at risk for suicide without comparable suicide rates. Such rates need to take into account the number of visitors and the average length of their stay in the park.

Much of what exists on suicide in national parks is written by journalists in newspaper articles and on assorted blogs by eye-witnesses. It is difficult to make rigorous generalizations about issues such as social and psychiatric factors that distinguish park suicides from other suicides. However, they can suggest propositions for hypothesis testing. In particular, this material can suggest some possible answers to one important issue: why people select a park for a stage for their suicide.

Why Do People Choose National Parks to Die by Suicide?

To answer the question "Why choose a national park for suicide?" one needs to ask suicidal people how they would go about selecting a location for suicide. Even better, persons who attempted suicide in a national park, but failed, could be interviewed on this matter. Unfortunately, there are no such studies of this kind. This is, however, a standing limitation of research on suicide as a whole. One exception is the work on why suicidal persons chose or would choose to suicide at the Golden Gate Bridge (Bateson, 2012; Rosen, 1975).

There is much anecdotal evidence that suggests that many seek out national parks for suicide because the park is a special place for them (e.g., Bytnar, 2010; Deutsch, 2009; Vanderbilt, 2009). Many go to great trouble, hiking long distances, to a noted beautiful spot. They sometimes return to a park where they have been before. Some have been reportedly seeking a beautiful place to die. A twenty-four-year-old female hiker in Bandelier National Monument was found comatose after an overdose she took in a very remote area of the park. She was found in a small cave by expert trackers on July 22, 1982, and ultimately survived (Farabee, 2005, p. 364).

Some persons seeking natural stages for suicide are outdoors people, such as climbers and hikers. For example, a rock climber shot himself, but only after having made his last ascent, the long climb to the top of the Visor of the Half Dome in Yosemite National Park (Deutsch, 2009). It takes considerable effort, endurance, and skill to climb up the cliffs leading to this popular destination. Specialized ropes, cables, pulleys, and other equipment are needed for the long ascent. Rock climbers come from all around the world to meet the challenge of this arduous climb. Many climbers have fallen hundreds of feet to their deaths at this very spot in Yosemite. In any event, rock climbers who witnessed the situation had the opinion that the place must have been a special place for the suicide (Deutsch, 2009). He chose not to fall to his death like many others who failed to make it to the top or slipped to their deaths on the way down. He conquered the Visor of the Half Dome, and only then did he shoot himself. He apparently planned to give one last outstanding performance before he ended his life. A helicopter had to be called in to remove the body from this dangerous location high above the canyon below. It is plausible that a series of accidental deaths at a natural location, such as Yosemite's Half Dome, might draw some suicidal individuals to the spot. For some, there may be an attraction to death hotspots, not just suicide hotspots.

Another example of a suicidal person going to some trouble to reach a beautiful natural area for their suicide is Bruce Colburn. Colburn, aged fifty-three, was an unemployed executive from Reading, Pennsylvania (Vanderbilt, 2009). He took a flight on October 7, 2008, to Montana and spent the night in a hotel. On October 8 he received a ride from an acquaintance to Glacier National Park to a campground near Kintla Lake. On October 23, park officials were contacted by the man who had given Colburn a ride to the park. Colburn had not called the man as planned to be picked up. In the following days, an aerial and ground search was performed involving over thirty search and rescue staff. They found his body at a remote spot. He had hiked to the picturesque Kintla Lake. Leaving his pack on the trail, he had scrambled up to point approximately one third of a mile above the lake. He died by a self-inflicted gunshot wound to the chest. It was, apparently, Colburn's first visit to Glacier

National Park. Nevertheless, he apparently did his homework and chose one of the most beautiful spots in the park to stage his suicide.

For some persons, seeking a natural area may be motivated by an urge to return one's body and soul to nature. Dr. Jerry Wolff, aged sixty-five, a biology professor at St. Cloud State University in Minnesota, was familiar with the topography and beauty of Canyonlands National Park. He had traveled there in the past as part of his research program. He was last seen on May 11, 2008. In a note to his family he said, "I am gone in a remote wilderness where I can return my body and soul to nature. There is no reason for anyone to look for me, just leave me where I am" (*New York Times* 2008).

Another way of indirectly assessing the motivation for seeking suicide in a national park is through reading commentaries on the subject from park rangers and people who are knowledgeable about deaths in the parks. For example, Albert Nash, a spokesperson for the Yellowstone National Park, where five suicides have occurred since 1997, reported, "Parks hold a special place in people's hearts. There are some individuals who feel it is important to have that kind of connection in those final moments" (*New York Times* 2008). Bruce Bytnar, who spent thirty-two years working for the National Parks, suggested that "many suicide[s] . . . look for places that are peaceful, private, perhaps where they had positive memories, and where they will not be disturbed but easily found after the act" (Bytnar, 2010). David Whittlesey, an expert on deaths in Yellowstone National Park wrote, "Perhaps these persons wanted their last moments to be spent in a beautiful or famous place, or perhaps they wanted their deaths somehow inextricably linked to nature" (Whittlesey, 1995).

However, it is unlikely that all those seeking to die in national parks intend to return their body and soul to nature. For some, the cliffs, lakes, waterfalls, and other structures provide the means for suicide. It may be that the availability of the means for suicide (e.g., cliffs in the GCNP) may also drive the selection of parks as a location for suicide. In addition, accessibility is a factor. The more easily accessible sites, such as cliffs along the road in the GCNP, may be selected over the more inaccessible but equally deadly remote sites (Estep, 2010).

Methodology

Data on suicide in the GCNP come from the medical examiner's office and national park files. They were provided by Ghiglieri and Myers (2005) and cover all known cases of suicide in the Grand Canyon (n = 47) from 1914 through 2004. A Google search using the names, years, and Grand Canyon keywords was also undertaken. Additional information was located on fifteen of these forty-seven suicides, including newspaper articles, National Park Service reports, and web-based blogs. Additional data included one suicide note (Mascolo, 2010) and a map of suicide locations in Grand Canyon National Park (Estep, 2010).

Data were coded into four categories: (1) basic demographic characteristics including age and gender; (2) evidence of social and health related strains including unemployment and stress in social relationships; (3) psychiatric morbidity including mention of depression, a history of suicide attempts, and a history of psychiatric hospitalizations; and (4) methods of suicide including jumping, driving a motor vehicle over the rim, firearms, and other methods.

Some caution needs to be exercised in interpreting the findings of the present study, especially with respect to the data on social and psychiatric strains. The reports go back to cases in the early twentieth century when the link between suicide and mental disorders had not yet been fully established or recognized by those responsible for certifying the cause of death in the GCNP. Many of the reports on the circumstances surrounding some of the suicides are very brief. It is likely that the data on these dimensions of suicide are underestimates of their true incidence. In contrast, data on other circumstances, such as sex, age, and suicide method, are complete, or nearly complete, and reliable.

Two control groups are employed for comparison purposes. First, the NVDRS data on 1,321 suicides in natural areas is incorporated as a comparison group (CDC, 2008). These data refer to all suicides occurring in natural areas during 2003–2006. Second, all other suicides, those not occurring in forests, mountains, beaches and other natural areas, in the NVDRS (n = 29,249) are used as a comparison group for suicides in the United States. The complete NVDRS database contains 30,570 suicides. While some of these may be in the national parks, none were from the GCNP because Arizona was not one of the seventeen member states contributing information to the NVDRS.

The calculation of the suicide rate in the GCNP followed procedures similar to those used to calculate the suicide rate in hotels in Las Vegas and Seattle (Gemar, et al., 2008; Zarkowski & Avery, 2006). Like guests in hotels, the average visitor to the GCNP does not stay for the whole year. Some adjustments need to be done for length of visitors' stays. Suicide rates in a city, for example, are based on the midyear population of the city. Midyear population is based on full-time residents, those who generally live at their homes year round, 365 days a year. For hotels and parks, since the vast majority of persons are temporary visitors, suicide rates need to be adjusted for average length of stay to make them comparable to standard suicide rates.

Data on the length of the average stay at the GCNP were taken from monthly public use reports available on the National Park Service web site.[1] This source provides year-to-date, annual estimates of full-time equivalent visitor days in its December reports. These were collected for a period of seven years, 2003–2009, to match the latest suicide count in the GCNP found in Newman, et al. (2010). The sum of year-end equivalent visitor days was then divided by 365 days to get full-year equivalent visitors. These data were then used to calculate a suicide rate per 100,000 per year.[2]

Results

The suicide rate in the GCNP for the period 2003–2009 was 59.86 per 100,000 per year or about five times the national average for the general population of Americans (Lester, 2000; Stack 2000). The sheer number of visitors to the GCNP was relatively stable beginning at 4,464,399 in 2003 and ending at 4,418,778 in 2009. Most visitors made brief day trips and did not spend an overnight in the GCNP. The number of full time visitor equivalents days varied between a low of 928,021 in 2009 to a high of 1,000,581 in 2007. Dividing these figures by 365 days per year yielded annual full-year population data for the GCNP between 2,571 year round people in 2003 to 2,542 year round people in 2009. The sum of full year equivalent populations for the GCNP for the seven-year period was 18,374 persons. Dividing the eleven known suicides by the estimated population of 18,374 yielded a suicide rate of 59.86 per 100,000 persons per year.

Table 11-2 presents the quantitative findings based on the forty-seven known suicides through 2004 in the GCNP. The findings are presented in terms of four variable sets: demographic variables, social strains, psychiatric morbidity and suicide method. After each quantitative set of data is presented, some case examples will be provided to put a face on the numbers.

Demographics

Men accounted for 80.9% of the suicides in the GCNP, a percentage somewhat lower than the 83.6% figure for men ending their lives in natural areas. The percentage of male suicides for the country as a

Suicide in the Grand Canyon National Park

Table 11-2. The distribution of suicides by demographic variables, social strains, psychiatric morbidity, and method of suicide. (A) GCNP (n = 47 suicides); (B) Suicides in all natural areas. NVDRS (n = 1,321), seventeen States, 2003–2006; (C) All other suicides, NVDRS (n = 29,249).

	(A) Suicides in GCNP	(B) All suicides in natural areas, NVDRS	(C) All other suicides in NVDRS
Demographics			
Percent male	80.9%	83.6%	78.2%
Mean age	31.3 years	42.0 years	45.5 years
Ethnicity: Asian	6.4%	2.3%	2.2%
Marital status: divorced	4.3%.	18.0%	21.6%
Urban resident	n.a.	n.a.	n.a.
Social & Related Strains			
Death of a loved one	0.0%	3.2%	6.0%
Physical health issues	5.4%	12.7%	20.6%
Financial problems	4.3%	8.8%	10.0%
Job problems	6.4%	9.2%	10.0%
Intimate partner problems	2.1%	24.6%	27.1%
Other relationship problems	2.1%	8.8%	8.9%
School problems	2.1%	3.6%	1.0%
Problems with the criminal justice system	8.5%	11.1%	9.2%
Victim of a violent crime	0 0%	0.8%	0.6%
Psychiatric Morbidity			
Alcohol problem	0.0%	12.2%	15.6%
Drug problem	0.0%	11.1%	13.4%
Depression	6.4%	36.9%	40.6%
Previous suicide attempt	4.3%	19.4%	17.4%
Mental disorder	4.3%	36.0%	38.0%
Current mental treatment	2.1%	30.7%	32.8%
Suicide note	19.1%	32.8%	29.5%
Method			
Cutting	0.0%	1.9%	2.0%
Fall/jumps	59.5%	5.9%	1.9%
Drowning	4.3%	16.5%	0.5%

(Continued)

Suicide as a Dramatic Performance

Table 11-2. (Continued)

	(A) Suicides in GCNP	(B) All suicides in natural areas, NVDRS	(C) All other suicides in NVDRS
Firearms	15%	42.7%	51.2%
Hanging	0.0%	22.1%	22.6%
Motor vehicle	21.3%	0.4%	1.3%
Poisons	0.0%	8.4%	19.1%
Other Characteristics			
Suicide pact	4.3%	n.a.	n.a
Park employee	2.1%	n.a.	n.a.
Modal season of occurrence	Winter		
Modal month	October	n.a.	

whole, column C, was 78.2%. Women were involved in both of the park's double suicides. Both occurred near Yaki Point, and both apparently involved male drivers launching their respective vehicles over the rim (Ghigliei & Myers, 2005).

Data on age were available for forty of the forty-seven suicides. The mean age of the GCNP suicides (31.3 years) was lower than the mean age for suicides at natural areas (forty-two). Both means for suicides in nature were lower than the overall national average age of 45.5. It is not clear why the suicides in the GCNP are younger than those found in natural areas.

The youngest suicide victim was only seventeen. Scott Beug was under a social strain—trouble in school. He took the family car and firearms and drove (a long distance) to the GCNP. He jumped off the rim on September 14, 1991. He had firearms, and so he could have used them for his suicide. Instead, he opted to jump 250 feet into the canyon. The oldest suicide in the GCNP was Richard Gibbs, aged fifty-two, on September 26, 2001. Gibbs came to the canyon by means of a tour bus from Las Vegas. Witnesses saw him sitting on the rim, arch his back purposefully and then jump. He fell over four hundred feet to his death (Ghigliei & Myers, 2005). Since he fell very quickly, it would have been difficult for a motivated rescuer to stop him.

Data on the ethnicity of the forty-seven suicides was rarely available, but from the last names of several, it is assumed that they were Asians.

138

At least 6.4% of the GCNP suicides were Asians, a percentage higher than that found in natural areas (2.3%). For example, Miss Myung Sun Kim, aged twenty-eight, jumped to her death on December 26.1980. This was the only known case where motivated rescuers from the suicide's family were present, but they were unable to prevent her suicide. Myung had been depressed. Her family reportedly pleaded with her not to get close to the rim but, when they looked away, she leapt over the edge. Opportunity theory, which argues that the presence of motivated guardians decreases the odds for suicide, is not always correct. Suicides do happen in the presence of motivated rescuers, especially when they look away, when a loved one is primed for suicide, and falling off the rim can be accomplished as quickly as a gunshot. It is difficult to intervene.

The state and city of residence is not provided in the reports for most of the GCNP suicides. However, at least ten came from out-of-state locations, some rather far away such as Massachusetts.

Social and Related Problems

Some cases were associated with relationship stress (4%). For example, Bruce Ciniello, nineteen, traveled to Arizona and lept off the rim of the Grand Canyon, falling five hundred feet, on October 15, 1992. He attributed his suicide to the strain involving his being gay and to his manic depression. He believed he was headed for a "peaceful afterlife." His suicide note read:

> Dear Family and Friends,
> I'm sorry it had to end this way but it was my fate. I couldn't handle life anymore. You see, the reason I ran away before to commit suicide is the same reason I did again. I'm gay. I never wanted to be and I always wished it would change, but it didn't. I wanted to live a normal life but God created me this way for some reason and there was nothing I could do to change it. I was born this way. Believe me, I would not choose this way of life for I know how hard and unaccepted it is. I'm painfully sorry you all had to deal with this, but I couldn't deal with it. This way, I could live a peaceful afterlife instead of a life of fear, agony and manic depressiveness.
>
> Please realize, I did not want to hurt anyone. I just wanted to end my own pain. I love you all dearly and will someday see you all again, hopefully with your understanding hearts and souls. I just hope God will bring me to heaven.
>
> Love always and eternally, Bruce.
> (Mascolo, 2010)

Physical illness played a contributing role in several suicides (6.4%). These illnesses included terminal cancer and a male infected with HIV. Job problems were noted in 6.4% compared to 9.2% of suicides in natural areas. One involved an unemployed airline pilot who jumped off the rim at Yavapai Point. Another involved an artist, Edward Walters, who wrote in his suicide note, "The show received terrible reviews from the critics, myself included. All I have done in my life is to bring distress and worse to others."

Financial issues were involved in 4.3% of the GCNP suicides, less than the 8.8% of suicides in natural areas. Two were so financially strapped that they did not have enough cash for a vehicle fee to enter the park. Determined to die, they left their cars behind, and they walked a long distance to the sites of their suicides. Trouble with the criminal justice system was present in 8.5% compared to 11.1% of cases in natural areas and 9.2% in the nation as a whole. Suicide was apparently an alternative to impending arrest for crimes including robbery and child molesting. Such crimes have a higher than average probability of incarceration.

An example is a double suicide involving a couple fleeing from the police in California. This happened on June 29, 1986, from the East rim of the canyon at a spot just past Yaki Point. Laura Allen, thirty, had been cohabitating with Richard McMillan, aged fifty, for about two years. Laura had two children, a son eight years old and a daughter nine years old, but she did not have full custody of them. They usually spent their time with their biological father and stepmother. During the children's last visit, they had both been sexually molested by her partner, Richard McMillan. After the children returned home they described what had happened to their biological father and stepmother. Laura's mother apparently tipped Laura off about the upcoming arrest by the local police on seven counts of child molestation (Associated Press, 1986; *The Bulletin* 1986). Both Richard and Laura had criminal records involving violent crimes. A past criminal record is often considered a risk factor for harsh treatment by the criminal justice system for current offenses. Laura, it should be noted, was also despondent over her physical disability (Ghigliei & Myers, 2005). The fear of arrest prompted the couple to flee. They traveled in McMillan's car across the Coconino Plateau to the GCNP. McMillan drove his car at high speed off the rim.

In other case of a suicide pact, a couple drove to the GCNP on their prized motorcycle. Having a special affection for their motorcycle, they rented a Hertz rental car to carry out their suicide. They left their prized motorcycle safely in the park (Ghigliei & Myers, 2005).

Psychiatric Morbidity

Data on the etiology of park suicide is sparse. However, if we combine reported depression with other mental disorders, one in ten, or at least 10.7%, of the GCNP suicides were related to mental problems.

In October of 1971, a Dorothy Dowd, aged forty-nine, had recently been released from a mental institution. She was reported as disturbing the guests at Bright Angel Lodge, a popular hotel on the rim inside the park. After receiving a query on the disturbances, the park ranger called the psychiatrist at the mental institution. The psychiatrist reportedly assured the ranger that Dowd represented no danger to others or herself. He added that she was not welcome to come back to his institution. Shortly thereafter, however, she put a paper bag over her head, and shot herself in the head with a pistol. She chose a ledge just below the rim as the site for her suicide.

Gregory Bansberg, thirty-two, was reportedly a troubled Vietnam veteran, possibly suffering from PTSD. He jumped off the rim on October 13, 1978.

One in five, or 19.1%, of the GCNP suicides left a suicide note. This is less than suicides in natural areas (32.8%).

Suicide Methods

The methods for suicide differed considerably from the national data. Adding together the two categories of falling from the rim, driving a car over the rim, and jumping, falls accounted for 80.1% of the Grand Canyon suicides. Specifically, there were ten cases (21.3%) of persons driving off the rim in motor vehicles. Three of these used rental cars. There are numerous places where one can jump off the rim. Nearly six out of every ten suicides, or 59.5%, involve jumping. Only a small portion of the rim is accessible by car, and almost all of the suicides by jumping occur along the road inside the park. There are many places where one could jump from seven miles of trails going down to the Colorado River. Nevertheless, few suicides occur along the trails by jumping.

The GCNP has considerably more suicides due to falls and motor vehicles than natural areas. While 59.5% of suicides are by falls in the GCNP, this is true for only 5.9% of suicides in natural areas as a whole.

Even fewer use this method nationwide (1.5%). Motor vehicles are the instrument of death in 21.3% of the GCNP suicides, but only 0.4% in natural areas and 1.3% in the nation as a whole.

All known cases of drowning were in the Colorado River, accounting for 4.3% of the GCNP suicides. This is less than that found in the nation's national areas (16.5%), but more than the suicides in the seventeen states (0.5%). Getting to the Colorado River is difficult given that it is at least a seven-mile hike down the Bright Angel Trail to the bottom of the canyon. For example, it took the present authors five hours to hike from the top of the rim down to the Colorado River, a mostly a downhill hike.

The remaining park suicides (15%) used mainly firearms, compared to the national data where most suicides (51.2%) are by firearms. Importantly, suicides do not hang themselves (there are few trees) at the GCNP. There were no recorded cases of suicide by hanging. In contrast, this method is used by about one fifth of the suicides in natural areas (22%) and in the seventeen state NVDRS region (22%). There were also no suicides using poisons or cutting.

The GCNP apparently attracts people wishing to die from a fall, either by jumping or by driving off the rim. The setting of the GCNP, being one of the world's most famous natural areas, is also an apparent draw. Many of the suicides came long distances to stage their suicide in the canyon.

Other Factors

A key issue in the opportunity theory of suicide concerns the availability or accessibility of the means for self-destruction. Cliffs that are accessible by taking a car down a road and then a short walk are likely to be used more, all else being equal, than those that require an arduous journey. There are hundreds of miles of deadly cliffs deep inside the GCNP, but one would have to hike along unmarked paths, often in one-hundred-degree-plus heat to get to them. While some of the suicides were located deep in the back country and remote areas of the park, most occurred along the main thirty-mile park road. While many of the suicides coming to the GCNP exerted considerable effort to travel long distances to reach the park, once there, they were satisfied with ending their lives near the rim.

Table 11-3 provides data on the specific sites of suicide in the GCNP. Only those sites with two or more suicides are shown. All are located at points reachable from the main roads within the GCNP. The present authors have visited the GCNP and determined that all seven listed

Suicide in the Grand Canyon National Park

Table 11-3. Specific sites of suicides in GCNP: Sites with two or more suicides, 1914–2004.

Site	Number of Suicides (years)
Yaki Point, East Rim Drive	5 (1974, 1974, 1986, 1986,1989); site of both of the GCNP's double suicides.
Mather Point, East Rim Drive	5 (1971, 1991, 1994, 1996, 2002)
The Abyss, West Rim Drive	4 (1985, 1990, 1993, 2000)
Moricopa Point, West Rim Drive	3 (1951, 1972, 1998)
Yavapai Point, East Rim Drive	3 (1987,1998, 2001)
First Trail view Outlook	2 (1980, 2000)
Pima Point, West Rim Drive	2 (1980, 1993)

sites are included on the maps distributed to visitors to the park. Half of the forty-seven suicides in the GCNP have occurred in the areas around these seven sites. It is apparently not known if persons choosing any of these specific sites were aware of any of the previous attempts at those locations.

Copycat Suicides

It is noteworthy that several suicides were marked by the same manner of death, that is, driving a car off the rim, as featured in a popular feature film, *Thelma and Louise* (1991). Suicide in films can be used as a point of identification for suicidal individuals, and, as such, increase suicide risk (Stack & Bowman, 2012). In *Thelma and Louise*, two troubled midlife women go on a road trip as a relief from their angst. Thelma had been abused by a jealous, possessive husband. They are unhappily married and perhaps headed for a divorce after Thelma runs off with Louise. Thelma and Louise go dancing, and Thelma is stalked by a man of questionable character. Louise shoots and kills him in an effort to prevent his raping Thelma. Their misadventures continue. They are eventually robbed of all their money. They raise funds for their trip by carrying out a robbery. Ultimately, they are corned by the police. Facing jail time, they choose to drive their 1966 Ford Thunderbird over the edge of a cliff. (The cliff scene was filmed in Dead Horse Canyon, not the GCNP.) Thelma's abuse and strife-ridden marriage may have served as a point of identification for copycat suicides among divorced women (Stack, 2000).

In real life, a recently divorced thirty-six-year-old woman, Patricia Locke/Astolfo, watched the film. Her mother reported that Patricia had watched the movie over and over again—about fifty times. Patricia drove her Chevy Suburban over the rim at the Abyss in the

143

GCNP, but its suspension got stuck on a rock outcropping. Still alive she got out and jumped off the ledge. However, she fell only twenty feet onto another ledge. Badly hurt, she crawled towards the edge, leaving a trail of blood. Determined to die, she finally slid off of this second ledge to her death (Ghigleri & Myers, 2005; Seidler, 2010). Two additional suicides in 1993 involved driving vehicles off the rim.

In addition, a man, Miguel, who had nearly died after cutting himself, reported that his attempt was influenced by media reports. He had recently broken up with his girlfriend and had stopped taking his antidepressants. He had read accounts of one of the recent suicides by car over the rim. He was so inspired he decided to pick the Grand Canyon to stage his own suicide. Miguel traveled to the GCNP from Nevada. He decided against jumping and bought a knife and backpack to kill himself on one of the trails down into the canyon. Fortunately, Miguel was rescued before he bled to death (Ghiglieri & Myers, 2005).

Seasonality

Suicide in the park follows a seasonal pattern. Suicides in the GCNP peak in the off-season (two thirds are in October through March), the months lowest in tourism. Suicide tends to peak in the spring nationally. The off-season is the period when there are fewer tourists around, some of whom might be motivated to stop a suicide in progress, such as someone leaning over the rim about to jump. The modal month is October.

Suicide in the GCNP overwhelmingly involves tourists. There was only one case of a suicide by a park employee. The rest were visitors to the park.

Unusual Case Characteristics

The manner in which the suicide act was carried out seemed unusual or poetic in some cases. Christopher White, twenty-five, smashed his wristwatch on the rock of the rim before jumping on December 30, 1994, perhaps to symbolize the end of time, at least for him (Ghiglieri & Myers, 2005).

Tim Clam, aged twenty-five, tried to get a seat on a helicopter tour over GCNP but was not able to do so during his first day in the park. He secured a ticket on his second day. While over the canyon, he opened the door of the helicopter. The pilot desperately tried to stop him, but the helicopter started to get out of control, and Tim jumped (*Los Angeles Times*, 2004). It is the only case of a suicide by jumping out of an aircraft in the GCNP. This is an unusual method for suicide both in society and in cinematic representations of suicide (Stack & Bowman, 2012).

A Note on Suicide in State Parks

Another possibility for a public location for suicides in nature is a state park. In results not fully reported here, a web-based search was undertaken entering the key words" suicide" and "park." The first one hundred hits were read and assessed for any mentions of possible suicide hotspots involving county or state parks.

The best example of a suicide hotspot was the Hoking County Parks in Hoking County, Ohio. Twenty-seven suicides had taken place there in the previous five years (Lecker, 2006), an incidence that far exceeds the GCNP, where there are fewer than two suicides a year. Apparently, no one has done a rigorous scientific study of this hotspot. Another apparent hotspot was the bridge in the Rocky River Reservation located in Fairview Park, Ohio. The bridge was the site of six consecutive suicides in 2004 (Guevara, 2004). This exploratory analysis suggests the existence of local suicide hotspots in natural areas. Essentially nothing is known in the scientific community about this localized phenomenon.

Conclusions

Suicide in the nation's national, state, and local park systems is a largely unstudied area of suicidology. Only one previous investigation has focused on national parks (Newman, et al., 2010), and that study provides information on a limited number of characteristics of suicides (e.g., age, gender, and method). Most of what is written on the subject consists of case studies authored by journalists and others (e.g., Deutsch, 2009; Estep, 2010; Guevara, 2004; Lecker, 2005; Vanderbilt, 2009). No systematic work exists on national park suicide comparing the suicides with a control group such as those suicides located in natural areas. The present study fills this gap.

A recurrent question has been why some persons will travel, often long distances, to end their lives in a national park. A review of qualitative work on this including suicide notes, interviews with park rangers, and statements from authors of books on death in the national parks suggested several possible motivation sets (Bytnar, 2010; *New York Times*, 2008; Whittlesay, 1995). A peaceful setting where one's body and soul can become entwined with nature at death is one theme. A review of the limited work on other natural areas also echoes this general set of motivations (Bateson, 2012; Guevara, 2004; Lecker, 2005; Rosen, 1975).

Data from the NVDRS on 1,321 suicides in natural areas were used to compare the suicides from the GCNP. Patterns in the demographic, social and psychiatric variables and the methods of suicide are both similar and different between these two groups of suicides. As in a previous study (Newman, et al., 2010), the vast majority of suicides (83.4%) in the GCNP were men, compared to 80.8% of the suicides in natural areas. Suicides in the GCNP were younger than in the NVDRS sample of suicides in natural areas (thirty-one versus forty-two years). This difference was unanticipated and is in need of further work to uncover the possible reasons for the discrepancy.

Evidence for most of the commonly found social strains behind suicides in natural areas was also found in the GCNP. The same was true of most of the psychiatric factors associated with suicide. However, the prevalence levels of these strains were consistently lower in the GCNP compared to the prevalence reported in the NVDRS database. Further work is needed on this problem, but it is anticipated that there are more missing data on these matters for the GCNP cases. The latter cases are older than those in the NVDRS and apparently subject to less fastidious record keeping in the rural county housing the GCNP in Arizona.

The opportunity theory of suicide received some support in relation to access to the structural means for suicide in the GCNP—its many cliffs. Fully 81% of the suicides involve falls from the rim, while only 6% of the suicides in natural areas follow this method. Additional work on other parks might find that the method of suicide is related to structural opportunities in the park, such as a lake or ocean that can be used for drowning (Lester,1989; Ross & Lester, 1991) or woodlands for hanging (Morselli, 1882).

Following the lead of the present study, which was able to calculate the first known rate of suicide in a national park (59 per 100,000 per year), future work might calculate suicide rates for other parks. It would be easier to calculate reliable suicide rates for the larger parks where an adequate number of suicides have occurred. In this fashion, which parks serve as hotspots for suicide and which have the highest rates of suicide could be determined. More generally, work on additional parks could explore the epidemiology of suicide following the variables included in the present study.

Barriers of various kinds have been installed in an effort to prevent suicides by driving off the rim at the GCNP, but persons intent on driving off the rim have been able to scout out paths in between barriers. A video on YouTube illustrates the path taken by Gheorghe Chiriac in a recent suicide by car off the rim on July 12, 2009.[3]

146

Maps providing the location of suicides within in parks and natural areas can help to identify possible hotspots. Maps can also be used to determine how accessibility is linked to suicide (Estep, 2010). Three-dimensional mapping technology has been used recently to further highlight locating deaths, including suicides, in the GCNP (Field, 2012). Such new methods of displaying deaths graphically can be applied to other parks.

Notes

1. http://www.irma.nps.gov/stats/SSRSReports/Park SpecificReports/Monthly park recreation visitation (accessed June 23, 2014)
2. A suicide rate for the full period under study (1914–2004) could not be calculated. Monthly attendance reports providing annual data on visitor person days were not available before 1979. The period of 2003–2009 was chosen since it is assumed that the most reliable data on the number of suicides in the park are provided in the Newman, et al. (2010) report which uses that time period.
3. https://www.youtube.com/watch?v=eyzqWsTAXXU

References

Associated Press. (1986). Dead in canyon crash were sought for molestation, may have killed selves. *Associated Press, News Archive,* July 2.

Bateson, J. (2012). *The final leap: Suicide on the Golden Gate Bridge.* Berkeley, CA: University of California Press.

The Bulletin (1986). Canyon plunge was suicide. *The Bulletin, Bend Oregon.* July 2, p. A2.

Bytnar, B. W. (2010). *A park ranger's life: 32 years protecting our national parks.* Tucson, AZ: Wheatmark.

CDC (Centers for Disease Control). (2008). *National Violent Death Reporting System coding manual.* Washington, DC: Department of Health and Human Services.

Cohen, L., & Felson, M. (1979). Social change and crime rate trends: A routine activities approach. *American Sociological Review,* 44, 588–607.

Deutsch, R. (2009). Another suicide at half dome. http://mrhalfdome.word-press.com/2009/09/21/another-suicide-on-half-dome/ (accessed June 21, 2014)

Estep, J. (2010). Grand Canyon suicide map, www.janestep.com/?page_id=1055 (accessed June 23, 2014).

Farabee, C. (2005). *Death, daring and disaster: Search and rescue in the national parks.* New York: Taylor.

Field, K. (2012). Over the edge 3D: Designing the deaths in Grand Canyon National Park. http://blogs.esri.com/esri/aregis/2012/09/07/over-the-edge-3d-designing-the%20deaths-in-grand-canyon-map%20 (accessed June 21, 2014

Gemar, K., Zarkowski, P., & Avery, D. (2008). Hotel room suicide: Las Vegas and Clark County. *Social Psychiatry & Psychiatric Epidemiology,* 43, 25–27.

Ghiglieri, M. P. & Myers, T. M. (2005). *Over the Edge: Death in the Grand Canyon*. Flagstaff, AZ: Puma Press.

Guevara, D. (2004). Bridge over parkland is scene of six suicides. *Cleveland Plain Dealer*, December 27.

Heggie, T. W., & Amundson, M. E. (2009). Dead men walking: Search and rescue in U.S. national parks. *Wilderness & Environmental Medicine*, 20, 244–49.

Heggie, T. W., Heggie, T. M., & Kliewer, C. (2008). Recreational travel fatalities in US national parks. *Journal of Travel Medicine*, 15, 404–11.

Kiver, E. P., & Harris, D. V. (1999). *Geology of U.S. parklands*. New York: Wiley.

Lecker, K. (2006). A good place to die: What makes Hocking County's suicide rate Ohio's fifth highest? The scenery. *The Columbus Dispatch*, May 15.

Lester, D. (1989). The suicide rate by drowning and the presence of oceans. *Perceptual & Motor Skills*, 69, 338.

Lester, D. (2000). *Why people kill themselves*. Springfield, IL: Charles C. Thomas.

Los Angeles Times. (2004). Man leaps from chopper into canyon. *Los Angeles Times*, June 12.

Mascolo, M. (2010). The challenges of growing up gay, lesbian or bisexual *North Shore Children & Families*, November, p. 3.

Morselli, H. (1882). *Suicide: An essay on comparative moral statistics*. New York: D. Appleton.

Newman, S., Akre, D. C. E., Bossarte, R., Mack, K., & Crosby, A. (2010). Suicide in national parks: United States, 2003–2009." *Morbidity & Mortality Weekly Report*, 59, 1546–49.

New York Times. (2008). For some troubled visitors, national parks become chosen site to end life. *New York Times*, June 29.

Repanshek, K. (2009), Remains of professor who went missing in Canyonlands National Park found in Needles region. *National Parks Traveler*, April 3.

Rosen, D. (1975). Suicide survivors: A follow-up study of persons who survived jumping from the Golden Gate and San Francisco-Oakland Bay bridges. *Western Journal of Medicine*, 122, 289–94.

Ross, T. E., & Lester, D. (1991). Suicides at Niagara falls. *American Journal of Public Health*, 81, 1677–78.

Seidler, B. (2010). Driving your car off a cliff: A deadly trend. *Examiner.com*, October 19. http//:www.examiner.com/article/driving-your-car-off-a-cliff-a-deadly-trend. (accessed June 23, 2014)

Stack, S. (2000). Suicide: a 15-year review of the sociological literature. Part I. Cultural and economic factors. *Suicide & Life Threatening Behavior*, 30, 145–62.

Stack, S., & Bowman, B. (2012). *Suicide movies: Social patterns, 1900–2009*. Cambridge, MA: Hogrefe.

Surtees, S.J. (1982). Suicide and accidental death at Beachy Head. *British Medical Journal*, 284, 321–24.

Vanderbilt, A. (2009). Body of overdue hiker identified: Death considered a suicide. U.S. National Park Service www.nps.gov/glac/parknews/news08-56.htm (accessed June 20, 2014)

Wasserman, I., & Stack, S. (2008). Lethal locations: An application of opportunity theory to motel suicide. *Death Studies*, 32, 757–67.

Weisman, A. D., & Worden, J. W. (1972). Risk-rescue rating in suicide assessment. *Archives of General Psychiatry,* 26, 553–60.

Whittlesey, L. H. (1995). *Death in Yellowstone.* Lanham, MD: Roberts Rhinehart.

Zarkowki, P. M. & Avery, D. (2006). Hotel room suicide. *Suicide & Life Threatening Behavior,* 36, 578–81.

12

Suicide in Public

David Lester

Marcus Porcius Cato killed himself in 46 BC. His death became a symbol for the death of the Roman republic and the death of liberty. Cato came from a wealthy family, followed to some extent Stoic values, and was opposed to Julius Caesar whom he viewed as a threat to the republic. Cato reluctantly sided with Pompey in an effort to contain Caesar but was defeated. Caesar offered to spare Cato, but Cato felt that to accept Caesar's pardon would legitimize Caesar's rule. Cato decided, therefore, to kill himself.

As Edwards (2005) has noted, there were a noteworthy feature of Cato's suicide. Cato's death was witnessed. He first attempted to kill himself with his sword, but his arm had been injured, and he failed. His companions arrived and had a surgeon sew up the wound. In the presence of his companions, Cato tore open the wound and died.

Edwards noted that Cato's suicide became a model for other Romans wishing to die by suicide. His determination, his reading of philosophical works on the evening before his suicide, the theatricality of the act, and the presence (and role) of witnesses who later report the details of the suicide to others, all of these became standard elements of Roman suicide by the elite. Witnessing such a suicide became a privilege.

Cato also managed to change his image by his suicide. From a political point of view, Cato failed since Caesar won the war and initiated an autocratic era in Rome as a succession of Emperors seized power from the Roman Senate. But Cato's suicide also made Cato a hero and gave him a moral victory.

When is Witnessing a Suicide Inappropriate?

On September 11, 2001, after the twin towers in Manhattan had been hit by airplanes, some of those working on the higher floors jumped from the windows in order to avoid death by incineration, asphyxiation, or crushing. These deaths can be viewed as suicides. The media, on the whole, did not show pictures or videos of these individuals in order to not compound the grief of the loved ones of those who died in the twin towers.

Edwards (2005) noted that, two years later, the Observer Sunday newspaper (September 7, 2003) printed photographs of one individual who jumped, with an accompanying essay. The newspaper received many letters of outrage that they had displayed such images. Some writers mentioned the feelings of those bereaved by the deaths that day; others felt that such images were obscene. Edwards suggested that observing a suicide is a shameful act, perhaps by suggesting that the viewer is complicit in the act. Edwards also suggested that potential viewers might fear a voyeuristic thrill when witnessing such a spectacle.

Witnessing (and Assisting) Suicide by Physicians

It is interesting to note in this context that some forms of physician-assisted suicide involve the physician actually administering the lethal injection. In most jurisdictions, Oregon for example , the physician prescribes a lethal dose of medication, but the person has to ingest it him or herself. In other cases, the physician administers the medication. For example, as Freud was dying from cancer in London, England, after his escape with his family from German-occupied Austria, his physician, Max Schur, administered a lethal dose of morphine as previously arranged between Freud and Schur.

Flemming (2005) noted that the Roman poet Lucan, who had fallen out of favor with the Emperor Nero and tried to overthrow him, was permitted to die by suicide (rather than execution). He had his physician cut his arteries. The Roman historian, Tacitus, gave many examples of suicides who had their physicians take such actions. These physicians were presumably the personal or household physicians of these wealthy men. Flemming argued that the lack of any information on the fate of these physicians most likely indicates that no action was taken. The careers of these physicians were unaffected by their involvement in the suicides of their patients. She also noted that the behavior of these physicians is at odds with the modern view of the role of doctors.

Assisted Suicide

In many cases of assisted suicide, people are often present as the person dies by suicide. These witnesses are typically significant others, but they may also be friends and helping staff members at clinics established to assist suicidal individuals. In recent years, several countries (such as Belgium, the Netherlands, and Switzerland) and a few American states (Montana, New Mexico, Oregon, Vermont, and Washington) have passed laws to permit assisted suicide and physician-assisted suicide. Typically, the individual has to have a terminal illness and be free of psychiatric disorder, and the decision has to be reviewed by a panel of qualified professionals. There is a growing trend for more countries and states to permit assisted suicide, and for the strict requirements to be weakened. For example, the requirement of a terminal illness is being relaxed in some regions. These options present a new way for people to stage their suicides.

Over one hundred years ago, Alfred Nobel, founder of the Nobel Prizes, proposed that a luxurious institute should be built on the French Riviera overlooking the Mediterranean Sea where people could go in order to commit suicide in beautiful surroundings (Sohlman, 1962; Seiden, 1986). Nobel's proposal was fanciful at the time, but today his proposed place exists. Dignitas in Switzerland has set up suicide clinics where people wishing to die and who meet the criteria established by Dignitas can go to die by suicide. In other places, the individual has to die by suicide at home.

The rules and regulations vary from region to region. In Oregon, for example, a physician provides the lethal medication, but individuals have to take the medication themselves. Typically, the physician is not present at that time. In the film *A Death of One's Own*[1] (2000), one patient decided to delay taking the medication until her brother visited, but then she was incapable of taking the medication herself and so was unable to hasten her death.

The possibility of assisted suicide presents individuals with many decisions to make. In the context of the present book, this means staging the act. Lester (2003) has presented advice and guidance for those making such a decision.) What method to use? For example, Dignitas uses medication (pentobarbital) most often, but helium gas can be used. Who to ask to be present? How to dress? To whom to write or e-mail? In one example, documented in the film *The Suicide Tourist*[2] (2007), Craig Ewert was a fity-nine-year-old retired university professor who suffered from ALS (Lou Gehrig's Disease). He was assisted by Dignitas in Zurich, Switzerland, and died in bed with Mary, his wife of thirty-seven years, at his side.

There have been many recent examples of such suicides in the United States, including the psychologist Sandra Bem, a renowned psychologist, and Brittany Maynard[3]. Jo Roman was diagnosed with advanced breast cancer, and she killed herself when she was sixty-one, in March 1978, in line with the principles that she had worked out. A book on her thoughts and decisions was published posthumously (Roman, 1980).

Four years prior to her death, Sandra Bem was diagnosed with Alzheimer's Disease, and she decided to end her life when the disease made it too difficult to continue. [4] Bem and her husband made her suicide a public process for their family and friends. As she approached the age of seventy, Bem's cognitive abilities began to decline severely, and she could no longer always recognize her relationship to her daughter or sister. If Bem delayed her suicide much longer, she would no longer be able to carry it out.

Six months before her death (on May 20, 2014), she stopped all treatments and, with the aide of a book (*The peaceful pill handbook*), she chose phenobarbital for her death. Bem and her husband decided on a date. She had a ceremony with her family two days before her death during which, in her presence, her family and friends recounted many of her achievements during her life and their thoughts and feelings about her. For her death, she requested that her husband stay with her while her family and friends met together at the home of Bem's best friend. She and her husband went for a walk, watched a movie (*Mary Poppins*, a movie Bem could still follow), and had dinner together. As reported on National Public Radio (Spiegel, 2014), after taking the phenobarbital alone in her bedroom (assisted suicide is not legal in New York), she asked her husband to lie in bed with her and hold her, which he did. She died in his arms. Afterwards, Bem's family and friends agreed that the process Bem had arranged made dealing with her death much easier.

Jumpers and Baiting by Onlookers

When an individual stands on a roof or ledge and threatens to jump in public, often bystanders gather below. Mann (1981) noted that reactions vary. On July 27, 1938, thousands gathered in New York City for up to seven hours until John Warde jumped from a the ledge of a window on the seventeenth floor of a hotel. Sometimes the crowd urges the individual to jump, but sometime they applaud when the man is talked down, as they did when Muhammad Ali talked a man down on January 19, 1981, in Los Angeles.

Mann studied this by collecting forty-nine cases in which a person threatened to jump and 117 when they jumped and died. Using the

New York Times, he found fifteen cases where spectators were mentioned, all men, and fourteen occurring in New York City. In four cases, the spectators baited the jumper. Mann searched other newspapers and added six incidents from the United States and around the world. Mann provided a typical newspaper report.

> A Puerto Rican handyman perched on a 10th floor ledge for an hour yesterday morning as many persons in a crowd of 500 on upper Broadway shouted at him in Spanish and English to jump. Even as cries of "Jump!" and "Brinca!" rang out, policemen pulled the man to safety from the narrow ledge at 3495 Broadway, the north-west corner of 143rd street. (p. 704)

In his analysis of these cases, Mann noted that baiting was rare. Only 17% of the fifteen cases with crowds involved baiting. Mann also noted that the crowd's anger was genuine and not mock serious. In one case, the crowd jeered when the man was rescued and threw stones and debris at the rescue squad. Baiting was more likely with large crowds (three hundred or more) suggesting that large crowds facilitate feelings of anonymity and diminished self-awareness. Baiting was also more common in evening and night incidents. Baiting was more common if the individual was lower (on or below the twelfth floor), the reverse of Mann's prediction. He felt that the lower the jumper, the less dehumanization would occur. Baiting was also more common in the incidents that lasted longer (more than two hours) suggesting the role of boredom in the crowd. Baiting was also more common in the summer (as are riots)

Suicide in the Presence of Others

Many individuals attempt to kill themselves in the presence of others. If the method is not very lethal (as in an overdose), then the others can intervene and prevent suicide. The use of a gun, however, means that the others witness the death, which is often messy. Thus, it is reasonable to hypothesize just from this circumstance that the suicide is angry with his or her significant others and wants them to suffer a trauma. The trauma is often made worse by the fact that the police have to ensure that the situation is not one of murder. I heard from the wife of a police officer who shot himself in her presence in their house, and she had to remain in the room for a couple of hours, covered with his remains, while the police tested her hands to see if she had fired the gun.

Sometimes, of course, death by suicide ends up being messy inadvertently. Flemming (2005) noted that when Seneca decided to die by suicide, he did not find the task easy. He opened veins in his arms and then his legs. When this failed to kill him, he asked his friend Statius Annaeus to find him some hemlock to poison himself with, but this had little effect. He finally managed to suffocate himself in a steam bath.[5]

Steer, et al. (1988) compared attempted suicides who were interrupted with those who were not interrupted during their suicide attempt prior to admission. In the follow-up (five to ten years), 14.6% of the interrupted attempters died by suicide versus only 4.8% of those who were not interrupted, and they died sooner (after thirty-two months versus fifty-four months), although not significantly so. As expected, those attempters who were interrupted took fewer precautions against being discovered during the index attempt, but did not differ in seriousness of the attempt or in the amount of planning.

In the next chapter, dying by suicide on social media, a phenomenon of the modern era, will be discussed.

Notes

1. http://gailpellettproductions.com/a-death-of-ones-own/
2. www.pbs.org/wgbh/pages/frontline/suicidetourist/
3. www.cnn.com/2014/10/07/opinion/maynard-assisted-suicide-cancer-dignity/
4. www.post-gazette.com/news/obituaries/2014/05/23/Obituary-Sandra-Bem-Psychologist-feminist-pioneer-in-gender-roles/stories/201405230080
5. Some suicides take pains to avoid a mess. For example, Willard Hershberger, a back-up catcher for the Cincinnati Reds, slashed his throat on August 3, 1940, in a hotel bathroom while sitting in the bathtub. In contrast, his father had shot himself in the family bathroom on November 21, 1929, leaving a bloody mess for his family to find.

References

Edwards, C. (2005). Modelling Roman suicide? *Economy & Society*, 34, 200–22.

Flemming, R. (2005). Suicide, euthanasia and medicine. *Economy & Society*, 34, 295–321

Lester, D. (2003). *Fixin' to die*. Amityville, NY: Baywood.

Mann, L. (1981). The baiting crowd in episodes of threatened suicide. *Journal of Personality & Social Psychology*, 41, 703–9.

Roman, J. (1980). *Exit house*. New York: Seaview Books.

Seiden, R. H. (1986). Self-deliverance or self-destruction. *Euthanasia Review*, 1(1), 48–56.

Sohlman, R. (1962). Alfred Nobel and the Nobel Foundation. In H. Schuck (Ed.), *Nobel: The man and his prizes*, pp. 15–72. Amsterdam, the Netherlands: Elsevier.

Spiegel, A. (2014). How a woman's plan to kill herself helped her family grieve. www.npr.org/sections/health-shots/2014/06/23/323330486/how-a-womans-plan-to-kill-herself-helped-her-family-grieve

Steer, R. A., Beck, A. T., Garrison, B., & Lester, D. (1988). Eventual suicide in interrupted and uninterrupted attempters. *Suicide & Life-Threatening Behavior*, 18, 119–28.

13

Suicide on Television and Online

David Lester

In recent years, an increasing number of individuals have communicated their suicidal thoughts and actions online through such avenues as Facebook, MySpace, YouTube, blogs, and Twitter. As a result, those concerned with suicide prevention have urged that online sites provide links to suicide prevention resources, and they have suggested monitoring web searches, postings, and tweets for risk factors that would identify potential suicides both at the individual and regional level (Gunn & Lester, 2012).

For example, Jashinsky, et al (2014) looked for regional trends by analyzing 1.6 million tweets over a three-month period, with over 37,000 identified as at-risk for suicide. They found a higher number of at-risk tweets than expected in the Midwestern and Western states, and the excess of at-risk tweets was associated with the suicide rates of the American states. Similarly, Gunn and Lester (2013) found that the volumes of Google searches for "commit suicide" and "suicide prevention" by state were positively associated with the states' suicide rates.

The present chapter examines actual suicidal behavior live on television and online.

Suicide on Live Television

Budd Dwyer

On rare occasions, individuals have killed themselves on live television. R. Budd Dwyer was the Treasurer of Pennsylvania from 1981 to 1987, but was convicted in 1986 of taking a bribe from a company seeking a contract with the state. Throughout his trial and after his conviction, Dwyer maintained his innocence and claimed that he had been framed. Dwyer was scheduled to be sentenced on January 23, 1987. On January 22, Dwyer called a news conference. Reporters were there, presumably to hear of his resignation. Dwyer was agitated and nervous. He protested his innocence and read from a prepared text. When he stopped reading, he gave three envelopes to his staffers, which later turned out to be a suicide note to his wife, an organ donor card, and a letter to the Governor of the state. He then pulled a .357 Magnum Smith & Wesson Model 27 revolver out of a manila envelope and suggested that the press leave the room. They pleaded with Dwyer to put the gun down. Some ran for help while others tried to approach Dwyer. Dwyer put the gun in his mouth and killed himself. Witnesses screamed and cursed while the television cameras ran.

The television stations made different decisions as to how much of the footage to show. Some stations froze the action just prior to the gunshot, while a few ran the complete scene. The ethical dilemmas in the decision-making process have been debated (e.g., Parsons & Smith, 1988), as have the decisions by newspaper editors of which photos to show (e.g., Baker, 1988; Kochersberger, 1988). For example, Baker (1988) found that medium circulation newspapers and those more than one hundred miles from where the suicide took place were more likely to show graphic still photos.

Bjelić (1990) examined Dwyer's press conference moment by moment and noted that the structure of the occasion was confounded. Dwyer saw it as a suicide ceremony, whereas the press saw it as a boring news conference. The occasion began smoothly until Dwyer pulled the gun from a manila envelope. At that point, flashbulbs went off, and Dwyer obtained what he had planned, namely "the story of the decade." Dwyer apparently expected that the reporters would sit there quietly while he read the past pages of his statement. However, some reporters thought of taking the gun from Dwyer, and so Dwyer had to change his plan. Dwyer monitored the actions of the reporters approaching him on the left and the right and abandoned his idea of reading the full statement. He put the gun into his mouth and fired. He was not able to die exactly as he wanted, but neither could the media prevent his dying.[1]

Christin Chubbuck

Another well-known suicide on television was by Christine Chubbuck, a news reporter who died by suicide live on television in Sarasota, Florida, on July 15, 1974, at the age of twenty-nine. Chubbuck had suffered from depression and suicidal ideation for a long time and had discussed her problems with her family. She had attempted suicide with an overdose in 1970, and was seeing a psychiatrist in the weeks before her death. Her major problem seemed to be her lack of intimate relationships. A colleague on whom she had a crush was involved with another reporter. She had recently had one ovary removed and was told that, if she did not have a baby in the next few years, she would be unable to conceive. Her colleagues described her as brusque and defensive in interpersonal contacts, and self-deprecating and self-critical.

She asked to do a piece on suicide and, in the course of preparing the piece, visited local law enforcement officials to find out about methods for suicide. She purchased a gun. Three days before her death, one of her segments was cut (in favor of covering a shoot-out), and she had an argument with the news director over this. On July 15, Chubbuck opened her show *Suncoast Digest* by reading a newscast, which she had never done previously. She covered three national news stories and then a shooting at a local restaurant. The film for that incident jammed, and Chubbuck said on-camera: "In keeping with Channel 40's policy of bringing you the latest in blood and guts, and in living color, you are going to see another first—attempted suicide." She drew out a gun and shot herself behind her right ear. She was pronounced dead fourteen hours later at Sarasota Memorial hospital. She left a script of the program, including the shooting, and an account to be read by the staff.

Both of these individuals were angry, and both were facing crises in their lives. Dwyer was facing a prison term for an offense he claimed he had not committed, while Chubbuck was facing a romantic crisis and conflict with her supervisor at work. Both planned their deaths carefully and in detail, and both made a public statement of their motives for killing themselves.

Court Cameras

Some suicides take place in courtrooms in the presence of others. Because it is common to televise or videotape courtroom proceedings, these incidents are sometimes broadcast live and can also be broadcast later on television and on the Internet.

On June 28, 2012, an Arizona millionaire, Michael Marin, aged fifty-three, was convicted for purposely burning down his $3.5 million house in Phoenix after he was unable to keep up with the mortgage payments. He faced up to sixteen years in prison. After the guilty verdict was read in court, he appeared to place something in his mouth. He then experienced convulsions, collapsed and died. The autopsy showed that he had killed himself with cyanide.[2]

A similar incident occurred on July 1, 2013, when Steve Parson, aged forty-eight, swallowed a cyanide pill in a Missouri courtroom after being convicted of raping a fourteen-year-old girl.[3] This incident seems likely to have been modelled on the suicide of Michael Marin one year earlier.

Other incidents that are captured on video and sometimes shown on television involve police chases of alleged offenders. Television stations now have helicopters that can fly to venues of interest, and they often capture offenders killing themselves. Pridmore and Walter (2013) reported two such incidents. In the first, in Los Angeles in 1998, Daniel Jones, aged forty, parked his car on the Harbor Freeway at 2:30 PM pointed a shotgun at passing cars, unfurled a home-made banner saying, "HMOs are in it for the money. Live free, love safe or die." He went back to his truck, which then burst into flames. Jones's hair and clothes were on fire, but he extinguished the flames. He then shot himself in the head with his shotgun.

In the second incident, in 2012, Jordon Romero, aged thirty-three, was pursued by police officers in Phoenix. Romero fired at the police cars chasing him and at a police helicopter. Eventually, Romero exited the car and, while running through the desert, shot himself in the head with a pistol. Both of these incidents were shown on live television and were later available on the Internet.

Suicide Online

Many individuals communicate their suicidal intent online, using websites such as Twtitter and Facebook. For example, Cash, et al., (2013) presented an analysis of suicide statements on MySpace. In chapter 4, I discussed two suicides who used Twitter and YouTube to post their suicidal distress and intentions. Some postings have gone further.

On November 30, 2013, a twenty-year-old student at the University of Guelph (Canada) announced anonymously online on a chat room that he intended to kill himself. He then posted the real-time video showing him lighting a fire in his dormitory room, turning off the lights, and crawling under his bed.

> Hi/b/ It begins. This is it. Tonight I will be ending my own life. I've been spending the last hour making the preparations and I'm ready to go through with it. As an oldfag who's been on 4chan since 2004, I thought I would finally give back to the community in the best way

possible. I am willing to an [sic] hero on cam for you all. All that I request is for you guys to link me to a site where I am able to stream it for you guys, then I will gladly fulfill my promise.[4]

Several of those on the website urged him not to do it. The fire was reported at 8 PM and was extinguished by the Guelph Fire Department who had been called. The student suffered serious, but non-life-threatening injuries.

Those involved with suicide prevention were greatly concerned by the fact that many personal suicide prevention pages shared this story on Facebook while not providing much education about prevention. They were worried that broadcasting the news of this event might lead to contagion and copycat incidents.

Discussion

Some of the incidents presented in this chapter were planned by the suicides to appear live on television or the Internet. In others, however, as in the case of the police chases, the offenders did not plan to die by suicide on television. For those that did choose to die in public, the role of anger and the desire to connect with others, even in their dying, seem present. These (as well as other possible motives) also seem to be present in those who die by suicide in the presence of others.

Notes

1. Bronner (1988) has analyzed the jokes that circulated after Dwyer's suicide. For a study of suicide jokes and humor, see Lester (2012).
2. http://www.nydailynews.com/news/crime/autopsy-shows-michael-marin-arizona-man-wall-street-trader-killed-cyanide-hearing-guilty-verdict-article-1.1123692
3. http://www.nydailynews.com/news/national/man-kills-court-sentencing-sodomizing-girl-14-article-1.1388294
4. http://cdn0.dailydot.com/uploaded/images/original/2013/12/1/stephenfire.png

References

Baker, R. L. (1988). Portraits of a public suicide. *Newspaper Research Journal,* 9(4), 13–23.

Bjelić, D. I. (1990). Public suicide as a deed of optionless intimacy. *Symbolic Interaction,* 13, 161–83.

Bronner, S. J. (1988). Political suicide: The Budd Dwyer joke cycle and the humor of disaster. *Midwestern Folklore,* 14(2), 81–89.

Cash, S. J., Thelwall, M., Peck, S. N., Ferrell, J. Z., & Bridge, J. A. (2013). Adolescent suicide statements on MySpace. *Cyberpsychology, Behavior, & Social Networking,* 16, 166–74.

Gunn, J. F., & Lester, D. (2012). Media guidelines in the Internet age. *Crisis*, 33, 187–89.

Gunn, J. F., & Lester, D. (2013). Using google searches on the Internet to monitor suicidal behavior. *Journal of Affective Disorders*, 148, 411–12.

Jashinsky, J., Burton, S. H., Hanson, C. L., West, J., Giraud-Carrier, C., Barnes, M. D., & Argyle, T. (2014). Tracking suicide risk factors through Twitter in the US. *Crisis*, 35, 51–59.

Kochersberger, R. C. (1988). Survey of suicide photos use by newspaper in three states. *Newspaper Research Journal*, 9(4), 1–10.

Lester, D. (2012). Reflections on jokes and cartoons about suicide. *Death Studies*, 36, 664–74.

Parsons, P. R., & Smith, W. E. (1988). R. Budd Dwyer: A case study on newsroom decision making. *Journal of Mass Media Ethics*, 3, 84–94.

Pridmore, S., & Walter, G. (2013). The predicaments of people whose suicide was captured on film. *Malaysian Journal of Medical Sciences*, 20(4), 64–70.

Part 3

The Methods Chosen for Suicide

14

The Methods Chosen for Suicide

David Lester

The major hypothesis about the choice of methods for suicide is that people choose a method readily available. Clarke and Lester (2013) and Lester (2009) have conducted studies and reviewed the research of others to show that, the more available and accessible a method for suicide is, the more often people choose that method for suicide. For example, fencing in a bridge from which people jump to their deaths cuts the number of suicides from that bridge (e.g., Bennewith, et al., 2007), while removing the fences from a bridge increases the number of jumpers from that bridge (e.g., Beautrais, 2001).

Idiosyncrasies in Choice of Method

Many papers document odd methods for suicide.[1] A thorough search of the medico-legal literature finds such methods as using chopsticks (Leung, et al., 1995), driving nails into one's head (Johansson & Eriksson, 1988) and decapitation while driving a car (Turk & Tsokos, 2005). Why did the people choose such eccentric methods for their suicide? Rarely do the investigators examine the motives for this choice of method for suicide.

Grumet (1989) reported the case of a male registered nurse, thirty-five years old and married, who took an overdose of imipramine and then connected a defilibrator to his head and released the electric charge through his brain. The man was a perfectionist and viewed himself as a failure. He frequently experienced guilt and depression. He also feared having a heart attack after suffering a mild one at the age of thirty-one. Grumet saw the choice of electricity as a symbolic way of execution for his sins (akin to convicted prisoners dying in the electric chair) and as a symbolic way of curing himself (akin to electroconvulsive therapy). Thus, the choice of method for suicide for this man had a very personal meaning. We need more studies of individuals similar to Grumet's study.

Suicide by Airplane

Some methods for suicide are more dramatic than others. For example, occasionally the pilot of a commercial aircraft chooses to die by suicide and kills the others on the airplane with him. It has been documented that pilots flying solo have crashed their planes in order to die by suicide (Maulen, 1993). Lester (2002) noted examples of possibly suicidally-motivated crashes of commercial airplanes. For example, the copilot of EgyptAir flight 990, Gameel al-Batouti, is suspected of crashing his plane (a Boeing 767) into the Atlantic Ocean on October 21, 1999, killing the 217 people on board. The plane crashed about sixty miles south of Nantucket Island. The American NTSB concluded that the copilot had caused the crash (for reasons unknown), while the Egyptian Civil Aviation Authority disputed this and concluded that the crash was caused by mechanical failure of the elevator control system of the plane. One set of crew made the take-off and was scheduled to fly the plane for the next four hours. However, al-Batotuti entered the cabin after twenty minutes and demanded to take over. After he took over, the captain went to the toilet. Thirty seconds later, al-Batouti said in Arabic "I rely on God." A minute later, the autopilot was disengaged, and al-Batouti again said "I rely on God." Three seconds later the throttles for both engines were reduced to idle, and both elevators were moved three degrees down. Al-Batouti then repeated "I rely on God" seven more times. The captain, who had returned, kept asking "What is happening?" The engines were then shut off, and the Captain asked al-Batouti whether he had shut off the engines. The plane crashed into the ocean soon afterwards. Later, in February 2000, another Egypt Air pilot, Hamdi Hanafi Taha, sought asylum in England claiming that he knew why al-Batouti had killed himself. According to the informant, al-Batouti had recently been demoted (possibly for sexually harassment) by an Egypt Air executive who was on board the plane.

In an earlier incident, a similar disagreement occurred between the NTSB and the national investigating agency. On December 19, 1997, SilkAir flight 185 (a Boeing 737), en route from Jakarta, Indonesia, to Singapore, crashed into the Musi River in southern Sumatra, killing all 104 people on board. The NTSB concluded that the crash was the result of deliberate input into the flight controls, most likely by the captain, Tsu Way Ming, a forty-one-year-old citizen of Singapore. (The copilot was twenty-three-year-old New Zealander, Duncan Ward.) The Indonesian National Transportation Safety Committee stated that it could not find a cause for the crash. The plane was flying normally when it began a nearly vertical dive. During the dive, the plane reached the speed of sound, and parts of the plane started to separate. The pilot had suffered recent financial losses of more than $1 million, and his trading privileges had been suspended ten days prior to the flight because of nonpayment. His income was less than his family's living expenses, and he had large credit card debts. One week before the flight he took out an insurance policy that went into effect on the day of the crash. He had also been disciplined by the airline on several occasions recently and had conflicts with Ward and other copilots who questioned his competence. In addition, eighteen years earlier, on the date of the crash, three of his squadron mates in the Singapore Air Force had died in a plane crash during training.

Passengers can cause crashes too. On May 7, 1964, Francisco Gonzales, twenty-seven years old, was on board Pacific Air Lines flight 773. He shot the pilot and copilot causing the plane to crash, killing all forty-four people on board. Prior to the flight, Gonzales had told several friends prior to the flight that he planned to kill himself, and he had purchased $105,000 of insurance before the flight. On January 6, 1960, National Airlines flight 2511 crashed killing all thirty-four people on board. An explosion had occurred near row seven and was thought to be from a bomb carried on board by Julian Frank as part of his plan to die by suicide. Frank had recently purchased a $1 million insurance policy.

Explaining Choice of Method

Although most theorists would resist the idea that the properties of a method may significantly influence the decision to commit suicide, it has been recognized since Durkheim (1897) that psychological and cultural factors influence choice of method. This observation received little careful attention, however, until the early 1960s (Hirsh, 1960; Dublin, 1963). Dublin distinguished three determining factors in choice of method: (1) availability or accessibility, (2) suggestion or infectiousness, and (3) personal and symbolic factors. With slight modifications, this classification provides a convenient starting point for the following discussion.

Availability and Accessibility[2]

The most "available" methods for suicide are, in fact, not the ones most frequently used. This point was made by Marks and Abernathy (1974):

> What are the most physically available methods in the United States for an individual to kill himself? Submersion? Cutting? Hanging? Burning? Jumping from a high place? Jumping in front of a speeding motor vehicle? Surely these are some of the most physically available methods for a person who wants to kill himself; however, these available methods of suicide . . . cannot be based solely on the logic of the physical presence (availability) of any given method for self-destruction" (p. 7).

Combining the notion of *accessibility* with *availability* makes for a better hypothesis because it permits the influence of geography to be used as an explanation of the choice of method as well as differences in the suicidal person's physical and mental capacities. For example, a city worker with an office in a tall building may have much greater access to jumping as a method of suicide than his suburban neighbor who works locally. Country dwellers may find it easier to find a private place to hang themselves (for example, a secluded tree) than people living in towns and cities. People with cars might more easily get to places where they could drown or throw themselves from a height. Anyone with a bit of technical competence is in a better position to use exhaust gas than someone without. Those who cannot swim can more easily drown themselves. Police have greater access to guns for suicide (Friedman, 1967) and chemists to poisons (Li, 1969). Gas suicide may have been less common in the Netherlands than in England because the design of gas fires and cookers in the Netherlands made them difficult to use for that purpose.[3]

These and other practical aspects of availability and accessibility may be important in causation since, quite early in the process of contemplating suicide, people have to think about what method to use. Failure to identify a suitable method or to resolve the practical difficulties involved could result in the idea of suicide being abandoned.

Suggestion and Symbolism

Phillips (1974) was one of the first researchers to document the possibility that publicity following suicides may increase the rate of suicide and that there are fashions in the methods used. He found that front-page news stories on suicide were followed by an increase in the number of suicides in the following month, and in another study (Phillips & Carstensen, 1988), he found a similar effect following television news reports of suicides. Many examples of suggestion have also been found in literature, in both historical accounts of imitation or mass suicide and case histories of individuals.

One of the most famous of these examples is the wave of suicides in the late eighteenth century triggered by Goethe's romantic novel, *The Sorrows of Young Werther*, about a lovesick youth who kills himself with his successful rival's pistol. Copies of the book were found on the bodies of so many suicides that a Protestant pastor denounced Goethe as a murderer, sale of the book was banned in Leipzig, and the clergy in Milan purchased the entire printing of the Italian edition.

A better-documented example of the power of suggestion and symbolism is to be found in the story of Mount Mihara in Japan, which became a suicide shrine in the early 1930s (Ellis & Allen, 1961). Until that time, Mount Mihara, which is on an island some sixty miles from Tokyo, attracted only a few tourists who went to see the sulfur clouds from its volcano. However, in January 1933, a pupil from an exclusive girls' school in Tokyo jumped into the crater, only to be followed a month later by another girl from the same school. The deaths attracted enormous publicity, and the legend took hold that those who jumped were instantly cremated and their souls sent heavenward in a plume of smoke. Crowds of sightseers flocked to the island and on one Sunday in April, six of these sightseers plunged into the crater while another twenty-five had to be forcibly restrained. By the end of 1933, 143 known suicides had occurred and many more were suspected. Despite strenuous policing efforts (by the end of 1934 the police had forcibly prevented more than 1,200 people from jumping into the volcano), the problem continued, with 619 deaths in 1936 alone. A fence was built which, along with some other preventive steps, reduced the lure of the mountain. Suicides did not cease, however, until 1955 when a badly injured young couple who had leaped like so many before were rescued from five hundred yards deep in the crater. Their rescue destroyed the myth of instant cremation that seemed to have exerted so powerful a fascination on so many people.

A less remarkable series of events, but one that recently caused considerable consternation in the northeastern United States, originated in a well-publicized case of suicide by four teenagers in Bergenfield, New Jersey. The facts are as follows. At 6:30 AM on March 12, 1987, four teenagers were found dead in a car with the engine running, parked in a thirteen-car garage of an apartment complex in Bergenfield (a community of 25,000 people about ten miles from the George Washington Bridge, which links New Jersey to Manhattan). A suicide note signed by all four said that they wanted to be buried together. The time of death was estimated at between 4–5:30 AM. The four belonged to a group of teenagers who were known as the burnouts. In the previous summer, four of the group had died in accidents, including one who fell from the Pallisade Cliffs to his death while walking with one of the victims in the car.

In the following week several teenage suicides by car exhaust were reported in other cities, including one by a youth in Clifton, New Jersey, on March 17. Then in Bergenfield, on March 18 at just after 4 AM, two teenagers, a boy and a girl, were found by the police in a car in the same garage used the previous week by the four suicides. The boy had turned off the engine when he heard the police arrive. The two teenagers knew the four who had died the previous week. The girl had made three suicide attempts in recent years and had received psychiatric treatment. The day before her suicide attempt, her sister had told the police that the girl was suicidal, and she had been taken to see a psychiatrist. Because of the anxiety in Bergenfield in the days following the first four suicides, suicide crisis hotlines had been set up, and every hour the police checked the garage in which the four had died. It was this precaution that saved the two teenagers, for they had only one hour to commit suicide in the garage before it was checked again. After this second use of the garage to attempt suicide, the police removed the door.

A well-documented case study of suggestion and symbolism was done by Seiden and Spence (1983–84) on suicide from the Golden Gate and Bay Bridges, which link San Francisco with the counties of northern California and the cities on the East Bay, respectively. During the approximately forty years from their openings in 1937 and 1936, respectively, nearly eight hundred suicides were confirmed at these locations. However, suicides from the Golden Gate Bridge outnumbered those from the Bay Bridge by more than five to one (671 to 121).

Seiden and Spence's study investigated the reasons for this difference in risk between the two bridges, which are similar in many other respects. They were opened within a few months of each other, they are in close proximity of each other, and they are of approximately the same height (two hundred feet above the water). Certain other factors might have been expected to favor the Bay Bridge as a suicide site. It is about eight times as long and carries about twice as much traffic (about 194,000 vehicles per day compared with 98,000 for The Golden Gate Bridge). One important difference favoring the Golden Gate Bridge, however, is that it is accessible to pedestrians. The Bay Bridge is open only to vehicles. Of 555 suicides from the Golden Gate Bridge studied by Seiden and Spence, 230 had been on foot. This was the case for only five out of the 112 suicides from the Bay Bridge. Nevertheless, three times as many suicides from the Golden Gate drove onto the bridge in cars compared to the Bay Bridge, suggesting other factors were at work than accessibility.

This conclusion is reinforced by the fact that, for East Bay residents (served primarily by the Bay Bridge) who used a car to get to their suicide site, as many jumped from the Golden Gate (fifty-eight) as from the Bay Bridge (fifty-seven). Indeed, about half of the fifty-eight who used the Golden Gate would have to cross the Bay Bridge to get there. In addition, as Seiden and Spence observed, "There are even a few people from outside the State of California who travel to San Francisco to jump off the Golden Gate Bridge. The Bay Bridge, however, has never had a jumper who was not a resident of the State of California" (p. 207).

Seiden and Spence see these facts as evidence of the "symbolically determined and romanticized attractiveness of the Golden Gate Bridge vis-à-vis the Bay Bridge" and of "a commonly held attitude that often romanticizes suicides from the Golden Gate in such terms as 'aesthetically pleasing' and 'beautiful' while regarding Bay Bridge suicides as 'tacky' and 'declassé'" (p. 207). In support, they quote Rosen's (1975) interviews with a handful of Golden Gate Bridge suicide survivors, as a result of which he characterized the bridge as "suicide shrine" with unique meaning to the jumpers, a meaning associated with death, grace, and beauty.

Personal Requirements and Cultural Norms

All of us fear death, but some forms of death are more terrifying than others. Thus, most of us dread a long terminal illness with severe pain and progressive loss of functions. Indeed, quality of dying and death may be as meaningful a concept to many people as quality of life. However, the factors affecting decisions about death, in particular a suicidal death, depend on personal circumstances. Most suicidal individuals are concerned about the physical pain involved and many, particularly women (Marks, 1977), about the damage to their faces and bodies. Some individuals, for religious reasons or to safeguard insurance payments for their relatives, may want to conceal the suicidal nature of their deaths, while others, particularly those who commit suicide in a public way such as by jumping under a subway train (Guggenheim & Weisman, 1972), may wish the opposite. Punishing those they consider responsible for their plight may be important for some suicides, whereas others may wish to cause the minimum of distress to their significant others.

All of these considerations are likely to influence the choice of method, although they have not been studied much. Dublin's (1963) own work concentrated mainly on the concept of lethality of intent. For example, he sought to explain the greater use of firearms by males primarily on the grounds that men who engage in suicidal behavior have more lethal intent than women whose suicide attempts are more often manipulative. For manipulative or ambivalent individuals, slower methods are usually preferred since these might allow either a last minute change of mind or for fate to have a hand, for example, through the chance intervention of a lover or friend.

In contrast, Marks and Abernathy (1974) argued that men's greater use of firearms reflects, instead, their greater familiarity with and acceptance of guns. Marks also put forward the same reason for the generally greater use of guns in suicide in the southern states (Marks & Stokes, 1976).

Indeed, the concept of differential socialization has wider relevance than merely for the use of guns. For example, Durkheim observed that Englishmen rarely hang themselves, perhaps because hanging is the traditional punishment in England for traitors and murderers. Car exhaust suicides may be more common in the United States because of the salience of the car in everyday life and, as Noomen (1975) has observed. Commenting on the high incidence of suicide by drowning in Holland, he said, "The Dutchman knows about death, because he knows about the water" (p. 168).

Choice Structuring Properties of Methods of Suicide

Marks and Abernathy (1974) identify five variables that would help to explain an individual's preference for a particular method of self-destruction: its physical availability, the suicide's knowledge of the method, his familiarity with the method, his personal or social accessibility to the method, and his evaluation of the method. Drawing on the work of others discussed previously, their list can be considerably extended, and Clarke and Lester (2013) suggested twenty "choice structuring properties" that impact in various degrees the method of suicide chosen (poisoning, cutting, suffocation and hanging, drowning, electrocution, shooting, jumping, etc.):

1. Availability (e.g., owning a car)
2. Familiarity with the method (e.g., car exhaust gases)
3. Technical skills needed (e.g., hanging, gassing)
4. Planning necessary (e.g., buying a gun, saving up drugs)
5. Likely pain (e.g., cutting wrists)
6. Courage needed (e.g., high building, train)
7. Consequences of failure (e.g., disability, publicity)
8. Disfigurement after death (e.g., hanging versus overdose)
9. Danger and inconvenience to others (e.g., car crash, subway leap)
10. Messiness and bloodiness (e.g., wrist cutting)
11. Discovery of body (e.g., by loved ones or strangers)
12. Contamination of nest (i.e., avoiding home)
13. Scope for concealing or publicizing death-shame, insurance (e.g., car-crash, drowning, subway leap)
14. Certainty of death (perceived or actual)
15. Time taken to die while conscious (e.g., poisons, wrist cutting)
16. Scope for second thoughts (e.g., swim back to shore, switch off gas)
17. Chances of intervention (e.g., "fate," estranged lover)
18. Symbolism (e.g., cleansing by fire, seppuku)
19. Masculine/feminine (e.g., guns)
20. Dramatic impact (e.g., lover's leap versus overdose)

These properties are largely self-explanatory and require no further illustration. Their relative importance is unknown, however, and other significant properties may have been omitted. Further, some of the properties are related in practice (for example, most bloody methods may need courage). Finally, some of the costs and benefits have both positive and negative valences, depending on the motivation of the individual concerned. For example, one individual may wish to spare relations the shock of discovering the body whereas someone else may deliberately inflict this them.

Closer investigation of the reasons for choosing particular methods could help in predicting the likelihood and extent of displacement following changes in the availability of methods. In the case of completed suicides, it may not be possible to do more than infer reasons for choice on the basis of the actions completed. An alternative source of data would be systematic questioning of samples of people, either groups of the suicidally inclined or the general population, to discover what people know about the various methods and how they evaluate them.

Little research has been conducted along these lines, although a study by Marks (1977) illustrates the approach. He questioned 642 college students about their preferences for method in an effort to understand differences in the choice of methods between men and women. Significant differences were found between the two groups in their evaluations of six of nine methods. Women associated painlessness and efficiency with drugs and poison, whereas men associated masculinity, efficiency, and knowledge of method with firearms.

Perception of Different Methods

Lester (1988a) studied undergraduates' perceptions of two relatively common methods of suicide: shooting and overdosing. The students were asked to state their preference for guns or an overdose of pills as a method of suicide. They then rated each method of suicide on seven-point rating scales for the ten properties judged to be particularly important for the two methods: quick/slow, painful/painless, difficult/easy, irreversible/reversible, good/bad, courageous/cowardly, dramatic/banal, masculine/feminine, messy/tidy, and impulsive/planned.

The respondents viewed suicide by guns and by overdose of pills as different on nine of the ten properties. Suicide by guns was seen as quick, painful, difficult, irreversible, dramatic, masculine, and messy, as well as moderately courageous and impulsive. In contrast, an overdose of pills was seen as slow, painless, easy, cowardly, feminine, tidy, and planned, as well as moderately reversible and banal. (Good versus bad ratings did not differentiate the methods.)

Males and females did not differ in their rating of guns as a method for suicide on any of the ten scales and differed on only one of their ratings of on overdose of pills. The females saw pills as a little more painless than did the males (5.79 and 5.26, respectively, on a scale of one to seven). Students who chose an overdose of pills differed from those students who chose guns in their perception of an overdose of pills on four scales. They saw pills as more slow (means 6.32 and 5.28), more painless (means 5.72 and 4.79), less planned (means 4.79 and 5.79), and less bad (means 4.79 and 5.95).

Thus, the methods of suicide considered in this study (guns and pills) were perceived very differently, and these perceptions were not greatly affected by the sex of the respondent or by the method that the respondent would choose for suicide. In an earlier study, Lester (1979) found that given a choice between drugs such as sleeping pills versus a gun or hanging, men and women undergraduates did not differ in their choice, and their choice was not associated with the fears of death and dying.

Lester (1988c) presented undergraduates with eleven methods for suicide and asked them to rate them as acceptable on a scale of one to five. The methods were overdose of sleeping pills/antidepressants, shooting yourself with a gun, car exhaust, swallowing acid or a caustic substance, drowning in a pond/ocean/pool, jumping off a building/cliff, hanging yourself, eating insecticide or other poison, setting fire to yourself, suffocation with a plastic bag, and cutting your wrists with a razor/knife. A factor analysis of the ratings identified two clusters for the men, but four clusters for the women, indicating that the women thought about the methods in a more complex manner than did the men. For example, for the women, using fire was on one cluster by itself, whereas for the men it was in the same cluster with eight other methods.

Reasons for Choice of Method

Although the previous studies showed that different methods of suicide are perceived very differently, further research is needed to explore why one method of suicide is preferred over another, and under what conditions people would switch methods if their preferred method were not available. Lester (1988b) investigated of the first of these questions by asking undergraduates which method they would choose for suicide and why. They were asked (1) which method they would choose for suicide; (2) whether they chose that method because it is quick, painless, does not disfigure, or is easily available (answered on a five-point rating scale from "not at all" to "definitely"); and (3) how much seven consequences of death concerned them (answered on a five-point rating scale from "doesn't concern me much at all" to "concerns me a lot"). The seven consequences were as follows:

1. I could no longer have any experiences.
2. I am uncertain as to what might happen to me if there is a life after death.
3. I am afraid of what might happen to my body after death.
4. I could no longer care for my dependents.
5. My death would cause grief to my relatives and friends.
6. All my plans and projects would come to an end.
7. The process of dying might be painful.

As expected, there were sex differences in the choice of method. Among the most common methods, females chose an overdose of medication more than males, with a ratio of 1.57:1; guns far less often, with a ratio of 0.35; and carbon monoxide/car exhaust equally often, with a ratio of 1.04.

Overall, the females rated painlessness, less disfigurement, and availability as more important reasons for choosing a method for suicide than did the males, and they rated availability as less important. For those students who chose an overdose of medication (the most common method chosen), females rated the painlessness and availability as more important reasons than did the males. Those who chose guns (rather than an overdose or carbon monoxide) rated quickness as significantly more relevant to their choice and the disfigurement as less important, but they did not differ in their ratings of the importance of pain and availability.

To check the importance of lack of disfigurement, the concern for "I am afraid of what might happen to my body after death" was examined. Those who chose guns had significantly less concern about this than those who chose overdoses and carbon monoxide, and males had less concern than females. (None of the other six consequences of death were significantly differentiated among those choosing different methods of suicide.)

The results of this study of college students showed that the quickness, painfulness, degree of disfigurement, and availability of methods for suicide do play a role in the hypothetical choice of method for suicide. In particular, females are more concerned about the appearance of their body after death, as are those who choose overdose and carbon monoxide. Also, females are more likely to choose overdoses than males. This suggests that making lethal medications less easily available may indeed lower the overall suicide rate, since people for whom disfigurement is a concern may well not switch to a more disfiguring method of suicide. Similarly, those who choose guns appear to want a quick death and may not switch to a slower and perhaps less certain method.

Can Death by Suicide be an Art Form?

Joyce Carol Oates (1980) raised the question of whether suicides are artists and whether death by suicide can be an art form? Oates noted that some suicides are artistic in that they engage in an act of self-destruction "*as if it were a kind of creation*" (p. 163) (italics in the original). If this were so, then the method chosen for suicide may be important.

However, Oates herself sees this as mistake. In her view, such suicides see death as a liberation when it is a destruction, an ultimate *deadness*.

She views such individuals as failed artists and their "art-work a mockery of genuine achievement (p. 163). Oates gives two examples of such suicides, Sylvia Plath (1932–1963) and Anne Sexton (1928–1974), both American poets who died by suicide. In her poem, *Lady Lazarus*, Oates notes that Plath seems proud of her self-destructive behavior.

> Dying
> Is an art, like everything else.
> I do it exceptionally well
>
> I do it so it feels like hell.
> I do it so it feels real.
> I guess you could say I've a call.

Oates views this poem as "close to hysteria" and the poem as full of self-loathing. Oates labels Plath's poems and her death as "adolescent gestures" with so little self-knowledge.

Oates's judgment is rather harsh. In her poem, *Daddy*, Plath shows great insight into her choices in life. She knows that her suicide is an attempt to get back to the father who abandoned her when he died (of natural causes) when she was eight. She knows that her choice of a husband (the British poet Ted Hughes) was a search for a father substitute. More importantly, Plath's suicide gave her life and her creative writing tremendous fame. Her act of dying may not have been an artistic action, but its impact on her art was enormous.

Oates also noted Sexton claimed that suicides were special people. In one of her poems, Sexton says:

> But suicides have a special language.
> Like carpenters they want to know *which tools*.
> They never ask *why build*.

Oates saw this poem as characterized by dignity and restraint.

Oates listed as *noble suicides* those not acting blindly in a confused emotional state, such as the deaths of Socrates (who did not flee execution but drank poison), Cato, Jesus, and, in literature, Othello, Anthony, and Cleopatra. Other suicides refuse to play the game, in Oates's view. They leave the party too soon and make others uncomfortable. The private gesture becomes a public act. But noble suicides can skillfully articulate their death wishes. She ends her essay by quoting lines from a poem of John Berryman (1914–1972), another American poet who died by suicide.

Life, friends, is boring. We must not say so.
After all, the sky flashes, the great sea yearns,
we ourselves flash and yearn,
and moreover my mother told me as a boy
(repeatingly) 'Ever to confess you're bored
means you have no

Inner Resources.' I conclude now I have no
inner resources, because I am heavy bored.

Notes

1. See also chapter 16.
2. This section is based on Clarke and Lester (2013).
3. The doors of the gas ovens opened down from the bottom rather than from the side.

References

Beautrais, A. L. (2001). Effectiveness of barriers at suicide jumping sites. *Australian & New Zealand of Psychiatry*, 35, 557–62.

Bennewith, O., Nowers, M., & Gunnell, D. (2007). Effects of barriers on the Clifton suspension bridge, England, on local patterns of suicide. *British Journal of Psychiatry*, 190, 266–67.

Clarke, R. V., & Lester, D. (2013). *Suicide: Closing the exits*. New Brunswick, NJ: Transaction.

Dublin, L. (1963). *Suicide: A sociological and statistical study*. New York: Ronald.

Durkheim, E. (1897). *Le suicide*. Paris, France: Felix Alcan.

Ellis, E. R., & Allen, G. N. (1961). *Traitor within: Our suicide problem*. Garden City, NY: Doubleday.

Friedman, P. (1967). Suicide among police. In E. S. Shneidman (Ed.), *Essays in self-desctruction*, 414–49. New York: Science House.

Grumet, G. W. (1989). Attempted suicide by electrocution. *Bulletin of the Menninger Clinic*, 53, 512–21.

Guggenheim, F. G., & Weisman, A. D. (1972). Suicide in the subway. *Journal of Nervous & Mental Disease*, 155, 404–9.

Hirsh, J. (1960). Methods and fashions of suicide. *Mental Hygiene*, 44, 3–11.

Johansson, B., & Eriksson, A. (1988). Suicide by driving an awl into the brain. *American Journal of Forensic Medicine & Pathology*, 9, 331–33.

Lester, D. (1979). Preferences for method of suicide and attitudes toward death in normal people. *Psychological Reports*, 45, 638.

Lester, D. (1988a). The perception of different methods of suicide. *Journal of General Psychology*, 115, 215–17.

Lester, D. (1988b). Why do people choose particular methods for suicide? *Activitas Nervosa Superior*, 30, 213–14.

Lester, D. (1988c). The perception of different methods for suicide. *Perceptual & Motor Skills*, 67, 530.

Lester, D. (2002). Suicide and aircraft. *Crisis*, 23, 2.

Lester, D. (2009). *Preventing suicide: Closing the Exits revisited.* Hauppauge, NY: Nova Science.

Leung, C. M., Poon, C. Y., & Lo, M. K. (1995). Chopsticks and suicide. *Singapore Medical Journal*, 36, 90–91.

Li, F. (1969). Suicide among chemists. *Archives of Environmental Health*, 19, 518–20.

Marks, A. (1977). Sex differences and their effect upon cultural evaluations of methods of self-destruction. *Omega*, 8, 65–70.

Marks, A., & Abernathy, T. (1974). Towards a sociocultural perspective on means of self-destruction. *Life-Threatening Behavior*, 4, 3–17.

Marks, A., & Stokes, C. (1976). Socialization, firearms and suicide. *Social Problems*, 23, 622–29.

Maulen, B. (1993). An aeronautical suicide attempt. *Crisis*, 12, 68–70.

Noomen, P. (1975). Suicide in the Netherlands. In N. L. Farberow (Ed.), *Suicide in Different Cultures*, 165–177. Baltimore, MD: University Park Press.

Oates, J. C. (1980). The art of suicide. In M. P. Battin & D. J. Mayo (Eds.) *Suicide: The Philosophical Issues*, 161–168. New York: St. Martin's Press.

Phillips, D. P. (1974). The influence of suggestion on suicide. *American Sociological Review*, 39, 340–54.

Phillips, D. P., & Carstensen, L. L. (1988). The effect of suicide stories on various demographic groups 1968–1985. *Suicide & Life-Threatening Behavior*, 18, 100–13.

Rosen, D. H. (1975). Suicide survivors. *Western Journal of Medicine*, 122, 289–94.

Seiden, R. H., & Spence, M. (1983–1984). A tale of two bridges. *Omega*, 14, 201–9.

Turk, E. E., & Tsokos, M. (2005). Vehicle-assisted suicide resulting from decapitation. *American Journal of Forensic Medicine & Pathology*, 26, 292–93.

15

The Rehearsal: Nonfatal Suicidal Behavior as a Precipitant of Suicide

John F. Gunn III

When actors or musicians are preparing for a performance, they rehearse. Rehearsals are the practices that occur prior to the main event—before the play or concert's opening night. The dress rehearsal is the final rehearsal prior to the act and is done in full costume. As the title of this chapter indicates, I will argue that nonfatal suicidal behavior can be viewed as a "rehearsal" for death by suicide.

There is a common joke regarding Carnegie Hall, with many variants, in which a man lost in New York City asks another how to get to Carnegie Hall, only to have the other person respond, "Practice." Practice increases the chance of success[1] in most endeavors. It also applies to suicide. Death by suicide is not easy. Humans have evolved with a strong instinct to survive, and going against this evolutionary drive is not easy. Therefore, in order to die by suicide, practice is often necessary. This practice often takes the form of nonsuicidal self-injury (NSSI) and nonfatal suicide attempts. It is the premise of this chapter that nonfatal suicidal behavior is very often the rehearsal for death by suicide.

Throughout this chapter, I will discuss the literature that connects both nonsuicidal self-injury and previous suicide attempts to eventual death by suicide. I will also discuss one current and prominent theory of suicide, the Interpersonal-Psychological Theory of Suicide (IPTS), which explains how these behaviors influence death by suicide.

Nonsuicidal Self-Injury (NSSI)

NSSI refers to self-harm that is independent of suicide intent. The criteria for a diagnosis of NSSI in the Diagnostic and Statistical Manuel, 5th Edition (American Psychiatric Association, 2013, pp. 803) are:

A. In the last year, the individual has, on 5 or more days, engaged in intentional self-inflicted damage to the surface of his or her body of a sort likely to induce bleeding, bruising, or pain (e.g., cutting, burning, stabbing, hitting, excessive rubbing), with the expectation that the injury will lead to only minor or moderate physical harm (i.e., there is no suicidal intent). Note. The absence of suicidal intent has either been stated by the individual or can be inferred by the individual's repeated engagement in a behavior that the individual knows, or has learned, is not likely to result in death.

B. The individual engages in the self-injurious behavior with one or more of the following expectations:

> To obtain relief from a negative feeling or cognitive state
> To resolve an interpersonal difficulty
> To induce a positive feeling state

C. The intentional self-injury is associated with at least one of the following:

> Interpersonal difficulties or negative feelings or thoughts, such as depression, anxiety, tension, anger, generalized distress, or self-criticism, occurring in the period immediately prior to the self-injurious act
> Prior to engaging in the act, a period of preoccupation with the intended behavior that is difficult to control
> Thinking about self-injury that occurs frequently, even when it is not acted upon

D. The behavior is not socially sanctioned (e.g., body piercing, tattooing, part of a religious or cultural ritual) and is not restricted to picking a scab or nail biting

E. The behavior or its consequences cause clinically significant distress or interference in interpersonal, academic, or other important areas of functioning

F. The behavior does not occur exclusively during psychotic episodes, delirium, substance intoxication, or substance withdrawal. In individuals with a neurodevelopmental disorder, the behavior is not part of a pattern of repetitive stereotypies. The behavior is not better explained by another mental disorder or medical condition (e.g., psychotic disorder, autism spectrum disorder, intellectual disability, Lesch-Nyhan syndrome, stereotypic movement disorder with self-injury, trichotillomania [hair-pulling disorder], excoriation [skin-picking] disorder)

NSSI is typically undertaken to reduce negative emotions (such as anxiety) or as a means of self-punishment. Those who engage in NSSI often report an immediate calming of their negative emotions and report experiencing a "high" associated with self-injury. This high can become addictive.

What is the relationship between NSSI and suicidal behavior? A paper reviewing research on self-harm and suicide by Hawton and James (2005) cites a risk of suicide after deliberate self-harm as between 0.24% and 4.30% (p. 892). However, their definition of deliberate self-harm does not seem to match entirely with the definition of NSSI presented above as they include in their definition attempted suicide and parasuicide.

Nock, et al. (2006) examined NSSI among adolescents and found a high rate of suicide attempts among those who engaged in NSSI. They report that, "70% of adolescents engaging in NSSI reported a lifetime suicide attempt and 55% reported multiple attempts" (p. 65). However, this study examined only whether a relationship existed between NSSI and suicide attempts and asked participants only about their NSSI behavior in the previous year. Plener, et al. (2009) examined the differences in NSSI and suicide attempts among samples of American and German students and found "important co-occurrences between suicidal behaviors and NSSI. Globally a majority of students who reported a suicide attempt also reported having engaged in NSSI" (pp. 1554–55).

Andover and Gibb (2010) looked at the relationship between NSSI, attempted suicide, and suicide intent in a sample of psychiatric inpatients. In this study, the number of NSSI episodes was significantly related to the presence and number of suicide attempts reported. More importantly, they found that a history of NSSI was associated more strongly with a history of suicide attempts than a number of other risk factors for suicide, including depressive symptoms, hopelessness, and symptoms of borderline personality disorder. NSSI and suicide ideation were similar in the strength of their association with a history of suicide attempts. Finally, they found that those who had a history of NSSI reported a significantly greater lethal intent for their most severe attempt.

However, while the research cited thus far points to a relationship between NSSI and suicidal behavior, we must keep in mind that NSSI is more common than suicidal behavior. In a study examining the co-occurrence of NSSI and suicidal behavior, Cloutier, et al. (2010) found that the co-occurrence of suicide attempts and NSSI among adolescents was 4% while "[h]alf of the adolescents presenting to emergency crisis services had self-harmed within the previous 24 hours" (p. 259).

Suicide Attempts

The single greatest predictor of death by suicide is a previous suicide attempt (Mann, 2002; Sher, Oquendo, & Mann, 2001). We will discuss in detail why this might be later in the chapter when we discuss the IPTS. However, let us first consider a number of key points. To start we must discuss what the rehearsal looks like according to the words of those who have made a suicide attempt. Then we will discuss the relationship between the method of attempted suicide and subsequent suicide, and, finally, the relationship between the frequency of suicide attempts to death by suicide.

In Their Words

What does the rehearsal look like? This question can best be examined by looking at what those who have survived suicide attempts have to say. Pavulans, et al. (2012) interviewed ten people who had made a recent nonfatal suicide attempt and found a number of themes that stood out, one of which was "being on the road towards suicidal action." This theme had to do with events prior to the suicide attempt and was subdivided into "to be or not to be" and "to pass the point of no return."

The "to be or not to be" subcategory is fairly easy to comprehend. Here the individual is making the decision as to whether they should go on living or die. One common aspect of this subcategory was the weighing of pros and cons. Here the individual considers the benefits and the disadvantages of suicide. The typical drawback cited was hurting loved ones, while the typical advantage was the cessation of pain. Interestingly enough "[t]he process of weighing pros against cons was sometimes described to generate such a high level of anxiety that getting away from these thoughts became an additional motive for attempting suicide."[2] This heightened state of anxiety and pain caused a shift of focus away from the drawback of hurting loved ones and toward the advantage of escape. As one of the patients interviewed states,

> [t]he only thing that spoke against suicide was that I'd hurt my family. The things that spoke for suicide were so many more, for instance then that my family would be better off without me, since my influence on their lives was negative. (male aged 47 years).

We will return to this notion of "better off without me" later in the chapter with our discussion of the IPTS.

From here the patients reported reaching a "point of no return." The authors indicate that this could occur following a "defined event or by an inexplicable impulse from within." They quote one patient as stating that it "simply felt like it was time." According to the testimonials reported by Pavulans and colleagues, once a patient was past this point of no return, they reported altered states of mind such as "chaos," characterized as a confused, panicked state, and "tunnel vision and turned off emotions," characterized by a preoccupation with suicide and a feeling of emotional numbness or dissociation.

Methods

What information is available on the relationship between choice of method and suicidal behavior? Giner and colleagues (2014) investigated how violent and serious suicide attempts differed from less-serious and less-violent suicide attempts. Interestingly they found that those who used more violent methods (such as a gunshot or an overdose requiring hospitalization) also reported more suicide attempts, while those who used less violent methods were less likely to report multiple attempts. Additionally, those who used violent methods were more similar to completed suicides than were less violent suicide attempters.

Bergen and colleagues (2012) examined how nonfatal self-harm relates to eventual death by suicide. Their work found that "[c]utting, hanging/asphyxiation, CO/other gas, traffic-related and other self-injury at the last episode of self-harm were associated with 1.8 to 5-fold increased risks (versus self-poisoning) of subsequent suicide" (p. 526). Furthermore, methods that involved "self-injury" had a greater risk of subsequent suicide than self-poisoning. Self-injury included the categories of hanging/asphyxiation, drowning, jumping from heights, jumping before moving object, firearms/fire-related, CO/other gas, and cutting/sharp/blunt object, whereas self-poisoning included analgesics, antidepressants/tranquillizers, and all other substances. This caused the authors to conclude that "[i]ndividuals using more dangerous methods (e.g., hanging, CO/other gas) should receive intensive follow-up" (p. 526).

Wilcox (2011) also investigated whether or not the method used in an "unsuccessful" suicide attempt predicts eventual completed suicide. The author found that certain methods were significantly related to eventual death by suicide, including hanging, drowning, firearms or explosives, jumping from a height, and gassing. In contrast, self-poisoning and cutting/piercing were not significantly related to eventual death by suicide.

As can be seen from this research on the relation between the method of attempting suicide and death by suicide, the more violent means of suicide predict eventual death by suicide. Why this may be so is discussed later in the chapter.

Frequency

Before we begin a discussion on frequency of suicide attempts and subsequent death by suicide, consider if you will the following statement taken from a news article concerning the death of Francisco Solomon Sanchez in California.

> After at least 10 documented suicide attempts spanning several years, Francisco Solomon Sanchez finally succeeded in killing himself last Friday, reports the *Pasadena Star-News* . . . Sanchez had actually jumped from the same overpass in 2003, and used prosthetic legs as a result of that failed attempt (*Huffington Post*, 2011).

Ignoring the inappropriate use of the word "succeeded," this quotation illustrates that there is occasionally a high frequency of suicide attempts prior to eventual death by suicide. What does the scientific literature have to say about frequency of attempt and death by suicide? Are multiple attempters more at risk than those with a single attempt history?

Rudd, Joiner, and Rajab (1996) compared the differences between young adults who were suicide ideators, suicide attempters, and multiple suicide attempters (that is, had made two or more attempts). Multiple attempters were found to experience more severe suicidal symptoms (such as the desire to die and a greater intensity and duration of suicide ideation).

Using self-reports and clinical interviews, Forman, et al. (2004) compared multiple suicide attempters with suicide attempters who had made only a single attempt. Those with a history of multiple attempts showed a higher level of risk factors for suicide (such as personal experience of childhood emotional abuse, and suicide in family members). They also showed more psychopathology (such as depression), more suicidality, and more pronounced decreases in interpersonal functioning. Summarizing their findings, the authors stated:

> . . . the current study demonstrates that individuals with histories of multiple suicide attempts have a particularly severe clinical profile

characterized by an extremely high degree of psychopathology, suicidality, and interpersonal dysfunction (Forman, et al., 2004).

How Might NSSI and Suicide Attempts Lead to Eventual Death by Suicide

The next question is how can we best conceptualize this "rehearsal" in a theoretical framework? The answer comes in the form of the "acquired capability for suicide," which is one of the triad of risk factors proposed by the Interpersonal-Psychological Theory of Suicide (IPTS: Joiner, 2005).

The IPTS posits that suicide occurs when three risk factors co-occur: (1) perceived burdensomeness, (2) thwarted belonging, and (3) the acquired capability for suicide. Perceived burdensomeness and thwarted belonging are two cognitions associated with the motivation to die by suicide, while the acquired capability for suicide relates specifically to the suicidal act (i.e., the actual behavior). Perceived burdensomeness is the perception that one is a burden on those around them and that others would be better off without them. Thwarted belonging is the perception that one is alone and that one has poor social support (e.g., loneliness). Both perceived burdensomeness and thwarted belonging can be cognitive distortions or they can be factual.

The acquired capability for suicide, the part of the theory most relevant to this chapter, is the ability to engage in lethal self-harm. The acquired capability for suicide requires that one become habituated to the fear of death and to the pain necessary for death by suicide. In Joiner's own words:

> It may be that few people *want* to die by suicide, but also, and perhaps more important, that even fewer people *can*. Self-injury, especially when severe, has the potential to be painful and fear inducing. Who can tolerate such high levels of pain, fear, and the like? The view taken here is that those who have gotten used to the negative aspects of suicide, and additionally, who have acquired competence and even courage specifically regarding suicide, are the only ones capable of the act—anyone else is unable to complete suicide, even if they want to (Joiner, 2005, p. 49).

The acquired capability for suicide requires that an individual both habituate to the painful, provocative experiences linked to suicide and that they also acquire the necessary knowledge about how to actually kill themselves.

In this theoretical framework, NSSI and nonfatal suicide attempts can be viewed as rehearsals for death by suicide. They allow an individual to test the waters. An individual who is still afraid of the pain necessary for suicide to occur might take to cutting or asphyxiating themselves in order to build up to the act. From there they may move beyond the fear of the pain and then test the waters with regard to fear of death, in which case nonfatal suicide attempts may occur. However, NSSI and nonfatal suicide attempts are not the only way for an individual to acquire the capability for suicide. Individuals who live more violent and pain-inducing lives will be better equipped to die by suicide then those who have not had the same violent and painful experiences. For example, an individual who has experienced childhood sexual abuse is more likely to acquire the capability for suicide than an individual who has not experienced such a painful and aversive event.

It may, therefore, be concluded that, for many suicidal individuals, in order to die by suicide, one needs to rehearse.

Notes

1. Keep in mind that by using the word "success" I am not implying that those who survive are failures.
2. This article was not paginated.

References

American Psychiatric Association. (2013). *Diagnostic and statistical manual of mental disorders* (5th ed.). Arlington, VA: American Psychiatric Publishing.

Andover, M. A., & Gibb, B. E. (2010). Non-suicidal self-injury, attempted suicide, and suicidal intent among psychiatric inpatients. Psychiatry Research, 178, 101–5.

Bergen, H., Hawton, K., Waters, K., Ness, J., Cooper, J., Steeg, S., & Kapur, N. (2012). How do methods of non-fatal self-harm relate to eventual suicide? *Journal of Affective Disorders,* 136, 526–33.

Cloutier, P., Martin, J., Kennedy, A., Nixon, M. K., & Muehlenkamp, J. J. (2010). Characteristics and co-occurrence of adolescent non-suicidal self-injury and suicidal behaviours in pediatric emergency crisis services. Journal of Youth & Adolescence, 39, 259–69.

Forman, E. M., Berk, M. S., Henriques, G. R., Brown, G. K., & Beck, A. T. (2004). History of multiple suicide attempts as a behavioral marker of severe psychopathology. *American Journal of Psychiatry,* 161, 437–43.

Giner, L., Jaussent, I., Olie, E., Beziat, S., Guillaume, S., Baca-Garcia, E., Lopez-Castroman, J., & Courtet, P. (2014). Violent and serious suicide attempters: one step closer to suicide? *Journal of Clinical Psychiatry,* 75, 191–97.

Hawton, K., & James, A. (2005). Suicide and deliberate self harm in young people. *British Medical Journal, 330,* 891–894.

Huffington Post (2011, June). Francisco Solomon Sanchez kills himself after 10 tries. Retrieved from www.huffingtonpost.com/2011/06/06/francisco-solomon-sanchez-suicide_n_872173.html

Joiner, T. E., Jr. (2005). *Why people die by suicide.* Cambridge, MA: Harvard University Press.

Mann, J. J. (2002). A current perspective on suicide and attempted suicide. *Annals of Internal Medicine,* 136, 302–11.

Nock, M. K., Joiner, T. E., Jr., Gordon, K. H., Lloyd-Richardson, E., & Prinstein, M. J. (2006). Non-suicidal self-injury among adolescents: Diagnostic correlates and relation to suicide attempts. Psychiatry Research, 144, 65–72.

Pavulans, K. S., Bolmsjo, I., Edberg, A., & Ojehagen, A. (2012). Being in want of control: Experiences of being on the road to, and making, a suicide attempt. *International Journal of Qualitative Studies on Health & Well-Being,* 7, #16228.

Plener, P. L., Libal, G., Keller, F., Fegert, J. M., & Muehlenkamp, J. J. (2009). An international comparison of adolescent non-suicidal self-injury (NSSI) and suicide attempts: Germany and the USA." Psychological Medicine, 39, 1549–58.

Rudd, M. D., Joiner, T. E., & Rajab, M. H. (1996). Relationships among suicide ideators, attempters, and multiple attempters in a young-adult sample. *Journal of Abnormal Psychology,* 105, 541–50.

Sher, L., Oquendo, M. A., & Mann, J. J. (2001). Risk of suicide in mood disorders. *Clinical Neuroscience Research,* 1, 337–44.

Wilcox, H. C. (2011). Method used in an unsuccessful suicide attempt predicts likelihood of future completed suicide. *Evidence-Based Mental Health,* 14, 16.

16

Suicide by Fire: Ethnicity as a Predictor of Self-Immolation in the United States

Steven Stack & Seth B. Abrutyn

Most of the research on suicide by fire is based on samples from Asian nations (e.g., Ahmadi, 2007; Fernando, et al., 2011; Laloe, 2004). Three countries from the Asian continent alone (India, Sri Lanka, and Iran) accounted for nearly half of the world's known published cases (Laloe, 2004), and burn centers in these three nations saw, on average, forty cases of self-immolators each year. Burn centers in other areas in the world report far fewer cases per year. No burn center in the United States, for example, has reported more than six cases of self-immolation per year (Laloe, 2004). Prevalence rates of self-immolation among patients reporting to burn centers are low in Western nations, ranging between 1% to 9%. In contrast, prevalence rates reported in Asia, the Middle East, and portions of Africa are higher, reaching 28% in some locales (McKibben, Ekselius, Girassek, et al., 2009).

The startling examples of self-immolation in Asia are often based on long-standing historical patterns and sometimes marked by links to Eastern religions. For example, the suicide by fire of Indian widows (sati) has been the subject of much scholarly work and has been the subject of many artistic representations for centuries (Lester, 2013). Like any behavioral repertoire or pattern, suicide or, more particularly, the "appropriate" means to suicide, varies culturally and regionally (Farberow, 1975) and is transmitted through various social media, including language, but also various forms of art (Kral, 1994; van Hooff, 2004). The motives for suicide by fire include dowry disputes wherein the in-laws of a wife demand additional dowry payments, demands that apparently contribute to considerable stress on Asian wives involved in these disputes (Kumar, 2003; Thombs, et al., 2007). A recent meta-analysis of nineteen studies focused on the incidence of suicide in the WHO-designated East Mediterranean region (EMR), which extends from Morocco to Afghanistan and is comprised of twenty-two nations. The pooled proportion of suicides by fire was 17.4%. Of suicides by females, 29.4% were by self-immolation, while 11.3% of the male suicides in the EMR were by the same method (Morovatdar, et al., 2013). In some areas, the incidence of self-immolation is even higher. For example, half of the suicides in Kurdistan, Iraq, are by fire, while 82% of the suicides of women in Ilam, Iraq, are by fire (Jangborbani & Sharifirad, 2005). In Iran, over 80% of female suicides are by burning, and most of these women are impoverished, illiterate, and married (Maghsoudi, et al., 2003) In contrast, in Europe and the United States, generally less than 1% of the suicides are by fire.

Given the prevalence of suicide by fire in the cultural traditions of many Eastern nations, it is hypothesized that Americans of Asian descent may be more likely to choose fire as a means of suicide than other Americans. However, no American based-study to date has explored this hypothesis.

Previous American Studies of Suicide by Fire

A search for previous studies using Medline with "suicide" as the subject and "fire" or "immolation" as keywords produced 301 hits. In order to be included in the present review, a study had to report findings on at least one case of suicide by fire in the United States. A total of seventeen studies meeting these criteria were found. The key elements are summarized in table 16-1. This research has a number of limitations.

(1) *Small non representative samples.* Nearly all of the studies, as noted in column two of table 16-1, are based on small samples of fewer than forty cases. This opens the door to the reporting of random fluctuations in the characteristics of self-immolation. In addition, it is difficult to capture patterns involving risk and protective factors. If there are few or no Asians in local samples, this ethnic risk factor may go undetected in small samples.

(2) *Local samples.* Column three of table 16-1 provides the location for each study. Most of the research is based on local samples, which may hinder the exploration of ethnic risk and protective factors.

(3) *Burn center samples.* As noted in column three of table 16-1, nearly all of the studies are based on patients presenting themselves for treatment at burn centers. This eliminates the self-immolators who

Table 16-1. Previous studies of suicide by fire in the United States: senior author/year, number of fire suicides/attempts, years of data, location, type of control group, and selected key findings.

Author (Year)	Number of suicides/suicide attempts by fire; (years of study data)	Location	Control or comparison group	Key findings
Adair (2006)	N = 2 fatal (2005)	Colorado, police files	none	Mean age = 60; females: 0%.; ethnicity: n.a.; Case A: Male, set fires and shot self; economic strain: unemployed & exhausted savings, fire destroyed house to be inherited by ex wife upon death. Case B: Male, set fires & hung self; economic strain: about to be evicted; set fire in protest of eviction. Neither case had a mental illness history. Both were complex (multi-method) suicides
Andreason (1975)	N = 14 (5 fatal) (years n.a.)	Iowa City, IA, burn center.	none	Mean age = 42; 71% female; ethnicity: n.a.; 93% mental disorder; fire selected as a punishment for sins; location: 43% at home, 57% institutionalized
Antonowicz (1997)	N = 7 (1 fatal) (1994–1995)	Allentown, PA, burn center	none	Mean age = 32; 29% female; 14% married; ethnicity: n.a.; 100% past psychiatric history; 57% previous suicide attempt; 29% alcohol/drug involvement
Daniels (1991)	N = 15 (8 fatal) (1980–1989)	Tampa, FL, burn center	none	Mean age = 31 years; 40% female; ethnicity: 72% white, 14% black, 14% Hispanic; 13% married, 60% single, 7% widowed, 20% divorced/separated; 47%Catholic, 27% Protestant, 26% unk; 7% foreign born; 60% previous mental disorder; 47% previous suicide attempts; 60% family history of mental disorder
Davis (1962)	N = 5 fatal (4 years)	Miami, FL, burn center	none	Mean age = 37; females: 60%; ethnicity: 40% black, 40% white, 20% Asian; 100% psychiatric disorder

(Continued)

Table 16-1. (Continued)

Author (Year)	Number of suicides/suicide attempts by fire; (years of study data)	Location	Control or comparison group	Key findings
Erzurum (1999)	N = 11 (3 fatal) (1987–1995)	Pittsburgh, PA, burn center	none	Mean age = 36; 36% female; ethnicity: 91% white, 9% black; 82% single, 9% widowed, 9%married; 91% lived alone; 91% mental disorder; 55% alcohol abuse; 64% previous suicide attempt; location: 81% home; economic strain: 91% unemployed;
Hammond (1988)	N = 33 (19 fatal) (1979–1984)	Miami, FL, burn center	none	Mean age = 49; 73% female; 27% white; 61% Hispanic, 12% black; health problem 21%; spouse unfaithful 12%
Krummen (1998)	N = 36 (10 fatal) (1978–1995)	Akron, OH, burn center	N = 2,237 accidental burn injuries	Mean age = n.a.; 38% female vs.27% controls; 29% vs. 7% controls died; ethnicity: n.a.; 65% vs.8% prior psychiatric diagnosis; 44% previous suicide attempt; 35% vs. 4% alcohol-related & 20% vs 2% drug-related; 65% related to failures in personal relationships; 6%physical illness
Layton (1983)	N = 5 fatal (1978–1982)	Pittsburgh, PA, burn center	none	Mean age = 45 years; 40% female; 100% white; 60% married; 60% medical illness; 80% previous mental disorder; 40% homicide/suicide; 100% at home
Modjarrad (2007)	N = 782 (163 fatal) (1994 & 2002)	National Nat'l Burn Repository (30 states)	accidental/ assaultive burn subjects	Mean age = 35 vs. 29 controls; females: 35% vs. 30% controls; whites: 52% vs. 65%; blacks: 35% vs. 20%, other races 11% vs. 15%
Nielsen (1984)	N = 32 (11 fatal)	San Diego, CA, burn unit	none	Mean age: n.a.; 44% female; ethnicity: n.a.; 88% psychiatric disorder; 66% prior suicide attempts

Pham (2003)	N = 32 (8 fatal) (1996–2001)	Sacramento CA, burn center	none	Mean age: 36; 41% female; ethnicity: n.a.; 19% married, 25% divorced; 91% previous psychiatric illness; 47% previous suicide attempt; 41% substance abuse; 67% physical illness or disability; economic stress: 67% unemployed; 16% homeless; 47% intimate partner problems
Scully (1983)	N = 15 (5 fatal) (1978–1981)	Denver, CO, burn unit	none	Mean age = 33; 60% female; ethnicity: n.a.; 100% mental disorders; 53% previous suicide attempt
Squyres (1993)	N = 17 (2 fatal) (1988–1991)	Augusta, GA, burn center	none	Mean age = 38; 59% female; 47% white, 53% black; 41% married, 29% single, 29% other; 70% psychiatric disorder; 59% substance abusers
Swenson (1990)	N = 8 attempters (1 year)	La Jolla, CA, burn center	none	Mean age: n.a.; 75% female; ethnicity: n.a.; 63% substance abusers; 38% psychiatric illness
Thombs (2007)	N = 1,466 fatal (1995–2003)	National data	suicides by all other methods	Mean age: 44 yrs for fire suicides vs. 43 years other suicides; female suicides by fire: 30.4% vs. all other methods 19.5%; ethnicity: n.a.
Tuohig (1995)	N = 15 (3 fatal) (1980–1991)	Salt Lake City, UT, burn center	16 self-mutilators	Mean age: 39 immolators vs. 29 mutilators; female: 47% vs. 88%; ethnicity: n.a.; married: 60% vs. 25%, single: 7% vs. 37%, divorced: 13% vs. 31%, separated: 13vs. 6%; psychiatric disorders 87% vs. 94%.; alcohol dependent: 47% vs. 47%; drug dependent: 33% vs. 40%; eating disorders: 0% vs. 25%; history of sexual abuse: 0% vs. 25%; unemployed: 53% vs. 69%.
mean age				Range: 31–60 years, median: 36 years
Percent female				Range: 0%–73% female, median: 41% female

died at the scene of their immolation. To the extent that persons who die and are never brought in for treatment at a burn center are different from those who survive the attempt and receive treatment, investigations restricted to burn center samples may have a bias in their results.

(4) *No control groups.* As shown in column four of table 16-1, most studies lack a control or comparison group. This often makes the identification of risk factors difficult. For example, in Miami, 61% of the suicides by fire were Hispanics (Hammond, et al., 1988), but to assess risk of suicide by fire we also need to know what percentage of all suicides in Miami were Hispanics. If 61% of suicides by all methods involved Hispanics, then being a Hispanic person would not be associated with a greater than expected number of fire-oriented suicides.

(5) *Mixed Samples of attempts and completions.* Column two of table 16-1 presents data on the number of fatal and nonfatal self-immolations in each study. Nearly all the studies mixed persons who died by self-immolation with persons who attempted suicide but did not die from their burns. To the extent that attempters and completers come from somewhat different populations (Lester, 2000), completed suicides need to be studied separately from attempters.

Only two large national investigations national were found (Modjarrad, et al., 2007; Thombs, Bresnick & Russell, 2007). The first of these is based on a compilation of 782 self-immolators (163 of which were fatal) found in the National Burn Repository (NBR). Being based on burn center data, it leaves out subjects who died on the scene of their suicides, never making it to a burn center for treatment. The findings report an average age of 35.3 years. Females make up 35% of these cases. European Americans make up 52%, while 37% are African Americans and 11.1% all other races. These data, when compared to those of other studies of overall suicide rates (Lester, 2000), indicate that women and African Americans are over-represented and European Americans are underrepresented in suicides by fire. However, no data were reported for other ethnic groups separately, including Asians, Hispanics, and Native Americans. Furthermore, there were no data on psychiatric variables and other social and economic circumstances surrounding self-immolation in the NBR.

Thombs, et al. (2007) reported on completed acts of self-immolation (n = 1,466) at the national level using data files compiled by the Centers for Disease Control (CDC). Unfortunately, not much information was extracted from these files. Nevertheless, as in the Modjarrad, et al. study, women were over-represented (given that they account for only one fourth of suicides overall), comprising 31.4% of self-immolation deaths. The Thombs, et al. study did not report on the ethnicity of the self-immolators, a focus of the present investigation.

The last column of table 16-1 provides information on the reported demographic, psychiatric, and social correlates of self-immolation. Data on ethnicity, a focal concern in the present study, is not available in most studies. In addition, only one study (Davis, 1962), restricted to just five case of suicides by fire, reports information on Asians, the ethnic group of prime interest in the present investigation. The data on suicide by fire by gender shows that there is considerable variation in these previous studies and ranges from a low of 0% to a high of 73%. The median percentage of females among suicides by fire is 41%. The range in average age is from thirty-one to sixty years. The median age for the subjects in the seventeen studies is thirty-six years old.

The present study is able to address the five limitations of the previous work by using the data in the NVDRS. The sample is large, containing over thirty thousand suicides of which 149 were by fire. This is a national sample with data from seventeen states. The large sample assists in having an adequate number of population subgroups such as Asians and other ethnic groups. The data refer to all deaths from self-immolation including those who die at the scene of the suicide and who never make it to a burn center for treatment. Furthermore, the present investigation has a control group comprised of all other suicides, enabling us to explore what factors distinguish the suicides by fire from the suicides by other methods. Finally, the study is restricted to completed suicide so that generalizations will not be contaminated by the inclusion of attempted suicides who follow somewhat different pathways to suicide.

Why Fire?

Suicide, like any symbolic act, must *mean* something to the individual who chooses one method versus another and, presumably, he or she believes it will *mean* something to loved ones or, as in the case of a Buddhist monk protesting the Vietnam War, to observers. As a performance, then, suicide by fire makes available (consciously or not) subjective meanings that the immolator believes others share because the performance contains a "grammar" and "syntax" embedded in a system "of collective representations" found in broader cultural "narratives and codes" (Alexander, 2004, p. 530). The meanings may be moral or emotional but, again, like all performances, suicides are "evaluated for their dramatic effectiveness" (ibid.) as this not only reveals the performer's authenticity, but a grave performance presses the audience to consider more deeply the performer's message.

It comes as no surprise that the hypotheses given for why fire may be the method of choice for a few suicidal individuals all point to the intersection of cultural, moral, or emotional directives and the desire to *send a message*. These include religious teachings, an expression of a sacrifice, a political protest such as the Buddhist monks protecting the Vietnam War (Crosby, Ree, & Holland, 1977), an expression of rage, and a desire for a dramatic ending (Romm, Combs, & Klein, 2008).

In Asian nations suicide by fire can be viewed as an aggressive act associated with "cultures of victims." In particular, women can show their anger and get revenge on their families (Morovatdar, et al., 2013). Indeed, in clinical and social scientific research, it has been shown repeatedly that women suffer more from sociocultural environments that foster what Lewis (1976) has referred to as "engulfed shame," or the imposition of rigid, unbending obligations and the near constant use of shame both as preemptive regulation and as a means of punishing women for not living up to these expectations. Not surprisingly, others have found that, unlike men who often repress the shame and lash out in anger, women did the opposite. They turn the anger on themselves, feel even greater shame, and thus more anger (Scheff & Retzinger, 2001). Eventually, the emotional and psychological pain may become so unbearable, along with the physical, emotional, or psychological coercion from others, that suicide becomes an option. The culturally "accepted" means of suicide conveys the victim's motives.

Much of the writing on self-immolation focuses on the Hindu rite of sati during which grieving widows throw themselves on the funeral pyres of their husbands (Lester, 2013). However, death by fire also has roots in Christian religious cultures, the main cultural roots of the United States. Fire is defined as a major source of punishment for sinners in Christian definitions of Hell. In this view, upon death, sinners will burn forever in the fires of Hell. In the Judeo-Christian tradition, flames are associated with both damnation and purification (Andreason & Noyes, 1975; Hammond, et al., 1988). Andreason and Noyes (1975) found that seeking punishment for one's perceived sins against God's will was the driving force behind the selection of suicide by fire. In colonial America, persons suspected of witchcraft were sometimes burned at the stake. Peter the Great in Russia gave members of the deviant religious sect, the Old Believers, a choice between self-immolation or being burned at the stake. They opted to burn themselves inside their church (Romm, et al., 2008). Conceivably, some persons selecting fire as a means of suicide may define themselves as sinful and are seeking punishment. In addition, death by fire is sometimes thought of as a ritual that purifies the individual, taking away sin as noted in the film *Act of the Heart*. The use of fire in suicide may, in some cases, be a form of anticipatory socialization to the perceived forthcoming pain in hell.

The empirical work on self-immolation in the United States often explains it using standard psychiatric and social categories. For example, the incidence of psychiatric disorders is typically higher among self-immolators than the general population (Erzurum & Varcellotti 1999; Krummen, James, & Klein, 1998). However, these patterns do not explain why self-immolators select fire as a means of suicide over hanging, poisons, jumping, and other methods. Mental disorders, as well as social disorders such as divorce and unemployment, are typical predictors of suicide. A meta-analysis of the best-designed investigations reported that 90% of suicides are marked by mental disorders (Cavanaugh, et al., 2003). Hence, a mental disorder may be a necessary but not sufficient condition for choosing suicide by fire. Something else is necessary, in combination with a mental disorder, in order for a person to select fire as a means for suicide.

Religious teachings may provide one answer. One American qualitative study with open-ended interviews of fourteen self-immolators found a religious-based theme underlying the selection of fire as a method. Fire produces substantial pain, and the individuals were seeking harsh punishment for their perceived sins against God (Andreason & Noyes, 1975).

Death by fire, like firearms, is nearly always fatal. Besides the cultural and emotional explanations, we cannot discount the fact that suicide is typically a choice and requires some degree of planning. The immolator is typically making a "rational" decision. In a case, presented by Shneidman (1996), in which a girl attempted to kill herself by immolation, all three aspects of the theoretical argument are present. The girl provides her own psychological autopsy and points to two major triggering events: the death of her father, with whom she had a terrible relationship, and her own failed suicide attempt by pills. Both events were discussed in the language of shame. The cultural aspect came when she addressed the "why fire" question. She had read about Buddhist monks in high school, and there was something "romantic" and "active" in the message sent. Finally, when it came down to choosing, she simply noted that it was a "sure deal." That being said, this discussion remains at the speculative and theoretical level as most studies generally do not employ an open-ended qualitative component in their research designs on self-immolation, a research component that is necessary in order to discover the reasons for selecting fire, in particular, as a method.

In the film, *Act of the Heart* (1970), Martha Hayes (Genevieve Bujold) is an impoverished woman fanatically devoted to Jesus Christ. She sings in the church choir. She falls in love with Father Michael Ferrier (Donald Sutherland), a handsome, sensual Augustinian monk who is a guest conductor for the choir. Father Ferrier makes frequent allusions to fire in his religious teachings. He speaks of how St. Augustine is often pictured with a flaming heart in his hand. He tells her that fire burns away sin. He leaves his order to be with her in a lustful relationship. She increasingly feels that she is sinful and feels guilt over a forbidden love. She immolates herself. Director: Paul Almond. Quest Pictures.

Methodology

The present investigation is based on data from the NVDRS (see chapter 8). The central dependent variable is type of suicide, a dichotomous variable comprised of suicides by fire (coded as 1), and suicides by all other methods (coded as 0). The core predictor variables involve ethnicity. The available ethnic categories in the NVDRS were each coded into a binary variable: Asian, African American, Hispanic, and Native Americans. Caucasians serve as the reference category.

Results

Table 16-2 presents the results of a simple bivariate analysis. A series of bivariate, two-by-two contingency tables were constructed. The percentage of each group's share in the total number of suicide by fire is compared to their percentage share of suicides by all other means. Asians accounted for 7.4% of all suicides by fire, whereas their share of all other suicides is only 2.1%, a statistically significant difference. African Americans were also significantly more likely to choose fire over other means of suicide compared to all other races. African Americans contributed 14.8% of the suicides by fire but only 7.4% of suicides by all other means. Females accounted for 36% of the suicides by fire versus 21.5% of the suicides by other methods, a statistically significant difference. The differences for Native Americans were not statistically significant.

Table 16-2. Comparison of the risk of suicide by fire and suicide by other means by ethnic group, gender, problems contributing to suicide, and demographic group.

Variable	Percent suicides by fire	Percent suicides by other means	Chi-square test of significance (df = 1)
Ethnicity			
Asian American	7.4%	2.1%	19.23*
African American	14.8%	7.4%	11.58*
Hispanic American	7.4%	4.9%	1.95 ns
Native American	2.7%	1.7%	0.844 ns
Gender:			
Female	36.2%	21.5%	18.91*
Problems			
Health problem	20.3%	9.4%	10.9*
Financial problem	13.4%	9.9%	2.00 ns
Job problems	10.1%	10.0%	0.001 ns
Demographics			
Married	38.9%	37.0%	0.22 ns
Widowed	6.0%	6.7%	0.092 ns
Divorced	16.8%	21.4%	1.91 ns
Separated	0.0%	0.6%	0.85 ns
Single	36.2%	32.2%	1.08 ns
Age	44.16 years	45.37 years	

* $p < .05$
ns = difference is nonsignificant

Table 16-3 provides the results of the multivariate logistic regression analysis. Controlling for the other predictors in the model, Asians were 3.61 times more likely to choose suicide by fire than were Caucasians. In addition, African Americans were 2.48 times and Hispanics 1.91 times more likely than Caucasians to choose fire as a method for suicide. Native Americans were no more likely than Caucasians to choose fire as a method for suicide. As anticipated, gender was also a significant predictor of suicide by fire. From the odds ratio, women were 2.17 times more likely than men to choose fire-based suicide.

Two problems of living were predictive of suicides by fire. The presence of health problems decreased the risk of fire suicides by 41%. Financial problems, however, increased the risk of suicide by fire

Suicide as a Dramatic Performance

Table 16-3. Ethnicity, gender, problems, and demographic predictors of suicide by fire (N = 149) vs. all other methods of suicide (N = 30,421); multiple logistic regression analysis, United States (17 states), 2003–2006, National Violent Death Reporting System.

Variable	Logistic regression coefficient	Standard error	Odds ratio
Ethnicity			
Asian American	1.28*	0.322	3.61
African American	0.908*	0.24	2.48
Hispanic American	0.647*	0.324	1.91
Native American	0.689	0.518	1.99
European American (reference)			
Gender:			
Female	0.778*	0.174	2.18
Male (reference)			
Problems			
Health problem	-0.94*	0.29	0.39
Financial problem	0.43*	0.25	1.54
Job problem	-0.01	0.28	0.99
Demographics			
Married	-0.06	0.21	0.94
Widowed	-0.33	0.42	0.71
Divorced	-0.36	0.26	0.69
Separated	-3.88	7.47	0.02
Single (reference)			
Age	0.009	0.006	1.01
Constant	-5.98*	0.275	

*$p < .05$
Nagelkerke r-squared = .034
-2 Log Likelihood = 1821.44*
Cases correctly predicted: 99.51%

by 54%. Job problems were unrelated to the risk of suicide by fire, and none of the demographic variables were able to significantly differentiate the suicides by fire from the suicides from other methods. The model correctly classified 99.51% of the cases as fire versus non-fire-based suicides.

Conclusions

The results of the present study indicate that Asian Americans are over three times more likely to choose suicide by fire than are Caucasians. In addition, controlling for other predictors, American women are more likely than men to suicide by fire. This pattern was obscured in previous research based on small, local samples and lacking in control groups.

Intimate partner problems have been tied to suicide by fire in contemporary Asia (Kumar, 2003). A recent study of Sri Lanka of fifty-one self-immolations determined that spouse or marital disharmony and related family disputes were the causes in 61% of the fire-based suicides. Only 6% of the cases were linked to mental disorders or substance abuse. Of these cases, 76% of the cases were women, and the principle precipitating factor was conflict with the spouse or lover (Fernando, et al., 2011). It is likely that, given exposure to their Asian cultural heritage, American Asians are more familiar with fire-based suicides and more likely than Caucasian Americans to have internalized the idea that fire is an appropriate method for suicide. Future work will be necessary to test this hypothesis by, ideally, distinguishing between those Asian Americans who are first generation immigrants versus those who were born in the United States. If there is a strong cultural component, it would be expected that the moral directive and cultural narrative surrounding death by fire would dissipate or be replaced by other means more common to American suicides.

That Asians and women are more at risk for suicides by fire than other groups is consistent with some artistic representations of suicide. One of the more commonly portrayed suicides by fire in art is that of a woman: Dido, Queen of Carthage. Dido's lover, Aeneas, has just left her. He has been called off to war. Dido packs up his belongings and uses them in her funeral pyre as fuel.

To the best of our knowledge, suicide by fire is only a minor theme in American art. For example, an analysis of an updated version of the database from Stack and Bowman (2012) found only seven films that involved self-immolation out of 1,665 depictions of suicide in American movies. These ranged from a silent film where the central character commits sati after the death of her husband (*The Beckoning Flame*, 1916) to a minor character in *Trespass* (1992) who dies by suicide as a result of guilt over a perceived sin (a large theft) against the church. Of the film characters who completed suicide by fire, 40% are women.

Only one is Asian. There is a synergy between film and society for this manner of suicide. The degree of attention drawn to fire-based suicides in American film largely reflects their incidence in the real world. Only 0.42% of suicides in American film are by fire. This figure parallels the percentage of such suicides in society 0.49% (149 out of 30,570) in the present study.

While suicide by fire is rare in the American cinema, future work is needed to assess the degree to which the Asian cinema portrays suicide by fire. It is plausible that a higher proportion of cinematic suicides would involve self-immolation in Asian films. In a Korean film, for example, (*Spring, Summer, Fall, Winter and Spring* 2003), a Buddhist monk dies by fire at the end of the film. He feels shame after his only pupil has been convicted of murder. It is plausible that Asian Americans may have a higher rate of exposure to Asian suicide films than other Americans. If so, there may be an artistic influence on Asian American suicide.

The finding that American women are more likely than American men to use fire as a method of suicide was reported in the one previous study of national data on completed acts of self-immolation. Thombs, et al. (2007) reported that the reasons for this gendered pattern are unknown. However, the same pattern has been found in other areas of the world, including many Asian nations (Morovatdar, et al., 2013).

The present chapter suggests that the American pattern may be interpreted from the standpoint of religious teachings regarding fire, hell, and punishment and because these individuals are more often shamed. On the one hand, American women generally score higher in religiosity than men. Women, for example, are more likely to hold religious beliefs, including those regarding an afterlife, hell, and God, than are men. Women's participation in religious practices, such as attending church, is also higher than that of men. These patterns are usually thought to be protective against suicide as noted elsewhere (Stack, 2000). However, a belief that fire purifies or is a just punishment for wrongdoing may have an appeal to religious or formerly religious women who are contemplating suicide (Andreason & Noyes, 1975).

While religious devotion protects most women from suicide, among religious women who do opt for suicide, fire may have a special attraction. This is something of an enigma. On the other hand, women are more likely to be subjected to emotional, psychological and physical coercion from partners, family members, media stereotypes, and other sources. For many women, living with shame and self-hatred, especially in the United States, is a normative situation and, unfortunately, one with potentially deadly consequences. Shame has been strongly linked to eating disorders (Scheff, 1989), for example, and shame itself has been linked to various types of violent actions, including suicide (Lester, 1997; Abrutyn & Mueller, 2014). The choice of death by fire may be a performance that expresses to the immolator and, more importantly, to her tormentors, the rage and anger that has been directed inward. Irrational as it may seem, suicide is like any act that carries symbolic meanings encoded in myth, art, and cultural narrative. The choice to burn oneself is one that conveys, consciously or not, a set of meanings to the performer and to the audience (Alexander, 2004). In any event, while fire is a rare form of suicide, American women are twice as likely as men to select it. Further work is needed to unravel the roots, one of which may involve a reaction to religious guilt, as in the films *Act of the Heart* (1970) and *Trespass* (1992), and in the qualitative empirical work of Andreason and Noyes (1975).

Finally, further work is needed to rigorously explore the meanings of suicide in Eastern religions and Eastern cultures. These social phenomena may influence persons from Asia even after they have migrated to other regions of the world. For example, the Hindu rite of Jauhar was a medieval culturally approved practice of mass suicide for people about to be overrun by Muslim invaders. When defeat by the invaders of a village or city was imminent, the cultural expectation was for the men to go out and die with honor on the battlefield while the women would die by fire on a funeral pyre. For women, suicide by fire was a way to avoid rape and dishonor at the hands of the invaders. Death was considered preferable to conquest and degradation (Adityanjee, 1994). While Jauhar has apparently not been practiced for centuries, its notion of condoning suicide when faced with dishonor may have endured in some quarters of Asia. The suicides of women over dowry rights and troubled marriages could be interpreted, in part, to protests or reactions to dishonor (Kumar, 2003). Possibly the Asian "cultures of victims," where women show their anger and get revenge on their families through suicide by fire (Morovatdar, et al. 2013), have been transported to or reinvented in the United States.

References

Abrutyn, S., & Mueller, A. (2014). The socioemotional foundations of suicide: A microsociological view of Durkheim's suicide." *Sociological Theory*, in press.

Adair, T. W., & Fisher, A. (2006). Suicide associated with acts of arson: Two cases from Colorado. *Journal of Forensic Science*, 51, 893–95.

Adityanjee, M. (1994). Jauhar: mass suicide by self-mutilation in Waco, Texas. *Journal of Nervous & Mental Disease*, 182, 727–28.

Ahmadi, A. (2007). Suicide by self-immolation: Comprehensive overview, experiences and suggestions. *Journal of Burn Care & Research*, 28, 30–41.

Alexander, J. C. (2004). Cultural pragmatics: Social performance between ritual and strategy. *Sociological Theory*, 22, 527–73.

Andreason, N., & Noyes, R. (1975). Suicide attempted by self-immolation. *American Journal of Psychiatry*, 132, 554–58.

Antonowicz, J. L., Taylor, L. H., Showalter, P., Farrell, K. J., & Berg, S. (1997). Profiles and treatment of attempted suicide by self-immolation. *General Hospital Psychiatry*, 19, 51–55.

Cavanaugh, J. T. O., Carson, A. J., Sharpe, M., & Lawrie, S. M. (2003). Psychological autopsy studies of suicide: A systematic review. *Psychological Medicine*, 33, 395–405.

Crosby, K., Rhee, J. O., & Holland, J. (1977). Suicide by fire: A contemporary method of political protest. *International Journal of Social Psychiatry*, 23, 60–69.

Daniels, S. M., Fenley, J. D., Powers, P. S., & Cruze, C. W. (1991). Self-inflicted burns: A ten year retrospective study. *Journal of Burn Care & Rehabilitation*, 12, 144–47.

Davis, J. H. (1962). Suicide by fire. *Journal of Forensic Science*, 7, 393–97.

Erzurum, V. Z., & Varcellotti, J. (1999). Self-inflicted burn injuries. *Journal of Burn Care & Rehabilitation*, 20, 22–24.

Farberow, N. L. (Ed.). (1975). *Suicide in different cultures*. Baltimore, MD: University Park Press.

Fernando, R. F., Hewagama, M., Priyangika, W. D, Range, S., & Karunaratne, S. (2011). A study on suicide by self-immolation. *Ceylon Medical Journal*, 56, 182–83.

Hammond, J. S., Ward, G., & Pereira, E. (1988). Self-inflicted burns. *Journal of Burn Care & Rehabilitation*, 9, 178–79.

Janghorbani, M., & Sharifirad, G. (2005). Completed and attempted suicide in Ilam, Iran (1995–2002). *Archives of Iranian Medicine*, 8, 119–26.

Kral, M. (1994). Suicide as social logic. *Suicide & Life-Threatening Behavior*, 24, 245–55.

Krummen, D. M., James, K., & Klein, R. (1998). Suicide by burning: A retrospective review of the Akron regional burn center. *Burns*, 24, 147–49.

Kumar, V. (2003). Burnt wives: A study of suicides. *Burns*, 29, 31–35.

Laloe, V. (2004). Patterns of deliberate self-burning in various parts of the world: A review. *Burns*, 30, 207–15.

Layton, T. R., & Copeland, C. E. (1983). Burn suicide. *Journal of Burn Care & Rehabilitation*, 4, 445–46.

Lester, D. (1997). The role of shame in suicide. *Suicide & Life-Threatening Behavior,* 27, 352–61.

Lester, D. (2000). *Why people kill themselves.* Springfield, IL: Charles Thomas.

Lester, D. (2013). Sati. In E. Colucci & D. Lester (Eds.). *Suicide and Culture,* 217–36. Cambridge, MA: Hogrefe.

Lewis, H. (1976). *Psychic war in men and women.* New York: New York University Press.

Maghsoudi, H., Garadagi, A., Jafary, G. A., Azarmir, G., Aali, N., Karimian, B., et al. (2003). Women victims of self inflicted burns in Tabriz, Iran. *Burns,* 30, 217–20.

McKibben, J. B. A., Ekselius, L., Girasek, D. C., Gould, N. F., Holzer, C., Rosenberg, M., et al. (2009). Epidemiology of burn injuries II: Psychiatric and behavioral perspectives. *International Review of Psychiatry,* 21, 512–21.

Modjarrad, K., McGwin, G., Cross, J. M., & Rue, L.W. III. (2007). The descriptive epidemiology of intentional burns in the United States: An analysis of the national burn registry. *Burns,* 33, 828–32.

Morovatdar, N. ,Moradi-Lakeh, M., Malakouti,S. K., & Nojomi,M. (2013). Most common methods of suicide in Eastern Mediterranean region of WHO: A systematic review and meta-analysis. *Archives of Suicide Research,* 17, 335–44.

Nielson, J. A., Kolman, P. B. R., & Wachtel, T. L. (1984). Suicide and parasuicide by burning. *Journal of Burn Care & Rehabilitation,* 8, 335–40.

Pham, T. N., King, J. R., Palmieri, T. L., &Greenhalgh. (2003). Predisposing factors for self-inflicted burns. *Journal of Burn Care & Rehabilitation,* 24, 223–27.

Romm, S., Combs, H., & Klein, M. (2008). Self-immolation: Cause and culture. *Journal of Burn Care & Research,* 29, 988–93.

Scheff, T. (1989). Cognitive and emotional components of anorexia: Re-analysis of a classic case. *Psychiatry,* 52, 148–60.

Scheff, T., & Retzinger, S. M. (2001). *Emotions and violence: Shame and rage in destructive conflicts.* Lanham, MD: Lexington Books.

Scully, J., & Hutcherson, R. (1983). Suicide by burning. *American Journal of Psychiatry,* 140, 905–6.

Shneidman, E. S. (1996). *The suicidal mind.* Oxford, UK: Oxford University Press.

Squyres, V., Law, E. J., & Still, J. (1993). Self-inflicted burns. *Journal of Burn Care & Rehabilitation,* 14, 476–79.

Stack, S. (2000). Suicide: A 15 year review of the sociological literature. Part I: Cultural and economic factors. *Suicide & Life Threatening Behavior,* 30, 145–62.

Stack, S., & Bowman, B. (2012). *Suicide movies: Social patterns, 1900–2009.* Cambridge, MA: Hogrefe.

Swenson, J. R., & Dimsdale, J.E. (1990). Substance abuse and attempts at suicide by burning. *American Journal of Psychiatry,* 147, 809–10.

Thombs, B. D., Bresnick, M. G., & Magyar-Russell, G. (2007). Who attempts suicide by burning? An analysis of age patterns of mortality by self-inflicted burning in the United States. *General Hospital Psychiatry,* 29, 244–50.

Tuohig, G. M., Saffle, J. R., Sullivan, J. J., Morris, S., & Lehto, S. (1995). Self-inflicted patient burns: Suicide vs. mutilation. *Journal of Burn Care & Rehabilitation,* 16, 429–36.

van Hooff, A. (2004). Paetus, it does not hurt: Altruistic suicide in the Greco-Roman world. *Archives of Suicide Research,* 8, 43–56.

17

Have Gun, Will Travel

Steven Stack

In his boyhood days, Vincent Foster lived across the street from to-be president William Clinton. For eight years the two were close friends before the Clintons moved away. Foster was a high achiever in school both in academics and athletics.[1] He graduated first in his class at law school and became a highly successful partner in an Arkansas law firm. He became close friends with Hillary Rodman (Clinton) being instrumental in hiring her at his firm. Foster reportedly was a perfectionist and would often work long hours into the night on a case he feared he might lose in court, although he seldom lost any (DeParle, 1993; Von Drehle & Schneider, 1994; Gerth & Labaton, 1995; Schmidt, 1997; Starr, 1997).

When asked by President Bill Clinton to come to Washington, he somewhat reluctantly agreed to help his friends. It involved switching careers from law in private practice with limited national visibility to politically oriented work with national exposure as White House deputy counsel. His work in Washington was during the tumultuous first six months of Clinton's presidency.

For the first time in his life, he experienced numerous failures at fulfilling the tasks assigned him. Appointments for various high-level positions in government, which he championed for President Clinton, were turned down or blocked by Congress. He reportedly took too much of the blame for failures, including "Travelgate" in which seven staff members of the travel bureau were fired because of allegations of financial malfeasance. He began to review the Whitewater scandal involving a tax underpayment for the sale of real estate in Arkansas by the Clintons. His fitness for his job was challenged in the press, with a perceived negative result on his reputation that laid the groundwork for an episode of depression. He had said that an unimpeachable reputation was of the utmost importance to him.

His wife and children had recently moved down to Washington to join him after his son had finished his year at high school. This aspect of belongingness was not enough to prevent his demise. He considered resigning, but feared the humiliation he would face if he returned to Arkansas defeated. He began to take antidepressants after confiding to his Arkansas family doctor on the phone.

On July 22, 1993, he went to work, had lunch and drove his 1989 Honda to Fort Marcy Park, a National Park seven miles outside of Washington DC. He walked seven hundred feet from his car to an old civil war cannon. Using a .38 revolver bequeathed to him by his father, he died of a gunshot wound to the mouth at approximately 4 PM.[2]

A letter, apparently one of resignation was found in his briefcase. It contains clues to his suicide. There are many references to occupational strains. As someone who placed a high value on honesty and integrity, he was apparently very troubled by the Washington scene where "ruining people is considered sport." His suicide note read:

> I made mistakes from ignorance, inexperience, and overwork. I did not knowingly violate any law or standard of conduct. No one in the White House, to my knowledge, violated any law or standard of conduct, including any action in the travel office. There was no intent to benefit any individual or specific group. The FBI lied in their report to the AG. The press is covering up the illegal benefits they received from the travel staff. The GOP has lied and misrepresented its knowledge and role and covered up a prior investigation. The Ushers Office plotted to have excessive costs incurred, taking advantage of Kaki and HRC. The public will never believe the innocence of the Clintons and their loyal staff. The WSJ editors lie without conscience. I was not meant for the job or the spotlight of public life in Washington. Here ruining people is considered sport.

As we shall see, Foster's case is representative of several of the general characteristics of persons who travel away from home and use a firearm to end their lives—a lethal location combined with a lethal method. He was: (a) male, (b) married, (c) had no history of substance abuse, and (d) his toxicology report was clean—no alcohol or nonprescription drugs were found. His decision to end his life away from his family may have been to shelter them from finding his body and having to clean up the mess from a gunshot wound. His apparent motive was occupational strain, which reportedly drove him into clinical depression. Press reports labeled the root cause of his death as "perfectionism" (e.g., DeParle, 1993).

Theoretical Framework: Lethal Location, Lethal Method and Gender Roles

As noted earlier in chapter 8, from the standpoint of the opportunity theory of location and suicide, suicide is more likely to be accomplished in the absence of motivated guardians. Motivated guardians include the significant others of a suicidal person (spouses, brothers, sisters, and children). Motivated guardians may prevent suicides in other ways besides physical interventions. There may be concern about traumatizing significant others if the suicide is performed at home because significant others are likely to discover the body.

In chapter 8, it was noted that men are more likely than women to die by suicide away from home. Data from the US General Social Surveys shows that women are five times more fearful than men on going out alone, based, in part, on the greater levels of fear of crime among women as compared with men (Snedker, 2012; Warr, 1985; Yavuz & Welch, 2010). Given that suicide is generally an act that is done alone, and that women are more afraid than men to travel alone, we would anticipate that women would be more apt to choose to die by suicide at home than away from home. In chapter 10, I showed that men are more likely than women to die by suicide in nature, which is consistent with traditional sex role stereotypes that men are more involved in outdoor activities in rural areas. For example, in a study of South Carolina, only 3.5% of women were hunters compare to 19.7% of men. Men were more likely than women to be involved in fishing, camping, hiking, and canoeing (Burger, et al., 1998; Floyd, et al, 2006). Differences in gender role socialization to outdoor activities may explain part of the gender differential in choosing locations away from home for suicide.

The higher suicide rate among men than women has been traced to a series of risk and protective factors including a higher use of guns among men, higher rates of substance abuse among males, and less help seeking and religious involvement among men compared to women (Lester, 2000; Stack, 2000). The greater preference among men than women for firearms as a means for suicide has been associated with a series of social factors, including men's greater participation than women in the military and men's greater participation in hunting and related activities with firearms, including professional and unprofessional target shooting. Anthropological work on the "American Gun Culture" has noted the greater participation in other aspects of firearms, including male dominance of the leisure pursuit of gun collecting (Kohn, 2004).

Artistic representations of firearms are also disproportionately focused on males. For example, the American Western has as one of its fundamental features skill with a firearm, and the bearer of the weapon is nearly always a male. The first Westerns of the 1920s and 1930s featured male stars, such as Harry Carey, skilled with weapons. John Wayne, the main pupil of Harry Carey, was also skilled with a firearm, such as his Winchester rifle in the movie classic, *Stagecoach*. Key television series of the 1950s and 1960s featured male stars skilled with handguns (e.g., *Have Gun will Travel*, with Richard Boone) and sometimes rifles (*The Rifleman*, with James Arness). Academic analyses of Westerns have noted a link between masculinity and the use of firearms to solve problems (Wright, 1977; Kitses, 2004). With the trend towards the demise of the classic Western with films such as John Wayne's last movie, *The Shootist* (1976), and Clint Eastwood's *The Unforgiven* (1992), the connection between maleness and skill with firearms was carried on through such genres as Hollywood's crime and police films. The *Lethal Weapon* series with Mel Gibson and the *Dirty Harry* series with Clint Eastwood connected gender and guns. Academic analyses of American crime films have strongly connected firearm use with masculinity (Clarens, 1997; Rafter, 2006).

Given artistic role models connecting masculinity with firearms, military socialization, and generalized gun culture, it is not surprising that suicidal men use firearms more than women. The degree of difference between men and women in the use of firearms in suicidal episodes (an episode includes both fatal and nonfatal attempts at suicide) is large, and the chances of an attempt with a firearm succeeding are high. For example, a study of 47,639 episodes of suicidal behavior, including 37,352 attempts and 10,287 completed suicides (Shenassa, Catlin, & Buka, 2003), determined that 96.5% of the suicide episodes that involved firearms resulted in deaths. In contrast, only 6.7% of episodes involved cutting and 6.5% of the episodes involved poisons resulted in death. Hanging/suffocation as a method was nearly as fatal as firearms with 90.4% of the persons using this method ending up dead. Using the Shenassa, et al. (2003) data, table 17-1 provides the data on the percentages of men and women who succeed in killing themselves by each method.

Comparing the figures in column three (males) with those in column four (females), we can see that women are less likely to use firearms in their suicidal acts: 20.2% of men employ guns in their episodes of suicide (either attempts or completions) compared to only 2.3%

214

Have Gun, Will Travel

Table 17-1. The percentage of suicide acts that are fatal by method and gender—Illinois, 1990–1997; 37,353 hospital admissions for attempted suicide and 10,287 completed suicides (Shenassa, et al., 2003).

Suicide method	Total: percentage of episodes using method (percent fatal)	Males: percentage of episodes by males using method (percent fatal)	Females: percentage of episodes by females using method (percent fatal)
Firearms (5,043 episodes)	10.6% (96.5% fatal)	20.2% (96.5% fatal)	2.3% (96.0% fatal)
Suffocation (2,574 episodes)	5.4% (90.4% fatal)	9.5% (90.7% fatal)	1.8% (89.0% fatal)
Crash/jump (676 episodes)	1.4% (74.0% fatal)	2.2% (76.1% fatal)	0.8% (68.8% fatal)
Exposure (to heat/cold, or electrocution) (183 episodes)	0.4% (56.3% fatal)	0.5% (64.0% fatal)	0.3% (43.5% fatal)
Cutting (2,409 episodes)	5.1% (6.7% fatal)	6.1% (9.9% fatal)	4.1% (2.6% fatal)
Poisons (35,476 episodes)	74.5% (6.5% fatal)	58.8% (11.1%fatal)	87.8% (3.9% fatal)
Other	2.7% (1.8% fatal)	2.5% (2.4% fatal)	3.9% (1.4% fatal)
Totals	47,639 episodes (10,287 fatal)	21,965 episodes (8,222 fatal)	25,674 episodes (2,065 fatal)

of women. Men are nearly ten times more likely than women to use guns in their suicidal acts. Importantly, the fatality rate is essentially the same for men and women who do use firearms (96.5% vs. 96.0%, respectively).

In contrast to the highly lethal method of firearms is the low lethality method of poisoning. Near the bottom row of table 17-1 are the figures for poisoning. Poisoning is the most common method in suicide episodes. Fully 74.5% of all suicidal episodes are by poison. However, only 6.5% of the acts of self-poisoning are successful. Still, the success rate for men for poisoning episodes is 11.1%, nearly three times the success rate for women using poisoning as a method (3.9%), illustrating an apparent greater intent to die among men than women. Importantly, 87.8% of female episodes involve the low lethality method of poisoning compared to only 58.8% of the episodes for men.

215

The present study coins the term the "Paladin Pattern" for suicide with guns away from home. Paladin was the central character, played by Richard Boone, in the hit television series, *Have Gun Will Travel*. The series had the third highest Neilson rating three years in a row, indicating that the values it expressed resonated with the public. While the Paladin Pattern does not in itself symbolize suicide (rather it symbolizes homicide), it has important parallels to suicidal events. Paladin traveled to the scene of a violent encounter with his adversaries. In like manner, persons involved in nonresidential suicides also travel to a site for the performance of their suicide. Paladin solved problems with violence. In a similar vein, suicidal persons use violence against themselves to solve their own problems (such as psychache, economic strain, and other issues). The suicidal persons studied in this chapter and Paladin both had a gun and traveled. The present chapter will use the more concise term, the Paladin Pattern for the longer expression "nonresidential firearm suicide."

The central hypothesis to be tested involves the gendered nature of the Paladin Pattern. Given the strong association between the cultural traditions of the American Western, and American society in general, men are more likely to be involved in gun culture than women, more likely to use guns in their suicides than women, and are more likely to choose to die by suicide away from home given their lesser fear of going out alone and being the victim of a crime. Taken together, the main thesis is that men are more likely than women to demonstrate the Paladin Pattern.

Methodology

As in the earlier chapters, the data are taken from the NVDRS for the years 2003–2006. Location at home was coded as 0; all other locations were coded as 1. Locations away from home included natural areas, hotels, the workplace, churches, and about two dozen very specific spots where suicides might occur. The final dependent variable is based on the intersection of place (away from home) with firearms as the method of suicide. In all there were 3,437 suicides by firearms away from home, thereby meeting both of the criteria for the Paladin Pattern. These are coded as 1. They are compared to a control group of 27,133 suicides comprising all suicides not meeting the conditions of the Paladin Pattern, coded as 0.[3,4] The 27 independent variables are those used in earlier chapters covering demographic, psychiatric, and social strain variables.

Results

In results not fully reported here, the bivariate relationship between each of five demographic, ten social strains, and twelve psychiatric strain variables was assessed using simple contingency tables. All five of the demographic variables were significantly associated with nonresidential firearm suicide, the Paladin Pattern, as were five of the ten social strain variables and nearly all of the psychiatric variables (eleven out of twelve). Table 17-2 presents some of the highlights of the significant bivariate relationships.

Males accounted for 90.3% of the Paladin suicides, but only 76.9% of all other suicides. Some 14% of the Paladin suicides involved legal problems with the criminal justice system compared to only 8.7% of

Table 17-2. Comparison of the percentage of the nonresidential firearm suicides (Paladin pattern) and all other suicides by selected variables (NVDRS, 2003–2006, 30,570 suicides).

Problem area	Percent Paladin Pattern suicide with characteristic	Percent all other suicides with characteristic	Chi-square test of significance
Demographic factors			
Male Gender	90.3%	76.9%	326.7*
Social strains			
Problem with the criminal justice system	14.0%	8.7%	100.7*
Violence perpetrator	8.6%	4.3%	125.1*
Violence victim	0.2%	0.7%	11.81*
Psychiatric morbidity			
Previous suicide attempt	8.7%	18.6%	208.51*
Current mental health treatment	17.7%	29.4%	207.8*

*$p < .05$

other suicides; 8.6% of the Paladin suicides involve violent perpetrators compared to half that many (4.3%) of other suicides. The reverse pattern holds for victims of violence who were less apt to show the Paladin Pattern. The psychiatric variables also showed the reverse pattern. For example, only 8.7% of the Paladin suicides had a previous suicide attempt compared to 18.6% of the other suicides.

Table 17-3 provides the results of the multivariate logistic regression analysis. For the purposes of clarity and brevity, only those variables that were significant predictors from the bivariate analysis were included in the multivariate model. Controlling for the other predictors, men were 2.24 times more likely than women to engage in the Paladin Pattern. Asian, Hispanic, and Native American were less likely than Caucasian Americans to follow the Paladin Pattern. Married persons were 1.39 times more likely than single persons to follow the Paladin Pattern. Each year of age decreased the odds of a Paladin Pattern by .04%.

Turning to social strains, three criminological strains were able to differentiate the Paladin from the non-Paladin cases of suicide. From the odds ratio, persons under strain from the criminal justice system were 1.35 times more likely than their counterparts to engage in the Paladin Pattern. Being a perpetrator of a violent crime enhanced the odds of a Paladin Pattern by 1.50 times. In contrast, being the victim (not the offender) in a violent crime decreased the risk of the Paladin Pattern by 71%.

Psychiatric variables tended to lower the odds of the Paladin Pattern: alcohol present (lower by 13%), opiate present (lower by 57%), reported alcohol abuse (lower by 33%), reported substance abuse (lower by 27%), depression (lower by 15%), a previous suicide attempt (lower by 42%), mental health problem (lower by 13%), and in current treatment (lower by 22%). Amphetamine use was not significantly related to the Paladin Pattern.

Only one psychiatric factor acted as a risk factor for the Paladin Pattern. Among those testing positive for marijuana the probability of the Paladin Pattern was 52% or 1.52 times higher. Finally, Paladin suicides were 1.4 times more likely than others to leave a suicide note.

The model as a whole provided a good fit, and a total of 88.76% of the cases were correctly classified.

Table 17-3. Multiple logistic regression analysis.

Variable	Logistic regression coefficient	Standard error	Odds ratio
Demographic			
Gender: male = 1	0.8*	0.06	2.241
Ethnicity			
Asian American	-0.42*	0.15	0.65
African American	-0.02	0.06	0.97
Hispanic American	-0.34*	0.09	0.3
Native American	-0.45*	0.16	0.63
Caucasian Americans = reference			
Marital Status			
Married	0.33*	0.04	1.39
Widowed	-0.17	0.1	0.83
Divorced	0.05	0.05	1.05
Single = reference			
Urban (location of suicide)	-0.32*	0.04	0.72
Age	-0.003*	0.001	0.996
Social & Related Problems of Living			
Death of a loved one	-0.04	0.08	0.95
Legal problem with criminal justice	0.3*	0.05	1.35
Victim of violence	-1.23*	0.42	0.29
Violence perpetrator	0.4*	0.07	1.5
Health problem	-0.46*	0.05	0.62
Psychiatric Morbidity			
Alcohol present	-0.13*	0.04	0.87
Marijuana present	0.42*	0.1	1.52
Cocaine present	-0.13	0.1	0.87
Opiate present	-0.82*	0.1	0.43
Reported alcohol problem	-0.39*	0.06	0.67
Reported substance abuse problem	-0.3*	0.06	0.73
Depression	-0.15*	0.04	0.85
Previous suicide attempt	-0.54*	0.06	0.58
Any mental health problem	-0.13*	0.06	0.87
In current treatment	-0.24*	0.07	0.78
Suicide note	0.34*	0.04	1.4
Constant	-2.29*	0.08	

*$p < .05$
Nagelkerke r-squared = .085
-2 Log Likelihood = 20157.38*
Cases correctly predicted: 88.76%

Conclusion

The present study focused on a combination of method and location, which suggests a high level of intent to die—firearms combined with a location away from home. The findings offer a window into the issue concerning which suicidal groups in society are the ones most determined to die.

Three broad variable sets were explored in searching for predictors of nonresidential firearm suicides, or the Paladin Pattern of "have gun will travel." As predicted, men were more than twice as likely as women to follow the Paladin Pattern. Gender role norms and expectations offered a partial interpretation of the gendering of the Paladin pattern. Married persons were 39% more likely than single individuals to follow the Paladin Pattern, which can be interpreted from the standpoint of the opportunity theory of suicide location. People may choose the Paladin Pattern in order to prevent interference by motivated guardians with the suicide performance or to shelter loved ones from finding the body.

The Paladin Pattern was significantly less likely to be found among persons with psychiatric problems. For example, persons with a past history of attempted suicide were 42% less likely to carry out a nonresidential firearm suicide. Given the emphasis on mental disorders as a cause of suicide in suicide research (e.g., Lester, 2000; Stack, 2000), one might be puzzled that a group with a relatively high intent to die (guns, away from home) would be less likely to be marked by psychiatric problems. This particular finding is in need of future theoretical and empirical work. It may be that certain social strains may trump mental disorders in the etiology of some important subgroups of suicides.

There are some implications for Joiner's theory of interpersonal suicide. Joiner (2005) argued that three conditions need to occur simultaneously in order for the probability of suicide to increase: thwarted belongingness (e.g., divorce), perceived burdensomeness, and the acquired capability for suicide. The acquired capability for suicide refers to a set of variables such as fearlessness regarding death and suicide and becoming accustomed to pain. Paladin suicides reflect a strong intent to die. Being a perpetrator of violence was linked to the Paladin Pattern. Previous research on the acquired capability for suicide has often failed to find a link to suicide attempts, but it has largely used attitudinal measures (with items such as "The best part of hockey games are the fights") rather than actual experience with violence. Actual experience with violence or being ready for violence (carrying a gun) is linked with the probability for attempting suicide (Stack, 2014). The present results also use a behavioral measure of violence (violence perpetration) and found it predicted highly lethal suicide stages (guns with travel).

Notes

1. He stood 6' 4".
2. For a critical review see Ruddy (1997)
3. It should be noted that suicides in jails or prisons, while involving trouble with the law, are not included as nonresidential suicides with firearms. Suicides in jails are generally carried though hanging, since it is difficult for prisoners to gain access to firearms or access to the means for other methods of suicide. (Tartaro & Lester 2009)
4. As before, since the dependent variable is a dichotomous variable, logistic regression techniques are appropriate. (Pampel 2000)

References

Burger, J., Sanchez, J., Whitfield-Gibbons, J., & Gochfeld, M. (2998). Gender differences in recreational use, environmental attitudes, and perceptions of future land use at the Savannah River site. *Environment & Behavior,* 30, 472–86.

Clarens, C. (1997). *Crime movies: An illustrated history.* New York: DaCapo.

DeParle, J. (1993). A life undone—A special report: Portrait of a White House aide ensnared by his perfectionism. *New York Times,* August 22.

Floyd, M. F., Nicholas, L., Lee, I., Lee, J. H., & Scott, D. (2006). Social stratification in recreational fishing participation. *Leisure Studies,* 28, 351–68.

Gerth, J., & Labaton, S. (1995). Whitewater papers cast doubt on Clinton account of a tax underpayment. *New York Times,* August 6,

Joiner, T. (2005). *Why people die by suicide.* Cambridge, MA: Harvard University Press.

Kitses, J. (2004). *Horizons West: Directing the Western from John Ford to Clint Eastwood.* London, UK: British Film Institute.

Kohn, A. A. (2004). *Shooters: Myths and realities of America's gun culture.* New York: Oxford University Press.

Lester, D. (2000). *Why people kill themselves.* Springfield, IL: Charles C. Thomas.

Pampel, F. (2000). *Logistic regression.* Thousand Oaks, CA: Sage.

Rafter, N. (2006). *Shots in the mirror: Crime films and society.* New York: Oxford University Press.

Ruddy, C. (1997). *The strange death of Vincent Foster: An investigation.* New York: Free Press.

Schmidt, S. (1997). Starr probe reaffirms Foster killed himself. *Washington Post,* October 11, p. A1.

Shenassa, E. D., Catlin, S. N., & Buka, S. L. (2003). Lethality of firearms relative to other suicide methods: A population based study. *Journal of Epidemiology & Community Health*, 57, 120–24.

Snedker, K. (2012). Explaining the gender gap in fear of crime. *Feminist Criminology*, 7, 75–111.

Stack, S. (2000). Suicide: A 15-year review of the sociological literature. Part I. Cultural and economic factors. *Suicide & Life Threatening Behavior*, 30, 145–62.

Stack, S. (2014). Differentiating suicide ideators from attempters: Violence. *Suicide & Life Threatening Behavior*, 44, 46–57.

Starr, K. (1997) The Starr report on the death of Vincent Foster. http://www.fbicover-up.com/starreport.htm (accessed June 27, 2014)

Tartaro, C., & Lester, D. (2009). *Suicide and self-harm in prisons and jails*. New York: Lexington Books.

Von Drehle, D., & Schneider, H. (1994). Foster's death a suicide. *The Washington Post*, July 1, p. A1.

Warr, M. (1985). Fear of rape among urban women. *Social Problems*, 32, 238–50.

Wright, W. (1977). *Sixguns and society: A structural study of the western*. Chicago, IL: University of Chicago Press.

Yavuz, N., & Welch, E.W. (2010). Addressing fear of crime in public space: Gender differences in reaction to safety measures in train transit. *Urban Studies*, 47, 2491–2515.

18

Unusual Suicides

Steven Stack

The field of deviant behavior is based on the study of actions that are against society's norms and are statistically infrequent, such as addiction, alcoholism, corporate price fixing, security fraud, homicide, and suicide. However, within each modality of deviance, there are unusual cases that are particularly against society's norms or extremely uncommon. Serial killers, mass murderers, and murders combined with other offenses such as torture or kidnapping are illustrations of deviance within the deviant act of homicide. Suicide is against society's norms and is also statistically infrequent (Clinard & Meier, 2004; Thio, 2006). Unusual cases of suicide constitute a form of deviance within deviance but, to date, there has been no systematic study of such cases. The present chapter focuses on deviant and unusual cases of suicide. The definition of what is unusual or deviant is left up to the authors writing research articles, many of which are by persons working close to the everyday reality of suicide, such as coroners and medical examiners.

The study of unusual or deviant behavior within suicidal behavior is important for a variety of reasons. First, a new, unusual suicide method may, in time, become a major method of suicide. One such possibility is suicide by inhaling the vapors of dry ice in an enclosed area. In a related vein, unusual suicides in a specific locale or country may signal an oncoming epidemic of such suicides through the process of contagion. For example, charcoal burning was an unusual method of suicide in Asia. A well-publicized suicide of a celebrity using charcoal burning was associated with more than a 400% increase in suicide by that method in South Korea (Chen, et al., 2014). Charcoal burning has now become even more common throughout Asia, but it is still uncommon in other parts of the world.

Second, unusual aspects of the suicide can assist officials in determining the cause of death. Forensic abnormalities in the staging of suicide can lead medico-legal authorities to misclassify some suicides as homicides or accidents. For example, in the vast majority of cases of firearm suicide, only one shot is fired. Unusual cases of suicide do occur where the individual shoots himself multiple times before achieving his goal of death. Inexperienced coroners without knowledge of such deviant cases might automatically label such cases as homicides.

Wound site is another issue in firearm suicides. While the vast majority of gunshot suicides to the head are in the front or side of the head, about 5% are to the back of the head. Coroners and lawyers sometimes assume a person with a gunshot to the back of the head has to be an "execution style" homicide, a common error (Stack & Wasserman, 2009). In some instances, the suicidal person may try to stage their performance so that it will look like a homicide, perhaps to get an adversary charged with murder.

Third, analysis of deviant methods and performances of suicide may provide a window into where and by whom new and creative formats for the performance arise. Are the new formats for suicide developed more by men or women? Do they come more from the developed or less developed world? Are they a function of differential opportunities for the new format such as access to pesticides or poisonous creatures such as snakes or spiders? To the best of the present writer's knowledge, this is the first analysis of a large sample of deviant cases of suicide—deviance within deviance.

Methodology

A search for unusual instances of suicide was conducted using Medline.[1] The search terms were the subject "suicide" combined with the keyword "unusual." This produced 516 hits. The first one hundred articles were reviewed. In order for an article to be included it had to report one or more completed suicides. Articles on suicide attempts or ideation were excluded. For example, an article on the unusual case of a woman who repeatedly, over the years, tried to kill herself by swallowing a thermometer was omitted. A twenty-year-old German male who attempted to kill himself through a snake bite but was rescued, was excluded. A total of eighty-six articles of the one hundred reviewed met the criterion. These contained 113 cases of unusual suicides in articles dating from 2003 to 2014. The present study did not enter into the analysis with a predetermined set of categories of types of unusual suicides. Instead, categories of the unusual were created from the reported cases.

Results

The first task of the analysis was to formulate a qualitative taxonomy of what researchers and medical examiners consider to be unusual suicides. A majority concerned a method of suicide considered atypical. Most of the 113 cases could be grouped by method of suicide into three broad categories: (1) violent methods (firearms, cutting and piercing, electrocution, explosions, fire, and hanging), (2) nonviolent methods (gases and vapors, suffocation using plastic bags and other methods not involving hanging, and poisons), and (3) complex suicides (involving two or more methods planned in advance or carried out spontaneously).

Exactly what makes a suicide by a particular method unusual varies among the cases. However, a statistically infrequent aspect of the suicide method is typically enough for the case to be considered unusual. A relatively large number of gunshot wounds, number of cuts or stabbings, number of different locations of wounds, and number of poisons used are common ways in which researchers define the unusual. A fourth category is that of other unusual suicides wherein some characteristic other than method is the focus of deviance.

Table 18-1 provides data on the number of unusual suicides in each category of the taxonomy. The first two categories (violent and

Table 18-1. Number of suicides in each category of the taxonomy (113 cases of unusual suicides, 2003–2014, described in 86 articles).

Category	Subcategories	Number of unusual suicides
Violent methods		
	Firearm	21
	Hanging	14
	Cutting & piercing	13
	Electrocution	2
	Fire & burns	2
	Explosions	4
	Jumping & falling	2
	Crushing	1
Nonviolent methods		
	Gases and vapors including CO, helium, nitrogen	18
	Suffocation (nonhanging) including tape, plastic bags	11
	Poisons	6
	Exposure (to cold)	1
Complex suicides	Complex suicides	14
Other unusual suicides	Odd circumstances to an otherwise regular suicide event	4

nonviolent methods) involve just one principal method. There were a total of fifty-nine cases of violent methods of suicide that were deemed unusual: twenty-one cases involving firearms as the principal method, fourteen hangings, thirteen by cutting and piercing, and two electrocutions. The second broad category, suicides involving nonviolent methods, included eighteen cases by gases and vapors, eleven by suffocation by means other than hangings, and six suicidal acts involving unusual cocktails of poisons. The third major category, complex suicides, involved between two and six methods. For example, in one instance, an individual shot himself the instant before driving his car into oncoming traffic. Finally there was a residual category where the circumstances surrounding the use of a single method enable it to meet the requirements for being unusual.

Unusual Suicides Using Violent Methods

The definition of what constitutes a violent suicide method follows previous conceptual work (Stack & Wasserman, 2005) and included firearms (handguns, shotguns, rifles and home-made firearms), hanging, cutting and piercing, electrocutions, fire and burns, explosions, jumping from high places such as bridges or tall apartment buildings, and crushing. There were a total of fifty-nine cases of violent methods of suicide. Several violent methods had only a few cases: two jumping, two fire/burns, two electrocutions, and one crushing.

Some extremely rare and unusual forms of violent suicide are missing, including being torn apart and/or eaten by a wild animal, such as a recorded case of a woman who climbed over the fence of a lion's cage at a zoo (Arun, et al., 2010). In addition, among the 113 cases at hand, none were found to have jumped off a bridge holding a child or one's pet, although rare cases have occurred in the past (Stack, 2014).

Unusual Firearm Suicides

There were twenty-one unusual suicides involving firearms as the sole means of suicide. Three cases from Czechoslovakia involved multiple gunshots, including two shots to the head. Homicides often involve multiple gunshot wounds, and so more information is often necessary to differentiate suicides from homicides. This information includes the presence of any suicide note and interviews with next of kin regarding the mental health of the deceased. Such cases represent a challenge to medico-legal authorities. The site of the wound is another criterion for the unusual. One case involved an execution style gunshot wound to the back of the head, typically thought to be a sign of homicide. In many unusual firearm suicides, extra investigative work is involved in determining if the death is a suicide or homicide.

Several firearm suicides were deemed unusual due to the presence of a homemade device serving as a gun. Nearly all firearm suicides are carried out using store-bought, manufactured guns, but a few individuals crafted their own weapons. A forty-three-year-old automobile mechanic was found dead of an apparent gunshot wound to the head in a bathroom at his workplace (Cuncliffe & Denton, 2008). Since investigators found no handgun or long gun in the bathroom, they initially believed the case to be a homicide. Afterward, while a worker was cleaning the stall, a device was found and identified as a homemade zip gun. It was small (three inches) and did not have the appearance of a typical firearm (it looked like a misplaced spark plug). It had been overlooked by investigators.

Unusual Suffocations: Hangings

In the United States in 2005, 22.2% of all suicides were by suffocation, and most of these are by hanging (deRoux & Leffers 2008). In many European nations, hanging is also the most common method of suicide. In Poland, 91.2% of male suicides are by hanging (Ajdacic-Gross, et al., 2008). Nevertheless, circumstances surrounding the style of hanging are sometimes unusual.

A thirty-four-year-old Bulgarian man staged his suicide by what was considered an unusual manner of hanging. He positioned his neck between two branches of a cherry tree that were v-shaped. The dead body hung from these branches with the feet 50 cm. off the ground (Doichinov, et al., 2008).

A rare form of double suicide was reported from Croatia. Approximately 1% of suicides are pacts or double suicides, of which nine out of ten involves male-female pairs. Hanging is an extremely rare method in suicide pacts. Two unemployed men in their twenties, close friends, hung themselves on the same tree in the backyard of one of the men (Marcikic, et al., 2011). Both had been drinking heavily in a pub before their suicidal act. One had been a psychiatric outpatient a few years prior to the double suicide. The other had just written about a sexual encounter with his girlfriend in his notebook.

Unusual Cutting and Piercing Suicides

There were a total of thirteen cases of suicides deemed unusual that involved cutting or piercing as the sole method of suicide. Many cases involved multiple cuts or piercings. These are often a sign of homicides in which the assailant has to wound the victim many times before he dies or where the assailant wishes to inflict as much pain on his adversary as possible. In such cases, additional investigation is often needed, such as a search for a suicide note and interviews with significant others of the deceased to determine suicidal intent.

A sign of a suicide by cutting is the presence of superficial wounds, which may be taken as warm-ups or confidence-building exercises before more fatal cuts are undertaken. Some suicides involve the use of great force or strength. Two cases involved driving a long kitchen knife deep into the skull of the individual. One blade was forced so hard that it broke off at the handle. Medications, in rare cases, can cause psychotic symptoms. One young man in France, on antimalaria medications taken for a trip to Africa, drove a large kitchen knife more than ten inches long into his skull through his own forehead. These types of wounds are generally forensic markers indicative of homicides. If cuts are combined with poison or other methods of suicide, they are categorized as complex suicides.

One subcategory of suicides by cutting and piercing are suicides by engineers. Some cases were found where the suicide built a complicated device or contraption to end his life. An eighty-year-old man in Australia built a complex apparatus designed to propel the side of his head into a metal bolt tightly secured to the floor. A very heavy metal weight on a rope was raised over a beam on the ceiling using a rope and pulley attached to the ceiling beam. The weight dangled over a 107 mm heavy bolt tightly screwed into the floor. The man placed his head over the bolt and used a kitchen knife to cut the rope (Austin, et al., 2012).

Suicide by Saws

Six cutting-oriented suicides were deemed unusual since the cutting instrument was not the typical knife. Several were found where a chainsaw was employed including one where an engineer designed her own guillotine-like device to guide the saw. Another involved an opportunistic chainsaw suicide at work by a man employed as a lumberjack. Others involved men (and one woman) at home, making use of table saws and band saws in their home workshops. In most cases these suicides involved men who had skills using these cutting devices, including backgrounds as carpenters or lumberjacks, but there were exceptions.

As noted, the number of cuts or stab wounds and the number of parts of the body that are cut or stabbed is a consideration in deeming a suicide event unusual. For example, a forty-three-year-old Italian woman with no history of mental disorders stabbed herself nine times in five different areas of the body. She was careful to stage her suicide in the bathtub to contain the blood.

Unusual Violent Suicides Using Motor Vehicles

The usual method in most suicides involving motor vehicles is marked by running a hose pipe from the exhaust to the inside of the vehicle, or the suicide leaves the car running in an enclosed space such as a garage (Straka, et al., 2013a). These are classified as nonviolent suicides. However, in some cases the car is used in violent crashes or as a tool for a hanging or other means of violent suicide.

In one case, a thirty-six-year-old man in Germany decapitated himself using his car. He tied one end of a rope to a tree. He then entered his van and buckled up with his seat belt. He put the noose at the other end of the rope around his neck. He then turned on the engine, put his foot on the pedal, accelerated his car, and removed his head. He had marked the spot on the ground beforehand where the rope would tighten (Blasser, et al., 2013). The man had led a double life with a sexual motivation and had suffered depressive episodes. In another deviant case, a complex suicide with two methods, a man was speeding in his car. He shot himself in the head an instant before crashing into oncoming traffic.

Unusual Electrocutions

Electrocution is a rare form of suicide. The tools for electrocution are widely available given the widespread availability of electricity in the home and elsewhere. However, few people take advantage of this means for suicide. There were only two cases of unusual suicides by electrocution. One subject, a Malaysian schoolboy, simulated the death penalty in the criminal justice system by means of an improvised electric chair. The victim strapped himself into a household kitchen chair, which had armrests. He fastened stripped electric wires to both of his wrists, which were wrapped around the arms of the chair. He then extended his foot to flick a switch to turn on the electricity (Murty, 2008).

This case of apparent imitation of capital punishment by electrocution for staging a suicide appears unique. However, there is a connection between methods of capital punishment and methods of suicide. Some forms of capital punishment have parallels to methods used in modern-day suicides. This is especially the case for hanging, a method of execution and also one of the most common methods of suicide in the modern world (Ajdacic-Gross, et al., 2008). Those who inject poisons into their systems are involved in an act similar to capital punishment using lethal injections. Suicide using firearms, a popular method in the United States, has a parallel to execution by firing squad. The use of these methods suggests that the suicides may be punishing themselves for bad behavior on their part.

Some forms of execution have not caught on, however, and are not represented even in the unusual cases in the present study. Crucifixion has remained essentially unknown in the suicide literature. Crucifixion, a common method of capital punishment in Biblical times and recently practiced by Islamic extremists, is a painful method, and it takes the individual a long time to die through this means. These features, plus logistic difficulties, act as deterrents to using crucifixion as a suicide method. The guillotine served as a major instrument of capital punishment for a period, including the decades surrounding the French Revolution in France and parts of Europe. As noted, there are several cases in the present study of guillotine-like devices used in suicides.

Unusual Suicides by Fire and Burns

Suicide using fire is an especially rare form of suicide. It accounts for less than one percent of the suicides in the United States and most other nations and localities (see chapter 14). Nevertheless the circumstances surrounding suicide by fire can be unusual. A twenty-one-year-old female in Colorado drove her automobile into the back roads of rural ranchlands. From forensic reconstruction of evidence, she apparently poured a can full of gasoline into the trunk, climbed in, locked the hood and lit her cigarette lighter. She apparently died of smoke inhalation before she was severely burned. Investigators found a possible link to the media. The woman played CD's by her favorite hip-hop group. Three of the songs dealt with locking a girl inside the trunk of a car. The woman had a history of depression, had made a previous suicide attempt by pills, and was obese, weighing over two hundred pounds (Adair, et al., 2003).

In another case, a building worker attempted suicide by jumping into a cement truck. He was ultimately fished out of the cement, but cement causes serious burns on human skin. The worker died from the burns twelve days later in intensive care in a Italian hospital (Catalano, 2013).

Explosions as Unusual Suicide Events

There were four cases of suicide by explosions in the present sample. This method of suicide is, at present, exceedingly rare (if we omit suicide bombers). Cases in the present analysis included one by a male with a hand grenade and one disconnecting the gas main to his house. The latter case is noteworthy since millions of people who heat their homes with natural gas have this means of suicide at their disposal. The fifty-five-year-old Canadian man disconnected the natural gas connection to his furnace. The ensuing explosion leveled his home and left only one wall standing. The man had a history of several failed suicide attempts (by other methods), and several personality and psychiatric disorders. He was also a heavy smoker (Demellawy & Fernandez, 2007).

An analysis of suicide movies found examples of suicide by this method (Stack & Bowman, 2012). This particular form of suicide by explosions could become a danger to public safety, especially if practiced in apartment complexes, where an explosion could set off a chain reaction, resulting in deaths and injuries to many people.

Unusual Cases Using Nonviolent Methods of Suicide

In all, there were fifty cases of unusual suicides that involved nonviolent methods. These included suicides by gases and vapors, suffocation (other than hangings), poisons, and one by exposure to cold. Generally, unlike most violent methods, such as firearms, cutting and explosions, there is little or no blood involved in many nonviolent methods. Such suicides generally represent fewer problems for medico-legal authorities in differentiating suicides from homicides. Homicides using gases or vapors are considerably less common than homicides using guns or knives. However, there can be serious problems in differentiating many of these nonviolent suicides from accidents, especially those from poisons.

Unusual Suicides with Gases and Vapors

There were a total of eighteen unusual suicides by gases and vapors. Three involved carbon monoxide and carbon dioxide. A twenty-five-year-old male used helium in a copycat suicide in the United Kingdom

(Gunnell, et al., 2012). Another person, on an oxygen-based life support system in a hospital, managed to redirect the oxygen into a medication tube inserted in his arm. One case of suicide by gas involved a new method employing industrial-strength nitrogen gas. A German student, on a three-day biking tour in the Slovak Republic, had brought his scuba gear with him. On the last day of the tour, he reclined on his bed in his hotel, naked. He fastened his scuba mask on. It was connected to a six-liter tank filled with high-pressure nitrogen gas. He died within minutes. There was only one previous similar case in the medico-legal literature using nitrogen as a method for suicide (Straka, et al., 2013b).

A Japanese man was found dead inside his car. There were signs that fifty kilograms (about 110 lbs) of dry ice had been brought to the car. Toxicology tests determined that he died of carbon dioxide poisoning from the decomposition of the dry ice inside the locked car. A clay cooking stove was in the car, but had not been used. Possibly this was a backup plan in case the dry ice method did not work. A simulation was carried out using a car under the same conditions. Carbon dioxide concentration increased to 22% and the oxygen concentration decreased to 16% in just twenty minutes (Norimine, et al., 2009). This is the only instance of suicide using dry ice that could be found. Given wide availability of dry ice in many nations, this particular finding is of some concern since the idea of using dry ice as a painless method of suicide could be contagious.

Suicide and Charcoal Burning

This set of twelve unusual case reports was dominated by early instances of suicide by charcoal burning inside an enclosed area. The first noted apparent suicide from carbon monoxide gas from burning charcoal in an enclosed airspace was in 1998 in Hong Kong. This method spread and helped raise the suicide rate in both Hong Kong and Taiwan by over 20%. It was still largely unknown in South Korea until 2007 when the first case appeared. In South Korea in 2007, charcoal burning was considered an unusual method (Huh, et al, 2009). However, after substantial media coverage of this new method in South Korea, its incidence has become more common and is no longer considered unusual (Chen, et al., 2014; Ji, Hong, Stack, & Lee, 2014). While common in Asia, charcoal burning is often viewed as an unusual method in Europe, especially in Eastern Europe (Katedry, et al., 2013).

Unusual Nonhanging Suffocation Suicides

There were eleven cases of unusual suicides carried out by these non-violent methods. The majority of nonhanging suffocation suicides use a plastic bag placed over the head (deRoux & Leffers, 2008). There were three cases of plastic bag suffocation suicides in the present sample. Other practices of suffocation included the use of toilet paper and washrags to block the passage of air through the nose and mouth. Two plastic bag suicides were staged to look like homicides.

Duct Tape Suffocation

An unusual and apparently relatively new method of suffocation is by duct tape. One report cited two cases in New York City of suicides using duct tape. A fifty-two-year-old male, depressed over gambling debts, checked into a hotel to stage the act after spending the night with his girl-friend. Another case involved a forty-seventy-year-old man diagnosed with paranoid schizophrenia. He wrapped duct tape around his head, covering both the nose and the mouth, staging the event in his basement. At least three other previous reports of suicide by duct tape have been reported in the literature (deRoux & Leffers, 2008). Fortunately, this method of suicide has not been the subject of major media attention. The authors noted that, before the publication of *Final Exit*, a book advocating suicide through putting a plastic bag over one's head, only 1.5% of the suicides in New York City used that method. After the publication of the book, fully 5% of the suicides in the city followed that method.

Suicide as Staged Homicides

There were two case reports of persons staging their suicides to make them look like homicides. An apparently altruistic sixty-one-year-old man in Italy had children with financial difficulties. He took out a life insurance policy that would be collectable only if his death was natural or a result of an accident or homicide. He managed to tie his hands behind his back after placing a plastic bag over his head. However, his efforts failed to convince the authorities, and his death was ruled a suicide (Aloja, et al., 2011).

The trick behind this technique of tying hands behind one's back after securing a plastic bag over one's head were disseminated through a film (*The Life of David Gale*, 2003) in which a woman uses the same technique, It is not clear if the man from Italy found the idea from the film, but the film was found at the scene of a similar suicide in France (Saint-Martin, et al., 2009).

Poisons

Six suicides by poisoning were deemed unusual. These often involved unusual cocktails combining different varieties of poisons. The poisoning suicide of a fifty-year-old anesthesiologist in Italy was seen as an unusual case because of his innovative use of lethal drugs. One poisoning in the United Kingdom was labeled unusual because the seventy-seven-year-old male found the recipe on the Internet (Gunnell, et al, 2012).

Exposure

There was only one case of suicide by exposure. A seventy-four-year-old German female climbed into a large rain barrel next to her house. She perished from hypothermia in the freezing weather (Doberenz & Madea, 2013). This method of suicide, although widely available in much of the world, is apparently rarely used.

Complex Suicides

Complex suicides are considered unusual since they involve two or more methods. A person may take poison and then jump off a cliff, as did a young man in Rocky Mountain National Park (Evans, 2010). Complex suicides account for a small proportion of all suicides, between 1.5% and 5.6% of all completed suicides (Jungman, et al., 2011). Seventeen complex suicides were labeled unusual in the 113 cases in the present sample.

Most complex suicides involve two or three methods, but a forty-four-year-old Serbian man used six. He staged a suicide at night in a field in his automobile. He drank insecticide, swallowed hydrochloric acid, cut his wrists multiple times with a razor, cut his neck, and pounded a screwdriver into his skull. He apparently rolled out of his car into the cold to further ensure his death, and hypothermia contributed to his suicide. He had no record of mental disorder. He wrote a note asking that the police tell his wife that he died in a car accident (Petkovic, et al., 2011).

A forty-year-old man in Serbia was the offender in a murder-suicide. He shot himself in the head with a rifle, but survived. He face was disfigured, and doctors implanted a tube in his neck to facilitate breathing. Six months later, in his prison cell, he stuffed the tube with paper and hung himself from the ceiling of his cell. This combination of two suicide methods (choking plus hanging), together with a set of unusual circumstance (a homicide followed by an attempted suicide with a rifle), qualified his event as being unusual. In particular, it is rare to survive a rifle shot to the head (Vapa, et al., 2012).

An unusual complex suicide with a starter's pistol took place in Italy. A sixty-seven-year-old retired dentist used a local anesthetic to facilitate cutting his wrists and also cut his throat. He then stabbed himself in the abdomen. To add to the unusual nature of his suicide, he next shot himself with a modified starter's pistol. The shooting event took place in his bedroom. The dummy handgun had been transformed into a deadly firearm through drilling (dentists have the necessary skills and tools) and other modifications performed by the dentist. He had been reportedly depressed over the separation from his wife and was living alone at the time of his suicide (DiNunno, et al., 2009).

A determined forty-three-year-old man in Germany, beset with financial problems, set his house on fire and shot himself twice, falling on a pile of ammunition boxes. Some of the ammunition exploded during the blaze and caused additional wounds to his burnt body. A Slovak man shot himself in the head an instant after swerving his car across the road and crashing into a truck (Straka, et al., 2013a).

In France, most complex suicides involve young to middle-aged males. However, in one case it was a sixty-seven-year-old female who had tried to end her life before but failed. She used three methods for her suicide. She took an overdose of drugs, cut herself, and electrocuted herself in her bathtub with a hair dryer (Pelissier-Alicot, et al., 2008).

Other Unusual Circumstances

Suicides in this category exhibited nothing unusual about the method of suicide, but were considered unusual for circumstances surrounding the suicide. A young Turkish boy ended his life directly after finding out that his dear pet, a chicken, had been slaughtered for the purposes of a family dinner. He staged his suicide with feathers from his dear pet stuffed into his pockets.

Other cases considered unusual included the homicide of an invalid thirty-four-year-old son followed by the suicide of his sixty-three-year-old mother in Florida. The case was deemed unusual because their bodies were not discovered until four years after the event. They lived in a residential area, but were socially isolated from neighbors. They did not speak English and lived most of the year in another residence in Germany. Most of their bills were paid electronically by a trust fund, except property taxes. There had been little reason to break into the home, until tax bills became years overdue and neighbors complained of a strange odor (Harding, 2011).

The Internet is a new way in which suicidal people can learn about techniques and characteristics of suicide methods and perhaps receive encouragement from other like-minded persons. A study of 593 suicides in the United Kingdom determined that nine (or 1.5%) were influenced by the Internet (Gunnell, et al., 2012).

Characteristics of the Unusual Cases

Gender

Males account for the majority of completed suicides in general (e.g., Lester, 2000; Stack, 2000), and they also account for the majority of unusual suicides, 96 of the 113 (85%). The share of females (15%) is somewhat lower than the 21% share they have of all suicides in the contemporary United States (Murphy, et al., 2013).

Age

The average age of the unusual suicides was 44.1 years. This is close to the average age of suicides in the contemporary United States, which is approximately forty-four (Murphy, et al., 2013). The ages ranged from thirteen (the boy in Turkey who hung himself after his much loved pet rooster was slaughtered for dinner) to ninety-nine (a man with multiple serious health issues who managed to hang himself in his bed in a German hospital).

Nation

Researchers in a total of twenty-eight nations contributed one or more articles on unusual suicides. However, more than half of the articles (see table 18-2) were produced by just eight nations. The United States and Germany head the list with fourteen and twelve articles respectively. England, Italy, France, South Korea, Czechoslovakia, and India each produced between five and eight articles.

All else being equal, we would expect nations that publish relatively high amounts of research articles on suicide would also be generally high in unusual articles. The United States, for example, published over eight thousand articles on suicide during this time period, far more than any of the other nations, and is first in unusual articles.

There is variation in the relative amount of attention that suicide researchers direct towards describing and assessing deviant suicides. This concern is evaluated in the last column of table 18-2. Column C

Unusual Suicides

Table 18-2. Number of articles on unusual suicide as a percentage of all suicide articles for nations with five or more articles on unusual suicides.

Nation	A. Number of articles on unusual suicides	B. Number of articles on suicide	Percentage of articles on unusual suicides
USA	14	8101	0.17%
Germany	12	1071	1.12%
England	8	1545	0.51%
France	7	636	1.10%
Italy	7	340	2.05%
South Korea	7	175	4.00%
Czechoslovakia	6	90	6.66%
India	5	472	1.05%

presents the percentage of unusual articles out of all articles. While the United States published the most articles on deviant suicides, only 0.17% of its articles are on unusual suicides. The relative amount of attention given to deviant cases of suicide is actually the lowest in the United States The nation calling the most attention to deviant suicides is Czechoslovakia, where 6.66% of all articles are on unusual suicides.

Conclusions

No study has previously developed a taxonomy of unusual suicides based on a representative sample of cases. A large sample of cases of unusual suicides can contribute to the understanding of suicides in several ways. It can detect new methods of suicide that may become common methods in the future. It can assist medico-legal authorities in determining the cause of death in cases where the death could be easily misclassified as a homicide or accident. Furthermore, it is important to ascertain who are the creative or innovative persons who develop new ways or new contexts for ending life. For example, are such inventive persons younger men from a given set of countries or regions of the world, or marked by a particular set of psychiatric disorders? Finally, a taxonomy of unusual cases can illustrate recurrent patterns in what kinds of suicides are labeled unusual in the scientific literature.

The present study presented a taxonomy of 113 unusual suicides described in 86 recent articles (2003–2014). A classification scheme by suicide method proved useful in organizing these deaths: violent methods of suicide, nonviolent methods of suicides, and complex suicide involving two or more methods. The literature paid about equal attention to violent suicide methods (fifty-nine cases) and nonviolent suicide methods (fifty cases). Complex suicides added another seventeen cases. A common theme underlying the labeling of a suicide as an unusual suicide was the number of wounds. Having two or more gunshots (especially to the head) was a defining characteristic of unusual firearm suicides. In cutting and piercing suicides, a distinguishing feature for an unusual case was also the number of wounds. The greater the number of parts of the body slashed or pierced increased the odds of a case being labelled an unusual suicide. Complex suicides received a disproportionate share of the unusual suicides. Representing 1–5% of the suicides in society, they represented 12.4% of unusual suicides.

Males were more likely than females to stage deviant suicides (85% vs. 15%). The gender gap in unusual suicides largely reflects the corresponding gender gap in ordinary suicides in society. However, the pioneering cases of suicides by new methods also seem to be dominated by men. This is the case in the reported instance of a new method by gases (dry ice) and in the first instances of charcoal burning (Chen, et al., 2014). Suicide by duct tape is also apparently a masculine method.

Age patterns were not dramatically different from those in society. There was a reasonable range in the ages of deviant suicides (thirteen to ninety-nine. The mean age of unsual cases, forty-four, was the same as the mean for ordinary suicides in the contemporary United States (Murphy, et al., 2014). The United States and Germany led the world in the number of papers on unusual suicides. However, if we are concerned with the degree of attention paid to unusual suicides, Czechoslovakia leads the world in the percentage of papers on suicide devoted to the unusual and strange cases of suicide (6.6%). In contrast, only 0.17% of American suicide papers deal with unusual suicides. Further work is needed to clarify what explains this variation in interest in unusual suicides.

New methods of suicide that are currently labeled unusual could conceivably follow the path of charcoal burning as a once uncommon but eventually commonplace method (Chen, et al., 2014). These included using dry ice in an enclosed area and the use of duct tape as a form of asphyxiation by occlusion of the nose and mouth (deRoux & Leffers, 2008; Norimine, et al., 2009). Both duct tape and dry ice are widely available and, unlike handguns, do not require a license to purchase them. One method rarely practiced to date, the explosion of natural gas in the home, could conceivably become more common.

The means are readily available for an increasing proportion of persons using natural gas to heat their homes (Demellawy & Fernandez, 2007). If widely practiced, such suicides would become a serious public safety concern, perhaps on a scale currently found in the current concern over firearms. Role models for explosion of natural gas suicides already can be found in the media (Stack & Bowman, 2012).

Complex suicides were commonly considered unusual in the sample of cases. These cases might provide a window on the measurement of intent to die. Future work might explore what differentiates complex, multi-method suicides from single method suicides. This might isolate factors related to a strong intent to die.

The availability of a means for suicide is often thought to be a risk factor (e.g., Lester, 2000, Stack, 2000). In the present study, however, some widely available methods were rarely used, including exposure to cold, explosions, and dry ice. Most of the world's population live in climates that, for at least part of the year, are cold enough to facilitate death through exposure. In many nations, suicide could be quickly achieved by disconnecting the natural gas line to one's house and waiting for an explosion. Recently, a case of suicide by dry ice, a quick and relatively painless method, has received some attention. Perhaps these methods would need to be used by a widely publicized celebrity suicide in order to become widely adopted (Chen, et al., 2014). Charcoal burning was once a rare method of suicide but, after widespread publicity of celebrity suicides, it has become more commonplace. Availability may need to be buttressed by media coverage in order for a method to become widespread.

Some caution needs to be exercised in interpreting the results of the present study. First, it relies on medico-legal authorities and researchers' perceptions of what constitutes an unusual case. There may be other conceptions of what constitutes unusual cases such as ones based on the location of suicides or a variety of odd combinations of uncommon psychiatric disorders. The search uncovered an apparent large number of cases from forensic journals. This might create a biased view. Second, the results of the keyword search using the search term "unusual" needs to be compared to related search terms. Alternative keywords such as "uncommon" might generate a different or somewhat different set of categories for a taxonomy of deviant suicides.

The present sample of cases is apparently biased in terms of the absence of some categories of what would probably be considered deviant acts of suicide. None of the unusual cases concerned mass murders who die by suicide after their acts, and none concerned suicide bombers. This may have to do with the extreme rarity of such cases so that they are unlikely to be available in research by medical examiners based on local cases of suicide. There was an absence of research studies in the present investigation carried out in the hotspots for suicide bombing, such as Iraq and Afghanistan. Some modalities of unusual suicides may be missed in nations where there are few suicide researchers. There were also few cases of homicide followed by suicide, although homicide/suicide is about as rare as complex suicides.

Future work is needed on both prospective and retrospective analyses of deviant suicides. Definitions of deviance change over long periods of time (Clinard & Meier, 2004; Thio, 2006). The present study was based on a sample of studies dating from 2003–2014, a twelve-year period. It is plausible that what was defined as unusual cases of suicide in previous eras could be somewhat different. For example, early cases of assisted suicide may have been discussed as unusual in the 1970s.

In order to understand better the motivations of these unusual suicides and the reasoning behind their choice of method, it is imperative in future research to interview those who survive these unusual methods. It may be the availability of the methods for those who are unable to procure the more commonly used methods, it may be that the unusual method chosen symbolizes some desire or thinking pattern of the individual, or the choice may reflect the psychiatric state of the individual wherein psychotic individuals may choose more unusual methods, especially if they are under the influence of command hallucinations.

Note

1.   Accessed 7-5-2014.

References

Adair, T. W., DeLong, L., Doberson, M. J., et al. (2003). Suicide by fire in a car trunk. *Journal of Forensic Sciences*, 48, 1113–16.

Ajdacic-Gross, V., Weiss, M. G., Ring, M., et al., (2008) Methods of suicide: International suicide patterns derived from the WHO mortality database. *Bulletin of the World Health Organization*, 86, 726–32.

Aloja, E., De Giorgio, F., Ausania, F., & Cascini, F. (2011). A case of suicidal suffocation simulating homicide. *Journal of Forensic Sciences*, 56, 810–12.

Arun, M, Palimar, V., Kumar,G. N. P., et al (2010). Unusual methods of suicide: Complexities in investigation. *Medicine, Science & the Law*, 50, 149–53.

Austin, A. E., Heath, K., Gilbert, J. D., & Byard, R. W. (2012). Head impalement—An unusual form of suicide. *Journal of Forensic & Legal Medicine*, 19, 264–66.

Blasser, K., Tatschner, T., & Bohnert, M. (2013). Vehicle assisted suicide with a nylon rope causing complete decapitation. *Archiv fur Kriminologie*, 232, 104–12.

Catalano, F., Martiano, F., Maina, G., et al. (2013). An unusual case of extensive self inflicted cement burn. *Annals of Burns & Fire Disasters*, 26, 40–43.

Chen, Y. Y., Yip, P., Chan, C. H., et al. (2014). The impact of a celebrity's suicide on the introduction and establishment of a new method of suicide in South Korea. *Archives of Suicide Research*, 18, 221–26.

Clinard, M., & Meier, R. (2004). *Sociology of deviant behavior*. Belmont, CA: Wadsworth.

Cunliffe, C., & Denton, S. (2008). An atypical gunshot wound from a home-made zip gun. *Journal of Forensic Sciences*, 53, 216–18.

Demellawy, D. E., & Fernandes, J. (2007). Suicide by explosion of natural gas: Case report and review of the literature. *American Journal of Forensic Medicine & Patho*logy, 28, 48–52.

deRoux, S., & Leffers, B. (2008). Asphyxiation by occlusion of nose and mouth by duct tape: Two unusual suicides. *Journal of Forensic Sciences*, 54, 1453–55.

DiNunno, N. D., Viola, L., Colucci, M., et al. (2009). A case of a suicide with a modified gun. *American Journal of Forensic Medicine & Pathology*, 30, 52–56.

Doberentz, E., & Madea, B. (2013). Death in a rainwater tank: Unusual death by hypothermia. *Archiv fur Kriminologie*, 231, 55–61.

Doichinov, I. D., Doichinova, Y. A., Spasov, S. S., & Marinov, N. D. (2008). Suicide by an unusual manner of hanging. *Folia Medica*, 50, 60–62.

Evans, J. R. (2010). *Death, despair, and second chances in Rocky Mountain National Park*. Boulder, CO: Johnson Books.

Gunnell, D., Bennewith, O., Kapur, N., et al. (2012). The use of the internet by people who die by suicide in England: A cross sectional study. *Journal of Affective Disorders*, 141, 480–83.

Harding, B. E., Sullivan, L., Adams, S., et al. (2011). Multidisciplinary investigation of an unusual apparent homicide/suicide. *American Journal of Forensic Medicine & Pathology*, 32, 208–12.

Huh, G. Y., Jo, G. R., Kim, K. H., et al. (2009). Imitative suicide by burning charcoal in the Southeastern region of Korea: The influence of mass media reporting. *Legal Medicine*, 11, S563–64.

Ji, N. J., Hong, Y. P., Stack, S., & Lee, W-Y. (2014). Is charcoal burning suicide a persistent epidemic in Asian countries? Epidemiological findings from South Korea. *Journal of Korean Medical Science*, 29, in press.

Jungman, L., Perdekamp, M. G., Bohnert. M., Auwarter, V., & Pollak, S. (2011). Complex suicide by ethanol intoxication and inhalation of fire fumes in an old lady. *Forensic Science International*, 209, e11–e15.

Katedry, Z., & Sadowej, Z. M. (2013). An unusual case of suicidal carbon monoxide poisoning committed using a portable barbeque grill. *Archiwum Medycyny Sadowej I Kryminologi*, 63, 15–20.

Lester, D. (2000). *Why people kill themselves*. Springfield, IL: Charles C. Thomas.

Marcikic, M., Vuksic, Z., Dumeenic, B., et al. (2011). Double suicide. *American Journal of Forensic Medicine & Pathology*, 32, 200–1.

Murphy, S., Xu, J., & Kochanek, K. D. (2013). *Deaths: Final data for 2010, National Vital Statistics Reports, 61*, May 8.

Murty, O. P. (2008). "Unusual self electrocution simulating judicial execution by an adolescent." *American Journal of Forensic Medicine & Pathology*, 29, 167–69.

Norimine, E., Ishizawa, F., Honda, K., & Uemura, S. (2009). Suicide case of carbon dioxide poisoning using dry ice. *Japanese Journal of Toxicology*, 22, 121–24.

Pelissier-Alicot, A. L., Gavaudan, G., Bartoli, C., et al. (2008). Planned complex suicide: An unusual case. *Journal of Forensic Sciences*, 53, 968–70.

Petkovic, S., Maletin, M., & Durendic-Brenesel, M. (2011). Complex suicide: An unusual case with six methods applied. *Journal of Forensic Sciences*, 56, 1368–72.

Saint-Martin, P., Prat, S., Bouyssy, M., & O'Byrne, P. (2009). Plastic bag asphyxia. *Journal of Forensic & Legal Medicine*, 16, 40–43.

Stack, S. (2000). Suicide: a 15-year review of the sociological literature. Part I. Cultural and economic factors. *Suicide & Life Threatening Behavior*, 30, 145–62.

Stack, S. (2014). "Impact of crisis phones on bridge suicide prevention, 1955–2012, Skyway Bridge, Tampa, Florida." Paper read at the annual meetings of the *Midwest Injury Prevention Association*, Ann Arbor, MI, September 30–October 1.

Stack, S., & Bowman, B. (2012). *Suicide movies: Social patterns*, 1900–2009. Cambridge, MA: Hogrefe.

Stack, S., & Wasserman, I. (2005). Race and method of suicide: Culture and opportunity. *Archives of Suicide Research*, 9, 57–68.

Stack, S., & Wasserman, I. (2009). Gender and suicide risk: The role of wound site. *Suicide & Life Threatening Behavior*, 39, 13–20.

Straka, L., Novomesky, F., Stuller, F., et al. (2013a). A planned complex suicide by gunshot and vehicular crash. *Forensic Science International*, 228, e50–e53.

Straka, L., Novomesky, F., Gavel, A., et al. (2013b). Suicidal nitrogen inhalation by use of scuba full face diving mask. *Journal of Forensic Sciences*, 578, 1384–87.

Thio, A. (2006). *Deviant behavior*. New York: Allyn & Bacon.

Vapa, D., Radosavkic, R., Maletin, M., & Veselinovic, I. (2012). *American Journal of Forensic Medicine & Pathology*, 33, 305–6.

19

Methods of Suicide Around the World

Steven Stack

In the United States, guns are the method of choice for suicide. In 1910, a year of the first available national data on suicide methods, firearm suicides accounted for only 30% of all American suicides. This figure reached 50% one hundred years later in 2010 (US Department of Commerce, 1913; Murphy, et al., 2013). However, from a global perspective on suicide, guns play a relatively minor role in suicide, and hanging dominates the suicide scene. In many nations, 80% to 92% of all suicides are by hanging. Hanging is nearly as lethal as guns. The fatality rates using these methods for suicide are, respectively, 89% versus 96% (Shenassa, et al., 2003). While there have been substantial efforts at controlling access to firearms through gun control legislation, such efforts may be fruitless in controlling suicide by methods such as hanging. A rope and a chair are all the equipment that is necessary, plus a place to hang the rope.[1]

The present chapter provides a brief overview of the methods used for suicide around the world, focusing on six methods in fifty-six nations by gender. Finally, historical changes in suicide method are explored over a period of 125 years for eight European nations.

The first rigorous compilation of data on the percentages of suicides carried out with various methods was published by Ajdacic, et al. (2008), and these data form the basis for this chapter. They are from the World Health Organization (WHO) database on suicide for fifty-six nations. A limitation of these data is that they do not provide information on some methods of suicide. In particular suicides by cutting and piercing are lumped into a residual category of "other methods." The residual category also includes suicides by electrocution, fire, crushing, and other means.

Table 19-1 presents the WHO data on suicide methods. The table is organized around six standard methods—three violent methods

Table 19-1. Percentage of suicides by each of six methods (P = other poisonings, Ps = pesticides, H = hanging, D = drowning, G = guns, F = falls), by gender (M = male, F = female), circa 1995–2004, annual averages. Source: Ajdacic-Gross, V. et al. (2008).

Region/nation	MP	MPs	MH	MD	MG	MF	FP	FPs	FH	FD	FG	FF
AFRICA:												
S Africa	6.6	3.6	68.7	0.0	12.6	0.2	22.7	12.5	41.2	0.8	9.2	0.8
AMERICAS:												
Argentina	0.7	1.7	49.1	1.5	37.6	2.4	3.4	4.1	38.0	4.2	25.9	10.3
Brazil	2.0	8.3	52.4	0.9	22.1	1.8	6.5	16.0	37.6	2.3	13.4	3.9
Canada	10.2	0.4	44.4	2.3	21.6	4.7	34.3	0.5	36.8	4.0	3.8	6.5
Chile	0.6	5.0	77.2	0.9	11.7	0.7	7.7	9.8	62.6	2.7	8.0	2.0
Columbia	5.9	20.1	27.7	1.1	37.0	3.1	12.5	45.7	17.4	1.2	15.0	4.2
Costa Rica	3.5	29.9	38.4	0.2	24.0	1.6	8.9	43.2	30.4	0.4	11.3	3.9
Cuba	1.7	8.9	76.8	0.6	3.4	2.0	11.5	10.3	27.4	1.3	0.7	3.0
Dominican Rep	2.5	22.4	42.8	2.5	20.2	1.5	7.8	34.9	31.9	3.6	8.4	3.0
Ecuador	1.6	32.2	41.3	1.6	19.2	0.1	2.3	64.3	23.9	0.8	5.3	0.1
El Salvador	0.4	86.2	8.4	0.3	3.8	0.1	0.0	95.1	3.2	0.0	1.4	0.0
Mexico	0.9	5.3	68.8	0.5	20.5	0.7	6.9	21.5	51.3	0.7	13.4	1.5
Nicaragua	1.8	61.4	25.7	0.6	7.4	0.1	7.7	84.6	4.8	0.1	1.7	0.0
Panama	1.4	18.3	63.5	0.0	11.9	3.2	2.9	46.3	44.1	0.0	2.2	3.7
Paraguay	0.6	15.4	42.9	1.6	30.4	1.2	2.5	38.5	27.1	1.9	21.5	2.8
Peru	2.3	54.6	14.1	3.3	11.8	0.3	1.8	83.0	7.3	2.4	1.2	0.0
Puerto Rico	4.8	1.6	67.6	1.7	17.6	1.5	19.2	6.2	42.3	1.5	6.9	7.7

United States	7.1	0.3	20.4	0.9	60.6	1.9	31.0	0.5	16.9	2.1	35.7	3.4
Uruguay	1.5	1.5	41.1	2.7	47.8	1.1	6.8	3.7	27.5	9.1	35.7	7.6
Venezuela	1.4	13.3	56.6	0.6	23.3	2.2	5.2	29.8	44.1	0.5	12.2	4.6
ASIA:											
Hong Kong	1.6	1.1	22.6	2.0	0.3	43.3	3.5	2.4	18.9	4.5	0.1	47.5
Israel	2.5	1.9	42	0.7	25.4	10.3	8.9	2.9	31.1	2.1	9.1	21.9
Japan	1.3	2.5	68.7	2.6	0.2	8.1	2.9	4.3	59.9	7.8	0.0	12.5
Kuwait	0.5	4.7	91.7	0.0	0.5	0.5	0.0	7.3	90.6	0.0	0.0	2.1
S Korea	0.4	37.5	39.2	3.2	0.4	9.5	0.8	42.8	26.0	3.8	0.1	18.5
Thailand	6.3	16.4	51.7	0.1	6.1	0.1	11.3	28.3	41.8	0.1	1.9	0.2
OCEANIA:											
Australia	8.0	1.1	45.4	1.3	11.5	3.6	26.5	0.7	36.4	3.9	2.6	4.6
New Zeal	6.4	1.0	48.4	1.9	11.2	2.5	19.7	0.4	42.5	4.4	2.2	6.4
EUROPE:											
Austria	5.6	0.3	48.1	3.3	20.7	8.9	17.7	0.6	35.2	10.7	2.6	18.1
Croatia	2.3	1.5	53.3	3.8	25.4	4.0	7.2	5.4	47.9	13.8	4.5	8.3
Czech	5.0	0.6	63.8	1.0	12.4	6.5	18.2	1.3	44.8	4.8	2.6	15.7
Denmark	13.7	0.7	40.7	4.8	14.5	5.1	36.9	0.7	29.6	13.2	0.8	7.9
Estonia	1.5	0.2	79.7	0.5	9.1	3.3	9.1	1.9	70.4	2.2	1.3	10.7
Finland	17.6	0.2	33.1	3.5	26.7	4.2	49.5	0.2	20.3	10.6	2.6	6.6
France	8.6	1.0	48.9	3.9	22.1	4.9	26.3	2.0	29.2	12.4	4.1	12.4

(Continued)

Table 19-1. (Continued)

Region/nation	MP	MPs	MH	MD	MG	MF	FP	FPs	FH	FD	FG	FF
Georgia	4.3	3.6	53.2	0.9	3.2	1.6	4.7	3.9	50.8	0.8	0.8	4.7
Germany	8.0	1.3	55.5	2.1	10.3	7.4	22.0	2.0	38.9	7.2	1.4	14.1
Hungary	7.0	4.6	70.3	1.4	4.0	4.9	28.1	7.0	43.4	4.5	0.6	9.9
Iceland	9.3	0.0	39	5.5	19.5	5.1	31.8	1.5	27.3	18.2	0.0	4.5
Latvia	0.9	1.0	85.1	0.8	6.5	2.3	6.2	4.1	72.6	3.9	0.9	7.8
Lithuania	1.1	0.4	91.7	0.3	2.7	1.3	6.3	1.6	83.1	2.2	0.3	4.4
Luxembourg	8.1	1.1	38.2	2.8	14.6	18.5	29.6	1.6	15.2	7.2	3.2	28.8
Malta	6.8	1.4	41.8	4.1	15.8	21.9	13.7	2.0	15.7	7.8	0.0	56.9
Moldova	0.9	7.0	80.3	2.0	2.4	2.6	5.0	18	55.7	9.1	0.5	5.4
Netherlands	11.7	1.4	47.9	6.6	4.4	7.8	24.0	1.8	33.6	11.0	0.6	10.7
Norway	11.1	0.2	37.9	4.6	27.1	4.7	33.3	0.5	32.3	13.5	2.0	7.1
Poland	1.8	0.3	91.2	0.5	1.1	2.1	7.9	0.8	77.6	3.0	0.2	6.5
Portugal	2.4	14	52.2	4.3	11.1	6.0	9.2	23.5	31.2	11.6	3.2	10.3
Romania	3.0	3.1	87.3	0.3	1.0	1.4	7.9	9.1	74.1	1.1	0.1	2.4
Serbia	1.6	2.9	57.6	3.3	20.1	2.3	4.2	9.8	57.2	7.9	5.2	4.0
Slovakia	3.2	1.7	70.0	0.8	12.3	5.0	17.0	2.8	50.2	2.8	2.9	17.2
Slovenia	2.5	1.8	64.7	2.5	11.8	3.6	8.6	3.1	53.1	12.2	1.2	9.0
Spain	3.5	2.6	52.7	3.9	7.1	18.4	8.3	5.4	29.4	7.6	0.9	36.9
Sweden	16.0	0.3	39.4	5.3	17.1	4.4	42.9	0.1	25.1	12.4	0.9	7.2
Switzerland	13.3	0.6	27.3	3.0	33.5	9.2	37.8	0.7	19.1	10.1	3.4	14.7
U.K.	14.7	0.4	55.2	2.4	3.5	2.9	41.1	0.3	35.9	4.7	0.6	3.7
Mean	4.8	9.1	52.5	2.0	15.3	4.9	14.8	15.2	38.6	5.2	5.3	9.4

(guns, hanging, and falls) and three nonviolent methods (pesticides, other poisons, and drowning). The focus is on male suicide methods since male suicides are more numerous than female suicides, and so the data for males are more reliable. We first explore male violent suicide methods, then male nonviolent suicide methods, and finally turn to a comparison of male versus female methods.

Violent Methods of Suicide: Men

Firearm Suicides

For men, suicide by firearm is the second most prevalent method of suicide. On average, the mean percentage of firearm suicides among the fifty-six nations is 15.3%. The percentage of suicides carried out by guns is highest in the United States where 60.6% of men use firearms for suicide. The nations with the next highest percentage of male suicides with guns are also located in the Americas—Uruguay (47.8%), and Argentina (37.6%). Switzerland leads European nations with 33.5% of male suicides using guns. At the other extreme, less than one percent of suicides by men are carried out with guns in several Asian nations—Japan (0.2%), South Korea (0.4%), and Kuwait (0.5%).

There has been substantial literature on the linkages between firearms and suicide rates, but much of the work has been based on the United States (Lester, 2009; Stack, 2000). From a cross-national perspective, the relationship between firearms and suicide is not clear. For example, in the United States firearms are the method of choice for men, and the use of firearms practically guarantees death. Approximately 95% of attempts at suicide with guns are successful (Shenassa, et al., 2003). Nevertheless, the United States' suicide rate is well below average by world standards. In results not fully reported here, the male suicide rate for the nations in table 19-1 for the year 2000 is 19.4 per 100,000 per year. The United States male suicide rate is only 15.9 (WHO 2014). Data from the International Crime Surveys indicate that the percentage of household owning guns was 32% in the United States in the year 2000, down from 46% in 1989 (Ajdacic-Gross, et al., 2006). The United States leads the world in the degree of household ownership of firearms, but its suicide rate is relatively low. In contrast, Japan's male suicide rate (27.1) is nearly double that of the United States, but less than one percent of Japanese households owns a gun (0.6%).

Using the data in table 19-1 and suicide rates from the WHO (2014), the percent of suicides using guns was unrelated to national male suicide rates (r = -0.15, p > .05). Guns play a minor role in suicide in nations with the highest suicide rates: 9.1% of suicides in Estonia involve guns, 6.5% involve guns in Latvia, 2.7% in Lithuania, and 12% in Slovenia. The male suicide rates in these nations are, respectively: 41.4, 50.6, 75.1, and 38.1 (WHO 2014). In contrast, 61% of male suicides in the United States are by firearms, and the male suicide rate is 15.9. It seems that high gun ownership rates at the national level may be reflective of a cultural system marked by low suicide acceptability (Stack & Kposowa, 2011).[2] People who do die by suicide may be likely to use firearms in such nations but, at the same time, the cultural system may be a protective factor against suicide. From a control theory of deviant behavior (Hirschi, 1967; Stack & Kposowa, 2011), the question is why there are so few suicides, not what causes the few that do exist.

Hanging Suicides

Attempts at suicide by hanging are nearly as fatal as attempts by guns. As noted by Shenassa, et al. (2003), 96% of efforts at suicide using guns are successful while 89% of efforts at suicide by hanging are successful. The data in table 19-1 show that hanging is a far more common method of suicide than firearms. On average, hanging accounts for more than three times as many suicides as do firearms. Fully 52.5%, on average, of male suicides employ hanging. For the Americas, hanging accounts for 77.2% of the suicides in Chile, and 76.8% in Cuba. For Asia, 91.7% of the suicides are by hanging in Kuwait. In Europe, Lithuania leads with 91.7% of its suicides by hanging, followed by Poland at 91.2%, and Romania at 87.3%. In contrast to guns, only one of the fifty-six nations has less than 10% of its suicides accounted for by hanging (El Salvador, 8.4%).

The percentage of suicides by hanging predicted national suicide rates. Using the data in table 19-1 supplemented by WHO (2014) male suicide rates for the year 2000, there was a significant correlation between percent of suicides by hanging and the male suicide rate (r = 0.39, p < .007).

Suicides by Falls

Falls include jumping off bridges and high buildings. Falls account for only a small percentage of male suicides, with an average incidence of male suicides from falls of 4.9%. The range is from 0.1% in Thailand to a high of 43.3% in Hong Kong. Small nations with predominately urban populations tend to have the highest percentages of male suicides by falling: Hong Kong at 43%, Luxembourg at 19% and Malta at 22%. In the United States, falls account for only 1.9% of male suicides.[3]

Nonviolent Methods of Suicide: Men

The three nonviolent methods for which data are available (pesticides, other poisons, and drowning) accounted for, on average, 15.9% of all male suicides.

Suicide by Pesticides

On average, poisoning with pesticides accounts for 9.1% of male suicides. Poisoning with pesticides is a major problem in rural Latin American countries. Pesticides account for a majority of suicides in El Salvador (86%), Nicaragua (61%), and Peru (55%). However, in most nations, pesticide's share of suicides is less than 5%.

Suicides by Other Poisons

Suicides by other poisons accounted for an average of 4.8% of male suicides. There is a tendency for other poisons[4] to be more popular in more developed than less developed nations. The nations with the highest usage of other poisons as a method for suicide were European - Finland (17.6% of all male suicides were by poison), the UK (14.7%), Denmark (13.7%), and Switzerland (13.3%). Nations where other poisons were an especially uncommon means of suicide were largely in Asia and South America. The smallest percentage of male suicides using other poisons was in El Salvador (0.4%), South Korea (0.4%), and Kuwait (0.5%).

Suicides by Drowning

The least common method selected by males was drowning, accounting, on average, for only 2.0% of male suicides. The nations with the highest use of drowning as a method were all located next to an ocean: The Netherlands (5.6% suicide by drowning), Iceland (5.5%), and Sweden (5.3%). Many nations had fewer than 1% of their suicides using drowning.

Male versus Female Methods of Suicide

Patterns in method of suicide between the genders were marked by both similarities and differences. Female suicide methods were related to male methods within nations. If suicide by hanging was common among males, it tended to be common among females as well. For example in Poland the respective male and female percentages of hanging suicides are 91.2% and 77.6%. The Polish male percentage of hanging suicides is nearly double that of the world average of 52.5%. The Polish percentage of suicides by hanging for females (77.6%) is double that of the average percentage of suicides by hanging for females (38.6%).

The correlation between the percentage of males using poison for their suicides and the percentage of females using poison for their suicides is very high (r = 0.95, p< .000). For other methods the link is also strong: for pesticides the correlation coefficient was r equal to 0.96, for hanging r equalled 0.91, for drowning r equalled 0.87, for guns r equalled 0.83, and for falls r equalled 0.9. When a method is popular with males it is also popular with females. There is more variability in choice of suicide method *between* nations than *within* nations by gender (Ajdacic, et al. 2008).

Nevertheless, females preferred some methods more than males. Males were more likely than females to choose violent methods of suicide. On average, 15.3% of male suicides were by guns compared to only 5.3% of female suicides. Of male suicides, 52.5% of male suicides hung themselves compared to 38.6% of female suicides. However, the gender order reversed on the less popular violent methods—falls. Only 4.9% of male suicides were by falls compared to 9.4%, on average, of female suicides.

Females were consistently more likely than males to choose nonviolent methods of suicide. Females were more likely to choose pesticides than males (15.2% vs. 9.1%) as well as other poisons (14.8% vs. 4.8%). Females were more than twice as likely as males to choose drowning as a method for suicide (5.2% vs. 2.0%). While the suicide methods of men and women are highly correlated across nations, women prefer nonviolent methods more than do men.

Suicide Methods: Historical Changes in Europe

Using data gathered by Morselli (1882) we can estimate long-term shifts in the suicide methods used in Europe. Morselli provides data for circa 1875 for eight nations for which comparable data are also available for the year 2000. Table 19-2 compares the percentages of suicides in 1875 with those 125 years later (in 2000) for five suicide methods.

The proportion of male suicides using guns increased, on average, from 11.6% in 1875 to 17.8% in the year 2000, an increase of 53%. For females the corresponding increase in the use of firearms in suicides was smaller, 27%. To the extent that firearms became more available during the 125 year period, we would expect an increase in their use for suicide.

Table 19-2. Percentage of suicides by each of five methods in 1875 and 2000 (P = poisonings, H = hangig, D = drowning, G = guns, F = falls), by gender (M = male, F = female), circa 1875–2000. Source: Ajdacic-Gross, V. et al. (2008) and Morselli (1882).

NATION	MP	MH	MD	MG	MF	FP	FH	FD	FG	FF
Circa 2000										
Austria	5.6	48.1	3.3	20.7	8.9	17.7	35.2	10.7	2.6	18.1
Denmark	13.7	40.7	4.8	14.5	5.1	36.9	29.6	13.2	0.8	7.9
France	8.6	48.9	3.9	22.1	4.9	26.3	29.2	12.4	4.1	12.4
Hungary	7.0	70.3	1.4	4.0	4.9	28.1	43.4	4.5	0.6	9.9
Norway	11.1	37.9	4.6	27.1	4.7	33.3	32.3	13.5	2.0	7.1
Sweden	16.0	39.4	5.3	17.1	4.4	42.9	25.1	12.4	0.9	7.2
Switzerland	13.3	27.3	3.0	33.5	9.2	37.8	19.1	10.1	3.4	14.7
U.K.	14.7	55.2	2.4	3.5	2.9	41.1	35.9	4.7	0.6	3.7
2000 mean	11.25	45.98	3.588	17.81	5.625	33.01	31.23	10.19	1.875	10.13
Circa 1875										
Austria	6.6	50.6	20.8	17.2	0.0	17.6	32.4	41.0	3.8	0.0
Denmark	0.6	82.5	11.1	3.7	0.0	2.6	58.3	35.9	0.0	0.0
France	1.6	48.0	24.2	13.5	2.4	3.7	32.3	42.1	0.7	5.0

(Continued)

Table 19-2. (Continued)

NATION	MP	MH	MD	MG	MF	FP	FH	FD	FG	FF
Hungary	2.4	61.5	10.8	16.7	0.4	4.2	55.6	31.2	1.7	0.0
Norway	0.0	66.4	18.4	5.4	0.0	0.0	54.7	33.2	0.5	0.0
Sweden	7.0	52.7	19.1	11.2	0.8	17.7	44.3	28.8	0.5	0.7
Switzerland	2.5	45.8	22.8	18.6	0.9	9.1	22.8	54.6	4.5	3.0
U.K.	7.0	40.7	15.5	6.6	1.9	15.6	28.1	32.4	0.1	3.8
1875 mean	3.957	56.03	17.84	11.61	1.28	8.813	41.06	37.4	1.475	2.5
Change										
1875–2000	184.3%	-18%	-80%	53.4%	339%	274%	-24%	-73%	27.1%	305%

Hanging was the most common method of both male and female suicide in 1875: 56.0% and 41.1% respectively. For males in 2000, hanging remained the method of choice with 46.0% of suicides carried out by that method. For females in 2000, hanging declined in popularity with 31.2% of female suicides using that method. It was surpassed only by poisons as the method of choice. Over the 125 years, hanging declined by 18% for males, and by 24% for females.

There were large increases in the percent of suicides by falls for both males (up from 1.3% to 5.6%, a 339% increase) and females (up from 2.5% to 10.1%, a 305% increase). Urbanization can create more opportunities for suicide by falls. Urban areas contain tall corporate buildings, apartment houses, and bridges.

Among nonviolent methods, there were large increases in the use of poisons and offsetting decreases in suicides by drowning. The percentage of male suicides by poisoning rose from 4.0% in 1875 to 11.3% in 2000, an increase of 184%. The percentage of female suicides by poisoning rose from 8.8% in 1875 to 33.0% in 2000, an increase of 274%. It is not clear what accounts for such a substantial increase in poisoning suicides. Modern autopsy methods may permit more careful procedures when classifying the cause of death. As better toxicology tests in autopsy cases were developed, perhaps some deaths formerly misclassified as accidental poisonings or undetermined poisons, became correctly classified as suicides. More likely, the increase in the availability and prescriptions of medications for physical illnesses, and especially for psychiatric disorders, has played a role. It would be of interest in the future to distinguish the use of medications, differentiating prescribed (such as antidepressants) and over-the-counter (such as paracetamol/Tylenol) from poisons *per se* for suicide.

In contrast to poisonings, there was a substantial drop in the percentage of suicides performed by drowning. The percentage of male suicides by drowning declined from 17.8% in 1875 to 3.5% in 2000, a decrease of 80%. The percentage of female suicides by drowning declined from 37.4% in 1875 to 10.2% in 2000, a decrease of 73%. It is unclear why suicides by drowning declined so substantially. Opportunities for drowning presumably remained about the same. Rivers, ponds, and oceans tend to remain intact over the centuries. Possibly media portrayals of alternative emerging forms of suicide (e.g., poisons) became more widespread and attractive.

Conclusions

The sources of the shifts in suicide methods over the last 125 years are not clear. It is possible that there will be shifts in suicide methods over the next century. Research is needed, both retrospective and prospective, examining and explaining long-term shifts in suicide methods. Not all suicides are preventable. If long-term trends are marked by a shift to a highly lethal, quick method for suicide, such as hanging, suicide will be less easily prevented than if long-term trends are toward the use of less lethal, slow acting poisons.

Notes

1. Incidentally, the rope does not have to be hung from a high point. A door handle will suffice.
2. In a study of twenty countries, Lester (1990) found that a measure of the extent of gun ownership was positively associated with the firearm suicide rate, but negatively associated with the nonfirearm suicide rate. Gun possession seems, therefore, to affect the choice of method for suicide but not the total suicide rate.
3. Lester (1994) found a positive association for the period 1960-1976 between the percentage of people living in high-rises in Singapore and the suicide rate by jumping (and also the total suicide rate), presumably because the percentage of suicides by jumping rose from 17% in 1960 to 51% in 1976.
4. Includes medication.

References

Ajdacic-Gross, V., Killias, M., Gadola, E., et al., (2006). Changing times: A longitudinal analysis of international firearm suicide data. *American Journal of Public Health, 96*, 1752–55.

Ajdacic-Gross, V., Weiss, M. G., Ring, M., et al. (2008). Methods of suicide: International patterns derived from the WHO mortality database. *Bulletin of the World Health Organization, 86*, 726–32.

Hirschi, T. (1967). *The causes of delinquency*. New York: Free Press.

Lester, D. (1990). The availability of firearms and the use of firearms for suicide. *Acta Psychiatrica Scandinavica, 81*, 146–47.

Lester, D. (1994). Suicide by jumping in Singapore as a function of high-rise apartment availability. *Perceptual & Motor Skills, 79*, 74.

Lester, D. (2009). *Preventing suicide: Closing the Exits revisited*. Hauppauge, NY: Nova.

Morselli, H. (1882). *Suicide: An essay in comparative moral statistics*. New York: D. Appleton.

Murphy, S., et al., 2013, *Deaths: Final Data for 2010*, National Vital Statistics Reports, 61, Table 18.

Shenassa, E. D., Catlin, S. N., & Buka, S.L. (2003). Lethality of firearms relative to other suicide methods: A population based study. *Journal of Epidemiology & Community Health, 57*, 120–24.

Stack, S. (2000). Suicide: A 15-year review of the sociological literature. Part I. Cultural and economic factors. *Suicide & Life Threatening Behavior*, 30, 145–62.

Stack, S., & Kposowa, A. J. (2011). The effect of survivalism—Self expressionism culture on black male suicide acceptability: A cross national analysis. *Social Science & Medicine*, 72, 1211–18.

US Department of Commerce, 1913, *Mortality Statistics*. Washington, D.C.: Government Printing Office, p.140.

World Health Organization (2014). WHO mortality database. http://apps. who.int/healthinfo/statistics/mortality/whodpms/param/php. Accessed, May 5, 2014.

Part 4

Cultural Scripts for Suicide

20

Russian Roulette and Duels

David Lester

Up to this point in the book, we have been looking at the ways in which suicidal individuals can script their suicidal act, for example, by choosing the method of suicide, the location of the act, and the writing of a suicide note. However, there are suicidal acts closely scripted by the culture in which the individual lives. Much like other ceremonies, such as baptisms, weddings, and funerals, cultures have laid down rules for the way in which some suicidal acts should occur. In this section, we will describe the scripts of Russian roulette, dueling, seppuku, protest suicide by self-immolation, victim-precipitated homicide, sati, sacrificial suicide among the Chukchi, and fasting to death in the Jain religion.

Suicidal actions do not always result in death. Many individuals survive, while others gamble (Lester & Lester, 1971), not knowing whether or not they will survive the self-destructive act. Russian roulette and dueling are good examples of this suicidal risk-taking.

Russian Roulette

In Russian roulette, an individual places one bullet in the cylinder of a six-shot revolver, spins the cylinder, places the gun to his head and pulls the trigger. The individual has a one in six chance of dying, and those who engage in this behavior would seem to have a self-destructive wish. The term "roulette" comes from the analogy with the gambling game of roulette. The "Russian" adjective is perhaps because this may have been a pastime played by members of the Czar's army in Russia or because of the Russian penchant for fatalism. One of the first mentions of the pastime is in a Russian novel, *A Hero of our Time*, by Mikhail Lermontov in 1840.

Who engages in this behavior? Fishbain and his colleagues (1987) identified twenty Russian roulette victims in Dade County, Florida, from 1957 to 1985, out of 6,534 suicides (0.31%). There were nineteen men and one woman. Compared to other firearm suicides, the Russian roulette suicides were more often unmarried, students, in poor health, African American and Hispanic, Roman Catholic, in the presence of other people, with alcohol/drugs in the body, substance abusers, and not US citizens. They were less likely to die in the bedroom, in the morning and with a history of recent depression. None left a suicide note. They were younger than the comparison group (twenty-eight years of age versus fifty-one on average).

Fishbain noted that 58% of the Russian roulette victims fired more than once, 26% had played the game previously, and 16% loaded more than one bullet into the gun. This suggests a strong death wish in these individuals. Baechler (1979) proposed a classification of types of suicides, and saw these individuals as risk-takers and as *ordeal suicides.* He saw those who witnessed the act as critical for its occurrence. In Fishbain's sample, the witnesses were friends (42%), girl-friends (26%) and family members (32%). The victims seemed to be risk-takers, drawn to gambling in this way, indulging in the illusion of omnipotent control over their destiny. They might have had low self-esteem and were trying to show-off in front of others. However, Fishbain did not carry out an intensive study of the interpersonal dynamics of the act by interviewing the onlookers who were there at the time of the act.

Marzuk and his colleagues (1992) compared fifteen victims of Russian roulette in New York City with a group of suicides by hanging. All Russian roulette individuals were men, mostly African Americans or Hispanic Americans (80%), unmarried and unemployed. None left suicide notes, and only one was known to have attempted suicide previously. The witnesses were primarily other men. The victims did not differ from the comparison group in age, sex, ethnicity, or alcohol in the body, but they were more likely to have cocaine in the body (64% vs. 35%).

One of Marzuk's cases was a middle-aged man who played the game alone at home whenever he was confronted with a serious problem. Surviving was a divine sign that he was meant to live. If he died, his problems were over. Others, especially those in the cocaine group, often challenged others to join in and prove that they were men.

Stack and Wasserman (2008) studied 1,412 suicides in Wayne County, Michigan, from 1997 to 2005 and found fifteen cases of death from Russian roulette. All were men. These fifteen suicides were compared with seventy-five men who died by suicide by shooting themselves in the head in the more conventional manner. The men dying from Russian roulette were more likely to be African American (80% vs. 31%) and to use revolvers than other types of guns (48% vs. 17%). They were younger (19 years of age vs. 49), more often single (87% vs. 36%), in the presence of others (73% vs. 5%) and discovered by a significant other (53% vs. 8%). They were less likely to have drugs in their body (7% vs. 32%).

Stack and Wasserman suggested that the stigma against suicide in the African American community (Early, 1992) may lessen their desire to die by suicide. Death by victim-precipitated homicide (where the victim of the murder goads the murderer into killing him), including suicide-by-cop (in which a victim goads the police into killing him) and Russian roulette, may be ways of dying, motivated by conscious or unconscious suicidal motivation, while avoiding the label of being a "suicide."

Wasserman and Stack (2011) followed up their study by looking at Russian roulette deaths nationwide for 2003–2006. They identified seventy-one deaths and, again as compared to men who died by suicide with gunshots to the head, those dying from Russian roulette were younger, more often African and Hispanic Americans, and more often single and divorced. More had alcohol in their system (48% vs. 23%), and less often currently in psychiatric treatment (8% vs. 18%) or had been in the past (6% vs. 24%). They were less often depressed (17% vs. 40%) or to have given evidence of suicidal ideation (14% vs. 25%). They did not differ in prior suicide attempts (10% vs. 9%), but none left a suicide note (0% vs. 9%). Those dying from Russian roulette less often had prior financial or job problems. The ethnic difference was greater for deaths in large counties than in small counties, suggesting a role for urbanization.

Shields and her colleagues (2008) compared twenty-four Russian roulette suicides with 1,485 suicides by gunshot to the head in Kentucky from 1993 to 2002. The Russian roulette suicides were younger (twenty-five years of age versus forty-two), all men, and more often African Americans. They had high levels of blood alcohol (50% vs. 27%) and drugs (69% vs. 43%). Most (80%) had never married. Only two had records of prior suicide attempts, and none wrote suicide notes. The father of one victim, a twenty-nine-year-old man, had died by suicide, using a shot to the head, one year earlier. Only one victim was alone.

One victim played the game with a friend, with each firing two shots. The victim died with the third shot. This individual was a twenty-two-year-old African American, a member of the university football team, studying electrical engineering with a 3.0 GPA. No alcohol or drugs were detected. A forty-six-year-old white man, employed as a custodian, played the game with a drinking buddy who had cancer. He placed two shells in the gun and died at the first shot. Four of the victims pulled the trigger at least three times before killing themselves.

A nineteen-year-old white man had a history of depression, several prior suicide attempts, and previous psychiatric hospitalizations. He played Russian roulette with his brother and two friends. He put five rounds into a .357 Taurus revolver, leaving only one chamber empty. He died on the first pull of the trigger. Postmortem toxicology revealed .01% blood alcohol and the presence of diazepam and nordiazepam. He had played Russian roulette on two previous occasions, each time with only one live round in the barrel.

Shields felt that the presence of others creates a group mentality that may persuade the individual to go through with the act to gain acceptance and approval, especially if the individual has taken drugs or alcohol.[1]

Duels

Dueling was popular in Europe and America for many hundreds of years. In the seventeenth and eighteenth centuries, duels were commonly fought with swords, but the use of firearms eventually took over. Duels were based on a code of honor and could end with first blood or death. By risking his life, a man could restore his honor, which had been tarnished by his opponent. There were formal rules of engagement (*code duello*) which included options for avoiding killing or wounding each other, if the participants so desired. Each participant could intentionally fire so as to miss the other, although some versions of the code prohibited this. However, the offended party could stop the duel at any time if he felt that his honor had been satisfied. Banks (2009) observed that duelists had to suppress their natural fears in order to protect their honor in this ritualized activity.

Banks (2009) commented on the role of the second, who could mediate the dispute between the rivals, make sure that the rules were followed, and, in the event of injury or death, arrange for medical care or funerals. Seconds were usually friends of the duelists, but sometimes strangers to the duelists, and they faced the same legal liabilities as the duelists if one of the duelists was killed. In 1842, Abraham Lincoln, an Illinois state legislator at the time, met to duel James Shields, but their seconds talked them out of it.

Freeman (1996) commented that, in American duels, the ritual was not one of violence or marksmanship with the aim of injuring or killing one's opponent, but rather "intricate games of dare and counter-dare, ritualized displays of bravery, military prowess, and, above all, willingness to sacrifice one's life for one's honor" (p. 294). In this case, the dare and counter-dare can arguably be attributed to suicidal desires (conscious or unconscious).

In his study of 367 duels in England between 1790 and 1845, Banks found that only twenty-five resulted in a trial, resulting in fifteen verdicts of not guilty, seven convictions for manslaughter, and three for murder. All of the sentences for murder were commuted from death to imprisonment. The death rate in duels in Italy in the late 1800s was only 0.5% (Hughes, 1998) but, in England, duels were more deadly. Simpson (1988) estimated a death rate of 14%, and Banks found 277 duelists killed in 834 duels (16.6%), and an additional 341 injured (20.4%).

Is there any evidence that some duelists had suicidal motivations? One famous case of a duelist being killed is Thomas Pitt, second Baron of Camelford (1775–1804), cousin to William Pitt the Younger, Prime Minister of England.[2] Camelford went to sea as a teenager and misbehaved throughout his seafaring career. Camelford was on George Vancouver's expedition to Canada in the 1790s, but continually got into trouble for disobeying orders. He ended up being placed in irons. Camelford was eventually given his own command, but he shot a fellow captain (Charles Peterson). He was court-martialed, but acquitted of murder. Camelford was frequently involved in violent acts, and many at the time thought him to be mad. In 1804, Camelford quarreled with and insulted his friend, Captain Thomas Best, knowing that Best was famous for his skill with a pistol. Best saw no option but to insist on a duel. The duel took place on March 7, 1804.

Tolstoy (1978) has described the actual duel. Best tried to persuade Camelford to withdraw his remarks that had provoked the challenge, but Camelford refused. Camelford's second proposed a distance of eight paces, but Best's second insisted on twelve paces saying that he had not come to see the men murder each other. The two men raised their pistols and leveled them, but Camelford could see that Best was deliberately aiming off to one side. He called across firmly and said, "That won't do." When Camelford's second called out, "Be quick," Camelford fired and missed. Best then fired and hit Camelford. Best's bullet paralyzed Camelford, and he died three days later.

Camelford, who knew that Best was sure to hit him with his shot, provoked the duel and refused to back down, even though he had insulted a good friend. His second tried to have them stand too close, and Camelford insisted that Best take good aim. It seems quite likely that Camelford intended to die.

The Duel between Alexander Hamilton and Aaron Burr

The most famous duel in the United States was between Alexander Hamilton and Aaron Burr on July 11, 1804. Hamilton told his friends that he had resolved not to shoot, and his friends warned him that this meant certain death. On July 10, Hamilton wrote a letter to be published if he was killed that confirmed his intentions. "I have resolved . . . to reserve and throw away my first fire, and I have thoughts of even reserving my second fire." He did withhold his fire, and he was mortally wounded in the duel. When the news of Hamilton's intentions was made public, many viewed his choice as suicide.

There was a growing antidueling movement in America at the time, and they seized on this opportunity to link dueling to suicide in order to stigmatize the practice as a fatal combination on murder and suicide. There was already a strong antisuicide attitude in America, and it was hoped that the stigma of suicide would help the cause. From 1801 to 1930, seventeen of thirty-one (55%) pamphlets examined by Bell (2009) featured suicide. Over time, Bell noted, the antidueling movement moved away from this focus on suicide and focused more on dueling as murder, especially after the duel between congressman Jonathan Cilley (from Maine) and fellow congressman William Graves of Kentucky on February 24, 1838, in which Cilley was killed.

Was Alexander Hamilton suicidal? Shneidman and Levine-Shneidman (1980) presented details of Hamilton's life relevant to this question. Hamilton's maternal grandmother abandoned her husband in America and took her daughter Rachael to St. Croix to live with her other daughter. Rachael married Johann Lavien, but the marriage failed, and Lavien had Rachael arrested for adultery and later divorced her. Rachael took up with James Hamilton and had two sons, Peter (in 1753) and Alexander (born in Nevis, in the British West Indies, in 1755). Hamilton abandoned the family in 1766 when Alexander was eleven and never saw his sons again. Rachel died on February 19, 1768, leaving the boys without any funds (John Lavien had been given all of her estate by the divorce court). The boys were taken in by James Lytton and his son Peter, but Peter died by suicide in 1769 and his father a few weeks later. The Hamilton boys were then apprenticed to merchants, Alexander to Thomas Stevens. Hamilton hated his origins and often lied about them.

In a study of thirty famous suicides (for whom detailed biographies were available), Lester (1989) found that fifteen had experienced loss of a parent during the latency period (ages six to puberty), primarily through death, but sometimes through divorce and separation. For example, Sylvia Plath lost her father to natural causes when she was eight; when he was thirteen, Leicester Hemingway (Ernest's younger brother) lost his father to suicide. Hamilton lost both parents during this stage of his life, one through abandonment and the other through death. Lester and Beck (1976) found that early loss sensitized people to later loss. In their study, people whose suicide attempt was triggered by an interpersonal loss were more likely to have experienced a loss in childhood and adolescence. The experience of the current loss seems to be made worse since it re-arouses the psychological pain experienced during that early loss.

Hamilton rose to become George Washington's chief of staff during the war of independence. He was Secretary of the Treasury and leader of the new Federalist Party. Hamilton had an affair with a married woman in 1791 (Maria Reynolds). When rumors spread about this, runors that eventually became public, it damaged his political reputation (and most likely his marriage).

Although on somewhat friendly terms with Aaron Burr, he helped Thomas Jefferson gain the Presidency after a tie with Aaron Burr in the electoral college. Hamilton helped defeat Burr as Governor of New York and made derogatory comments about Burr in the process. Although their friends tried to defuse the confrontation, Burr challenged Hamilton to a duel. It was scheduled for July 11, 1804.

Dueling was common in that period of American history. Hamilton's eldest son, Philip, had been killed in a duel in 1801 (at the same site). As noted above, Hamilton told his friends that he had decided to withhold his fire (or aim away from Burr). Had he announced this to Burr and his seconds, there were formal rules to be followed to avoid injury and death. Hamilton did not follow these rules. Burr's bullet hit Hamilton in the lower abdomen (probably inadvertently, given the inaccuracy of dueling pistols). Hamilton died the next day.

Discussion

In both Russian roulette and duels, a person may die, but the death is not attributed to suicide and, therefore, spares the deceased any stigma that he and his significant others think might attach to a suicide. Russian roulette is gambling, and the actor appears to be a brave risk-taker. In duels, people are protecting their honor, and death is seen as preferable to life with dishonor. However, both Russian roulette and duels may be unconsciously (or consciously) motivated by suicidal desires, and both are examples of the dramatic staging of the suicidal act.

Notes

1. Alcohol is associated with sensation seeking, impulsive behavior, and risk-taking.
2. My thanks to Stephen Banks for pointing out this case to me.

References

Baechler, J. (1979). *Suicides.* New York: Basic Books.

Banks, S. (2009). Dangerous friends. *Journal for Eighteenth-Century Studies,* 32, 87–106.

Bell, R. (2009). The double guilt of dueling: The stain of suicide in anti-dueling rhetoric in the early republic. *Journal of the Early Republic,* 29, 383–410.

Early, K. E. (1992). *Religion and suicide in the African-American community.* Westport, CT: Greenwood.

Fishbain, D. A., Fletcher, J. R., Aldrich, T. E., & Davis, J. H. (1987). Relationship between Russian roulette and risk-taking. *American Journal of Psychiatry,* 144, 563–67.

Freeman, J. B. (1996). Dueling as politics. *William & Mary Quarterly,* 53, 289–318.

Hughes, S. (1998). Men of steel. In P. Spierenburg (Ed.) *Men and violence,* pp. 64–81. Columbus, OH: Ohio University Press.

Lester, D. (1989). Experience of personal loss and later suicide. *Acta Psychiatrica Scandinavica,* 79, 450–52.

Lester, D. & Beck, A. T. (1976). Early loss as a possible "sensitizer" to later loss in attempted suicides. *Psychological Reports,* 39, 121–22.

Lester, G., & Lester, D. (1971). *Suicide: The gamble with death.* Englewood Cliffs, NJ: Prentice-Hall.

Marzuk, P. M., Tardiff, K., Smyth, D., Stajic, M., & Leon, A. C. (1992). Cocaine use, risk taking and fatal Russian roulette. *Journal of the American Medical Association,* 267, 2635–37.

Shields, L. B. E., Hunsake, J. C., & Stewart, D. M. (2008). Russian roulette and risk-taking behavior. *American Journal of Forensic Medicine & Pathology,* 29, 32–39.

Shneidman, J. L., & Levine-Shneidman, C. (1980). Suicide or murder? The Burr-Hamilton duel. *Journal of Psychohistory,* 8, 159–81.

Simpson, A. E. (1988). Dandelions on the field of honor. *Criminal Justice History,* 9, 99–155.

Stack, S., & Wasserman, I. (2008). Social and racial correlates of Russian roulette. *Suicide & Life-Threatening Behavior,* 38, 436–41.

Tolstoy, N. (1978). *The half-mad Lord.* New York: Holt, Rinehart & Winston.

Wasserman, I., & Stack, S. (2011). Race, urban context, and Russian roulette. *Suicide & Life-Threatening Behavior,* 41, 33–40.

21

Death by Seppuku

David Lester

Seppuku, the Japanese ritual of suicide by cutting the stomach and beheading, has occurred in Japan for over a thousand years (Kakubayashi, 1993). Although the method of suicide is consistent, the participants have varied greatly, from defeated warriors, servants whose lord has died, and wives in order to shame their husband (Rankin, 2011). It can be carried out as a solemn ceremony or as dramatic theater.

Rankin noted that seppuku survived and achieved the high status it has in Japan because of the way it was presented in works of history and in fiction. Cutting the stomach wall is incredibly painful, and most of those committing seppuku cry out in pain. The method is also extremely messy with blood and intestines spilling out. However, in reports in the past, this was minimized, and, instead, seppuku was presented as "poetry, courage, and comradely love" (Rankin, 2011, p. 16). Rankin called this "aesthetic cleansing," and it promoted the seppuku ideal. Rankin was of the opinion that, if seppuku had been presented realistically, it would have quickly died out as a ritual custom. Even the word *seppuku* is a euphemism. Originally, the Japanese called it *hara-kiri*, which means belly-cut. The word seppuku came from two Chinese characters meaning cut the stomach. This took over as the dominant term in the 1800s so that nowadays Japanese think that hara-kiri is a foreign word!

Rankin noted that cutting open the stomach is not a good way of dying. Occasionally, people survived and, even if they died, death took hours or even days. Hence combining the act with beheading became more popular in order to hasten death. Modern cases occur of seppuku outside of Japan, committed by ordinary people. For example, Di Nunno, et al. (2001) reported four cases from Italy, two by men (aged thirty-six and fifty-seven) and two by women (aged seventy-five and seventy-nine).

The fifty-seven-year-old man had first stabbed his wife to death, and his act resembled the classic cuts made in seppuku. The thirty-six-year-old man had suffered from schizophrenia for many years and had been hospitalized for this disorder on numerous occasions. The seventy-five-year-old women had bipolar disorder, while the seventy-nine-year-old woman suffered from depression. Both had previously attempted suicide, by stabbing and by overdose, respectively. The seventy-nine-year-old woman was found in the road near her house, and the police at first suspected homicide. However, the woman's relatives told the police that she kept her house very clean, and indeed the house was clean and tidy. It appears that she chose the road to kill herself in order to avoid soiling the house. All the cases gave evidence of multiple stab wounds to the intestinal loops, which Di Nunno, et al. interpreted as attempts by the individuals to accelerate death and stop the pain.

A Case Study of Seppuku: Yukio Mishima

In the Preface to this book, we mentioned the suicide of Yukio Mishima who, on November 25, 1970, in Tokyo, Japan, committed *seppuku*. He disembowelled himself and then had an assistant behead him. The report of his suicide by the media captured worldwide attention. The setting of his suicide, the manner of his suicide, and the timing of it all added to the dramatic aspects of the act.

Mishima liked the romantic image of dying as a samurai. By doing so, he would achieve hero status, and his death would bring together all of the threads in his life. The ideal of the samurai was the pursuit of Literature and the Sword, and Mishima set out to develop both paths.

There are several themes that were portents of Mishima's suicide. For example, in his literary endeavors, he began a long novel in four parts in 1965 that he would finish just prior to his suicide in 1970. Mishima was concerned about his physical body. He was a small man, about five foot four, and he had loathed his body when he was young. Starting in 1955 he planned a rigorous program of exercise, bodybuilding and sun tanning. He specialized in kendo (fencing with a blunt lance), eventually receiving the rank of fifth dan. He believed that it was best to die when your body was still in good shape, rather than as a decayed old man. He viewed his body as beautiful and even had photographs of it placed in a volume about Japanese body builders. However, in 1970, at the age of forty-five, although still in good shape, his body began to decline. He was often too stiff for some of the exercises, and he was not able to keep up with younger men.

Mishima was an exhibitionist. He appeared in movies and on the stage. He wrote for all kinds of magazines and newspapers in addition to his serious writings. He delighted in shocking people with his writings and his possessions. He posed for a book of nude photographs in 1963 and in the pose of Saint Sebastian in 1966. In this final decade of his life, Mishima developed a hero worship of the Emperor, together with a nostalgia for Japan's imperial and colonial past, and he became a favorite of the right-wing political groups.

In 1968, Mishima created his Tatenokai, a group of young men who functioned much like a private army. Using his connections, Mishima obtained permission for his group to train with the Japanese army and to be inspected on ceremonial occasions by military officers. He recruited right-wing students for the group and, at the first initiation ceremony, Mishima and the others cut their fingers and dripped blood into a cup. Each signed their name in blood on a sheet of paper, and then each sipped the blood.

As his ideas shifted to the right, Mishima fell further out of favor with the literary establishment, which leaned left. He broke with the theatrical group that produced his plays. Soon critics began to greet his new works with silence. His biographer (Stokes) felt that Mishima was essentially alone, without intimate friends, even though he was quite sociable. He found it hard to accept the love of others and could be repelled by and flee from their love. Mishima liked to hurt the object of his love. Thus, there was no one to challenge his lifestyle and his goals. His wife would not dare, and his mother was too uncritical of him.

In 1970 he began to plan his seppuku. He recruited four students to help, including the leader of his Tatenokai, Morita, prossibly his lover and who shared his right-wing views. Mishima changed the plan a number of times, but in the end, on November 25, 1970, the group visited a local military unit, captured General Mashita (the commander of the Eastern Army) and ordered Mashita's officers to gather the troops to hear a speech from Mishima. Mishima tried to get them to rise up and take over the government in the name of the Emperor, but the soldiers laughed at him. He went back into the General's room and disemboweled himself, whereupon Morita tried twice to behead him. One of the three assistants, Furu-Koga, took the sword and completed the beheading. Then Morita tried to disembowel himself, but failed, whereupon the Furu-Koga cleanly beheaded him. The assistants were ordered by Mishima not to commit seppuku, and they were sentenced to four years in prison for their participation in the seppuku.

Japanese culture is tolerant toward suicide (although far from having the highest suicide rate in the world). There was a mass seppuku of the military leaders after the defeat in the Second World War, and Mishima spent part of the war in a factory making the planes for the kamikaze pilots who sacrificed themselves for their country. The list of Japanese writers who have killed themselves is long: Bizan Kawakami 1908, Takeo Arishima 1923, Akutagawa 1927, Shinichi Makino 1936, Osamu Dazai 1948, Tamiki Hara 1951, Michio Kato 1953, Sakae Kubo 1958, and Ashihei Hino 1960. Mishima had met Dazai and probably was aware of the other contemporary writers who had killed themselves. For someone who had developed a fascination with bloody death at a young age, these suicides must have been especially potent events.

There is another factor that is relevant here. In 1960, Mishima wrote a short story titled Patriotism.[1] It tells of a newly married couple in 1936 in Japan. The husband is a Lieutenant in the Imperial army. Six months into their marriage, the husband's colleagues in the army are involved in a mutiny against the Emperor, and the husband is immediately called upon to help quash this mutiny.[2] Yet, the soldiers he must kill are his friends, and he decides that he cannot do this. He and his wife decide to die together. The husband disembowels himself with his sword in front of his wife and, with her assistance, stabs himself in the neck in order to complete the act. His wife then kills herself with a knife.

Mishima described in detail the preparations that the husband and wife take—arranging the house, writing notes, leaving the front door of their house open. Once the killing begins, the acts, the impact on their bodies, and the mental states are described in lyrical and graphic detail, and it seems to the reader as though Mishima relishes these details and is living them vicariously through his protagonists.

Mishima's seppuku did not occur exactly as staged in his short story. His assistant beheaded him rather than Mishima stabbing himself in the neck. It occurred on an army base and not at home. Mishima was trying to lead a mutiny, but it was a mutiny to restore the Emperor to his rightful place rather than, as in the story, to depose him. In life and in the story, Mishima was on the side of the Emperor, but it is possible that this story written in 1960 helped Mishima write the script for his seppuku in 1970.

Comment

There is at least one other type of ritual suicide in Japan. *Jigai* is practiced by the wives of samurai who have committed seppuku or suffered disgrace, as did the wife in Mishima's short story. Jigai was also committed in order to prevent rape or capture by an enemy. Jigai involves cutting the arteries in the neck with one stroke of a knife (such as a *tantō* or *kaiken*). Often the women tied their legs together to preserve a dignified pose in death. Unlike seppuku, jigai can be completed alone since it does not require an assistant to complete the act. These days, only about 0.2% of suicides in Japan are carried out using this method.

Although jigai is a feminine counterpart of seppuku, a recent case of jigai committed by a man in Italy was reported by Maiese, et al., (2014). A fifty-eight-year-old man who was a devotee of Japanese culture was found dead in his bathtub with his internal jugular vein cut with a tantō.

Notes

1. http://www.mutantfrog.com/patriotism-by-yukio-mishima. The story was published in 1961, and Mishima codirected a film of the story in 1966.
2. The story is based on a real incident that occurred in 1936, known as the February 26 Incident.

References

Di Nunno, N., Costaninides, F., Bernasconi, P., & Di Nunno, C. (2001). Suicide by hari-kiri *American Journal of Forensic Medicine & Pathology, 22*, 68–72.

Kakubayashi, F. (1993). An historical study of hara-kiri. Australian *Journal of Politics & History, 39*, 217–25.

Maiese, A., Gitto, L., Dell'aquila, M., & Bolino, G. (2014). A peculiar case of suicide enacted through the ancient Japanese ritual of jigai. *American Journal of Forensic Medicine & Pathology, 35*, 8–10.

Rankin, A. (2011). *Seppuku.* New York: Kodansha International.

Stokes, H. S. (1974). *The life and death of Yukio Mishima.* New York: Farrar Straus & Giroux.

22

Self-Immolation as a Protest

David Lester

On November 2, 1965, at the age of thirty-one, Norman Morrison placed his one-year-old daughter, Emily, down on the sidewalk, doused himself in kerosene and set himself on fire outside the window of the Pentagon office of the US Secretary of Defense Robert McNamara in order to protest the war in Vietnam. Five days after Morrison died, a Vietnamese poet, Tố Hữu wrote a poem entitled *Emily, My Child*. A street in Hanoi was named after Morrison (as was a road in Da Nang), and a Vietnamese postage stamp was issued in his honor. When the President of Vietnam, Nguyễn Minh Triết in Da Na, visited the United States in 2007, he visited the site of Morrison's suicide and read Tố Hữu's poem.

As a form of political protest, self-immolation is unmatched in power. The sight of the Tibetan young man (Jampa Yeshi, twenty-six years old) protesting the actions of China in Tibet, engulfed in flames running through the streets of New Dehli in March 2012 appeared in many news outlets (including *Time*) and shocked us.[1] Today, with the fast transmission of such images across the world in a matter of minutes, people everywhere are made aware of this type of sacrifice. Indeed, such sacrifices can even bring about revolutions, as did that of Tarek al-Tayeb Mohamed Bouazizi, a Tunisia street vendor who self-immolation on December 17, 2010, to protest of the confiscation of his wares and his harassment by a municipal official, an act that became a catalyst for the Arab Spring.

Suicide by Self-Immolation

The use of self-immolation for suicide is not uncommon, especially in Arab and Asian countries. The journal *Burns* (as well as other similar journals) has published scores of reports on this method for suicide. In recent years articles have appeared on suicide by self-immolation in

Afghanistan, China, Egypt, India, Papua-New Guinea, South Korea, Sri Lanka, Turkey, and Zimbabwe (Laloë, 2013). In Western countries it is common for immigrants from these regions to use self-immolation for suicide.

Of the 4,267 suicides in Iran (a rate of 6.4 per 100,000 per year) in 2003 to 2004, 1,156 (27%) were by self-immolation (Ahmadi, et al., 2008). The modal suicide was female (with a female/male ratio of 2.4:1) and young (mean age of twenty-nine), and the rate was higher in rural areas than in urban areas. Suicide by self-immolation was higher in the Kurdish and Torkaman ethnic groups and lower in the Turkish and Baluche populations.

In contrast, in the United States, from 1995 to 2003, Thombs, et al. (2007) found that only 0.1% of the suicides were from burns. The rate for suicide by this method was greatest in those aged forty to forty-nine. For Berlin (Germany) from 1990 to 2000, Rothschild, et al. (2001) reported on forty-six cases of suicide by self-immolation. They comprised 0.8% of all of the suicides during that time period. Most were men (76%), and their mean age was forty-three. The most common place was outdoors (65%), most often in a park or forest, while those indoors were in their house or apartment. Gasoline was the most common substance used, and the cause of death was burn shock (35%), severe burns plus smoke intoxication (28%) and multiple organ failure due to severe burns (20%). Only a third (33%) had measurable blood alcohol, and only two of the forty-six suicides had a political motive.

Poeschla, et al. (2011) have provided a comprehensive review of suicide by self-immolation. Whereas in high income countries, most suicides by self-immolation are men, in low income countries, most suicides by self-immolation are women (especially young women), and the women were often socially-oppressed and disadvantaged.

Laloë (2013) noted that those burning themselves in the West and Middle East usually have a psychiatric disorder (especially depression or schizophrenia), and their actions are less lethal. In other countries, the motivation usually concerns personal reasons. These suicides are younger than European suicides, mostly women, recently married and lacking conflict-solving skills. They have often heard of other similar suicidal actions using burning and may be unaware of the serious and often fatal consequences. Those who survive often claim that the burning was accidental, and they face abandonment by their husband, and their own family may be unsupportive. The young woman will be disfigured and no longer be marriageable, and she becomes a burden to her family (Laloë, 2013).

Many cultures have suicide by self-immolation in their myths and in their history. The mythical Greek hero Heracles (son of Zeus and Alcmena) threw himself onto a funeral pyre after his wife smeared his chest with toxic blood from a centaur. The Stoic philosopher Empedocles (490–430 BC) jumped into Mount Etna, a volcano in Italy, and Peregrinus Proteus (100–165 AD), a philosopher, immolated himself on a funeral pyre at the celebration of the Olympic Games (Romm, et al., 2008). In Hindu mythology, Sati, the daughter of Daksha (the son of Brahma) fell in love with Shiva and married against her father's wishes. Shiva refused to pay obeisance to Daksha, and Daksha snubbed Sati and Shiva, whereupon Sati immolated herself on a sacrificial fire. Self-immolation as a way of death was viewed as quite acceptable by Buddhists in China, along with prohibitions against killing and suicide in general. Benn (2007) in his book *Burning for the Buddha* gave many examples of self-immolation. In an early documented case in 526 AD, a Buddhist monk, Daodu, who had grown weary of life, died by self-immolation even though the Emperor Laing Wudi disapproved.

Romm, et al. (2008) also provide examples of self-immolation in fiction (the last ruling steward of Gondor dies on a pyre in *The Lord of the Rings*), opera (Brünnhilde in Richard Wagner's *Götterdämmerung*), films (*The act of the heart*), and popular culture (the Japanese rock band Sadaharu's *Better living through self-immolation*).

Romm et al. speculated that self-immolation expresses both rage and expiation for sin (a way of purifying oneself or making amends for living an unsatisfactory life) as well as being a way of sacrificing oneself or protesting against evil. The mythical bird, the phoenix, burns to death in its nest, but a new phoenix arises from the ashes, and so there may be an element of rebirth fantasies. Perhaps self-immolation appeals because it is one of the most painful methods of dying (and so a severe punishment for past misdeeds) or because it leaves a ghastly image for loved ones and significant others and for the onlookers.

Self-Immolation as Political Protest

There are several ways of dying as a protest. Hunger strikes have long been used as a method of protest, and they not infrequently result in death. One famous protest of this type was made by Bobby Sands, a member of the Irish Republican Army in Northern Ireland, who was imprisoned by the British courts for his activities. He went on hunger strike while in prison and died in H Block of HMP Maze (Long Kesh) prison on May 5, 1981, at the age of twenty-seven. Sands was born in 1954 in Rathcode, a predominantly loyalist district of north Belfast. As a result of his final arrest and imprisonment, he was sentenced in September 1977 to fourteen years. He was denied the category of "political prisoner" and imprisoned instead as an "ordinary prisoner." The prisoners so labeled protested this action in various ways (such as refusing to wear the prison uniform), and then some of the prisoners decided to go on a hunger strike. The second hunger strike started on March 1, 1981, and Sands died on the sixty-sixth day of his hunger strike, on May 5, the first of ten prisoners to die. He left a diary covering the first seventeen days of his hunger strike (Sands, 1998).[2]

Hunger strikes often take place in private (for example, in prison) although some do occur in public. In 2013, in England, fifty-five-year-old Gyanraj Rai endured fifteen days of a hunger strike in freezing weather outdoors in Whitehall, London, in order get the Government to respond to the demands of the Gurkhas for equal rights.[3] Another way of dying sacrificially to protest and fight for change is by becoming a suicide bomber. However, self-immolation in public also has a dramatic impact.

Self-immolation as a form of political protest has a long history. At the end of the seventeenth century and into the mid-nineteenth century, roughly twenty thousand men and women burned themselves to death in Russia (Robbins, 1986). They belonged to a break-off group of the Russian Orthodox Church, and they died rather than being taken into captivity. Those who were captured were starved in the prisons or simply executed, and so suicide seemed to be a reasonable alternative to this persecution.

Several self-immolations from the last sixty years have remained in our collective memory and are frequently cited. Norman Morrison's self-immolation in Washington, DC, in 1965 to protest the Vietnam War was mentioned above. Two years earlier, on June 11, 1963, Thich Quang Duc died in this way in Saigon, South Vietnam, to protest the persecution of Buddhists by the President Ngo Dinh Diem, and on January 16, 1969, Jan Palach died in Prague, Czechoslovakia, to protest the Soviet invasion of Czechoslovakia. But these few "famous" self-immolations barely touch the extent of self-immolations over the past sixty years and the epidemic in recent years in many regions of the world. The website http://www.savetibet.org lists 125 Tibetans who have self-immolated in Tibet and China between February 27, 2009, and February 4, 2014. Wikipedia lists twenty-three protest self-immolations in the year of 2011.

Biggs (2005) has compiled a list of 533 protest suicides between 1963 and 2002, and estimates that the actual number is between eight hundred and three thousand individuals. In Biggs's sample, there were no cases from Africa or the Middle East,[4] Three quarters of protest suicides took place in three countries: India, Vietnam and South Korea. Most took place in urban areas and in countries with democratic governments. The most common method for protest suicide was fire (about four out of five choose fire), but in South Korea many set themselves alight and then jumped from buildings. In about one in eight cases, the protest suicide was thwarted. The chance of surviving a protest suicide was about 30%, but this varied by country. In Vietnam, almost all died; in India, only about two-thirds died.

Biggs classified the motivations of these protest suicides into two main categories.

(1) Selfless motivations, including advancing some cause and appealing to others to change their behavior, such as galvanizing them to engage in protest. Selfless motivations also include appealing to a supernatural agency to intervene.
(2) Egocentric motivations, including cheating the enemy out of capturing the individual, transfiguration (attaining a more exalted existence), attention seeking, and redemption from personal failings.

Self-immolation can enhance the commitment of others to the cause and convert others. About one sixth of the protest suicides in Biggs's sample resulted in people protesting afterwards in the streets or attending the funeral *en masse*. It also inspires others to imitate the sacrifice, and protest suicides often occur in waves. As we will see later, the self-immolation of Norman Morrison may have been one of the critical incidents that changed the opinion of Robert McNamara, the Secretary of Defense, toward the war in Vietnam.

Biggs noted that political movements that involve self-immolation do not typically involve suicide terrorism (the exception is the Kurdistan Workers Party in Turkey) and usually involve a grave cause. However, the wave of self-immolations in India in the 1990s involved a proposed law to reserve university positions for members of the lower castes, hardly a grave cause. (The law had been proposed, but not passed at the time.)

The Staging of Self-Immolation

It is important for the present book to examine how self-immolation is staged, and two incidents have been documented more than others—those of Thich Quang Duc and Norman Morrison.

Thich Quang Duc[5]

Thich Quang Duc, a Vietnamese Mahayana Buddhist monk, was born in 1897 in the village of Hoi Khanh in Central Vietnam, one of seven children. He left home at the age of seven to study Buddhism with his maternal uncle and spiritual master. He became a novice at the age of fifteen and a monk at the age of twenty. He spent three years in solitary contemplation before rising through the ranks of the Buddhist movement in Vietnam, supervising the construction of Buddhist temples and becoming the abbot of the Phuc Hoa pagoda.

The self-immolation of Thich Quang Duc arose from the persecution of Buddhists by the President of South Vietnam, Ngo Dinh Diem, who was Roman Catholic. The regime banned the display of Buddhist flags in Hué on May 8, 1963, Buddha's birthday, although the city had flown Vatican flags just recently. In the mass demonstration, police killed eight or nine protestors, including children.

The initiative for the self-immolation came from Quang Duc himself, and the Buddhists leaders initially rejected his offer. One monk, however, had good relations with foreign journalists and saw the potential for the act. After seven days of prayer and fast, the leadership gave Quang Duc permission. The monks experimented with different fuels, and they dropped hints about Quang Duc's plan.

On the day of the act, June 11, 1963, a procession of roughly 350 monks and nuns marched through the streets, led by a car carrying banners in both Vietnamese and English. Meanwhile, some monks and nuns prevented fire engines from reaching the location of the self-immolation by lying under the wheels. Journalists were alerted and were there with cameras. Quang Duc's self-immolation took place outside the Cambodian Embassy at the traffic intersection of Phan Dinh Boulevard and Le Van Duyet Street, a few blocks south of the Presidential Palace.

Quang Duc got out of the car with two other monks. One placed a cushion on the road for Quang Duc to sit on while the other monk took a five-gallon can of gasoline from the trunk of the car. Quang Duc sat down calmly on the cushion surrounded by a circle of marchers. A monk poured the gasoline over Quang Duc who rotated a string of wooden prayer beads and recited *Nianfo* (a homage to Amitabha Buddha). Quang Duc ther. struck a match and dropped it onto himself. A monk was present with a loudspeaker to announce the act, and others distributed the text of Quang Duc's declaration *in English*. After ten minutes, the body toppled on to its back. Monks covered the corpse in yellow robes and tried to place it into a coffin, but the limbs could not be bent for the corpse to fit properly. The coffin was taken to a nearby pagoda.

Among those witnessing Quang Duc's death was David Halberstam, a reporter for the *New York Times*.

> Flames were coming from a human being; his body was slowly withering and shriveling up, his head blackening and charring. In the air was the smell of burning flesh; human beings burn surprisingly quickly. Behind me I could hear the sobbing of the Vietnamese who were now gathering. I was too shocked to cry, to confused to take notes or ask questions, too bewildered to even think. (Halberstam 1964, p. 211).

A photograph by Malcolm Browne of the Associated Press of Quang Duc in flames appeared around the world, although the *New York Times* refused to print it. Browne won the World Press Photograph Award for 1963.[6] After further persecution of the Buddhists, the President of South Vietnam, Ngo Dinh Diem, was overthrown by a military coup and executed on November 2, 1963.

Norman Morrison[7]

Norman Morrison was born on December 29, 1933, in Erie, Pennsylvania. He graduated from Chautauqua High School in Chautauqua, New York in 1952 and from the College of Wooster (Ohio) in 1956, majoring in religion. He earned certification to teach high school history and social studies. He attended the Western Theological Seminary in Pittsburgh and received a bachelor of divinity degree in 1959. That year he changed from being a Presbyterian to being a Quaker. He met his wife, Anne, in Chautauqua, where she was working as a waitress in the summer of 1955. She was from Georgia. She found him a little quirky at first but eventually fell in love with him. They married in 1957. Morrison organized a Quaker group in Charlotte, North Carolina, taught in East Mecklenburgh High School in Charlotte, and then moved the family to Baltimore in 1962 to work as executive secretary of the Stony Run Quaker Meeting.

Morrison was greatly concerned over America's involvement in Vietnam, and he was appalled by the indiscriminant killing of civilians,

Suicide as a Dramatic Performance

especially women and children. He wrote to representatives and senators in Washington, DC, as well as "Letters to the Editor," planned peace vigils and conference, and lobbied in Washington. Morrison was moved by the self-immolation of Thich Quang Duc in Vietnam in 1963 and also the self-immolation of Alice Herz, an eighty-two-year-old Quaker, on March 16, 1965, in Detroit, to protest America's involvement in the war there. (She died from her injuries ten days later.)

On the day of his death, Morrison stayed home with a cold and worked on preparations for a class he planned to teach. He did not seem distraught or depressed, but rather quite calm. His wife was home too with their one-year-old daughter Emily. Morrison did ask her, "What would you do if anything happened to me?" When Anne went to pick up their other two children (Ben aged six and Christina aged five) from school, Morrison took Emily and drove from their home in Baltimore to Washington, DC, in a car they were taking care of for friends. On the way there, he posted a letter to his wife which arrived the day after his death. In the letter, he said that he had read *that morning* an article about the bombing with napalm of a village in South Vietnam which killed most of the villagers, but spared a Catholic priest who reported the atrocity.[8] "Know that I love thee, but I must go to help the children of the priest's village."[9] Reading about that incident seemed to precipitate his decision, although a friend noted afterwards that he and Morrison had discussed self-immolation on several occasions.

The details of Morrison's self-immolation are far from clear. Witnesses had different versions, and some witnesses changed their testimony later. At dusk, during rush hour, he parked the car and walked to the river entrance of the Pentagon, roughly forty feet from Robert McNamara's office in the Pentagon. He paced back and forth for forty-five minutes. He then doused himself with kerosene from a one-gallon glass jug, and struck a match on his shoe. The flames shot ten feet into the air. Two military officers rushed to smother the flames with their hands and coats, receiving burns in the process, but to no avail.[10]

> The fire shot ten to twelve feet into the air . . . The flames, people said, made an envelope of color around his asphyxiating body. The sound of it, one witness said, was like the whoosh of small-rocket fire. (Hendrickson, 1996, p. 188)

What is unclear is what happened to Emily. Some say that Morrison gave her to a bystander; some that he sat her down on the sidewalk; others that he held her until bystanders screamed that he should save her and he threw her out of his arms. The medical examiner's report said that he dropped Emily into a bush. His wife says that, when she picked Emily up later that night, Emily was completely unharmed. She did not have a scratch, cut, or burn on her, and she did not smell of kerosene. Did Morrison mean to sacrifice Emily as Abraham was prepared to sacrifice his son Isaac (described in the Old Testament)? Did he take her simply to remind himself of the children killed and burned in Vietnam and help him face his own personal sacrifice? Emily believes the latter: "By involving me, I feel he was asking the question, 'How would you feel if this child were burned too?' . . . I believe I was there with him ultimately to be a symbol of truth and hope, treasure and horror altogether."[11] In his letter to his wife, Morrison wrote, "At least I shall not plan to go without my child, as Abraham did" (Welsh, 2008, p. 36). This sounds as if Morrison meant her to die with him, yet he packed Emily's diaper bag with extra milk, diapers, and pacifiers, which seems that he knew that Emily would need them after his death.

Hendrickson (1996) is convinced that Morrison's protest helped change the opinion of Robert McNamara about the war.

> And yet what I fervently believe, and cannot prove, is that the fire in the garden became the deep sensitizing agent for a revelation that began seeping into the secretary of defense about a fortnight later. (pp. 198–99)

The presence of Emily, only eleven months old, added to the power of Morrison's act. The poem written by the Vietnamese poet Tố Hữu a few days after Morrison's death was entitled *Emily, My Child* (Welsh, 2000), and begins:

> Emily, come with me
> So when grown up you will know the way
> And not be lost.
> Where are we going, Daddy?
> To the riverbank, the Potomac.
> What do you want me to see, Daddy?
> I want you to see the Pentagon.
> O my child, with your round eyes,
> O my child with your golden hair,

Ask me no more questions, darling?
Come, I will carry you.
Soon you will be home again with Mommy.

As noted earlier, Morrison became a hero in Vietnam, with streets named after him and a commemorative postage stamp issued. When Anne visited Vietnam in 1999 with her daughters,[12] she was amazed how people there remembered Morrison's sacrifice, and Anne experienced the reverence and appreciation they had for Morrison. The visit in 1999 helped the family heal and assuage the loss of their husband and father thirty-four years earlier.[13]

Conclusions

I have chosen two well-known cases of self-immolations because these have been explored and documented in great detail. Self-immolation is a startling act, especially as we imagine what it must feel like to die in that way. It needs no other accompaniments. But we have seen in the self-immolation of Thich Quang Duc how his fellow monks and nuns helped him plan and prepare the setting for his act and how the staging of the act gave it incredible significance globally. For Morrison, the place chosen (outside McNamara's office in the Pentagon) and the presence of his baby nearby gave his death much greater significance. There were other self-immolations to protest that particular war, but Morrison's act remains the symbol of that era.

Notes

1. http://india.blogs.nytimes.com/2012/03/26/tibetan-in-delhi-sets-self-alight-to-protest-chinese-leaders-visit/?_php=true&_type=blogs&_r=0
2. For a discussion of the hunger strikes in 1981 in Northern Ireland, see Dingley and Mollica (2007).
3. www.getreading.co.uk/news/local-news/reading-gurkha-ends-hunger-strike-6329253
4. This has changed in recent years for the Middle East.
5. This section is based on Biggs (2005) and other sources.
6. http://www.ap.org/explore/the-burning-monk/
7. The fullest account of Norman Morrison's life is by his wife at the time, Anne Welsh (2008).
8. The article was a reprint of one in *Paris-Match* on October 2, 1965, and reprinted in *I. F. Stone's Weekly* on November 1, 1965.
9. http://www.thenation.com/blog/156433/when-antiwar-protest-turned-fatal-balld-norma-morrison.
10. Col. Charles S. Johnson and S/Sgt. Robert C. Bundt.
11. http://www.theguardian.com/lifeandstyle/2010.oct/16/norman-morrison-vietnam-war-rotest.

12. Their son, Ben, died from cancer at the age of 16.
13. For a moving account of Anne Morrison Welsh's visit to Vietnam in 1999, and many examples of how the Vietnamese revere Morrison, even after all these years, see Welsh (2008).

References

Ahmadi, A., Mohammadi, R., Stavrinos, D., Almasi, A., & Schwebel, D. C. (2008). Self-immolation in Iran. *Journal of Burn Care & Research*, 29, 451–60.

Benn, J. A. (2007). *Burning for the Buddha*. Honolulu, HI: University of Hawaii Press.

Biggs, M. (2005). Dying without killing. In D. Giambetta (Ed.), *Making sense of suicide missions*, pp. 173–208. New York: Oxford University Press.

Dingley, J., & Mollica, M. (2007). The human body as a terrorist weapon: Hunger strikes and suicide bombers. *Studies in Conflict & Terrorism*, 30, 459–92.

Halberstam, D. (1964). *The making of a quagmire*. New York: Random House.

Hendrickson, P. (1996). *The living and the dead*. New York: Vintage.

Laloë, V. (2013). A medical-surgical perspective for suicide attempts. In A. Shrivastava, M. Kimbrell & D. Lester (Eds.), *Suicide from a global perspective: Risk assessment and management*, pp. 119–25. Hauppauge, NY: Nova Science.

Poeschla, B., Combs, H., Livingstone, S., Romm, S., & Klein, M. B. (2011), Self-immolation. *Burns*, 37, 1049–57.

Robbins, T. (1986). Religious mass suicide before Jonestown. *Sociological Analysis*, 47, 1–20.

Romm, S., Combs, H., & Klein, M. B. (2008). Self-immolation. *Journal of Burn Care & Research*, 29, 988–93.

Rothschild, M. A., Raatschen, H. J., & Schneider, C. (2001). Suicide by self-immolation in Berlin from 1990 to 2000. *Forensic Science International*, 124, 163–66.

Sands, B. (1998). *Writings from prison*. Dublin, Ireland: Mercier Press.

Thombs, B. D., Bresnick, M. G., & Magyar-Russell, G. (2007). Who attempts suicide by burning? *General Hospital Psychiatry*, 29, 244–50.

Welsh, A. M. (2000). Norman Morrison, dead of life, dead of death. *Winds of Peace*, January, 2, 4–5.

Welsh, A. M. (2008). *Held in the light*. Maryknoll, NY: Orbis Books.

23

Victim-Precipitated Homicide[1]

David Lester

As Wolfgang (1958) pointed out, one way of committing suicide is by provoking someone else to murder you. In that way, you die while avoiding any stigma attached to suicide in your culture or subculture. In this chapter I will present several examples of this behavior.

Primitive Cultures

Many cultures have behaviors (or syndromes) in which people become violent toward others and are killed. One of the common terms in our language for this is "berserk." MacDonald (1961) suggested that this term comes from Norse (Scandinavian) mythology in which Starkadder (who had eight hands) and Alfhilde had a grandson named Berserk, so named for the furious way he went into battle without wearing armor, increasing the chances therefore of being killed. His name Berserk derived from the bearskin he wore as a shirt (*ber sark*) and was applied to groups of marauders found in the Viking community from 870 AD. to 1030 AD, after which they were banned by law.

Men who went berserk were characterized by a wild fury, which increased their strength and made them insensitive to pain. They behaved like wild animals and killed everyone they met, friend or foe. Afterwards, they would be exhausted and physically feeble for days. Fabing (1956) suggested that this state was brought on by eating toxic mushrooms, which brought on temporary psychoses, but he notes that others have suggested that it was simply an ecstatic fury appearing in a group of aggressive psychopaths.

Crazy-Dog-Wishing-To-Die

Andriolo (1998) has described a number of cultures in which people commit suicide by getting others to kill them. For example, among

Suicide as a Dramatic Performance

the Plains Indians, such as the Crow, a man who was tired of living would tell his kin that he wanted to seek death in battle. His relatives would try to dissuade him but, if he persisted, they would go along with his choice. The man was now accorded special status. He wore special clothes, used a special rattle and danced and sang special songs. In these he would talk "crosswise," that is, expressing the opposite of his real intentions and doing the opposite of what he was told. He was allowed to eat whatever he wished and to have sex with whomever he desired. His death in battle would then become a glorious memory for the tribe to recall and retell. If he failed to be killed, he was released from his vow and accorded high prestige. If he changed his mind or fled, he was ridiculed and scorned. Andriolo noted that this form of suicide was not open to women. The women in these societies who killed themselves did so in conventional ways and were stigmatized because ordinary suicide was frowned upon.

This method of committing suicide has been called indirect suicide, vicarious suicide, or masked suicide. Masked suicide is a public performance and, therefore, a public property. The suicide conforms to the cultural norms and values and thus confirms them. The suicidal person of this type also does not act impulsively, but rather seeks a cause, and the scenario offers solemnity, symbolism, and purpose. The ritual induces control and calmness in the suicide. Lowie (1913) has provided an example.

> Hunts-to-die knew of another Crazy Dog, who lived in his grandfather's time. He was the handsomest Indian ever seen, and was called Good-crazy-dog; his real name was He-strikes-the-enemy-with-his-brother. At one time the Sioux attacked a Crow band, killing all, including some of Good-crazy-dog's relatives. Good-crazy-dog said, 'I am going to die, I will be a Crazy Dog.' He bought red flannel for the sashes, making one for each side. He made a rattle out of a buffalo paunch, and tied eagle feathers to one end of it; inside he put beads and little stones. He wore a fine war-bonnet on his head and tied skunk skin ornaments to his moccasins. His necklace was of bapà'ce shells, and his earrings of sea-shells. In the back he wore a switch and in front little braids of hair. He rode a fine spotted horse with docked tail; for its trappings he sewed together red and green flannel. When he rode through the camp. He began to sing and the old women cheered him. He was killed in battle. (Lowie, 1913, p. 194)

Juramentado

Andriolo noted also that in Muslim societies, which typically disapprove of suicide in general, dying in the context of a *jihad*, a religious obligation, is considered a glorious death that enables the deceased to enter heaven immediately. In *juramentado*, a man who wished to die would go to place where there were many Christians and kill as many as possible before being killed. Today, these deaths are seen in the suicide bombers in Middle Eastern countries, who tie bombs to themselves or drive cars loaded with bombs to a crowded street and die in the explosion.

This pattern is also found in Muslims in the Philippines, the Jivaro of Peru, and the Yanomano of Venezuela.

> ... when a [Jivaro] man "no longer wants to live," he does not commit suicide in the ordinary sense, but rather suddenly starts leading assassination raids against the men who are his enemies, insisting on taking the principal risks, such as being the first to charge into the enemy's house. Sooner or later, of course, he will himself be killed, which apparently surprises no one ... (Harner, 1972, p. 181)

Running Amok

"Running amok" is no mere figure of speech, but a real homicidal syndrome. Burton-Bradley (1968) has provided an eye-witness account of such a case. The subject approached some of his relatives and the witness at dusk one evening while they were sitting outside a house. The subject had a spear, which he threw at one of the relatives, who was hit in the side. The victim was carried inside the house by some of the others. While this was being done, the subject threw another spear that hit another relative, who removed it herself. All ran away, defending themselves in the process. The eyewitness reported that the subject said. "Where are you all? I am coming after you." The witness hid until daybreak. He then found two bodies: one inside the house and one outside. With five other villagers, he searched for the subject and found him in the bush wounded in the chest, with five spears stuck in the ground beside him. He was then overpowered by the villagers. In addition to having attacked and killed people, he had damaged and destroyed yams in the yam house.

When arrested, the subject said that he had been in the bush for two days without food prior to the offense. He claimed to have amnesia for his acts but admitted that it was said that he had killed a man and a woman and speared three others. However, he later admitted that at the time of the offense he was aware that his actions were wrong in the eyes of both his own people and the administration, and that they might lead to his death. He was evaluated at a psychiatric hospital, but no mental disorder was noted.

Amok is a behavior characterized by previous brooding, homicidal outbursts, persistence in reckless homicide without apparent motive, and a claim of amnesia. It is most commonly known as a behavior of the Malays in Malaysia. Various authors have seen its cause in malaria, pneumonia, syphilis infections that have spread to the brain, hashish, heat stroke, paranoid states, and mania. However, Van Wulfften-Palthe (1936) suggested that running amok is a standardized form of obtaining emotional release. The community recognizes it as such and expects it of a person who is placed in an intolerably embarrassing or shameful situation. Malaysian social structure emphasizes strong ties between relatives and kinfolk. This results in tensions arising from these inter-personal obligations. Amok is rare (if not absent) in Malays who live in Europe and who do not have these obligations to kinfolk, as well as among Malays in Malaysia who have left their kin groups.

Burton-Bradley (1968, p. 252) summarized the cases he had come across. They were all young men, and none had serious mental disorders (such as schizophrenia) or epilepsy.

A healthy adult is quieter than usual or "goes bush" for a few days. There may be a history of slight or insult. He may regain his normal composure, or the condition may continue and remain unchanged (an abortive attack), or it may become worse. In this case, suddenly and without warning, without anyone expecting such an immediate response at this point in time, he jumps up, seizes an axe or some spears, rushes around attacking everyone and even destroying inani-mate objects, such as yam houses or hospital property. Within a very short period of time, a number of people will be dead or wounded. He shouts "I am going to kill you," and everyone in the neighborhood seeks safety in flight. All are now fully aware that the man is suffering from a special form of *kava kava* or *long long* (insanity), and that he will not stop of his own accord. They recognize that this and other similar types of reaction are available methods of tension reduction, used from time to time as acts arising from despair. The man continues in this fashion until overpowered, by which time he has become exhausted. He may also be killed or wounded. The attack may be aborted at any time by anyone who is brave enough to attempt it. On the subject's recovery, it is usually claimed that there is no recollection of the events that occurred during the acute phase.

Lester and Lester (1975) suggested that these killings may be seen as a means of delivering the person from unbearable situations. Experiencing nihilistic feeling of despair, the man sees his life as intolerable and has nothing to lose but life, and so he trades his own life for those of others. The amok episode rehabilitates him in the eyes of his group, but he runs the risk of being killed in the process. In other cases of amok, however, the man is not making a rational decision. He loses control completely, and his strong emotions take over.

Running amok is found most commonly in Malaysia, but it has been reported in Papua and New Guinea, Trinidad, India, Liberia, Siberia, Africa, and Polynesia. It seems to be rare among the Chinese. Westermeyer (1972, 1973) described eighteen cases of amok in Laos in which the men used grenades. All the murderers were male, and fifteen were soldiers. Sixteen had fathers who were farmers. The men were living away from home, drinking at the time, and ten of them killed themselves after the attack. Most of the attacks took place at night, on weekends, in crowded places and were a reaction to the loss of a loved one, money or prestige. Those who killed in these amok attacks were younger than other murderers in Laos, killed more victims, killed more often in crowded places, and more often used a grenade. They were more often living away from home and on active duty in the military, and they were more likely to have been drinking and to kill themselves after the murders than other murderers.

Kiev (1972) viewed amok as a homicidal mania, but he felt that it could occur in states of delirium, agitated depression, and acute anxiety reactions. Andriolo (1998) thought that the psychiatric state preceding amok was a bipolar affective disorder (manic-depressive psychosis). The outburst appears to be manic, and the state of exhaustion afterwards depressive, but I see no close correlation between manic-depressive disorder and amok, and certainly no psychiatrist has diagnosed those who run amok without already knowing about their outburst.

The Wiitiko Psychosis[2]

According to Parker (1960), the Wiitiko psychosis is a behavior pattern found among the Algonkian-speaking Canadian-Natives in the forested central northeastern Canada, including the Saulteux, Cree, Beaver, and Ojibwa Indians. Kiev (1972) viewed it is a "classic depressive disorder," but he felt that schizophrenia and mania could also be involved.

It affects mainly males who have spent time hunting unsuccessfully for food in frozen forests. Initially the subject feels morbidly depressed and nauseated, and he experiences distaste for ordinary foods. He may have periods of semi-stupor. Gradually he becomes obsessed with the paranoidal belief that he is bewitched, and he starts having homicidal and suicidal thoughts. He feels that he is possessed by the Wiitiko monster. As the psychosis develops, he begins to see those around him as fat, luscious animals that he desires to devour. Finally, he enters a stage of violent, homicidal cannibalism. The Indians believe that if he reaches this point, he is incurable and must be killed.

There may be genetic factors, brain damage, and traumatic experiences that contribute to the cause of this disorder. However, Parker focused on the stress from the environment and the child-rearing techniques in the Ojibwa culture. The Ojibwa child is at first handled permissively and indulged, but between ages of three and five, a drastic change occurs. The child is weaned from his dependency and prodded to assume adult responsibilities. He is hardened by practices such as being made to run naked in the snow. He is goaded by the adult men to become a hunter, and he is taught by his mother how to trap animals. By age nine, he has his own hunting grounds, and by age twelve he is a competent hunter, staying away for long periods, hunting in the silent, frozen forests. The boy is made to fast until eventually he can go for long periods with only one meal a day. Punishment is often administered by withholding food. Finally, at puberty, he is sent out into the forest without food and expected to remain there until he is able to communicate with the supernatural by means of a vision.

Parker summed up the important results of this experience as follows: (i) the period of indulgence followed by harsh weaning from dependency leads to the development of covert dependency cravings; (ii) there is a close association of food, eating and self-esteem in which to be hungry is an expression of defeat and shame; (iii) power, acceptance, and affection are secured by self-denial and suffering; and (iv) security and self-esteem are vulnerable and must constantly be reaffirmed by the external symbols of success.

As adults, the Ojibwa are characterized by a high level of interpersonal hostility, which they express in indirect ways, such as hypersensitivity to insults, exaggerated pride, and paranoid tendencies. The Ojibwa's childhood experiences lead to unsatisfied dependency cravings and repressed (unconscious) hostility. However, the social structure of Ojibwa society does not allow acceptable outlets for these needs, and the adult Ojibwa treads a narrow path between his quest for affection and his desire to give vent to his rage. Failure in hunting can easily lead to a psychiatric breakdown. Failure to obtain food threatens starvation and loss of self-esteem. The paranoid feelings may result from the belief that your bad luck is the result of others practicing magic against you, a belief which develops easily in those who have repressed their anger. Failure as a hunter is a stress that leads to a breakdown of the normal defense mechanisms. Rage and aggression are then expressed in a direct and overt manner, rather than being turned inward as depression.

A mild case of Wiitiko psychosis can be treated successfully by having other people prepare a dish of melted bear grease and berries, which the patient drinks. This action simultaneously lessens hunger by providing a good many calories (important in the old days when the long winters were particularly stressful for the Ojibwa) and satisfies dependency cravings since the person is fed and cared for by others as he was when he was a child. There may also be some significance in the choice of bear grease since bears are considered by the Ojibwa to be magically important animals.

Suicide at the Hands of the State

Martyrs

Baechler (1979) suggested that the term *indirect suicide* could be used to label victim-precipitated suicides. Baechler gave an example from the seventh century. A married priest, Petros of Kapitolion (in the province of Damascus in Syria), liked the idea of becoming a martyr. To achieve this, he made a series of comments that offended the Muslims who ruled the region in which he lived. (He may have been trying to convert Muslims to Christianity.) Although the Muslim rulers were remarkably tolerant[3], he eventually forced them to execute him.

Some martyrs may be seen as motivated in part by suicidal desires, although, of course, many other motives may also be present. In a discussion of martyrs in the Ottoman Empire in the fifteenth through nineteenth centuries, Constantelos (1978) noted many reasons for martyrdom, including political protest and social agitation, atonement for converting to Islam, and imitation of earlier martyrs. For example, Romanos from central Greece went on a pilgrimage to Jerusalem and was inspired by listening to the Acts of the Martyrs read in the monastery there to become a martyr. He succeeded in getting himself executed in 1694.

Suicide by the Hand of the Government

It has been suggested that some murderers are trying to commit suicide, perhaps unconsciously, by getting the state to execute them, at least in countries where the death penalty is in force. For example, Dorpat (1968) noted that Lee Harvey Oswald, the presumed assassin of President John F. Kennedy, left many clues to his identity, including fingerprints on the rifle. He also brought attention to himself by going to a movie theater after the crime and shooting a police officer who approached him. It has been observed that some inmates on death row eventually volunteer to give in to the process leading to their execution. They stop all appeals and accept the death sentence. However, it is by no means clear that they felt this way before their crime or immediately after conviction.

Baechler provided the example of a French murderer, Claude Buffet, who had demanded the death penalty, but who was instead sentenced to life imprisonment. Buffet then tried to escape, taking hostages and killing two in order to force the authorities to execute him, which they did in December, 1972. Buffet had reasoned that, since the Christian religion forbids suicide, the only way to exit this life prematurely and without sinning was to be killed. Buffet wrote to the French President, "To kill in order to commit suicide, that's my morality" (Baechler, 1979, p. 36). Baechler cites a French report that identified twenty-eight such murderers in France.

Hughes (1986), in his history of Australia, noted that in the early 1800s, Australian authorities sent their worst criminals to Norfolk Island, one thousand miles offshore in the Pacific Ocean, where conditions were horrendous. One way of committing suicide was as follows. A group of men would draw straws to select two of their number. These two would then draw straws to choose who would kill the other. Thus, one of the men would escape Norfolk Island by death. The murderer would then have to be shipped back to Sydney on the mainland for trial. This gave the man a slim chance for escape. If he failed to escape, then he would be tried, convicted of murder and hung. Thus, the second man would escape Norfolk Island by being executed by the state.

Several classic cases of this type occurred in olden times, including Antigone and Socrates.

Antigone

Oedipus is famous for inadvertently murdering his father (he did not know the identity of his victim) and then marrying his mother (again unknowingly). When he discovered the reality of his actions, his mother/wife committed suicide, and he blinded himself. He eventually died, leaving four children. Eteocles allied himself with the new king, Creon, while the other son, Polynices, led a rebellion and lost. Both brothers were killed in the civil war.

Antigone decided to bury her brother Polynices against Creon's orders, knowing that the punishment was to be stoned to death. After failing to persuade her sister Ismene to assist her, she asked Ismene to tell everyone what she is going to do. Her first attempt to bury her brother was discovered, and he was unburied. When she buried him a second time, she "screamed like an angry bird" (Sophocles, 1956, p. 137) so as to be sure to get caught.

Antigone anticipated a public death, and she compared herself with the public death of the daughter of Tantalus. The Chorus then reminded Antigone that Tantalus's daughter (Niobe) was a goddess, while Antigone was a mere mortal, which upset Antigone. Creon ordered Antigone to be sealed in a cave rather than being killed in public. Antigone hung herself (using the same method for suicide as did her mother) after being placed in the cave.

In her death, Antigone succeeded in transforming her image. The child of an incestuous marriage, she defied Creon and died heroically, leaving Creon cast as the villain. She died by suicide by getting Creon to execute her. Only when she was deprived of her public execution, a victim-precipitated homicide, did she hang herself.

Socrates

Socrates was the son of Sophroniscus and Phaenarete from Alopeke, a town on the road from Athens to the marble quarries of Pentelicon. He was born in 470 B.C. or 469 BC and executed in 399 B.C. at the age of seventy. Socrates was put on trial in 399 B.C., found guilty, and sentenced to death. The traditional death sentence in Athens was to drink hemlock, but what makes Socrates' death a suicide was not simply his acquiescence to the death sentence, but the fact that he could easily have escaped a guilty verdict and the death sentence. According to a recent biographer, Stone (1988), he sought to be executed, and this is what makes his death truly suicidal.

Athens was a fully participatory democracy with freedom of speech as one of its main tenets. As a result, Athens attracted thinkers from all over who came there to exchange ideas and to debate one another. Socrates was one of the leading philosophers there, but his views were rather odd. First, Socrates was completely opposed to democracy. He favored authoritarian rule by experts. Just as shoemakers must know how to make shoes, rulers must know how to rule. Only those who have the correct knowledge should be allowed to rule. Then the ruler orders, and the ruled must obey. Clearly, Socrates and his followers were out of step with the Athenians.

Did Socrates threaten the leaders of Athens? Socrates used his wisdom to make the leaders appear to be ignorant fools and, by his tactics, he turned some of the young men of the city against the democracy and encouraged them to hold all Athenians in disdain. However, the playwrights frequently did this in their plays, and they were not censored, so this in itself is not sufficient cause for the trial of Socrates. Athens was based on participation by all in the government of the city, while Socrates preached withdrawal from political life. For himself, in seventy years, he hardly participated. Although he did not participate in either of the two movements that overthrew the democracy, neither did he participate in the restoration of democracy.

Important for understanding the reasons for his trial and conviction was the fact that two of his students helped overthrow the democratic government in Athens. Part of the charge against Socrates was that he led the youth to despise the established constitution and made them violent. In 411 BC the overthrow of the government was led by Alcibiades after which followed a period of rule by the Four Hundred. In 404 BC, a group of thirty overthrew the government, aided by Sparta, which had defeated Athens in the Peloponnesian War.

The rule of the Four Hundred lasted only four months, and the rule of Thirty only eight months, but there were many horrors committed during those brief periods. The possibility of new horrors must have scared the Athenians so much that Socrates's ideas were now seen as very dangerous. In both coups, the aristocracy joined with the middle classes to disfranchise the lower classes, and then the aristocracy turned against the middle class. The aristocracy proved to be cruel, rapacious, and bloody. The Thirty killed more than fifteen hundred Athenians in eight months, more than had died in the last decade of the Peloponnesian War. Although there was an amnesty after the coup of 404 BC, some of the Thirty refused to be reconciled and moved to the nearby town of Eleusis. The Athenians learned that the leaders of Eleusis were planning to attack Athens in 401 B.C. and attacked first and defeated them. Thus, Athens in 399 BC had much to fear from the followers of Socrates, and so they tried him.

Stone estimated that the vote for Socrates' guilt was probably 280 for conviction and 220 for acquittal. Socrates was surprised that so many voted for acquittal for, according to Xenophon, he did his best to antagonize the jury, particularly by being boastful and arrogant. It seemed as if seventy years of life was enough for Socrates, and he was worried about becoming frail and losing his hearing and vision. He acknowledged that trial and execution was a way to commit suicide.

Next came the vote for the penalty. Athenian juries could vote only for the penalty proposed by the prosecution or that proposed by the accused. The prosecution demanded the death penalty. Socrates offered first that he should be fed free of charge for the rest of his life as a civic hero. He next offered a fine of one mina, a trivial amount, but, following pressure from Plato and other followers, then suggested thirty minas of silver. The jury voted for the death penalty by a vote of about 360 to 140. A proposal of banishment from the city or a reasonable fine would have pleased the jury. He probably could have won acquittal by appealing to the Athenian commitment to free speech. But for Socrates to appeal to the Athenian system would have given the system a moral victory over him.

After the verdict, when Socrates was in prison, his followers arranged for his escape. Socrates refused. He said it was his duty to obey the court's verdict and die. So Socrates drank the hemlock that was provided to him by the court and died and, in doing so, fulfilled his own death wish.

Modern Cases

A number of authors have described more recent cases. Wertham (1949) described the case of a patient he had seen in psychotherapy, Robert Irwin, who had mentioned early in 1931 that he had thought of killing his girlfriend in order to be executed by the state. In 1937, he tried to kill an ex-girlfriend, but because she was not living at home, he killed her mother, sister, and a boarder instead, after which he gave himself up to the police. (Incidentally, he was not executed. He was sentenced to 139 years in prison.)

Sellin (1959) described many such cases from the 1700s and 1800s and noted that they must have been quite common since the Danish government decided in 1767 to waive the death penalty in cases where the offender murdered in order to be executed. Sellin mentioned two cases from the 1900s: a Frenchman, morally unable to kill himself, who stabbed a woman unknown to him in order to be executed by the state, and Frederick Field, who killed two people in London in 1931 in order to be executed. More recently, Bohm (1999) described the case of Daniel Colwell who was sentenced to die in the electric chair in Georgia in 1998. Colwell confessed that he was morally unable to kill himself, and so he shot two strangers in a parking lot so that the state would execute him. He later changed his mind and began appealing the death sentence. Van Wormer (1995) presented summaries of twenty

Suicide as a Dramatic Performance

such cases that she had located in both recent scholarly and newspaper articles on the death penalty, and one of the cases she summarized was that of Gary Gilmore.

Gary Gilmore was executed in Utah in 1977 for the murder of two men during the commission of armed robberies. No one had been executed in America for the prior ten years, a period during which the US Supreme Court deliberated the conditions under which executions were permissible under the Constitution. More than most recent murderers, Gilmore seemed to want to be executed. Indeed, he insisted upon his execution, and he seemed to be saying that state could not punish him because he desired to die by execution. The state apparently would help him in his final act of murder—that of himself. Perhaps also, although this is less clear, Gilmore murdered the men during armed robberies in part in order to ensure his execution.

One night in July 1976, he went driving with his girlfriend's sister, and with her in the truck, he went into a gas station, robbed the twenty-six-year-old attendant, Max Jensen, and shot him in the back of the head, twice. The next night, he walked into a motel in Provo, shot the receptionist, Ben Bushnell, in the back of the head and stole the cash box. He was recognized, and after he called a relative for help (he had shot himself in the thumb), he was caught in a roadblock.

At the trial a couple of months later, Gary stared at the judge and jury menacingly, refused to let his girlfriend (Nicole) testify, and offered his own testimony belligerently. On October 7 he was found guilty and sentenced to death. He told the judge he wanted to be shot rather than hanged. He waived the right to appeal and requested that his execution be carried out. The date was set for Monday November 15. The Utah governor ordered a stay, for which Gary called him a "moral coward." On November 16, both Gary and Nicole attempted suicide by overdosing on sedatives. Gilmore's brother, Mikal, considered appealing on Gary's behalf. On December 3, the US Supreme Court ordered a stay of execution but lifted it on December 13. The execution was rescheduled for January 17.

Mikal visited Gary to discuss appeals. Gary told Mikal:

> I killed two men. I don't want to spend the rest of my life in jail. If some fucker gets me set free, then I'm going to go get a gun and kill a few more of those damn lawyers who keep interfering. Then I'll say to you, 'See what your meddling accomplished? Are you proud?' (Gilmore, 1994, p. 339)

Gilmore's brother Frank felt that:

> Gary had reached the point of no return. He wanted the release of death . . . He had found the perfect way to beat the system by having them kill him. Then he's out of it. (p. 341)

Later, Gary told Mikal that, if his sentence was commuted, "I'd kill myself." (p. 343)

Gary Gilmore was executed by shooting on Monday morning, January 17, 1977.

Suicide-by-Cop

Suicide-by-cop refers to a situation in which, once police officers arrive on a scene, the individual purposely disobeys orders from the police to lay down his weapon and to surrender. The person then intentionally escalates the potential for the use of force through such acts as threatening the police officers or civilians in the area with a weapon, most commonly a gun. The police officers then are forced to escalate their response, often firing at the individual and killing the person in self-defense or to protect civilians. Suicide-by-cop is a lethal method of committing suicide because the would-be suicide knows that police officers are trained in the use of guns (and so in all likelihood will hit their target), are certain to have a gun, and will fire in life-threatening situations.

Jenet and Segal (1985) reported a typical case of suicide-by-cop. The perpetrator called 911 four times after 7 PM from a school reporting a burglary in progress. When the police arrived, they saw a man at the window who approached the front door. He opened it and fired one shot at the police officers. The stakeout unit and a police dog unit arrived and began to search the building. The suspect was spotted on the first floor, and he again fired a shot at the police and fled. The police dog detected the man on the second floor, whereupon he said, "I give up." The officers secured the dog, but as the officers approached the man, he crouched down and pointed the gun at them. They shot and killed him. The weapon was a .22 caliber starter pistol and incapable of firing live cartridges. The man turned out to be a male helper at the school, working split shifts. Seven months earlier, he had been admitted to a local psychiatric hospital after attempting suicide by cutting his wrists, and he was diagnosed as having a depressive neurosis.

Wilson (1998) and his colleagues described an incident in which a thirty-three-year-old white male was involved in a domestic dispute.

When the police arrived, he went into his bedroom and pointed his rifle toward his own chest. He refused to come out, cocked and uncocked the rifle, and begged to be killed. The police tried to get his Rabbi and his psychiatrist to come and talk to him, but both refused. After an hour, police shot tear gas into the bedroom, and a police officer wearing a mask entered the room. The man tore the mask off the officer and shouted "I'll kill you," whereupon the officer shot and killed him.

In another case, a twenty-one-year-old white male entered a police department with a loaded .357 Magnum pistol. He pointed it at the solitary police officer there and occasionally at himself, threatening to kill both of them. He fired two rounds and warned officers outside not to enter. He opened the door and fired at one officer but missed, whereupon two other officers shot and killed him. His blood alcohol level was 0.22%, and his urine indicated amphetamine use. He had been diagnosed as having a major depressive disorder and had previously attempted suicide several times.

The Motivation for Suicide-By-Cop

Van Zandt (undated) described the profile of the typical suicide-by-cop as follows. He is from the lower social classes and uses aggression as a way of responding to problems. He is seeking death because of depression and guilt, despair, or a desire to punish society for the wrongs it has committed against him. His philosophy of life leads him to view suicide as an unacceptable way of dying, whereas forcing others to kill him is acceptable because this makes him a victim of other people's aggression. Thus, he will provoke the police to kill him, even to the extent of killing innocent people or police officers. If he has killed a significant other prior to the confrontation with the police, then his death at the hands of the police may serve as a punishment for his crime. This suggests that, although he has apparently rebelled against the norms of society, especially in his violent behavior, he has internalized the values of the society, values that demand that criminal behavior be punished.

Mohandie and Meloy (2000) saw the possible motivations for suicide-by-cop as (1) an attempt to escape the consequences of criminal or shameful behavior, (2) using the confrontation with the police to try to reconcile with a significant other (such as a lover), (3) hoping to avoid the exclusion clauses in insurance policies that operate for the first year or two after taking out the policy,[4] (4) overcoming the moral prohibition against committing suicide, and (5) choosing an efficient method for suicide.

Mohandie and Meloy suggested that suicide-by-cop could be viewed as an *expressive behavior*, for example, a means of expressing hopelessness, depression, and desperation, a view of oneself as a victim, a need to save face by being forcibly overwhelmed rather than surrendering, a need for power, a way to express feelings of rage and revenge, or a need to draw attention to oneself or to one's issues. To illustrate this type of suicide-by-cop incident, they presented the case of a man who had been evicted from his house and who had recently lost both parents and a son. He was sporadically unemployed, drank a lot, and was described by associates as "down in the dumps." He confronted the police with a rifle and was shot to death. His manner of death expressed his hopelessness and his view of himself as a victim.

Geberth (1993) suggested that the two main motives for suicide by cop are that having another to kill you lessens the sinfulness of the act and the stigma associated with suicide. Some perpetrators are seeking punishment for their sins, real or imagined, while others do not have the courage to end their lives themselves. Some perpetrators may be seeking publicity in their deaths and so behave in a grandiose manner. Geberth also suggested a role for unconscious motives in that the police officer who kills and thereby punishes the perpetrator may be a surrogate or stand-in for the perpetrator's parents whom the perpetrator hated. The perpetrator ensures his own self-destruction and forces the police officer (who symbolizes a surrogate parent) to kill him, thereby causing the police officer to feel regret and guilt for his actions. Finally, if the perpetrator hates authority or is full of rage, then to die defiantly at the hands of the authority, perhaps killing others in the process, may be satisfying. This motive typically leads to a hostage situation in which the negotiations fail or where the perpetrator is a member of a terrorist or radical political group.

Homant, et al. (2000) collected together 123 suicide-by-cop incidents from several sources (including some of those reviewed above) and coded the information from each case. The perpetrators possessed firearms in 50% of the incidents, followed by a knife in 20%. In 22% of the incidents, it turned out that the police were not in any real danger—in 9% of these incidents the perpetrator had a firearm that was not loaded and in 12% the perpetrator used a toy firearm or an object that resembled a firearm. The police shot and killed the perpetrator in 72% of the incidents, in 6% the perpetrator committed suicide, in 8% the perpetrator was wounded by the police and survived, in 9% the perpetrator was overcome, and in 4% the perpetrator surrendered or the police left without incident.

Eighty-nine percent of the perpetrators were male, and their ages ranged from fifteen to eighty, with a mean age of thirty-two. Personal psychopathology or stress was reported for 76% of the perpetrators, most commonly family/domestic problems (33%) and drug or alcohol problems (33%). Some 22% had previously documented mental illness, and 20% a criminal history. Fifteen percent had made previous suicide attempts. Twenty seven percent had shown clear evidence that the perpetrator was planning suicide, and in a further 24% of the cases this was probable. A fatal outcome was much more likely if others were present at the scene of the incident.

A Typology of Suicide-By-Cop Incidents

Homant and Kennedy (2000) took a sample of 145 cases of suicide-by-cop and twenty-nine incidents that did not quite meet the criteria for such incidents (standoff or barricade situations, desperate escapes, interrupted suicides, and mistakes in which the police or the perpetrator reacted too quickly such as in response to a sudden movement). Homant and Kennedy found four categories of these incidents, each with several subtypes:

(1) Direct confrontation
  (i) Kamikaze attacks: In these, the perpetrator plans an attack on the police in order to be killed by them, and he makes a direct attack on the police.
  (ii) Controlled attacks: Here the perpetrator confronts the police, perhaps approaching them while holding a gun, and demands that they kill him.
  (iii) Manipulated confrontations: The perpetrator causes the police to investigate a situation, for example, by calling them to report a crime or a suicide attempt.
  (iv) Dangerous confrontations: These incidents are similar to (iii) but the perpetrator actually commits a crime or poses a danger to hostages.

(2) Disturbed intervention
  (i) Suicide intervention: Incidents in which the officers are called to prevent an individual from committing suicide.
  (ii) Disturbed domestic conflicts: Incidents in which the police officers respond to a domestic dispute that escalates into a suicide-by-cop incident.
  (iii) Disturbed person: These incidents involve disturbed individuals acting strangely and dangerously. When the police are called, the incident escalates into a suicide-by-cop incident.

(3) Criminal intervention
   (i) Major crime (such as burglary): The police arrive on the scene and prevent the perpetrator's escape. The subject appears to prefer death to arrest and acts so as to force the police to kill him.
   (ii) Minor crime (such as a traffic stop): Here the perpetrator appears to resist the police intervention, and the resistance escalates.

Homant and Kennedy found that the perpetrators were youngest in the criminal intervention incidents (mean age twenty-six) and oldest in the disturbed interventions (mean age thirty-six).[5] But the ages varied also by subtype. The danger to police and others was less in the direct confrontations, while the danger to the perpetrator did not vary with the type of incident. The distribution of female perpetrators among the three major types was similar to that for men.

Staging a Suicide-By-Cop

To die by suicide-by-cop, the act must be staged carefully. The staging can be described by studying the clues that are provided to police officers in order to classify a situation as a suicide-by-cop. Van Zandt (undated) provided a list of features of police-citizen confrontations which suggests that they may be suicide-by-cop situations.

(1) The person in a hostage/barricade situation refuses to negotiate with the police.
(2) He has killed a significant other, especially a child or mother.
(3) He demands that the police kill him.
(4) He sets a deadline for the police to kill him.
(5) He has recently learned that he has a life-threatening illness or disease.
(6) He indicates that he has an elaborate plan involving prior thought and preparation for his death.
(7) He says that he will surrender in person only to the officer in charge.
(8) He indicates that he wants to "go out in a big way."
(9) He presents no demand that includes his escape or freedom.
(10) He is from the lower social classes.
(11) He provides the authorities with a "verbal will."
(12) He appears to be looking for a macho or manly way to die.
(13) He has recently given away money or personal possessions.
(14) He has a criminal record that includes assaults and violent behavior.
(15) He has recently experienced two or more traumatic events in his life involving his family or himself.
(16) He expresses feeling of hopelessness and helplessness.

Mohandie and Meloy (2000) have also listed a set of clues that can indicate when an incident may be suicide-by-cop.

Verbal clues include:

(1) demands that the authorities kill him/her
(2) setting a deadline for them to kill him/her
(3) threatening to kill or harm others
(4) wanting to go out in a blaze of glory or indicating that he/she will not be taken alive
(5) giving a verbal will
(6) telling hostages or others that he/she wants to die
(7) looking for a macho way out
(8) offering to surrender to the person in charge
(9) indicating elaborate plans for his/her own death
(10) expressing feelings of depression and hopelessness
(11) emphasizing that jail is not an option
(12) making Biblical references (especially to the Book of Revelations and resurrection)

Behavioral clues include:

(1) displaying a weapon
(2) pointing the weapon at the police
(3) clearing a opening in the barricade in order to shoot
(4) shooting at police
(5) reaching for a weapon with police present
(6) attaching the weapon to his/her body
(7) counting down to kill hostages or others
(8) assaulting or harming hostages
(9) forcing a confrontation with police
(10) advancing on the police when told to stop
(11) calling the police himself to report a crime in progress
(12) continues acts of aggression after being wounded
(13) self-mutilation with police present
(14) pointing weapon at self
(15) refusing to negotiate
(16) making no demands to escape
(17) making no demands at all
(18) getting intoxicated in order to increase his/her courage

Discussion

In each of these types of suicide by victim-precipitated homicide, there is a script that the individual follows. Some of the scripts are determined by the culture and incidents that have occurred in the past. Other scripts have to be followed or else the individual will not be killed (as in suicide-by-cop). For all of the types of victim-precipitated homicide, the staging of the act is of critical importance.

Notes

1. This chapter is based on Lindsay and Lester (2004).
2. This is also called the Windigo psychosis.
3. They labeled him as mad in order to spare him.
4. Lester (1988) surveyed life insurance companies and found that the majority have a two-year exclusion clause permitting them to refuse payment if the person commits suicide in that time period. Occasional companies limit this exclusion period to one year. All companies surveyed, however, refund the premiums paid, sometimes with interest.
5. The mean age in the direct confrontations was thirty-one.

References

Andriolo, K. R. (1998). Gender and the cultural construction of good and bad suicides. *Suicide & Life-Threatening Behavior,* 28, 37–49.

Baechler, J. (1979). *Suicides.* New York: Basic Books.

Bohm, R. M. (19990. *Deathquest.* Cincinnati, OH: Anderson.

Burton-Bradley, B. G. (1968). The amok syndrome in Papua and New Guinea. *Medical Journal of Australia, i,* 252–56.

Constantelos, D. J. (1978). The "neomartyrs" as evidence for methods and motives leading to conversion and martyrdom in the Ottoman Empire. *Greek Orthodox Theological Review,* 23, 216–34.

Dorpat, T. L. (1966). Suicide in murderers. *Psychiatric Digest,* 27(June), 51–55.

Fabing, H. D. (1956). On going berserk. *American Journal of Psychiatry,* 113, 409–15.

Geberth, V. (1993). Suicide-by-cop. *Law & Order,* 41(7, July), 105–9.

Gilmore, M. (1994). *Shot in the heart.* New York: Doubleday.

Harner, M. (1972). *The Jivaro.* Garden City, NY: Doubleday.

Homant, R. J., & Kennedy, D. B. (2000). Suicide by police. *Policing,* 23, 339–55.

Homant, R. J., Kennedy, D. B., & Hupp, R. T. (2000). Real and perceived danger in police officer assisted suicide. *Journal of Criminal Justice,* 28, 43–52.

Hughes, R. (1986). *The fatal shore.* New York: Vintage Books.

Jenet, R. N., & Segal, R. J. (1985). Provoked shooting by police as a mechanism for suicide. *American Journal of Forensic Medicine & Pathology,* 6, 274–75.

Kiev, A. (1972). *Transcultural psychiatry.* New York: Free Press.

Lester, D. (1988). Suicide and life insurance. *Psychological Reports,* 63, 920.

Lester, D., & Lester, G. (1975). *Crime of passion.* Chicago, IL: Nelson-Hall.

Lindsay, M., & Lester, D. (2004). *Suicide by cop.* Amityville, NY: Baywood.

Lowie, R. H. (1913). Military societies of the Crow Indians. *Anthropological Papers of the American Museum of Natural History,* 11(3), 143–227.

MacDonald, J. M. (1961). *The murderer and his victim.* Springfield, IL: Charles C. Thomas.

Mohandie, K., & Meloy, J. R. (2000). Clinical and forensic indicators of "suicide by cop." *Journal of Forensic Sciences,* 45, 384–89.

Parker, S. (1960). The Wiitiko psychosis in the context of Ojibwa personality and culture. *American Anthropologist,* 62, 603–23.

Sellin, T. (1959). *The death penalty.* Philadelphia, PA: American Law Institute.

Sophocles. (1956). *The Theban plays*. Translated by E. F. Watling. Baltimore, MD: Penguin.

Stone, I. F. (1988). *The trial of Socrates*. Boston, MA: Little Brown.

Van Wormer, K. (1995). Execution-inspired murder: A form of suicide? *Journal of Offender Rehabilitation, 22*(3/4), 1–10.

Van Wulfften-Palthe, P. M. (1936). Psychiatry and neurology in the tropics. In C. D. de Langan & A. Lichtenstein (Eds.) *A clinical textbook of tropical medicine*, pp. 525–47. Batavia, NY: Kolff.

Van Zandt, C. R. (undated). Suicide by cop. Unpublished paper.

Wertham, F. (1949). *The show of violence*. Garden City, NY: Doubleday.

Westermeyer, J. (1972). A comparison of amok and other homicide in Laos. *American Journal of Psychiatry, 129*, 703–9.

Westermeyer, J. (1973). Grenade-amok in Laos. *International Journal of Social Psychiatry, 19*, 251–60.

Wilson, E. F., Davis, J. H., Bloom, J. D., Batten, P. J., & Kamara, S. G. (1998). Homicide or suicide? *Journal of Forensic Sciences, 43*, 46–52.

Wolfgang, M. E. (1958). *Patterns of criminal homicide*. Philadelphia, PA: University of Pennsylvania Press.

24

Sati[1]

David Lester

Sheth (1994) and Vijayakumar (2009) have both noted that suicide committed as a personal act motivated by emotions such as pride, frustration, and anger is censured in Hinduism. In contrast, other forms of voluntary self-termination of life are not considered to be suicide and are, therefore, not condemned. Self-sacrifice for the general good is admired, as is self-sacrifice to expiate sins such as incest. Ascetics are allowed to choose death by voluntary starvation, committed deliberately and without passion. For example, *mahaprasthana* (great journey) involves the individual going on a continuous walk after giving up all attachments and possessions and subsisting only on air and water. *Sati* is also a form of suicide that is permitted. As Weinberger-Thomas (1999) pointed out, sati refers to the woman who commits this act and signifies "a chaste and faithful virtuous wife" (p. 20), but the term is typically used, erroneously, to refer to the act itself.

It should be noted that the sacrifice (voluntarily or otherwise) of survivors of a deceased individual was not uncommon in India and other countries in historical times. It was thought in many cultures that a deceased emperor or warrior would need to have possessions and services in the after-life, and so possessions were buried along with the deceased and, sometimes, servants were also sacrificed. Sati is one of the few cultural customs where a survivor of a low-ranking individual was expected to sacrifice herself.

Sati[2] has a long history. Although best documented in India, it occurred in China, Mesopotamia, and Iran. It was practiced by queens, whose kings expected them to die with them. Rajput queens in India sometimes committed suicide by self-immolation even when their husbands were killed in battle far away. The first memorial to sati was found in Madhya Pradesh in India in 510 AD (Baig, 1988), but the earliest historical instance is of the wife of General Keteus who died in 316 BC (Vijayakumar, 2004). Sati is named after the consort of the god Shiva. Shiva and Sati's father (Daksha) had an argument, and Sati was so angry at her father that the fire of her anger destroyed her. Shiva retaliated by sending a monster to destroy Daksha's head but later relented and allowed Daksha to be fitted with a goat's head. The higher castes, Brahmans, Kshatriyas, and Vaishyas, have interpreted this myth as indicating the way in which a widow should join her dead husband on his death—by immolating herself (Freed & Freed, 1989).

The *Vedas*, the most important of the Hindu texts, does not demand that women commit sati, although there is disagreement over one word. Some argue that it is the word for "go forth" while others argue that it is the word for "to the fire" (Yang, 1989). Most now think the *Vedas* encourages widows to get on with their lives and even remarry.[3] The British banned sati in 1829 (Cassels, 1965; Mehta, 1966), but about forty cases have occurred since independence in 1947, the majority in Rajasthan.

There are two types of sati. *Sahamaran*a (or *sahagamana*) is where the widow ascends the funeral pyre and is burnt along with the body of her dead husband. In *Anumarana* the widow commits suicide, typically on a funeral pyre, after the cremation of her husband (Yang, 1989), usually with his ashes or some memento of him, such as a piece of his clothing. Stein (1978) noted cases in the eighteenth and nineteenth centuries in which women died on the funeral pyre of an important person, mothers died on a son's funeral pyre, and sisters died on their brother's funeral pyre. Weinberger-Thomas (1999) noted that pregnant women, women with infants, adulterous wives, prepubertal girls, women who were menstruating, women who had amenorrhea, and "disobedient" wives were not allowed to commit sati since they were considered to be impure in this state.

A debate has raged over whether widows went voluntarily or were forced (at knife point, sometimes bound and gagged) or drugged. To prevent widows changing their minds and trying to escape from the fire, exits from the fire were sometimes blocked, and roofs of wood were designed to collapse on the widow's head (Stein, 1978). This debate continues today in discussions of modern cases of sati. Daly (1978) observed that Indian men sometimes married children under the age of ten, and Narasimhan (1994) noted that eyewitnesses in the nineteenth century reported that child widows aged eight and ten were sometimes forced onto the funeral pyre and bound hand and foot if they tried to escape. Some widows were drugged with opium. On the other hand, some widows asked to be bound and thrown on the pyre to prevent them fleeing and escaping their duty (Vijayakumar, 2004).

Historical Data

Although there are few data on sati in modern times, some data can be found on sati in the nineteenth century. Inamdar, et al. (1983) noted that 2,366 cases of sati occurred in India in 1821. Yang (1989) reported data from cases of sati from Bengal from 1815 to 1828, during which time period there was an average of 581 cases each year. There were also satis in other regions (Bombay and Madras), but 90% occurred in Bengal. There were cases in both the upper castes and the lower castes, although the relative percentages varied from district to district.[4] In the whole of Bengal in 1825, 2.7% of the cases were aged nineteen or younger, and 4.7% were over the age of eighty, One widow was over the age of one hundred. The modal age group was forty to forty-nine (19.1%).

Yang noted that some widows committed sati many years after their husband's death. Sixty-year-old Jhunia committed sati fifteen years after her husband's death; seventy-year-old Karanja committed sati forty years after her husband's death; seventy-year-old Hulasi committed sati on the funeral pyre of her son sixteen years after her husband's death. For these women, Yang suggested that sati may have been a form of ritual suicide motivated at least in part by personal considerations. Yang noted that, after 1822, more of the widows came from impoverished families, and most left little property. In one sample of seventy-nine satis, twenty-five husbands had died wealthy, thirteen in middling circumstances, and forty-one in poor circumstances.

Sati in Modern Times

It has been estimated that about thirty women have committed sati in Rajasthan between 1943 and 1987 (Weinberger-Thomas, 1999), although the official count is twenty-eight. Weinberger-Thomas estimates that perhaps forty satis occurred in India as a whole in that time period. There was diversity in social class (one was even a street singer), but Rajputs accounted for nineteen of the thirty satis in Rajasthan.

Desite the frequent occurrence of sati in the last sixty years, there are few cases with good information. Altekar (1978) reported the sati of his sister in 1946 within twenty-four hours of the death of her husband. Inamdar, et al. (1983) reported the case of a sixteen-year-old girl (Om Kanvar) who died on the funeral pyre of her twenty-two-year-old husband, a van driver who had died of tuberculosis. They noted that she was the seventh reported case in the state of Rajasthan in recent years and the second that year. The site of her sati became a shrine for pilgrims, with reports of miracle cures of deaf and mute individuals.

Another case is that of Kuttu Bai, a sixty-five-year-old widow whose husband died after a prolonged illness in Panna in the province of Madhya Pradesh.[5] The sati took place the day after his death, on August 2, 2002. Accounts differ as to whether she went voluntarily and calmly or whether she was forced onto the pyre.[6] The crowd of two thousand who watched the sati is reported to have prevented police officers from stopping the ceremony. In the same village, another woman committed sati in 1950, and the site of this sati has become a shrine. This raises the possibility of modeling and imitation impacting the decision of a widow to commit sati.

On August 23, 2006, the BBC news website reported another case of sati. Janakrani immolated herself on the funeral pyre of her husband, (Prem Narayan) in the village of Tulsipur in Madhya Pradesh. Her sons reported that there was no ceremony and that she "slipped away" to commit the act by herself. On September 21, 2006, the BBC news website reported another case—Karua Devi, again in Madhya Pradesh. She was in her nineties and dressed in full bridal gear. One of her sons lit the funeral pyre. She is reported to have desired to commit sati and was encouraged by her sons and some villagers. She was a member of the upper-caste Hindu Rajput community. The report also noted that one widow in the state in the previous month had been prevented from committing sati by members of her family. Sen (2002) mentioned a sati on November 11, 1999, in the Bundelkhand region of Uttar Pradesh—a widow (Charan Shah) aged fifty-five, who had nursed her husband through tuberculosis for over twenty years. He died four years after one of her three sons had died, and the grief was too much for her, according to press cuttings.

Explanations for Sati

Sharma (1978) noted that Durkheim (1897) classified sati as *altruistic suicide*, and Vijayakumar (2004) followed this. Of the three types of altruistic suicide (obligatory, optional, and acute), Durkheim viewed sati as obligatory. Altruistic suicide occurs in societies where social integration is too strong, and obligatory altruistic suicide occurs when the sense of duty is a ruling factor. However, sati may fit better into Durkheim's category of *fatalistic suicide* since the newly widowed woman seems in some cases to be too strongly regulated. This might be the case if the woman is psychologically persuaded or forced into the act. (Physical force would change the act into murder rather than fatalistic suicide.) In order to accurately classify a sati into a Durkheimian typology, therefore, some knowledge of the sati's motives is essential, and this is rarely available. It may also be that any particular sati may have more than one of these motives and thus fits into two or even three categories. Those in India who favor sati see the benefits as accruing not just to the husband, but also to the wife and to her descendants. Therefore, Sharma (1978) viewed sati as a *sacrifice* rather than a *suicide*, and Sharma suggested a new term for the behavior—*suifice* (suicide + sacrifice).

In contrast to this view, Weinberger-Thomas (1999) saw sati as having *egotistical* elements. After exploring the history and mythology associated with sati, Weinberger-Thomas viewed the sacrifice as unrelated to duties toward the husband. The sati becomes a heroine, with temples established in her name, openly in the past and surreptitiously today. Cults develop centered around her. The sati represents the powers of femininity. Weinberger-Thomas quotes a Rajasthani saying: What matter that the husband dies if his wife's dream comes true? (p. 167).

Baig (1988) suggested that the psychodynamics underlying support for sati among the *men* in the society involve blaming for the wife for not keeping her husband alive and a fear that wives will not be faithful to their husbands, a fear that constrains widows even after their husbands' deaths. Parrilla (1999) noted that sati is believed by some to facilitate spiritual salvation for the husband, while the wife is subsequently revered as a goddess (Harlan, 1994). Sati is thought to ensure that the sati's descendants will be admitted to heaven for seven generations and that family members will be spared reincarnation.

Weinberger-Thomas (1999) documented how satis from earlier times are venerated in many regions of India, and recent satis are similarly venerated, even though any celebration of their lives and deaths is forbidden by the government. There are daily services at their shrines (often the home in which they lived), sometime surreptitiously and sometimes under the pretense of celebrating a sati from historical times.

There is also an economic rationale for sati. Under the law of inheritance in Bengal (*dayabhaga*), widows inherit their husband's estate, over-ruling the claims of his relatives. Sati, therefore, keeps the man's assets in his family. Vijayakumar (2004) noted that sati is rare in Kerala where matriarchy prevails, unlike Bengal where wives are entitled to half of their husbands' property, leaving his relatives eager to be rid of the wife. Abraham (accessed 2005) noted that the women in Rajasthan (where sati has been common) are extremely subjugated. Their illiteracy rate is among the highest in India, and the treatment of widows is particularly cruel there.

Can a wife avoid sati? Weinberger-Thomas noted that sprinkling the woman with water that has been colored with indigo is enough to make her too impure to become a sati. Being touched by an untouchable or a person a person of lower caste also prevents a woman becoming a sati. In olden days, being touched by a foreigner would also suffice, and cases have been documented of widows throwing themselves on foreign spectators to avoid becoming satis. Weinberger-Thomas notes that a person can be tricked into impurity, for example, by sprinkling indigo dye on the coconuts placed on the funeral pyre. However, sometimes, widows simply refused to become satis. Weinberger-Thomas noted a case in the early 1800s when, after the death of the Rajah Bhanswarrah, not one of his wives committed sati despite urging from others to do so.

Bala, who, at the age of forty, was prevented by the local police from becoming a sati after the death of her adopted son, has become a *jogini* (an emanation of divine energy) and has a temple in her honor.[8] Her case is interesting since her "husband" collapsed when he touched her at the wedding ceremony and died fifteen days later. Thus, she was seen as the "cause" of her husband's death. She was sixteen at the time.

Bala was born in 1903 near Pipar (in Jodhpur District), was widowed in 1919 and adopted her nephew. This son died in 1943, and Bala announced her intention to die on his funeral pyre along with the daughter-in-law. The daughter-in-law was tricked into drinking indigo water and a blue veil was thrown over Bala. Both were considered impure and unfit to be satis. Bala lived until 1986, but maintained a total fast for those forty-three years. This last point about her forty-three-year-long fast illustrates the myths that develop about satis, making it very difficult to distinguish fact from fiction in their lives.

Weinberger-Thomas makes the same point about Hem Kanvar, who committed sati in 1943, about whom many mythical stories have been told. For example, after the news of her husband's death and her decision to commit sati, she is said to have become white and radiant. Her house, which has become a temple in her honor, lived in and officiated by her in-laws, has become the site of pilgrimages and miracle cures.

> We must resign ourselves to the fact that we shall never know anything about the real life woman whose name was Hem Kanvar. . . .

> [T]he "life stories" of the new satis . . . resemble one another to the point of confusion . . . The same vignettes, and occasionally the same cover illustration [of the publications], reinforce the sense of *déjà vu* that permeates the corpus. (Weinberger-Thomas, 1999, p. 139)

Weinberger-Thomas noted that the customs and rituals make it very difficult for a widow who states her intention (willingly or under pressure) to commit sati to later recant.[9] If she does try to recant, she may be forced onto the funeral pyre. The case of Javitri who committed sati on July 11, 1979, in Jari (in Uttar Pradesh) is relevant here. Her husband and brother-in-law were killed by hoodlums. Javitri's in-laws greeted her with curses when the news was delivered because, in that subculture, Javitri was seen as guilty for having cast a spell on her in-laws.

Modeling

Weinberger-Thomas (1999) cited examples from historical times of ten or twelve satis occurring in a single family line. She also noted a case from 1822 where the sati chose as a venue the place where a sati had burned herself five months earlier. Weinberger-Thomas noted similar modeling in modern satis. Sometimes the villages where satis take place are only a few miles from one another, and these regions have many sites (marked by sati stones and temples) where satis took place in historical times. The case of one sati, Bala, is interesting since Bala claimed that she had been a sati in a previous life, but since she had cursed her in-laws in that previous life, she had to be reborn in order to die again, this time in an appropriate manner. Roop Kanvar's sati in 1987 took place in a village where two historical satis are commemorated, both of whom were wives in her husband's family line.

In the past, women in India died in mass suicides by immolation (and other means) in order to escape capture, rape, abduction, and death at the hands of invaders. Baig (1988) mentioned such cases from the tenth to the thirteenth centuries in India, and Lester (2010a) described mass suicides of Hindu women in India during the chaos after the partition of India (into Pakistan and modern India) in 1947. Baig suggested that these mass suicides by women may have contributed to the sati mentality in India.

Psychiatric Speculations

Bhugra (2005) felt that it was unlikely that women who committed sati were suffering from "formal mental illness." However, none of these women had been given a psychiatric evaluation prior to the sati, and so there are no data with which to test Bhugra's opinion. Bhugra also noted the possibility of the widows being in a possession trance or in a state of depersonalization as a result of severe bereavement.

In contrast to Bhugra's opinion, Inamdar, et al. (1983) noted that women committing sati were often young and childless or old women, and they faced miserable lives, but nonetheless:

> At a moment of great loss and stress and exposed to the multiple pressures of family and society, within a strong and ancient mytho-logical tradition, a vulnerable individual may assent to and commit a self-destructive act that is ultimately immortalized. (p. 133)

Weinberger-Thomas (1999) suggested viewing sati as a form of possession. In her description of sati occurring in Bali (Indonesia), she describes the sati as "breaking out" in the way a fever or passion breaks out. The sati herself is overcome by a frenzy, and the possessed woman is thought to become a vehicle for a god or spirit. Weinberger-Thomas noted also that this frenzy also overcomes the spectators sometimes. Weinberger-Thomas also noted that two satis in 1943 in India both began to shake and speak in a gravelly voice, and this was taken to indicate possession.

The Status of Women

Women are oppressed throughout the world. As Johnson and Johnson (2001) have noted, "*Today, in every corner of the globe*, some women are denied basic human rights, beaten, raped, and killed by men" (p. 1051). It has been noted that women have particularly low status in India where female feticide (the selective abortion of female fetuses), female infanticide, murder, dowry murder, and suicide are forces that decrease the female population relative to the male population (Freed & Freed, 1989).[10] Freed and Freed quoted a man in the village in which they stayed in 1958, "You have been here long enough to know that it is a small thing to kill a woman in an Indian village" (pp. 144–145).

In some countries, abandoned woman are social outcasts. In India, widows are treated very harshly. An article in *The Economist* (Anon, 2007) described 1,300 widows at an ashram in Vrindavan in Uttar Pradesh, who pray for three hours each day in return for a token which they can exchange for three rupees (seven cents) and a handful of uncooked lentils and rice. They are entitled to a state pension of $3.70 a month and the food ration that is given to poor Indians, but only about one quarter of the widows receive these. The article noted that widows are "unwanted baggage." In the past they were encouraged to die on their husband's funeral pyre, and those who did not were forbidden to remarry. Today, the law gives them better protection, but remarriage is still discouraged. Two fifths of the widows were married before they were twelve years old and a third were widowed by the age of twenty-four. Those widows interviewed said that they preferred to live in the ashram than go home where their treatment would be even worse. In some places, widows are permitted only one meal a day, sometimes no fish (because fish are a symbol of fertility), and must shave their heads.

The Case of Roop Kanwar

One case of sati has become extraordinarily famous, the sati of Roop Kanwar, an eighteen-year-old widow, who committed sati in Deorala, Rajasthan, on September 4, 1987 (Ali, 1987). Thousands watched her sati, yet the "facts" of the case are far from clear (Hawley, 1994). Roop Kanwar was a well-educated woman from the Rajput caste who was married for only eight months. Her twenty-four-year-old husband died from gastro-enteritis, appendicitis, or a suicidal overdose. He had recently failed an exam required for entry into medical school. Dressed in bridal finery, she was watched by a crowd of about four thousand as she died (Narasimhan, 1994). Although the government tried to prevent a celebration of this, some 250,00 people came to the village for a glorification ceremony. Money was donated to build a temple in her memory. Estimates were as high as $250,000 within two weeks. Roop Kanwar's brother-in-law and father-in-law were arrested but released without charges being filed. Roop Kanwar became a *sati-mata*, a deified woman with miraculous powers to grant favors (Narasimhan, 1994). There are rumors that she was forced into sati and may have been drugged (Kumar, 1995). She was escorted to the pyre by young men carrying swords who might well have stabbed her had she tried to flee (Narasimhan, 1994). She may have fallen from the pyre and needed assistance in mounting it (Hawley, 1994). Observers saw her flail her hands in the air as the flames touched her (Narasimhan, 1994), but one official claimed that she was blessing the crowd by this action. Others claimed that she cried out to her father for help (Hawley, 1994). As a result of this sati, Parilla (1999) noted that both women and men in Rajashan rallied to support the right to commit sati, while other groups fought to ban it (Kumar, 1995).[11]

Suicide as a Dramatic Performance

The sati of Roop Kanwar is the only one for which there is information about the circumstances leading up to the event. Mala Sen (2002), an Indian working in London, England, traveled on several occasions to India and, during her visits, became friends with Roop Kanwar's father-in-law, Sumer Singh. She also tracked down the first police officer to arrive at Deorala and who interviewed people in the village. What did she find out?[12]

The marriage had been arranged when Roop Kanwar was about five or six and Maal Singh was nine or ten. The contract was finalized in 1981, and they were married on January 17, 1987, in Jaipur. She was a city girl, and her father-in-law said that she was homesick in Deorala and so spent most of the marriage in Jaipur with her parents. Her husband was studying for his exams at this time. The low caste servants in the village were afraid to talk of the sati for fear of upsetting their employers, but they did tell Mala Sen's taxi driver that there was crying and shouting in the house during the time Roop Kanwar returned to her in-laws a few days prior to Maal Singh's death.

When the police officer, Ram Rathi, arrived on the scene, only the remains of the pyre were left. He visited the village several times afterwards and spoke to both the rich and the poor residents of the village. He found out that Roop Kanwar had not loved her husband. In fact, she had a childhood sweetheart whom she was not allowed to marry,[13] and she had been having an affair with him after her marriage in her home town of Jaipur, to which her lover had moved from Ranchi. When her parents found out, they were horrified and ordered her to return to her husband. She had become pregnant as a result of affair, but hid this from her parents. On returning to her husband, she tried to persuade her husband that the child was his. However, their marriage had never been consummated because her husband was impotent, and he had "mental problems," as did his mother.[14] Although he had a B.Sc. degree, Maal Singh was unemployed. Roop Kanwar had lived with her husband for only three weeks of their seven-month marriage, a brief period after the marriage ceremony and for a few days before his death. After Roop Kanwar came back to him, he tried to kill himself by swallowing a large quantity of fertilizer. His family covered up his suicide attempt, and a doctor took him to a distant hospital where he died on September 4, 1987.[15] His body was rushed back to Deorala for a quick cremation in order to prevent an autopsy.

The police officer was of the opinion that Roop Kanwar was "encouraged" to commit suicide. Although myths quickly grew surrounding her

314

death (that her eyes glowed red and her body generated an immense heat as she walked to her death), the children in the village told the police officer that she seemed unsteady on her feet, as if drunk or drugged, and stumbled several times on the way to the funeral pyre. She was surrounded by several youths armed with swords, and her eldest brother-in-law (who was fourteen years old) lit the funeral pyre.[16] Reports that she waved her arms as she burned and called out have been interpreted as agony and pain, but supporters of sati argue that it was joy being expressed.

Remember that wives are thought in this region of India to be responsible for illnesses and events that befall their husbands. If the husband dies or is killed, then she is responsible. In this case, the wife had been unfaithful to her husband and conceived a child by another man. In many families, Roop Kanwar would have been murdered for these behaviors. Whereas there are occasional modern cases where the parents of the bride saved her from committing sati, Roop Kanwar's parents disapproved of her true love and moved from Ranchi to Jaipur to put an end to the affair, to no avail. They, like her in-laws, celebrated her sati because now they were the parents of a new goddess and not simply business people who ran trucks between Ranchi and Jaipur.[17]

Roop Kanwar, therefore, like the female suicide bombers described by Lester (2010b, 2011), had few options. She could die on her husband's funeral pyre or face being murdered (or viciously persecuted for the rest of her life). Her suicide can be conceptualized as fatalistic in nature. By committing sati, she transformed her image from sinner to heroine. Or her death can be conceptualized as murder.

Discussion

Since not every widow chooses to die on her husband's funeral pyre, why do some become sati while others do not? The answer to this is that the choice was probably dependent on interpersonal and intrapsychic factors. For example, Stein (1988) reported the following:

> The first modern *sati* in the area occurred in 1954, in a family in which the family property had been equally settled among four sons. The death of the *sati* meant the consolidation of the property by the remaining three, since the wife of one of them, who was childless, was made the guardian of the dead woman's children. When this woman in turn became a widow shortly thereafter, rumors immediately started that she too would become a *sati*, the property going

to the remaining two brothers. She escaped immolation, however, by sending an urgent message to her father, who obtained a police escort for the funeral. (p. 474).

One widow committed sati, the other refused. Why? What psychological characteristics distinguished these two women? There is no research on this question.

From the viewpoint of the present book, sati is a scripted form of suicide that is staged by the widow's family and in-laws. What is unclear is the extent to which the widow plays a part in the scripting and to what extent is she forced into it, rendering the act more akin to murder rather than suicide.

Notes

1. This chapter is based on Lester (2013).
2. Sati is also spelled as suttee and sutty.
3. Lower castes see marriage with the deceased husband's younger brother as quite acceptable (Weinberger-Thomas 1999).
4. Yang presented no data on the relative proportions of each caste in the population.
5. news.bbc.co.uk/2/hi/south_asia/2176885.stm and 2180380.stm; www.indianexpress.com/oldStory/29260/
6. One group most definite in its view that this sati was involuntary is the Communist Party of India (Anon, 2002) (pd.cpim.org/2002/sept22/09152002_mp_sati.htm).
7. This is not the same as Durkheim's concept of egoistical suicide, which involves a very low level of social integration.
8. Weinberger-Thomas visited her at her temple.
9. The same is true of female suicide bombers (Lester 2010b, 2011).
10. Supplemented by maternal mortality as a result of unhygienic lying-in and postpartum conditions.
11. The role of pressure is illustrated by the case of Gayatri in 1983 where the village elders refused to cremate her husband unless she agreed to become a sati. The police watched her death along with thousands on onlookers (Narasimhan 1990).
12. One element, modeling, seems to be ruled out. Roop Kanwar's father-in-law said that there were no previous satis in his or his daughter-in-law's family.
13. He was from a different caste.
14. Her husband told Mala Sen that his wife suffered from depression.
15. After the sati, the doctor, Magan Singh, fled and was not found for many months. After he was found and charged, he was no longer allowed to practice medicine.
16. Her father-in-law claimed to have been in a hospital many miles from Deorala after collapsing and becoming unconscious when his son, Maal Singh, was brought to Deorala.
17. Other reports say that Roop Kanwar's father was a schoolteacher.

References

Abraham, S. (accessed November 29, 2005). The Deorala judgment glorifying suicide. www.hsph.harvard.edu/grhf/Sasia/forums/sati/articles/judgement.html.

Ali, S. (1987, October 8). A young widow burns in her bridal clothes. *Far Eastern Economic Review*, 138, 54–55.

Altekar, A. S. (1978). *The position of women in Hindu civilization*. Delhi, India: Motilal Banarsidass.

Anon. (2002). Stranglehold of obscurantism: Kuttu Bai didn't commit suicide; she was murdered. *People's Democracy*, 26(37).

Anon. (2007). Singing for supper. *The Economist*, 384(8542, August 18), 35.

Baig, T. A. (1988). Sati, women's status and religious fundamentalism. *Social Action*, 38(1), 78–83.

Bhugra, D. (2005). Sati. *Crisis*, 26, 73–77.

Cassels, N. G. (1965). The abolition of suttee. *Journal of British Studies*, 5(1), 77–87.

Daly, M. (1978). *Gyn/ecology*. Boston, MA: Beacon Press.

Durkheim, E. (1897). *Le suicide*. Paris: Felix Alcan.

Freed, R. S., & Freed, S. A. (1989). Beliefs and practices resulting in female deaths and fewer females than males in India. *Population & Environmentr*, 10(3), 144–61.

Harlan, L. (1994). Perfection and devotion. In J. H. Hawley (Ed.) *Sati, the blessing and the curse*, pp. 79–99. New York: Oxford University Press.

Hawley, J. S. (Ed.) (1994). *Sati, the blessing and the curse*. New York: Oxford University Press.

Inamdar, S. C., Oberfield, R. A., & Darrell, E. R. (1983). A suicide by self-immolation. *International Journal of Social Psychiatry*, 29, 130–33.

Johnson, P. S., & Johnson, J. A. (2001). The oppression of women in India. *Violence Against Women*, 7, 1051–1068.

Kumar, R. (1995). From Chipko to sati. In A Basu (Ed.) *The local feminisms*, pp. 58–86. Boulder, CO: Westview Press.

Lester, D. (2010a). Suicide and the partition of India. *Suicide-Online*, 1, 2–4.

Lester, D. (2010b). Female suicide bombers and burdensomeness. *Psychological Reports*, 106, 160–62.

Lester, D. (2011). Female suicide bombers. *Suicidology Online*, 2, 62–66.

Lester, D. (2013). Sati. In E. Colucci & D. Lester (Eds.), *Suicide and culture*, pp. 217–36. Cambridge, MA: Hogrefe.

Mehta, M. J. (1966). The British rule and the practice of sati in Gujarat. *Journal of Indian History*, 44, 553–60.

Narasimhan, S. (1990). *Sati*. New Delhi, India: Viking.

Narasimhan, S. (1994). India: From sati to sex-determination tests. In M. Davies (Ed.) *Women and iolence*, pp. 43–52. London, UK: Zed Books.

Parilla, V. (1999). Sati: virtuous woman through self-sacrifice. http://www.csuchico.edu/~cheinz/syllabi.asst001/spring99/parrilla/parr1.htm. Accessed November 29, 2005.

Sen, M. (2002). *Death by fire*. New Brunswick, NJ: Rutgers University Press.

Sharma, A. (1978). Emile Durkheim on suttee as suicide. *International Journal of Contemporary Sociology,* 15, 283–91.

Sheth, S. D. (1994, July–August). Those who take their lives. *Manushi,* 83, 24–30.

Stein, D. K. (1978). Women to burn. *Signs,* 4, 253–68.

Stein, D. K. (1988). Burning widows, burning brides. *Pacific Affairs,* 61, 465–85.

Vijayakumar, L. (2004). Altruistic suicide in India. *Archives of Suicide Research,* 8, 73–80.

Vijayakumar, L. (2009). Hindu religion and suicide in India. In D. Wasserman & C. Wasserman (Eds.) *Oxford textbook of suicidology and suicide prevention,* pp. 19–25. New York: Oxford University Press.

Weinberger-Thomas, C. (1999). *Ashes of immortality.* Chicago: University of Chicago Press.

Yang, A. A. (1989). Whose sati? *Journal of Women's History,* 1(2), 8–33.

25

Suicide as the Liberation of the Soul

David Lester

When suicide is engaged in as a sacrificial act, there is often a formal process and ceremony associated with the death. Willerslev (2009) has described the process of voluntary suicide among the Chukchi of north-eastern Siberia in which a family member kills another, often ill and aged, who expresses the desire to die, and this illustrates this type of staging.

Sacrificial Suicide among the Chukchi

Sacrificial death has been reported among several groups, including the Sami in Norway and the Caribou Indians, but this was often done without the sick person's consent. They sometimes were abandoned or left in the wilderness without food, and sometimes encouraged to take their own life. In the Chukchi, in contrast, the desire to die comes from the infirm individuals themselves. Furthermore, these deaths differ from other suicides among the Chukchi, which resemble those more that occur in our society and which are motivated by personal reasons, such as romantic crises.

Willerslev noted that elaborate rituals accompany these sacrificial suicides. He reports one death that was described to him.

> My grandfather must have been nearly 90 years old. One day he said, "I am tired, help me go to my relatives." He pointed at my father who got all pale, but did not dare to refuse him. My grandfather put on his funeral clothing and my mother and I prepared him the best food. We all sat together, taking turns telling good things about him. He said to us that he would continue to look after us and we should not fear him. Then all the females and children left the tent. I was later told that my father emptied a bullet of half of its gunpowder . . . My grandfather put the barrel on his forehead, and my father shot him dead. (p. 701)

They then covered the body with animal skins, and her father put dots of the grandfather's blood on everyone.

Superficially, this type of suicide seems to be consistent with the presence of perceived burdensomeness, which has been proposed by Joiner (2005) in his Interpersonal theory of Suicide. Joiner proposed that seeing oneself as a burden to others and having one's interpersonal relationships broken (thwarted belonging), combined with an acquired capacity for harming oneself, result in suicide. However, such an explanation fails to consider the spiritual beliefs of the Chukchi.

Willerslev noted that under Soviet and Russian rule, the living circumstances of the Chukchi had improved tremendously. They received medical and technical support and the availability of consumer goods. Therefore, the elderly were not a burden on their families. There were also cases of this type of suicide in able-bodied men and women in their prime. The Chukchi believe in a spirit world in balance with the earthly world. The spirit world provides souls for those on earth, but those on earth must return to the spirit world eventually. The Chukchi make sacrifices to their deceased members ranging from the easiest (stones and wooden images), up through sausages made from reindeer and reindeer themselves, to the most difficult of all—human sacrifice. While the Evens (another Siberian indigenous group) who converted to Orthodox Christianity in the 1700s see suicide as a sin, the Chukchi see it as a heroic act leading to the best of afterworlds. Death for the Chukchi is "an integral and necessary part of the creative circle of renewal. . . . [T]he living depend on the deceased for their supply of souls, so the deceased could be said to depend on the living to perform the acts of sacrifice that ensure the reproduction of their herds" (p. 696).[1]

Willerslev hypothesized that the highest offering (a human sacrifice) would be more common during times of great crisis. He found evidence that this was so, with examples from a devastating plague in 1810s (Wrangell, 1842) and in other epidemics (Batianova, 2006).

Fasting among the Jains

Fasting to death among the members of the Jain religion is not really a sacrifice, but it has elements of the ceremony associated with sacrifices. Fasting is of great importance to adherents of the Jain religion. The Jain religion is related to Buddhism and was founded at the same time, around the fourth century BC, in the same region of India. Jainism stresses renunciation, resulting in a life of asceticism. Those who follow the religion strictly live in small groups of two to a dozen, walking between towns, carrying all of their possessions with them, and teaching their worldview. The two most important values are nonviolence (toward every living thing—humans and animals) and nonpossession.

Laidlaw (2005) described the practice of fasting in Jainism. The most revered members of the group are all dead, and they died by fasting to death. Laidlaw described the life and death of Amarchand-ji Nahar, who married, had children, and became a successful businessman. After he retired, he moved to one part of his mansion where he lived an ascetic life, with a strict regimen of prayers, confession, meditation, and other rituals, including fasting. For many years, he fasted on every alternate day, and he became an expert in his community on fasting and also on breaking a fast, which can be dangerous. His final fast lasted for thirty-six days. For the final twenty-four days, he did not drink anything. People came from all around to see him, and he died while saying a meditational prayer with others around him. His room was preserved as a shrine by his family, who were very proud of him.

The practice of fasting in Jainism is called *sallekhana* or *samadhi-maran* (death in meditation). Such events are covered widely in the media. Large crowds gather, and there are lavish public ceremonies. The person who is fasting to death is viewed as an exemplar of nonviolence. Other Jains in the region may also fast until the samadhi-maran dies in order to honor him. The fasting until death begins with a formal binding vow, usually taken in front of witnesses. A senior official must check that this is not an ordinary suicide, motivated by personal reasons such as depression or anger. The goal must be to fulfill the goals of Jainism—the liberation of the soul guided by the two values of nonviolence and nonpossession.

Laidlaw saw samadhi-maran as similar in some respects to the Hindu practice in which devotees drown themselves in a sacred river or jump to their death from a sacred mountain, to death as a form of protest (*dharna*), and to *jauhar* among Rajputs in which the residents of a besieged city commit mass suicide rather than being taken by their enemies (the men riding out to fight to death and the women immolating themselves).[2] However, the aim of the individual in samadhi-maran is very different from those examples.

Discussion

In these two types of suicide, returning to the spirit world as a sacrifice and as the ultimate expression of an ascetic life, the procedures are known and followed. The script was written centuries ago, and the suicides today must follow the script for their death to be considered honorable. In many of the other examples in this book, the individuals who are choosing to die by suicide can write their own script but, when the script is culturally determined, individual deviation is less acceptable.

Notes

1. The Chukchi believe that the spirits have their own reindeer herds.
2. Laidlaw also included sati here but, as we saw in chapter 24, my view of sati is very different from these practices, more closely resembling murder.

References

Batianova, E. P. (2006). Ritual violence among the peoples of Northeastern Siberia. In P. P. Schweizer, M. Biesele & R. K. Hitchcock (Eds.), *Hunters and gatherers in the modern world*, pp. 150–63. New York: Berghahn Books.

Joiner, T. E., Jr. (2005). *Why people die by suicide*. Cambridge, MA: Harvard University Press.

Laidlaw, J. (2005). A life worth leaving. *Economy & Society*, 34, 178–99.

Willerslev, R. (2009). The optimal sacrifice. *American Ethnologist*, 346, 693–704.

Wrandell, F. (1842). *Narrative of an expedition to the Polar Sea, in the years 1820, 1821, 1822 and 1823*. New York: Harper & Brothers.

26

Conclusion

David Lester & Steven Stack

Four hundred years ago, William Shakespeare noted that "All the world's a stage, And all the men and women merely players." Almost one hundred years ago, Nicolas Evreinhoff made this idea into a more formal theory. Nikolai Nikolayevich Evreinov (1879–1953) was a Russian theater director, actor, playwright, stage-manager, and essayist. His plays were produced in Russia, Germany, France, England, the United States, and many other countries. In 1927, he wrote a book titled *The Theatre in Life*, in which he argued that all of us have a theatrical instinct, which leads us to transform ourselves, creating images from within ourselves that we use to change our appearance. We have a desire to be different, to do things that are different, and to imagine ourselves in different situations. Essentially, we are all theatrical beings. From primitive times on, we have decorated our bodies with scars and dyes and dressed ourselves in costumes. We have made ceremonies out of the birth of a child, education, hunting, marriage, wars, and funerals, and turned justice and religion into occasions for theater.

Evreinhoff quoted Erasmus of Rotterdam who said, What, after all, is human life if not a continuous performance in which all go about wearing different masks, in which everyone plays a part assigned to him until the stage director removes him from the boards (p. 46). Evreinhoff believed that we live our lives without realizing that we are acting, just as Molière's famous character Monsieur Jourdain did not realize that he was speaking prose. We constantly play a part when we are with others and when we think that we are being observed by others.

If everything in life is theatrical, why should our dying be anything less?

We set out in the present book to examine suicide from a perspective that has rarely, if ever, been applied previously. Could suicide be viewed as a dramatic act or performance, scripted and staged by the suicidal individual? Although some of the topics raised in the book have been studied in the past, such as the choice of method for suicide, the choices have never been studied from the perspective of the suicidal individual. What is in the minds of suicidal individuals when they make these choices and what do their choices tell us about them?

For example, choice of method for suicide has been studied for whether it predicts later death by suicide. Researchers have compared the methods chosen by men and by women and by the young and the elderly. The impact of restricting access to methods for suicide, such as by fencing off bridges from which people jump to their death, has been studied (Clarke & Lester, 2013). But how the choice of method by suicidal individuals fits into the drama they are staging has been ignored.

Suicides make many choices, from writing a suicide note, choosing a place to die, and a method to use, to how they will dress and whether they will drink alcohol or take drugs prior to their suicide. Consider the timing of the suicidal act. Suicides in most nations peak in the Spring (with a secondary peak in the Fall in some countries). Why does one person choose to die by suicide in the Spring and why does another reject that time? Suicides peak on Mondays. What plays a role in the decision by a person to choose a particular day? We do not mean simply looking for correlates by age or sex, but rather what are the psychodynamics behind the choice of day. What time of day do people choose for the action—afternoon or evening? Some individuals have imbibed alcohol (or ingested other drugs) prior to dying by suicide, while others die sober. Why?

We have attempted to argue here that these choices are not merely correlates of some personal characteristic (such as sex, age, or a personality trait), but rather well thought-out ideas about how to present their suicide to others. Perhaps the best example is the suicide of Mitchell Heisman (chapter 4) who dressed in white and went to the Yard at Harvard University where he shot himself at 11 AM in front of some twenty spectators, leaving a 1,900 page suicide note. He dressed for the occasion, chose a time and place, decided to use a gun, and left a unique suicide note for others to read. Our thesis is that suicidal individuals stage their suicide, devoting serious consideration as to how to present the act to others and how to obtain the desired reaction from family members, friends, and strangers. What proportion of suicides fit this thesis? Since the thesis is new, no one has yet examined suicidal acts from this point of view. However, it has not been difficult to find many examples to illustrate our thesis, and so it is likely that the majority of individuals stage at least some part of their suicidal act.

In this book, we have focused on some decisions that suicidal individuals make, especially concerning the communication aspects of the act (including the suicide note and the way in which their bodies will appear), the methods chosen, the venue for the acts, and the cultural norms that shape the suicidal act. But, as noted above, we have neglected some aspects, such as why some suicidal individuals choose to drink prior to the act and the timing of the act. For example, why did some people die by suicide in the 1930s while the song *Gloomy Sunday* was playing in their apartment or with the sheet music in their pocket (Stack, Krysinska, & Lester, 2007–2008)? These aspects are also worthy of study. We need more case studies and qualitative research into suicidal individuals to generate hypotheses, such as the study of the diaries of suicides (e.g., Lester, 2014) and interviews with attempted suicides (e.g., De Leo, 2010).

In today's world, there is much focus on the role of the Internet and websites such as Facebook and Twitter in shaping suicidal behavior, but the media in past eras also shaped suicidal behavior. In the past, novels, plays, operas, and newspapers have played a role in helping suicidal individuals stage their suicides. Krysinska and Lester (2006) documented how people in Japan in the 1700s copied the suicides in Kabuki plays, which were then banned as a result. Nicoletti (2004) has documented the fascination of newspaper and magazines in the 1800s in England with the suicides of women, reporting their suicides (along with their suicide notes and drawings of the acts), thereby leading to imitation by other women.

In asking the question of how people stage their suicides, we also moved easily into other disciplines, in particular anthropology (see Rubenstein's chapter on ritual dramatic performance (chapter 2).) All too often, scholars remain isolated in their own discipline and fail to unearth rich insights provided by related disciplines. Today, there are painters, playwrights, songwriters, and performance artists who occasionally choose suicide for their themes. What insight might they provide into the way in which people stage their suicides? To what extent do people use those themes to stage their own suicide?

Do All Suicides Stage Their Act?

Is every suicide a dramatic performance? Perhaps not. Some suicides are not well planned at all. Research has shown that a good proportion of attempted suicides (48% in one study (Deisenhammer, et al. 2009)) report that the time between first thinking about suicide and making the attempt was less than ten minutes. But many of those who *die by suicide* (if not most) do plan their suicidal act. In this, they are not mere automatons propelled by brain chemistry or psychiatric disorder into acts of self-destruction, but creative scriptwriters and actors who give much thought to the way in which they will die.

An important question to ask is what proportion of suicides fits this perspective. We would argue that all suicides do so. Every suicide has to choose a method, time, and place for their act, as well as how to dress and whether to leave a suicide note. Some may deliberate about these decisions for a long period of time (even months and years as we have seen in the cases of Mitchel Heisman and Martin Manley in chapter 4). Others may act more impulsively. So the question is not the proportion of suicides that stage their suicidal act, but whether and for how long they give thought to the decisions to be made and to what extent was their planning conscious.

In chapter 5, we discussed the case of a young man, crossing a bridge, who decided at that moment to kill himself by jumping from the bridge. Although the planning process took seconds, he chose a time (then) and a place (there) and a method (jumping). The brief decision process limited his choices, but he made those choices nonetheless.

Only a minority of suicides leave a suicide note. Estimates range from 20–40% in different studies, and we typically assume that about a quarter of suicides leave a suicide note. This is a sizable proportion, and these suicides have clearly decided to present themselves to others in a particular way. Those suicides who isolate themselves for their suicidal act, as well as those who kill themselves in the presence of others, have also made clear choices, choices that minimize the probability of others intervening or are guaranteed to traumatize those in the presence of the suicide (especially if a firearm is used).

The possibility that the suicidal acts of many, if not most suicides, contain some aspects of a performance is supported by national data on suicide plans. According to the latest national Youth Risk Behavior Surveys, 13.6% of high school youth answered affirmatively to the question: "During the past 12 months, did you make a plan about how you would attempt suicide?" Details on the components of such plans are not available (Stack, 2015a). However, it is probable that those who report having made a plan for suicide have thought about the method to be used. It also seems reasonable to assume that many have considered the location for the event—at home, away from home, at

Conclusion

school, in a beautiful natural area, and so on. In addition, suicide plans also often include whether or not to write a note, and what kind of note. What should go into a note? Does the plan involve retribution, an effort at blaming someone or some institution for one's suicide? Other considerations involved in planning can include a desire for an audience. In particular, who should be in the audience? Most suicides occur at home but the location within the home varies considerably. Plans can include a favorite spot within one's residence. Plans also can include the time of day, week, and even the season. In some cases, a holiday is selected as part of a plan.

While more than one of every eight high school students report having thought about an actual plan for suicide, this proportion is greater than that for the general population. According to data from the National Survey on Drug Abuse and Health, 1.0% of the adult population reports having thought about a plan for suicide during the past year (Centers for Disease Control 2011). There is some regional variation in adult suicide planning ranging from 0.9% in the Northeast to 1.2% in the Midwest. Nevertheless, 1% of the 2010 adult resident population over 19 is 2,254,000 persons (US Department of Commerce, 2012). The number of youths, as well as the number of adults who have actively considered the location, method, audience, time, whether or not to leave a note, and other considerations for a suicide performance, far exceeds the number of actual completed suicides (less than forty thousand).

Future research is needed ascertain the components of people's suicide plans. Since suicide planning involves over two million persons each year in the United States, survey research is possible. Large samples of people who report suicide plans could reveal details on what socio-demographic, personality, and opportunity factors, desires (e.g., for revenge), personality disorders and other psychiatric disorders affect how at-risk individuals plan their suicidal performance.

Location

Several chapters in this book have focused on the choice of location for a suicidal act. While much has been written on the lethality of various suicide methods, relatively little has been done on the lethality of suicide locations. Several chapters raised the question of what factors contribute to individuals selecting lethal locations, that is, places where there is likely to be a relative absence of motivated bystanders. Someone who takes an overdose with a spouse or children nearby is less likely to die than someone who takes the same dose in isolation in a hotel room or in a remote location in a national park. There is less chance of detection of the attempt by a potential rescuer in some locations than in others.

Women were found to be more likely to choose to die by suicide at home than were men. This may help to explain the gender gap in suicide. Women in the United States have a suicide rate one quarter that of men. Women more often choose to die by suicide at home, and home is the place where motivated rescuers are most likely to be found. Further research is needed to explain differences in the location of suicide within the home. For example, men may be more likely than women to be attracted to the garage or basement than are women given the masculine nature of activities in those places. Some persons choose to die by suicide in their bedroom, in bed. What does this signify? Does it symbolize a death in the context of sleep? Such issues could be addressed by an analysis of the locations desired or reported by currently suicidal individuals in their own suicide plans.

Data from suicides in the Grand Canyon National Park indicate that this location qualifies for a suicide hot spot. It is likely that other national parks may also be marked by relatively high suicide rates, acting like magnets for a small proportion of suicidal individuals. In addition, local bridges can attract a certain sector of the suicidal population. A recent study determined that, although the suicide rate in Florida declined over a twenty-year period, there was a significant increase in suicides from the Skyway Bridge in St. Petersburg, Florida (Stack, 2015b). Some suicides have special places in mind for their suicides and the better known ones include the Golden Gate Bridge and Niagara Falls. However, there is most likely a large number of locations that attract suicidal persons at the local level, and these include bridges, hotels, and state and local parks. Most of these, including hundreds of bridges, have never been subject to scientific scrutiny (Stack, 2015b).

Method

The choice of method is a critical element in planning a suicidal action. Many people have a preferred method and will not consider an alternative method. One of the authors of this book befriended a suicidal woman who had made multiple attempts to die using an overdose, but, each time, someone intervened and took her to a hospital where she was saved. She knew that hanging might be a better method, but she was afraid to use that method. Eventually, after another overdose,

Conclusion

she was placed on suicide watch in a psychiatric hospital, and as soon as the suicide watch was removed, she hung herself in the hospital.

A relatively uncommon method of suicide, suicide by fire, was explored and found to be linked to ethnicity. This rare method of suicide was found to have cultural roots. Asian Americans, perhaps the group with the closest historical link to fire as a method, were significantly more likely to choose fire than other ethnic groups for their suicide performance. A review of suicide methods around the world determined that hanging is the most common method in Europe. In Poland, for example, hanging accounts for more than 90% of suicides. While hanging is a method that is impossible to control through means of restriction (ropes and places to attach them are widely available throughout the world), the proportion of individuals who choose this method varies considerably. The method that is selected for performing suicide is, in part, culturally determined.

Further research is required for explaining the rise of new methods of suicide. For example, charcoal burning inside a car or van has been spreading in such areas as Southeast Asia. Suicide performances may use a new method if that method is used by a celebrity, someone who is well known and admired. For example, in South Korea suicide by charcoal was unknown until a popular movie star chose this method for suicide. After widespread publicity of this suicide, suicide by charcoal burning rose from 0.7% to 7.9% of all suicides, an increase of over eleven-fold (Ji, et al., 2014).

The chapter on "Have Gun will Travel" combined the work on a lethal location (suicide away from home) with a lethal method (firearms). This combination is more common among men than among women and may help explain the higher suicide rate by men. Men are not only more likely to choose guns than are women, they are also more likely to select lethal locations.

Future Research

Throughout this book, we have suggested areas where more research is needed. As noted above, temporal patterns in suicide have been well documented, with suicide peaks in the springtime, at the beginning of the month, on Mondays ("blue Monday"), and sometimes around holidays and ceremonial occasions (e.g., Lester, 2000). However, little is known at the individual level about what kinds of persons choose the springtime, Mondays, and holidays for their suicides. What determines the time of day chosen for a suicidal act?

Recent research has found that some people undertake a search for existential meaning when they approach a new decade in their life. Such persons, called nine-enders (those aged twenty-nine, thirty-nine, forty-nine, and fifty-nine) were found to have significantly higher desires for extra marital affairs and suicide rates than those at other ages (Alter & Herschfield, 2014). Future work is needed comparing the suicide plans of nine-enders with others to ascertain the extent to which a failed sense of meaning causes some suicidal persons to stage their performance while being a nine-ender.

Another issue is why some people seek an audience for their suicides while others go to great lengths to die by suicide in isolation. This particular issue could be unraveled through interviews with individuals who report having a suicide plan.

We have pointed out in many chapters that this research must go beyond simply looking for variables that correlate with the particular choice (of method, location, clothing, timing, etc.). What is needed is qualitative research involving interviews with those who have made serious attempts to die by suicide, but who survived. Qualitative research is less common in suicide research and is more difficult to get published in scholarly journals, but it is essential if we are to understand the factors that impact the decisions made by suicides as they plan the staging of the acts.

Final Comment

Our intent has not been to provide the final answer to the question of why people stage their suicides in the way that they do, but we hope that we have provided new insights into the suicidal mind and provoked you, our readers, to view suicidal behavior from this new perspective.

References

Alter, A. I., & Herschfield, H. E. (2014). People search for meaning when they approach a new decade in chronological age. *Proceedings of the National Academy of Sciences of the United States, 111*, 17066–70.

Centers for Disease Control. (2011). Suicidal thoughts and behaviors among adults aged 18 and ver—United States, 2008–2009. *Morbidity & Mortality Weekly Report, 60*(13), 1–22.

Clarke, R. V., & Lester, D. (2013). *Suicide: Closing the exits*. New Brunswick, NJ: Transaction.

De Leo, D. (2010). *Turning points*. Bowen Hills, Australia: Australian Academic Press.

Deisenhammer, E. A., Ing, C. M., Strauss, R., Kemmler, G., Hinterhuber, H., & Weiss, E. M. (2009). The duration of the suicidal process. *Journal of Clinical Psychiatry, 70*, 19–24.

Evreinhoff, N. (1927/1970). *The theatre in life*. New York: Benjamin Blom.

Ji, N. J., Hong, Y. P., Stack, S., & Lee, W. Y. (2014). Trends and risk factors of the epidemic of charcoal burning suicide in a recent decade among Korean people. *Journal of the Korean Medical Society*, 29, 1–4.

Krysinska, K., & Lester, D. (2006). Comment on the Werther effect. *Crisis*, 27, 100.

Lester, D. (2000). *Why people kill themselves, 4th edition*. Springfield, IL: Charles C. Thomas.

Lester, D. (2014). *The "I" of the storm*. Warsaw, Poland: De Gruyter.

Nicoletti, L. J. (2004). Downward mobility:Victorian women, suicide, and London's Bridge of sighs." *Literary London*, 2(1), March, online at www.literarylondon.org/london-journal/march2004/nicoletti.html.

Stack, S. (2015a). Internet bullying victimization distinguishes suicide ideators from suicide attempters: An analysis of the 2013 Youth Risk Behavior Survey. Paper presented at the *XXVIII World Congress of the International Association for Suicide Prevention*, Montreal, Canada, June 16–20.

Stack, S. (2015b). Crisis phones: prevention vs. suggestion effects: Skyway bridge, 1954-2012. *Crisis*, in press.

Stack, S., Krysinska, K., & Lester, D. (2007–2008). Gloomy Sunday. *Omega*, 56, 349–58.

US Department of Commerce. (2012). *Statistical Abstract of the United States: 2012–2013*. New York: Skyhorse Publishing.

About the Authors

Seth Abrutyn is an assistant professor of Sociology at the University of Memphis. His work emphasizes synthesizing disparate theories in order to develop more robust and comprehensive theoretical principles.

Barbara Bowman, JD is a researcher at the Center for Suicide Research in Troy, Michigan, and she practices corporate law with a large firm in Detroit, Michigan.

John F. Gunn III is an independent researcher with a BA from The Richard Stockton College of New Jersey (now Stockton University), and an MA in Psychology from Rutgers, The State University of New Jersey. His work focuses on testing theories of suicide typically through the use of material left behind by those who die by suicide.

David Lester has PhD degrees from Cambridge University (UK) and Brandeis University (USA). He is emeritus professor of Psychology at Stockton University and a former President of the International Association for Suicide Prevention (IASP). He has published extensively on suicide, murder and other issues in thanatology.

Jermaine Martinez is a PhD candidate in the department of Communication at the University of Illinois Urbana-Champaign. His research examines autobiographical accounts of depression and public discourses on clinical depression.

Joseph Rubenstein is a professor of Anthropology at Stockton University. He received his PhD from the New School for Social Research where he wrote his dissertation on the role of ambivalence in ritual drama.

Steven Stack, PhD, is a professor at Wayne State University in the department of Psychiatry and department of Criminology. He is the author of 318 articles and chapters, and three books, mostly on the social risk and protective factors for suicide.

Bijou Yang has a BA and MA from the National Taiwan University and a MA and PhD in economics from the University of Pennsylvania. Her research has focused on contingent employment, e-commerce and the behavioral economic approach to suicide and criminal behavior. She served as President of the Society for the Advancement of Behavioral Economics (SABE) from 2006–2008.

Senior Author Index

Abel, D., 31, 39
Abraham, S., 310, 317
Abrutyn, S., 207, 208
Adair, T. W., 195, 208, 230, 240
Adityanjee, M., 207, 208
Ahmadi, A., 193, 208, 274, 283
Ajdacic-Gross, V., 227, 230, 240, 243, 244, 247, 250, 251, 254
Alexander, J. C., 199, 207, 208
Ali, S., 313, 317
Aloja, E., 233, 240
Altekar, A. S., 307, 317
Alter, A. I., 330
American Psychiatric Association., 184, 190
Andover, M. A., 185, 190
Andreason, N., 195, 200, 201, 206, 207, 208
Andriolo, K. R., 285, 289, 303
Anon., 312, 316, 317
Antonowicz, J. L., 195, 208
Artaud, A., 7, 9
Arun, M., 226, 240
Asinof, E., 16, 20
Associated Press., 140, 147
Austin, A. E., 41, 49, 228, 240

Baechler, J., 53, 68, 260, 266, 291, 292, 303
Baig, T. A., 305, 309, 311, 317
Baker, R. L., 160, 163
Bakhtin, M. M., 56, 58, 59, 68
Banks, S., 262, 266
Barbour, J., 46, 49
Bateson, G., 65, 68
Bateson, J., 112, 115, 126, 132, 145, 147
Batianova, E. P., 320, 322
Baumeister, R. F., 56, 68

Beautrais, A. L., 167, 180
Bell, R., 264, 266
Benn, J. A., 275, 283
Bennewith, O., 167, 180
Bergen, H., 187, 190
Best, S., 14, 20
Bhugra, D., 311, 317
Biggs, M., 277, 282, 283
Bjelić, D. I., 160, 163
Blasser, K., 229, 241
Blaustein, M., 113, 115, 119, 126
Bohm, R. M., 295, 303
Braginsky, B., 13, 20
Bronner, S. J., 163
Buber, M., 60, 68
Burger, J., 111, 118, 125, 126, 213, 221
Burke, K., 57, 61, 68
Burton-Bradley, B. G., 287, 288, 303
Byard, R. W., 42, 49
Bytnar, B. W., 132, 134, 145, 147

Carpenter, B., 18, 20
Cash, S. J., 162, 163
Cassels, N. G., 306, 317
Catalano, F., 231, 241
Cavan, R., 114, 126
Cavanaugh, J. T. O., 201, 208
Centers for Disease Control., 79, 80, 93, 116, 127, 135, 147
Cheah, D., 45, 49
Chen, Y.Y., 223, 232, 238, 239, 241
Chicago Daily Tribune., 109, 127
Clarens, C., 214, 221
Clarke, R. V., 167, 174, 180, 324, 330
Clinard, M., 223, 240, 241
Cloutier, P., 185, 190
Cohen, L., 77, 93, 107, 111, 127, 129, 147

Cole, M., 52, 69
Constantelos, D. J., 291, 303
Crosby, K., 200, 208
Cunliffe, C., 227, 241

Daly, M., 306, 317
Daniels, S. M., 195, 208
Davis, J. H., 195, 199, 208
DeCatanzaro, D., 34, 39, 54, 69
Deisenhammer, E. A., 45, 49, 325, 330
De Leo, D., 325, 330
Demellawy, D. E., 231, 239, 241
Demirci, S., 41, 49
Denno, D. W., 48, 49
DeParle, J., 211, 212, 221
deRoux, S., 227, 233, 238, 241
Deutsch, R., 132, 133, 145, 147
Di Nunno, N., 235, 241, 267, 271
Diggory, J. C., 47, 49
Dingley, J., 282, 283
Doberentz, E., 234, 241
Doichinov, I. D., 227, 241
Dorpat, T. L., 291, 303
Dublin, L., 169, 174, 180
Durkheim, E., 5, 6, 9, 52, 60, 69, 95, 107, 114, 127, 169, 180, 308, 317

Early, K. E., 261, 266
Edwards, C., 151, 152, 156
Ellis, E. R., 171, 180
Erzurum, V. Z., 196, 201, 208
Estep, J., 130, 134, 135, 145, 147
Etkind, M., 15, 16, 17, 20, 62, 69
Evans, J. R., 234, 241
Evreinhoff, N., 323, 330

Fabing, H. D., 285, 303
Farabee, C., 131, 133, 147
Farberow, N. L., 193, 208
Fernando, R. F., 193, 205, 208
Field, K., 147
Firth, R., 47, 49
Fishbain, D. A., 259, 266
Flemming, R., 152, 156
Floyd, M. F., 117, 125, 127, 213, 221
Forman, E. M., 189, 190
Fortune., 109, 115, 127
Frank, A. W., 60, 69
Freed, R. S., 306, 312, 317
Freeman, J. B., 263, 266
Friedman, P., 170, 180

Gaylord, M. S., 42, 49
Geberth, V., 299, 303
Geertz, C., 6, 9
Gemar, K., 97, 107, 135, 147
Gerth, J., 211, 221
Ghiglieri, M. P., 130, 134, 138, 140, 141, 144, 148
Gilmore, M., 296–97, 303
Giner, L., 187, 190
Goffman, E., 8, 9, 55, 60, 63, 69
Good, B., 52, 69
Gould, M. S., 53, 69
Gross, C., 78, 79, 90, 93
Grotowski, J., 6, 9
Grumet, G. W., 167, 180
Guevara, D., 145, 148
Guggenheim, F. G., 174, 180
Gunn, J. F., 22, 26, 39, 159, 164
Gunnell, D., 232, 234, 236, 241

Halberstam, D., 279, 283
Halprin, A., 7, 9
Hammond, J. S., 196, 198, 200, 208
Hanzlick, R., 92, 93, 106, 107
Harding, B. E., 236, 241
Harlan, L., 309, 317
Harner, M., 287, 303
Hawley, J. S., 313, 317
Hawton, K., 185, 190
Hayakawa, S., 51, 69
Heggie, T. W., 110, 113, 116, 127, 131, 148
Hendrickson, P., 280, 281, 283
Hirschi, T., 248, 254
Hirsh, J., 169, 180
Homant, R. J., 299, 300, 303
Huffington Post., 188, 191
Hughes, R., 292, 303
Hughes, S., 263, 266
Huh, G. Y., 232, 241

Iga, M., 109, 115, 127
Inamdar, S. C., 307, 312, 317

Jacobs, J., 14, 18, 19, 20, 62, 64, 69
Janghorbani, M., 208
Jashinsky, J., 159, 164
Jason, D. R., 97, 107
Jenet, R. N., 297, 303
Ji, N. J., 232, 241, 329, 331
Johansson, B., 167, 180
Johnson, P. S., 312, 317

Senior Author Index

Joiner, T. E., Jr., 17, 20, 189, 191, 220, 221, 320, 322
Jungman, L., 234, 241

Kakubayashi, F., 267, 271
Katedry, Z., 232, 241
Kiev, A., 289, 303
King, E., 110, 113, 114, 127
Kitses, J., 214, 221
Kiver, E. P., 129, 148
Klein, A., 45, 49
Kleinman, A., 52, 69
Kochersberger, R. C., 160, 164
Kohn, A. A., 213, 221
Kposowa, A., 105, 106, 107
Kral, M., 51, 52, 53, 67, 69, 193, 208
Krummen, D. M., 196, 201, 208
Krysinska, K., 325, 331
Kumar, R., 313, 317
Kumar, V., 194, 205, 207, 208

Laidlaw, J., 321, 322
Laloe, V., 193, 208, 274, 275, 283
Layton, T. R., 196, 208
Lecker, K., 145, 148
Leenaars, A., 62, 69
Lester, D., 15, 20, 26, 37, 38, 44, 47, 49, 50, 51, 54, 67, 69, 77, 78, 79, 90, 91, 93, 95, 107, 110, 112, 113, 114, 116, 118, 124, 127, 131, 136, 146, 148, 153, 156, 163, 164, 167, 168, 176, 177, 180, 181, 193, 198, 200, 207, 209, 213, 220, 221, 236, 239, 241, 247, 254, 265, 266, 288, 303, 311, 315, 316, 317, 325, 329, 331
Lester, G., 261, 268
Leung, C. M., 167, 181
Lewis, H., 200, 209
Li, F., 170, 181
Lindsay, M., 303
Littlejohn, S. W., 51, 69
Los Angeles Times., 144, 148
Lowie, R. H., 286, 303
Luckenbill, D., 2, 3

MacDonald, J. M., 285, 303
MacDonald, M., 15, 20
Maghsoudi, H., 194, 209
Maiese, A., 271
Mann, J. J., 186, 191
Mann, L., 154, 156

Marcikic, M., 227, 242
Marks, A., 170, 173, 174, 176, 181
Marzuk, P. M., 260, 266
Mascolo, M., 135, 139, 148
Maulen, B., 168, 181
McKibben, J. B. A., 193, 209
Mehta, M. J., 306, 317
Menninger, K., 56, 69
Messner, B. A., 62, 64, 65, 66, 69
Miller, M., 77, 93
Modjarrad, K., 196, 199
Mohandie, K., 298, 302, 303
Moore, S. F., 7, 8, 9
Morovatdar, N., 194, 200, 206, 207, 209
Morselli, H., 95, 107, 110, 112, 114, 127, 146, 148, 250, 251, 254
Morson, G. S., 57, 58, 60, 69
Motely, M. T., 55, 70
Murphy, S., 236, 238, 242, 243, 254
Murty, O. P., 229, 242

Narasimhan, S., 306, 313, 316, 317
New York Times., 134, 145, 146
Newcomer, E. P., 31, 39
Newman, S., 110, 111, 116, 118, 127, 129, 130, 131, 136, 145, 146, 147, 148
Nicoletti, L. J., 325, 331
Nielson, J. A., 209
Nock, M. K., 185, 191
Noomen, P., 174, 181
Norimine, E., 232, 238, 242

Oates, J. C., 178, 181
Orbell, J., 15, 20

Pampel, F., 221
Parilla, V., 313, 317
Parker, S., 289, 303
Parks, S. E., 72, 75, 95, 96, 107
Parsons, P. R., 160, 164
Pavulans, K. S., 186, 191
Pelissier-Alicot, A. L., 235, 242
Petkovic, S., 234, 242
Pham, T. N., 197, 209
Phillips, D. P., 53, 70, 170, 171, 181
Plener, P. L., 185, 191
Poeschla, B., 274, 283
Pompili, M., 14, 20
Pope, W., 95, 107
Pridmore, S., 162, 164

Rafter, N., 214, 221
Rankin, A., 267, 271
Repanshek, K., 148
Robbins, T., 276, 283
Roman, J., 16, 20, 154, 156
Romm, S., 200, 201, 209, 275, 283
Rosen, D. H., 112, 126, 127, 132, 145, 148, 173, 181
Ross, T. E., 110, 113, 116, 118, 119, 124, 127, 146, 148
Rothschild, M. A., 274, 283
Rudd, M. D., 188, 191
Ruddy, C., 221

Saint-Martin, P., 233, 242
Sands, B., 275, 276, 283
Sartre, J., 55, 70
Scheff, T., 200, 207, 209
Schlenger, R., 97, 107
Schmidt, S., 211, 221
Scully, J., 197, 209
Seiden, R. H., 17, 20, 153, 156, 172, 181
Seidler, B., 144, 148
Sellin, T., 295, 303
Sen, M., 308, 314, 317
Sharma, A., 308, 309, 318
Shenassa, E. D., 214, 215, 222, 243, 247, 248, 254
Sher, L., 186, 191
Sheth, S. D., 305, 318
Shields, L. B. E., 261, 266
Shneidman, E. S., 19, 20, 52, 56, 62, 63, 70, 201, 209
Shneidman, J. L., 264, 266
Simon, O. R., 45, 50
Simon, R. I., 44, 48, 50
Simpson, A. E., 263, 266
Skegg, K., 113, 114, 127
Snedker, K., 111, 118, 124, 127, 213, 222
Sohlman, R., 153, 156
Sophocles., 293, 304
Spiegel, A., 154, 157
Squyres, V., 197, 209
Stack, S., 90, 92, 93, 95, 106, 107, 126, 127, 136, 143, 144, 148, 205, 206, 209, 213, 220, 221, 222, 224, 226, 231, 236, 239, 242, 247, 248, 255, 260, 266, 325, 326, 328, 331
Starr, K., 211, 221
Steer, R. A., 156, 157
Stein, D. K., 306, 315, 318,

Steiner, G., 55, 70
Stokes, H. S., 269, 271
Stone, I. F., 293, 304
Straka, L., 229, 232, 235, 242
Strauss, C., 52, 70
Stravynski, A., 59, 70
Strayed, C., 125, 127
Strom, S., 110, 127
Surtees, S. J., 113, 114, 118, 127, 131, 148
Swenson, J. R., 197, 209

Takahashi, Y., 53, 70, 110, 113, 118, 119, 121, 128
Tarde, G., 53, 70
Tartaro, C., 221, 222
Thayer, L. O., 58, 70
The Bulletin., 140, 147
Thio, A., 223, 240, 242
Thombs, B. D., 194, 197, 198, 206, 209, 274, 283
Time., 109, 128
Todorov, T., 61, 70
Tolstoy, N., 263, 266
Tuohig, G. M., 197, 210
Turk, E. E., 167, 181
Turner, V. W., 5, 6, 9, 10

U.S. Department of Commerce., 243, 255, 327, 331

Van Brunt, B., 44, 50
van Hooff, A., 193, 210
Van Wormer, K., 295, 304
Van Wulfften-Palthe, P. M., 288, 304
Van Zandt, C. R., 298, 301, 304
Vanderbilt, A., 132, 133, 145, 148
VanSteenhuyse, E., 43, 50
Vapa, D., 235, 242
Ven Gennep, A., 6, 10
Vijayakumar, L., 305, 306, 307, 308, 309, 318
Von Drehle, D., 211, 222

Warr, M., 111, 118, 128, 213, 222
Wasserman, I., 3, 73, 75, 77, 79, 92, 93, 96, 97, 98, 99, 106, 107, 111, 128, 129, 148, 261, 266
Watzlawick, P., 55, 70
Wedin, B., 49, 50
Weinberger-Thomas, C., 305, 306, 307, 309, 311, 312, 316, 318

Senior Author Index

Weisman, A. D., 77, 93, 96, 108, 128
Welsh, A. M., 281, 282, 283
Wertham, F., 295, 304
Westermeyer, J., 289, 304
Whittlesey, L. H., 126, 128, 134, 145, 149
Wilcox, H. C., 187, 191
Willerslev, R., 319, 322
Wilson, E. F., 297, 304
Windfuhr, K., 78, 90, 91, 93
Wolfgang, M. E., 285, 304

World Health Organization., 248, 255
Wrandell, F., 322
Wright, W., 214, 222

Yamazaki, M., 97, 108
Yang, A. A., 306, 307, 316, 318
Yang, B., 20, 49
Yavuz, N., 118, 128, 213, 222
Yeh, C., 110, 113, 114, 115, 118, 128

Zarkowki, P., 97, 98, 108, 128, 135, 149

Subject Index

acquired capability for suicide, 189
Act of the Heart (film), 202, 207
African Americans, 100, 203
age, 119, 122, 125, 146
  & Paladin pattern, 218
airplane suicide, 168
alcohol abuse, 125, 127
Ali, Muhammad, 154
ALS, 153
altruistic suicide, 5, 14, 308
American Association of Suicidology, 22
American gun culture, 213
amok, 287
Anglo-Saxons, 33
anomie, 9
anthropological perspective, 5
Antigone, 292
anti-semitism, 33
Applewhite, Marshall, 43
arab Spring, 273
art, representations of suicide in, 96, 97,110, 112, 143, 171, 179, 202, 205, 233, 275, 292, 325
ashrams for women, 312
Asian Americans, 101, 138, 202, 205, 329
asperger's syndrome, 35
assisted suicide, 5, 9, 152
Atta, Mohamed, 1
audience, 8, 51, 54
autopsy, 18
availability of suicide methods, 167, 170, 239

baiting, 154
Batman, 44
Beachy Head (UK), 114
The Beckoning Flame (film), 205
Belcher, Jovan, 2

belonging, thwarted, 18, 189
Bem, Sandra, 153
Berryman, John, 179
berserk, 285
birthday effect, 2
Black Forest (Mt. Fuji), 110, 114
blogs, 159
blue monday, 329
Bouazizi, Tarek-al-Tayeb Mohamed, 273
The Bridge (film), 110
Bridgman, 16
Brown, Malcolm, 279
Buddhist views on suicide, 275
burdensomeness, 17, 36, 63, 66, 189, 320
burn centers, 193–194
Burr, Aaron, 264
bystanders, 96, 106, 130, 134, 327

Caesar, Julius, 151
Camelford, Baron of, 263
camping, 125
canoeing, 125
cannibalism, 290
Canyonlands National Park, 134
car exhaust, 171
Caribou (tribe), 319
Cato Marcus Porcius, 151, 179
Centers for Disease Control, 22
charcoal burning, 223, 329
child & protective Services, 25
Chubbuck, Christine, 160
Chukchi, 319–320
Cilley, Jonathan, 264
cinema, representations of suicide in, 96, 97, 143, 205, 233
Civil War, American, 33
Cleopatra, 46, 49, 179
clothing/dressed for suicide, 2, 42–44, 97

code duello, 262
communication, non verbal, 55
  other directed intention, 55
  sentences, 56, 58
  utterances, 56, 58
complex suicides, 97, 144, 225, 234–235
costs & benefits of suicide, 186–187
courtroom suicide, 161
Crazy-dog-wishing-to-die, 285
criminological strains, 218
crisis of communication, 60
Crow (tribe), 286
cultural norms, 173, 325
cultural scripts, 199, 201
culture of victims, 200, 207

death of a significant other, 101, 120, 122
dementia, 34, 37
depression, 46, 85, 274, 298
destigmatization of suicide, 112
Detroit, MI, 99, 105, 261
Diagnostic Statistical Manual (APA), 184
Dido Queen of Carthage, 205
Dignitas, 153
Dirty Harry (film), 214
disfiguring, 46
dowry disputes, 193
dowry murder, 312
Dreyfus, Alfred, 16
drowning (method of suicide), 112, 121, 124, 126, 142, 250
  historical trends, 253
drug subculture, hotel suicide, 105–106
duels, 262–265
Dwyer, Bud, 16, 159

economic strain, 84
egotistical suicide, 309
Egypt Air, 168
Empedocles, 275
engulfed shame, 200
Erasmus, 323
erotic overtones, 46
ethnicity, 81, 88, 90, 100, 118, 199, 339
  & Paladin pattern, 218
Evens, 320
execution by the state, 291

Facebook, 13, 21, 41, 159, 163
falls (method of suicide), 121, 248
  historical trends, 253

familiarity with method of suicide, 174
fasting, 320
fatalistic suicide, 308, 315
fear of crime, 124
feticide, female, 312
financial problems, 203
firearms, 105, 121, 124, 213, 247–248
  historical trends, 250–252
  & masculinity, 213
fires of hell, 200
fishing, 125
The Forest (film), 110
Forrest Gump (film), 96
Foster, Vincent, 211
Freud, Sigmund, 154

Gas, 170
Gay suicides, 139
Gender, 81, 88, 90, 100, 104, 105, 117–118, 122, 124, 131, 136, 193–194, 203, 205–206, 213, 328
  & lethality of method, 215–216, 249–250
  & Paladin pattern, 218
  & unusual suicides, 236, 238
General Social Surveys, 213
gigadeaths, 34
Gilmore, Gary, 296
Glacier National Park, 133
Gloomy Sunday, 325
Goethe, 171
Golden Gate Bridge, 16, 92, 110, 112, 115, 118, 126, 172, 328
Götterdämmerung, 275
Grand Canyon National Park, 129, 136, 328
  calculated suicide rate, 138
  suicide methods, 137–138, 141–142
  suicide risk factors, 137–141
Graves, William, 264

Hale-Bopp comet, 43
Half Dome (Yosemite National Park), 133
Hamilton, Alexander, 264
hanging (suicide method), 122, 248
  historical trends, 253
hara-kiri, 267
Harvard University, 31
Have Gun, Will Travel (film), 214, 216
health problems, 85, 91, 101, 104, 105, 120, 122, 203
Heaven's Gate cult, 3, 43

Subject Index

Heisman, Mitchell, 31, 324, 326
Hemingway, Leicester, 265
Heracles, 275
Hershberger, Willard, 46, 156
Herz, Alice, 280
hiking, 125
Hindu views on suicide, 28, 305
Hispanics, 100, 203
Hitler, Adolf, 33
Hong Kong, 42
hotel suicide, prevalence, 74, 97
  as hotspots, 97
  review of literature, 97–98
  & substance abuse, 99, 102, 104
hot spot, suicide, 92, 97, 109–110, 114,
  118, 145, 148, 328
  Grand Canyon National Park, 136
hunters and hunting, 125
hunger strikes, 275

imitation, 143–144, 223, 239, 308, 325, 329
impression management, 8
impulsivity, 45
India, 305–316
indirect suicide, 286, 291
infanticide, female, 312
internet, 32
interpersonal theory of suicide, 189, 220
intimate partner problems, 120, 122, 205
Iran, 94
Iraq, 94
Irish Republican Army, 275
IS PATH WARM, 22

Jain religion, 320
jauhar (Hindu mass suicide), 207
Jesus, 179
jigai, 270
jihad, 286
jivaro, 287
jogini, 310
Joiner, Thomas, 189, 220
jumping, 123–124, 147,167, 248, 254
juramentado, 287

Kabuki, 325
kamikaze, 6, 14, 15, 270
Kanwar, Roop, 313–314
Kegan Falls (Japan), 115
Kevorkian, Jack, 44
Kurdistan Workers Party, 277

last wishes, 47
Lawyers Head (NZ), 114
Leaving Las Vegas (film), 97
legal strains, 84–85
Lermontov, Mikhail, 259
lethal locations, 3, 74, 77–78, 111
lethality of method, 214–215
Lethal Weapon (film), 214
liberation of the soul, 319
The Life of David Gale (film), 233
Lincoln, Abraham, 262
location for suicide, 3, 73–74, 77–159,
  327–328
  19th century, 95
Lord of the Rings, 275
Lou Gehrig's disease, 153
Lucan, 152

mania, 34
Manley, Martin, 34, 36, 37, 326
marital status, 82–83, 88–89, 101, 118–119,
  122, 203
martyrs, 291
masked suicide, 286
mass suicide, 207, 276, 311
mass transit railway (MTR), 42
McNamara, Robert, 277
mental age, 13
mental disorders, 126
Meta analysis, 201
method of suicide
  charcoal burning, 223
  drowning, 112, 121, 124, 126, 142, 249
  fire 193–207, 230–331
  firearms 105, 121, 213, 247–248, 252
  general, 132, 137–138,141–142, 167,
    328–329
  hanging, 122, 248
  helicopter, 144
  historical trends, 250–253
  jumping, 123–124, 141, 167, 248
  other nations, 245–250
  poison, 104, 122, 187
  violent, 182–183
Mishima, Yukio, 1, 16, 269
MMPI, 13
modeling, 308, 311
Molière, 323
Monroe, Marilyn, 46, 49
Morrison, Norman, 272, 276, 279
motel room, 3

343

Suicide as a Dramatic Performance

motivated rescuers, 96, 111, 138
motor vehicles (suicide method), 124, 142
Mount Mihara, 109–110, 171
murder, 2
MySpace, 159, 162

naked suicide, 44–46
national burn repository, 198
National parks, 3, 74, 110, 115–116,
 133–134, 328
 selecting them for a stage for suicide,
 132–134, 145
national violent death reporting system,
 73, 79, 99, 135, 199, 217
Native Americans, 101, 203
natural areas, 116
naturism (Japanese religion), 115
Nazis, 34
Nero, 152
New Forest (UK), 114
newspaper reports, 15
Niagara Falls, 115, 328
nihilism, 33
Nobel, Alfred, 153
non suicidal self injury (NSSI), 183–184
Norman conquest, 34

obligatory suicide, 308
obsessiveness, 34
occupational strain, 140, 212
Oedipus, 292
Ojibwa, 290
opiate drugs, 104
opportunity theory, 77, 96–97, 101, 105,
 106, 111, 120, 125, 129, 139, 142, 146,
 213, 220
oppression of women, 312
ordeal suicide, 260
Oswald, Lee Harvey, 292
Othello, 179
Ottoman Empire, 291

pain, 52
Palach, Jan, 276
Paladin pattern, 216–218
paranoia, 32, 290
partition of India, 311
perturbation, 52–53
pesticides (method), 248
Pheonix, 275
physician-assisted suicide, 152–153

Pitt, Thomas (duels), 263
Plath, Sylvia, 179, 265
point of no return, 187
poison (method of suicide), 104, 122,
 124, 187
 poison-historical trends, 253
Prinze, Freddie, 2
protest suicide, 273
Proteus, Peregrinus, 275
pseudocide, 14, 16
pseudo-commandos, 44
psychiatric morbidity, 81, 85, 89, 122
 & Paladin pattern, 218
psychosemantic fallacy, 19
psychosis, 45
Puritans, 33

qualitative research, 330
Quang Duc, Thich, 276, 278

Rajasthan (India), 306
rampage murder, 44
rationality, 33
rehearsal, 6
religion, 206
The Rifleman (film), 214
risk to rescue ratio, 52
risk-taking, 260
ritalin, 31
ritual, 5
Russian old believers, 200
Russian roulette, 259–261

sadaharu, 275
Sami, 319
Sands, Bobby, 275
sati, 193, 275, 305
scenography, of suicide, 3
schizophrenia, 13, 274
scripts, 6
self-immolation, 6, 193
self-mutilation, 22
self-sacrifice, 305
Seneca, 156
seppuku, 1, 267
sex differences, 47
Sexton, Anne, 179
Shakespeare, William, 323
shame, 207
Shiva, 306
The Shootist (film), 214

344

Subject Index

Siberia, 319
Sing Sing correctional facility, 47
skin, 41
Skyway Bridge, 92, 328
Smith, Sandra, 48
socialization, 174
social strains, 79–80, 83–84, 89, 101, 125, 218
  & Paladin pattern, 220–221
sociobiology, 32
Socrates, 179, 293
spring peak, 324
Spring, Summer, Fall, Winter, Spring (film), 206
Stagecoach (film), 214
Star Wars, 44
Stein, Gertrude, 1
stigma, 9
substance abuse, 45, 85, 102, 104, 106, 120, 122
subway trains, 174
suggestion, 170
suicide
  as an idea, 54
  attempt, 85, 185–187, multiple 188–189
  at volcanoes, 109
  bombers, 5, 6, 14, 276, 287
  -by-cop, 261, 297–302
  by fire, review, 194–199
  by motorcycle, 140
  intent, 185
  notes, 2, 13, 61–67, 104, 106, 122, 134, 139, 140, 141, 212, 234
    & Paladin pattern, 218
  online, 162
  pacts, 140
  plans, 326–327
  prevention, 109, 154
  in public,151
  tourism, 78, 144, 153
The Suicide Tourist (film), 153
suifice, 309
superaddressee, 59–60
symbolism, 170, 176

Tacitus, 152
TAT, 13
television, 2, 159
Thelma & Louise (film), 143
Tibetan protest suicides, 276–277
Tikopia, 47

timing, suicidal act, 2
trauma, 46
Trespass (film), 205
Tweets, 24
Twitter, 2, 13, 24, 38, 41, 159, 325

The Unforgiven (film), 214
unusual suicides
  chainsaws, 228
  complex, 97, 144, 225, 234–235
  cutting & piercing, 228
  definition, 223
  dry ice, 232
  duct tape, 233
  electrocution, 229–230
  explosions, 231, 239
  firearms, 226–227
  hangings, 227
  helium, 231
  homicides (staged), 233
  hypothermia, 234
  motor vehicles, 229
  by nation, 236–237
  nitrogen gas, 232
urbanism, 83, 101, 104, 122

Vedas, 306
Velz, Lupe, 16
vicarious suicide, 286
victim-precipitated homicide, 261, 285
Vietnam peace moratorium, 16
vikings, 285
violence, victims of, 85

websites, 37
Weismuller, Johnny, 16
Western bias, 45
widows, 101, 104, 125, 312
Wiitiko psychosis, 289
wilderness, 3
Wilson, Edward, 34
witchcraft, 200
witnesses to suicide, 153, 156, 260, 326–327
World Trade Center, 1
World War Two, 15, 38, 270

Yanomano, 287
Yellowstone national park, 134
Yosemite national park, 133
YouTube, 2, 21, 159, 162

345